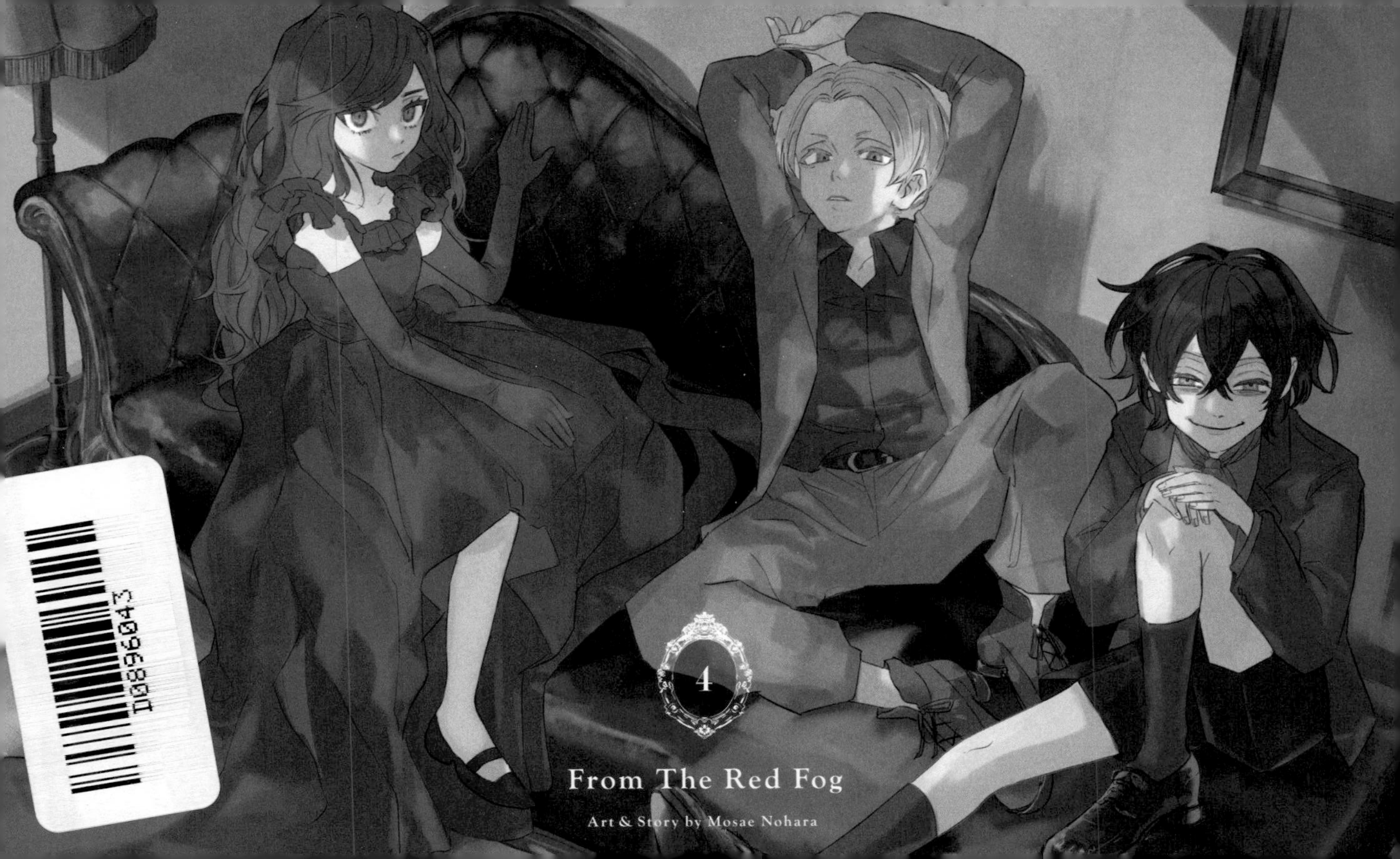
4
From The Red Fog
Art & Story by Mosae Nohara

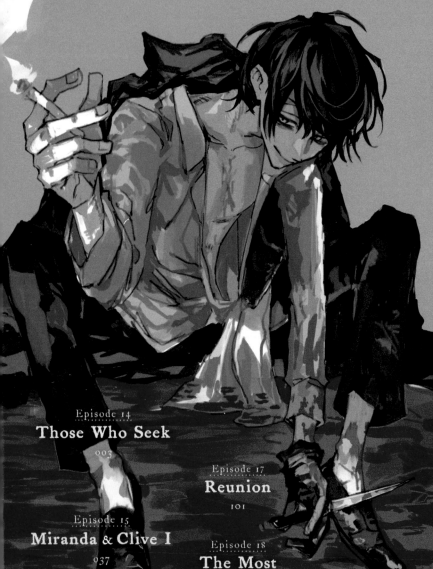

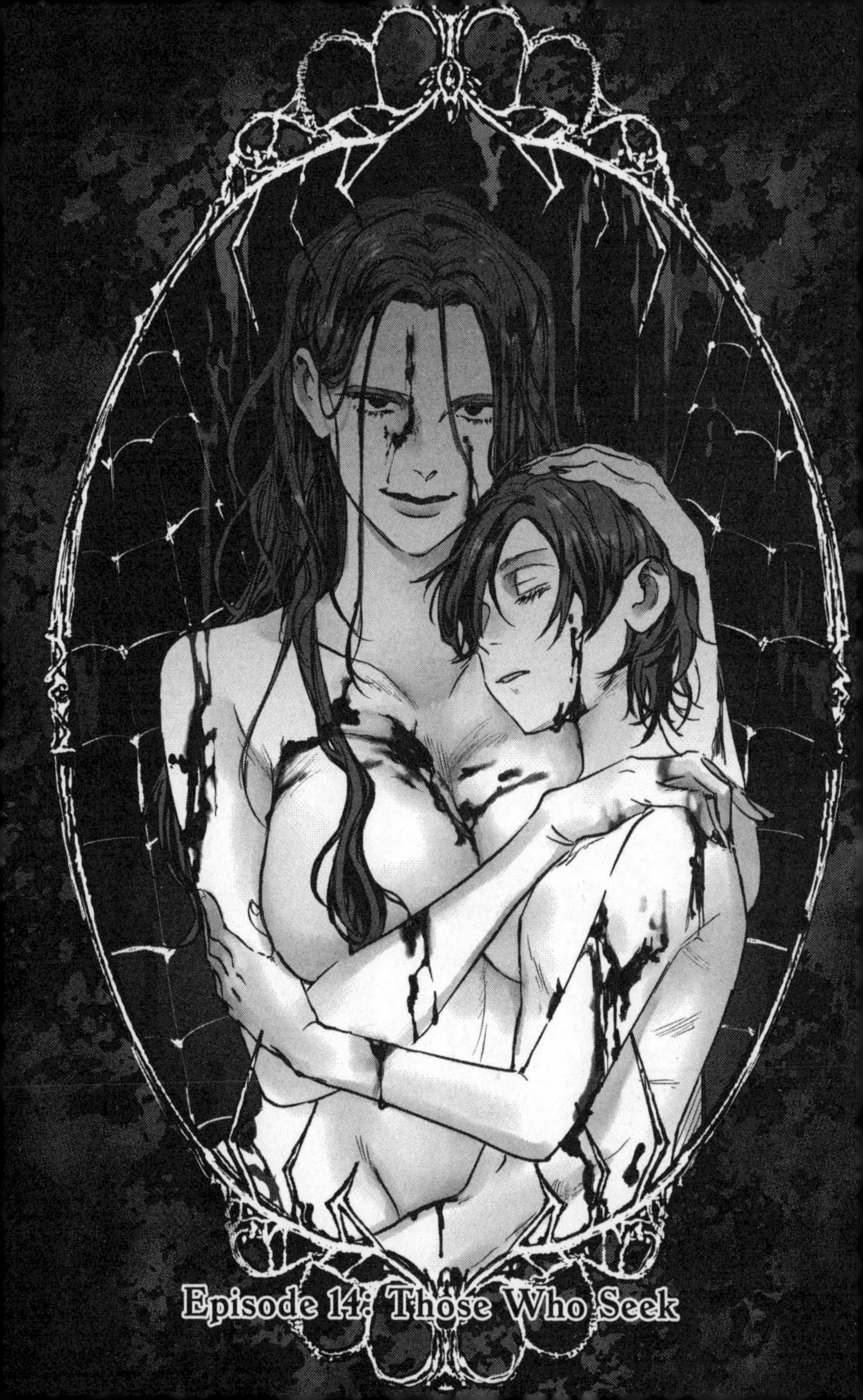
Episode 14: Those Who Seek

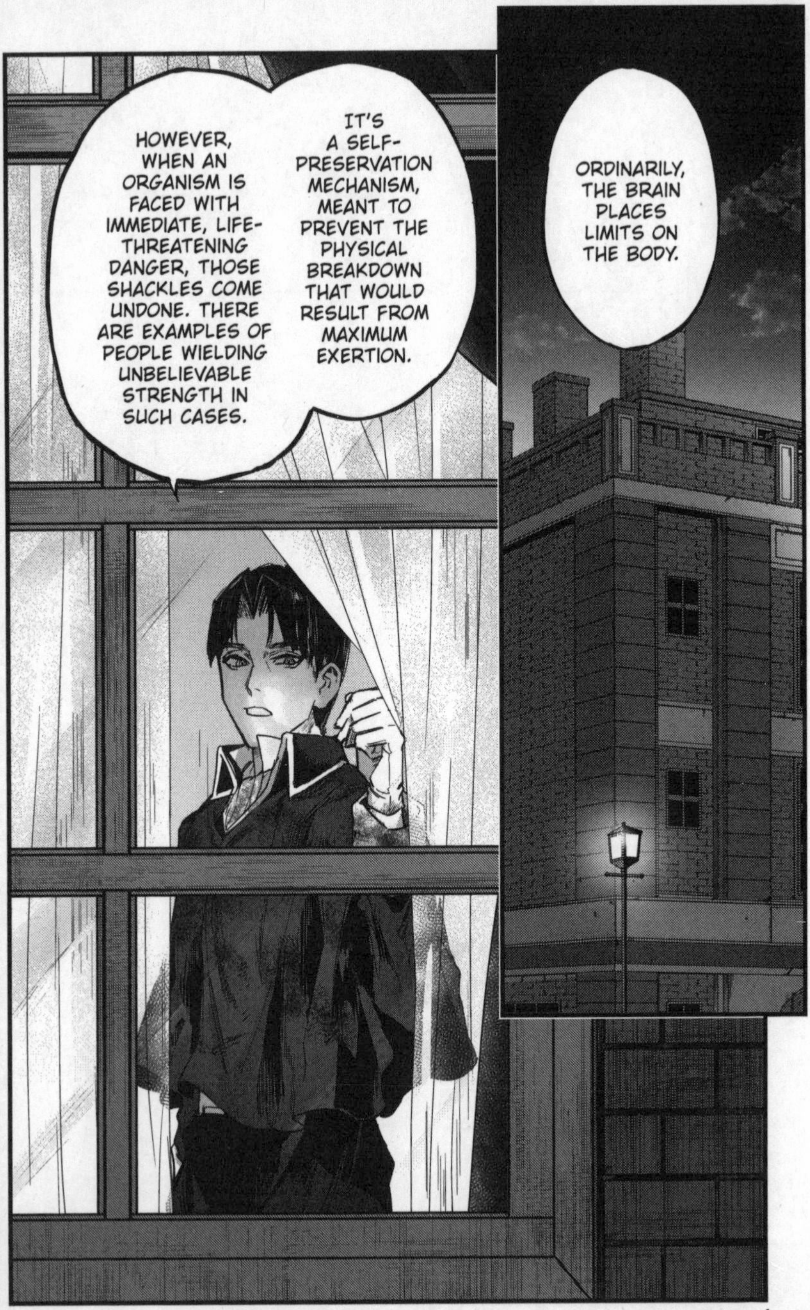
ORDINARILY, THE BRAIN PLACES LIMITS ON THE BODY.
IT'S A SELF-PRESERVATION MECHANISM, MEANT TO PREVENT THE PHYSICAL BREAKDOWN THAT WOULD RESULT FROM MAXIMUM EXERTION.
HOWEVER, WHEN AN ORGANISM IS FACED WITH IMMEDIATE, LIFE-THREATENING DANGER, THOSE SHACKLES COME UNDONE. THERE ARE EXAMPLES OF PEOPLE WIELDING UNBELIEVABLE STRENGTH IN SUCH CASES.

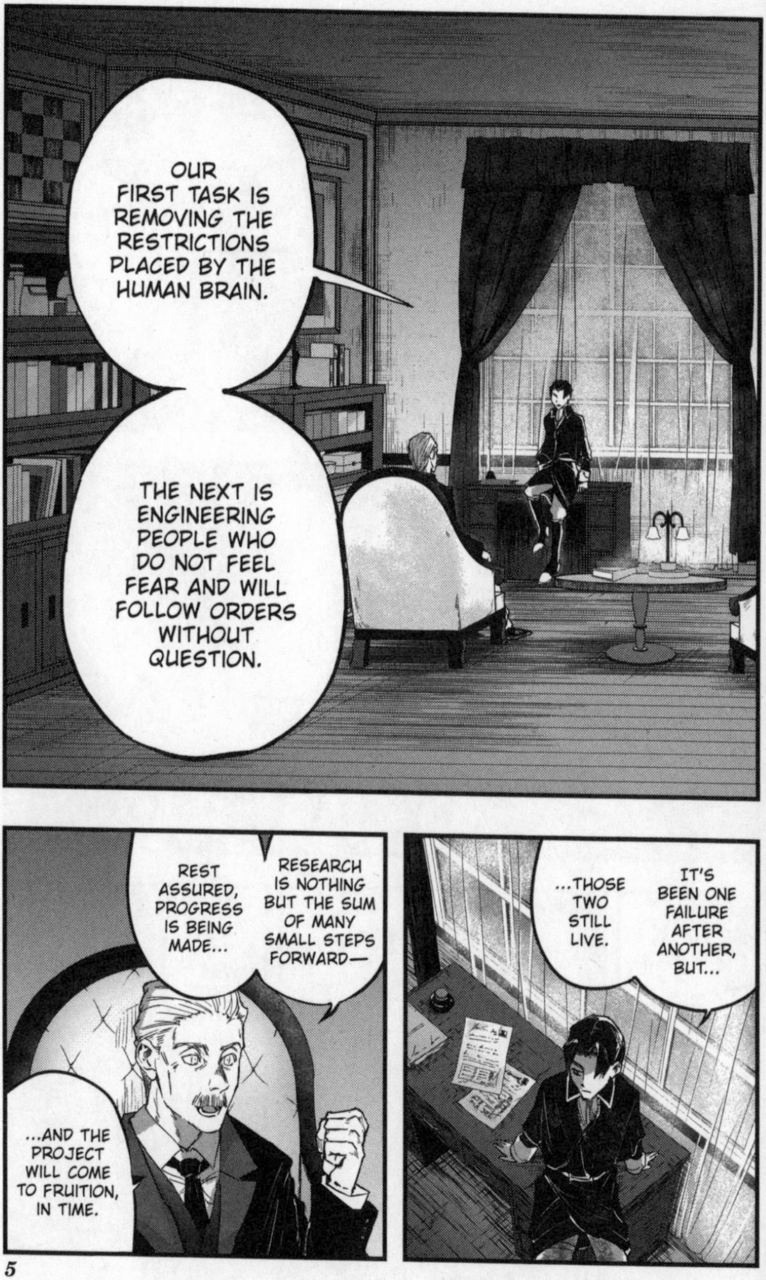
OUR FIRST TASK IS REMOVING THE RESTRICTIONS PLACED BY THE HUMAN BRAIN.
THE NEXT IS ENGINEERING PEOPLE WHO DO NOT FEEL FEAR AND WILL FOLLOW ORDERS WITHOUT QUESTION.
IT'S BEEN ONE FAILURE AFTER ANOTHER, BUT...
...THOSE TWO STILL LIVE.
RESEARCH IS NOTHING BUT THE SUM OF MANY SMALL STEPS FORWARD—
REST ASSURED, PROGRESS IS BEING MADE...
...AND THE PROJECT WILL COME TO FRUITION, IN TIME.

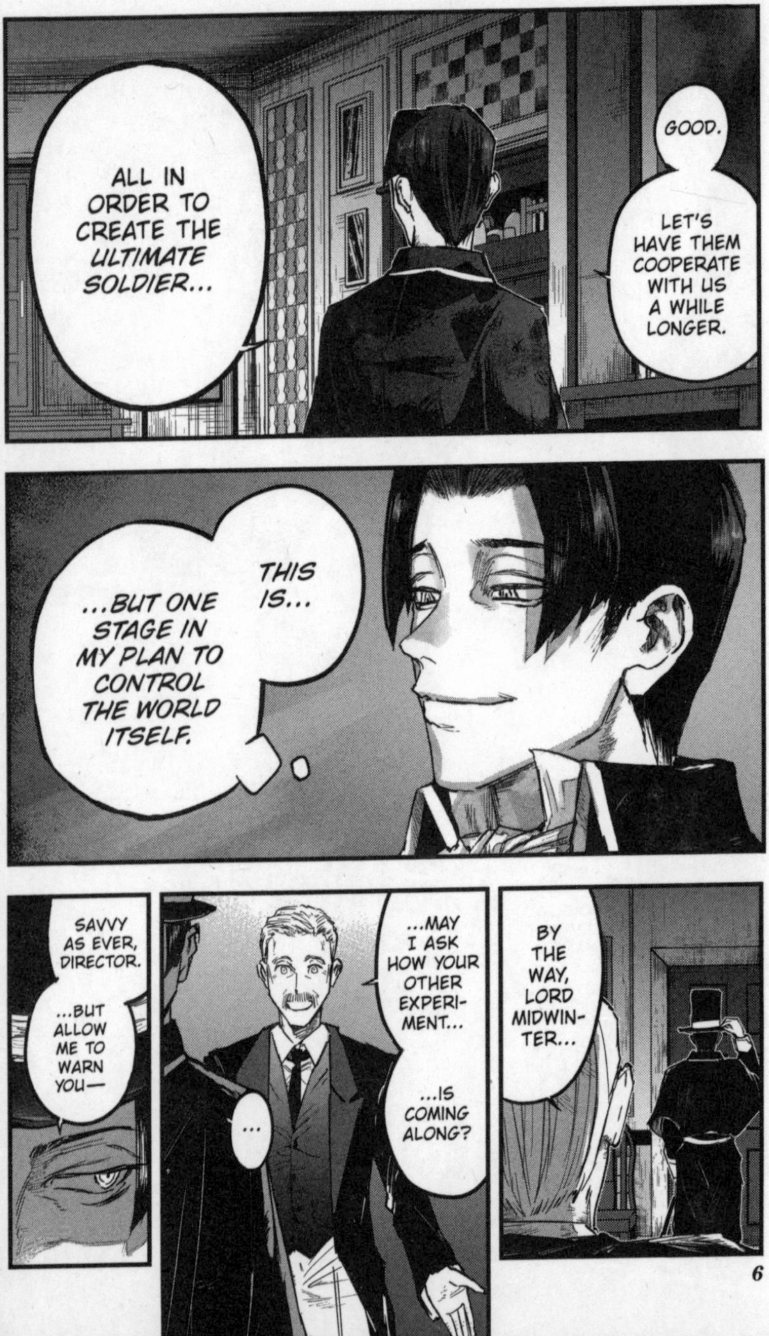
GOOD.
LET'S HAVE THEM COOPERATE WITH US A WHILE LONGER.
ALL IN ORDER TO CREATE THE *ULTIMATE SOLDIER*...
THIS IS...
...BUT ONE STAGE IN MY PLAN TO CONTROL THE WORLD ITSELF.
BY THE WAY, LORD MIDWINTER...
...MAY I ASK HOW YOUR OTHER EXPERIMENT...
...IS COMING ALONG?
...
SAVVY AS EVER, DIRECTOR.
...BUT ALLOW ME TO WARN YOU—

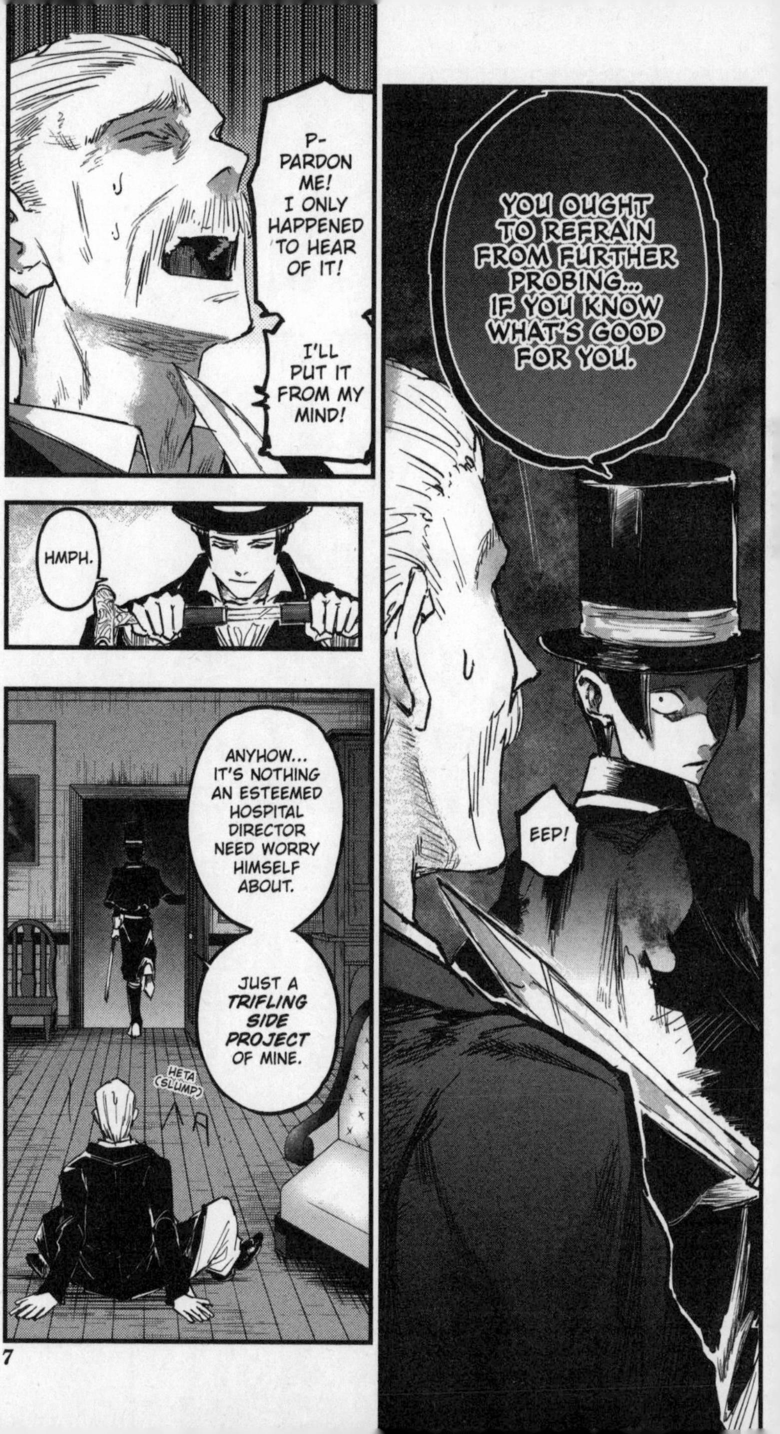
YOU OUGHT TO REFRAIN FROM FURTHER PROBING... IF YOU KNOW WHAT'S GOOD FOR YOU.
EEP!
P- PARDON ME! I ONLY HAPPENED TO HEAR OF IT!
I'LL PUT IT FROM MY MIND!
HMPH.
ANYHOW... IT'S NOTHING AN ESTEEMED HOSPITAL DIRECTOR NEED WORRY HIMSELF ABOUT.
JUST A *TRIFLING SIDE PROJECT* OF MINE.
HETA (SLUMP)

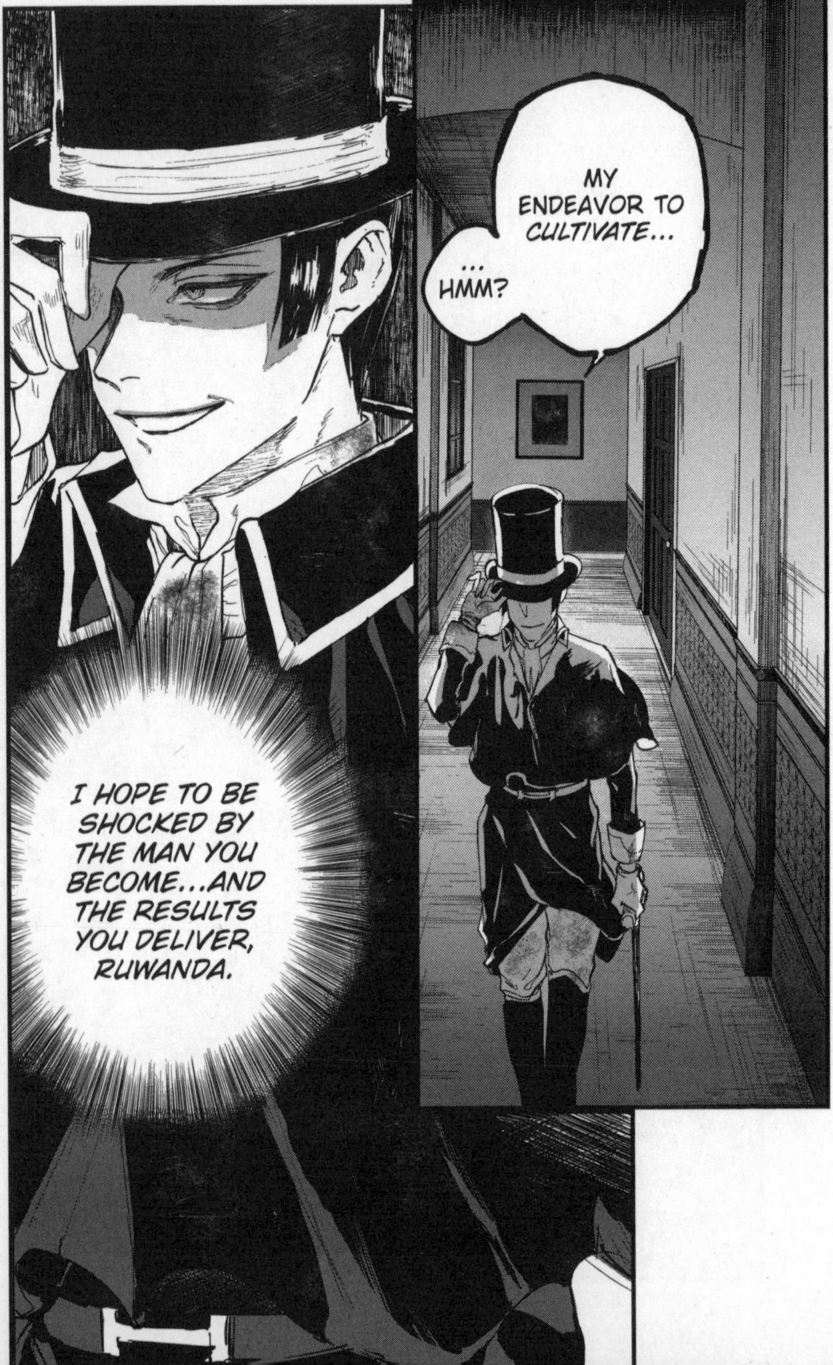
MY ENDEAVOR TO CULTIVATE...
...HMM?
I HOPE TO BE SHOCKED BY THE MAN YOU BECOME...AND THE RESULTS YOU DELIVER, RUWANDA.

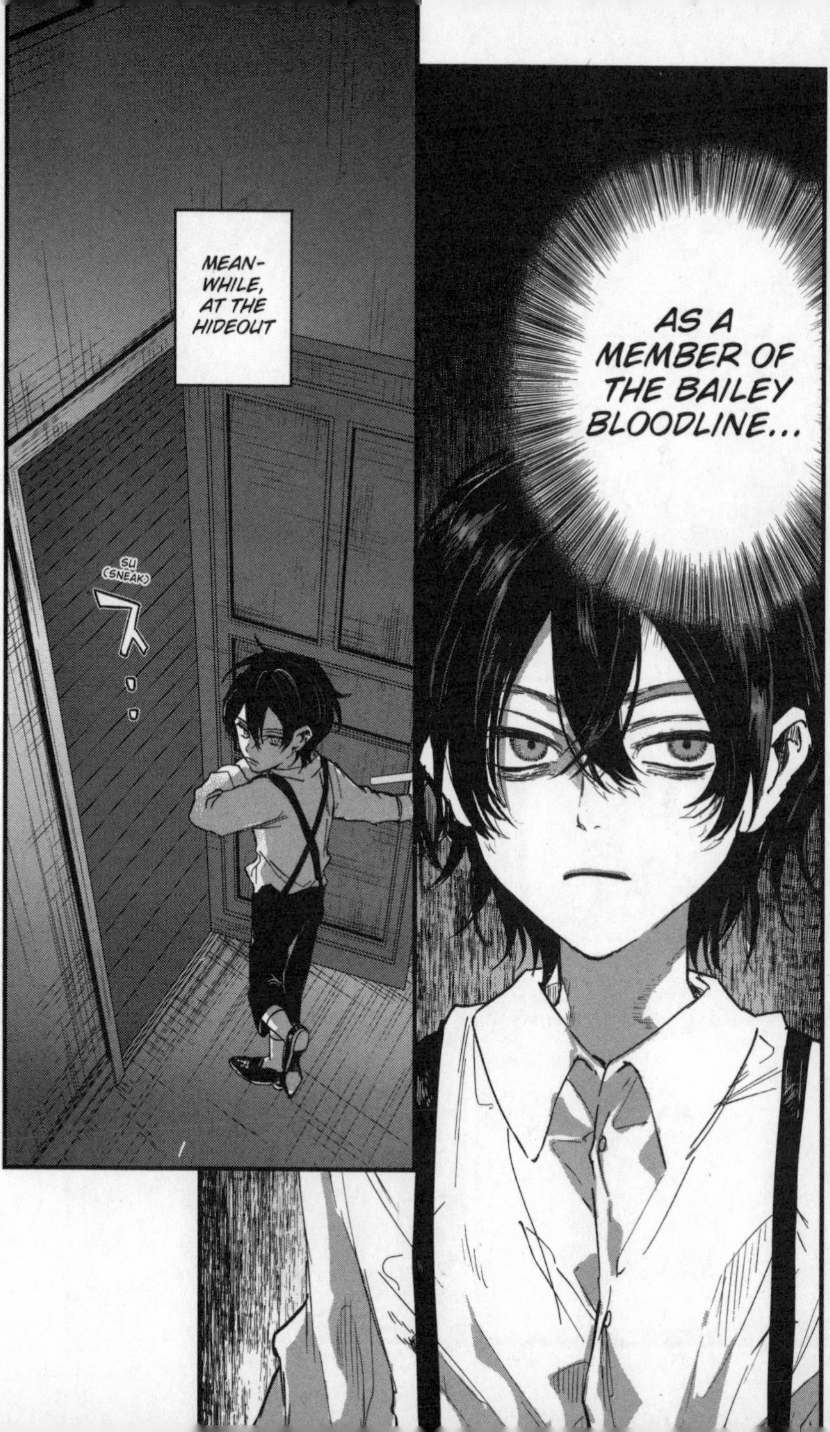
AS A MEMBER OF THE BAILEY BLOODLINE...
MEAN-WHILE, AT THE HIDEOUT
SU (SNEAK)
ス...

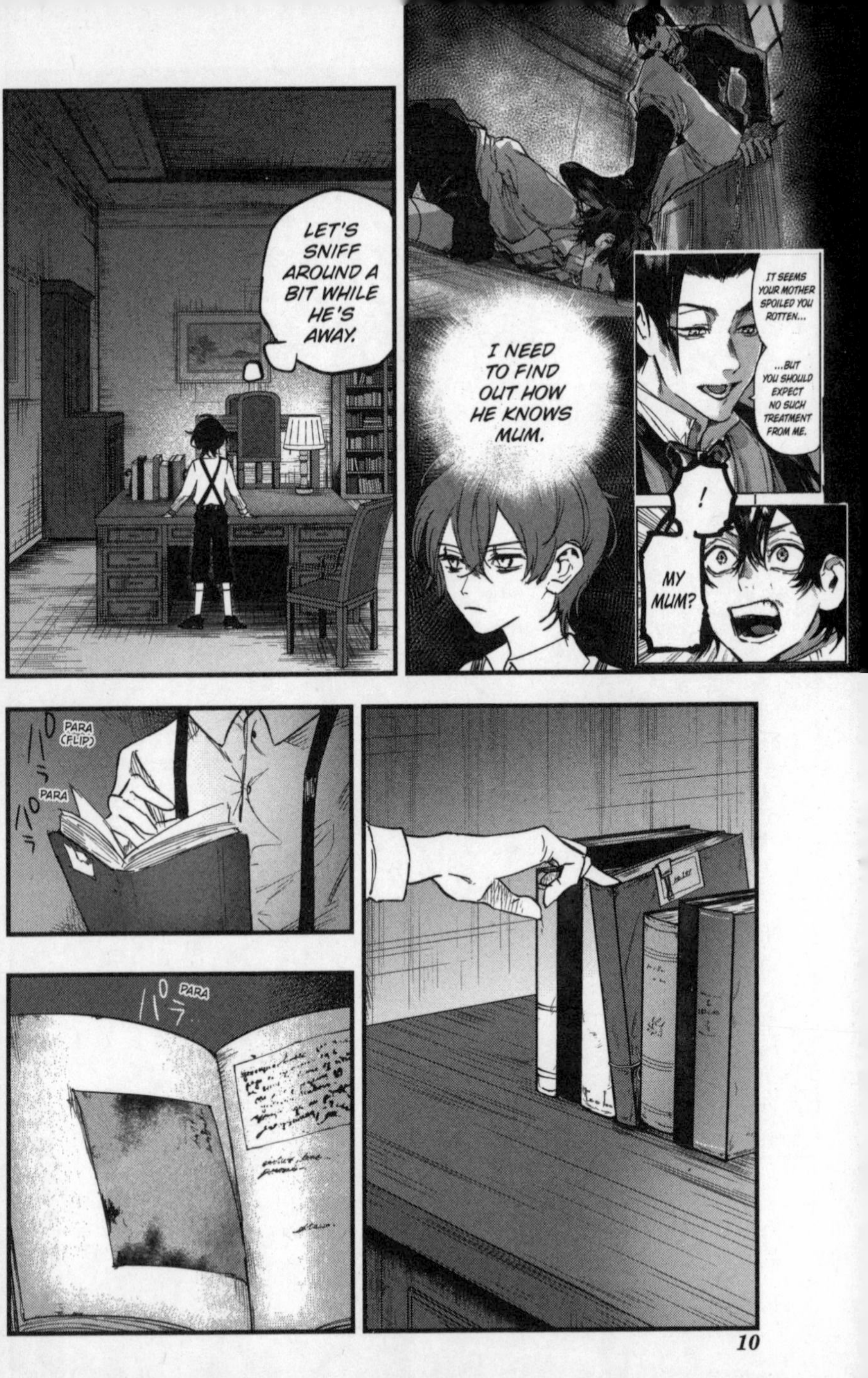
IT SEEMS YOUR MOTHER SPOILED YOU ROTTEN...
...BUT YOU SHOULD EXPECT NO SUCH TREATMENT FROM ME.
!
MY MUM?
I NEED TO FIND OUT HOW HE KNOWS MUM.
LET'S SNIFF AROUND A BIT WHILE HE'S AWAY.
PARA (FLIP)
PARA
PARA

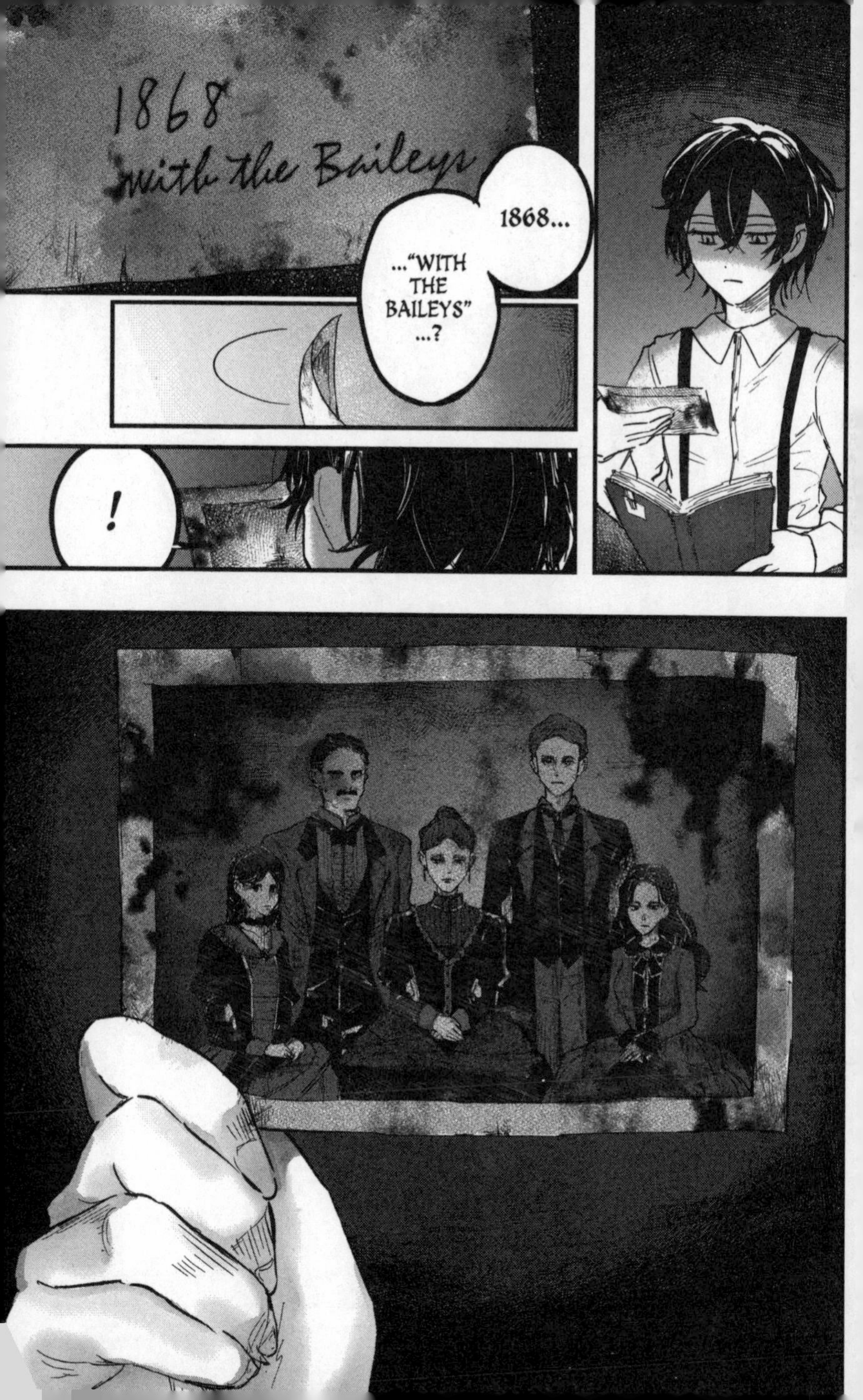
1868...
..."WITH THE BAILEYS" ...?
1868
with the Baileys
!

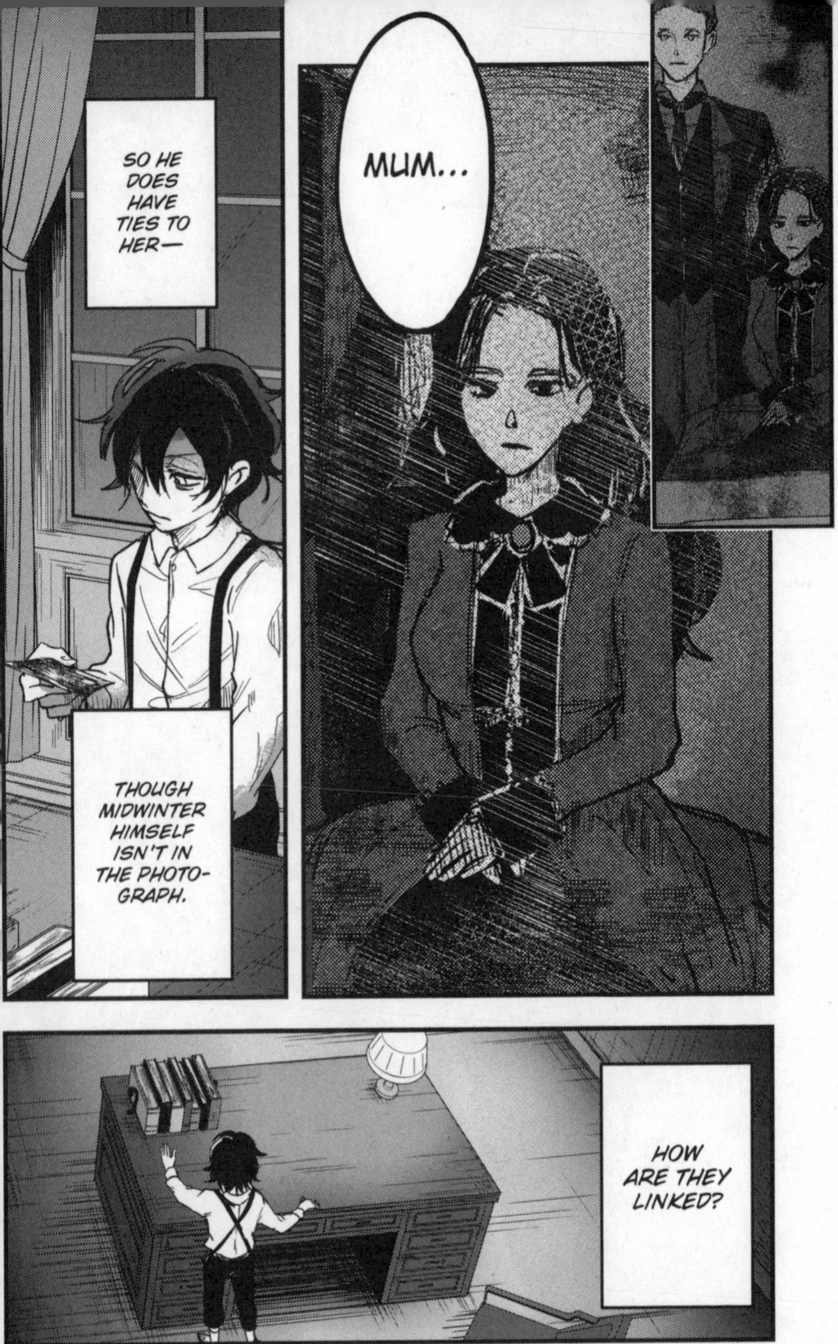
MUM...
SO HE DOES HAVE TIES TO HER—
THOUGH MIDWINTER HIMSELF ISN'T IN THE PHOTOGRAPH.
HOW ARE THEY LINKED?

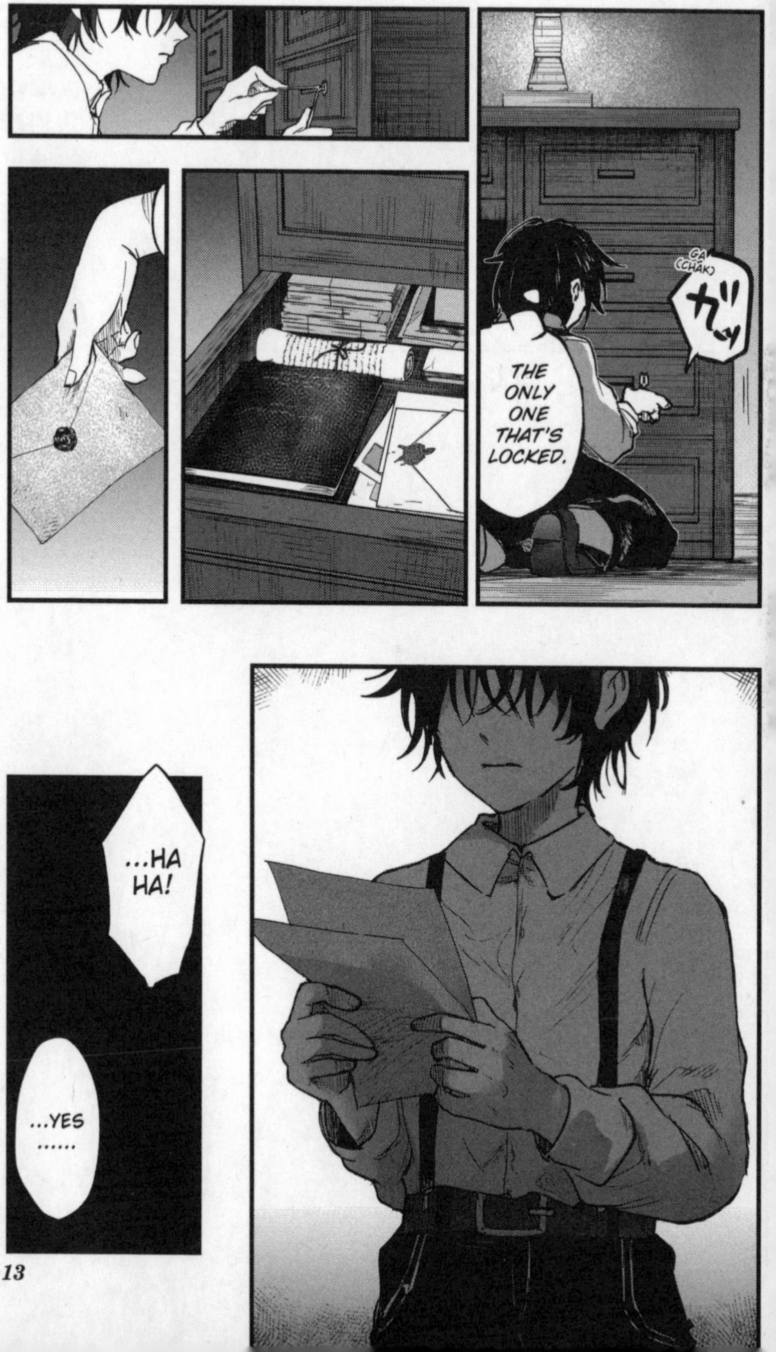
GA (CHAK)
ガッ
THE ONLY ONE THAT'S LOCKED.
...HA HA!
...YES ......

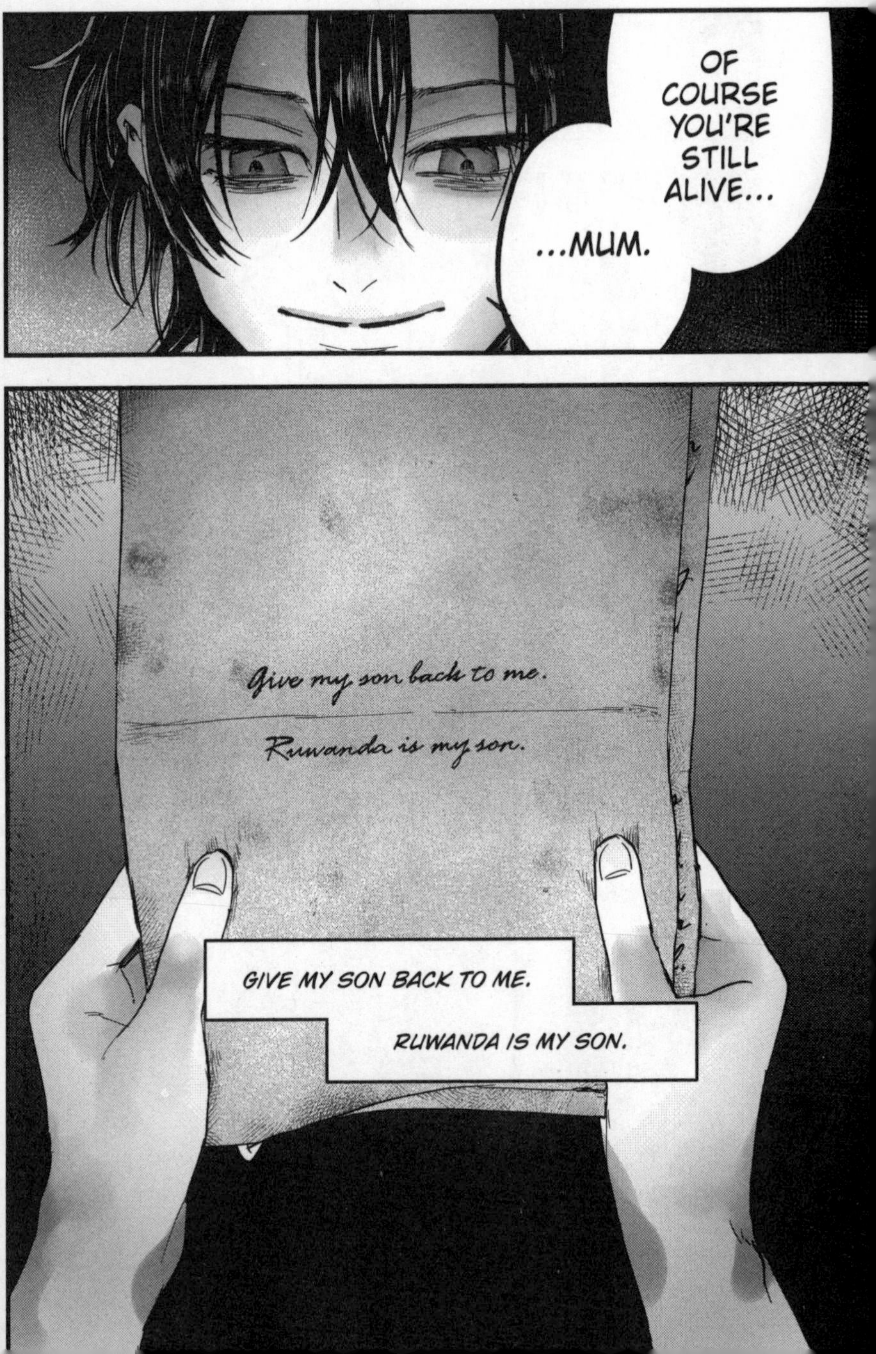
OF COURSE YOU'RE STILL ALIVE...
...MUM.
Give my son back to me.
Ruwanda is my son.
GIVE MY SON BACK TO ME.
RUWANDA IS MY SON.

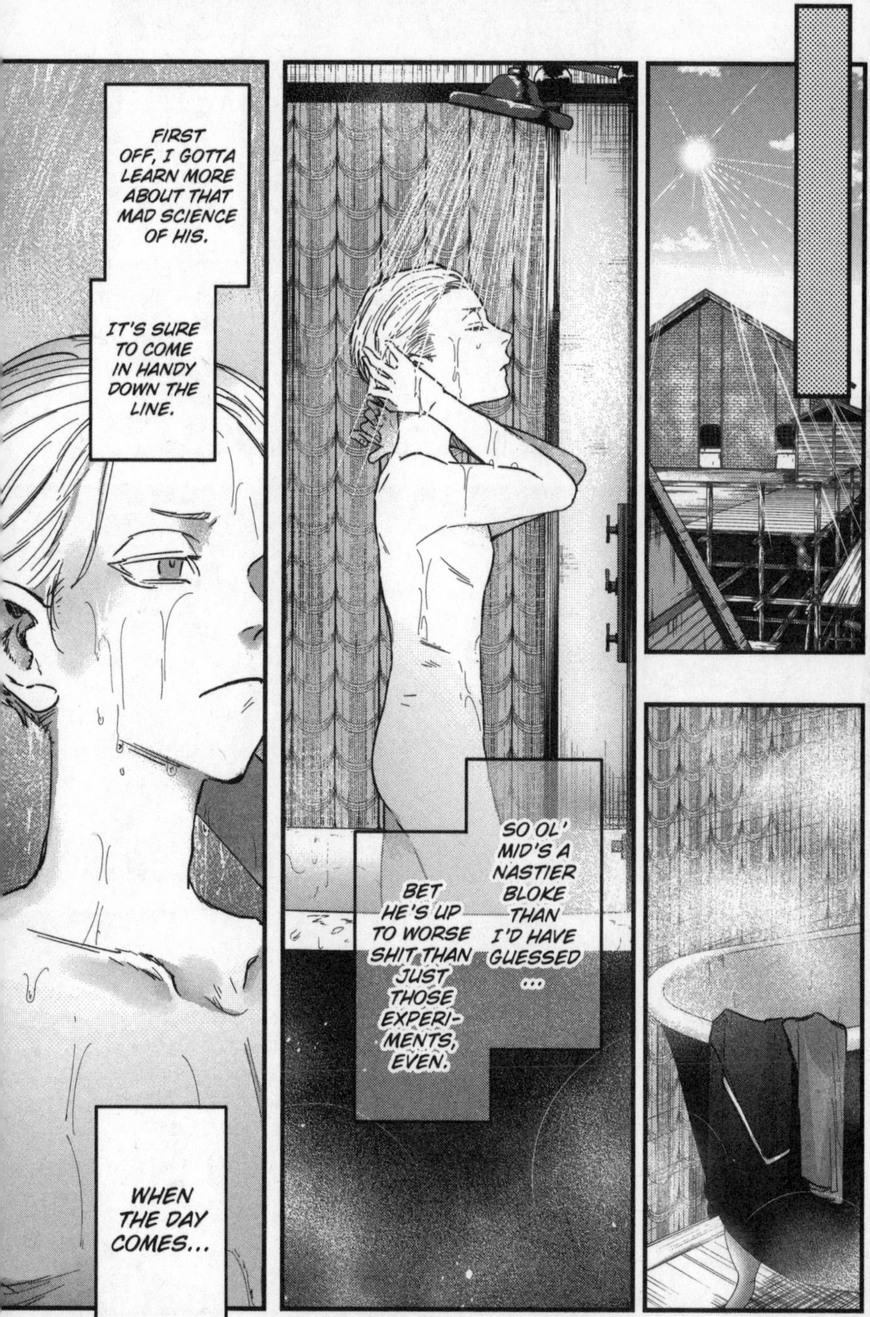
SO OL' MID'S A NASTIER BLOKE THAN I'D HAVE GUESSED...
BET HE'S UP TO WORSE SHIT THAN JUST THOSE EXPERI-MENTS, EVEN.
FIRST OFF, I GOTTA LEARN MORE ABOUT THAT MAD SCIENCE OF HIS.
IT'S SURE TO COME IN HANDY DOWN THE LINE.
WHEN THE DAY COMES...

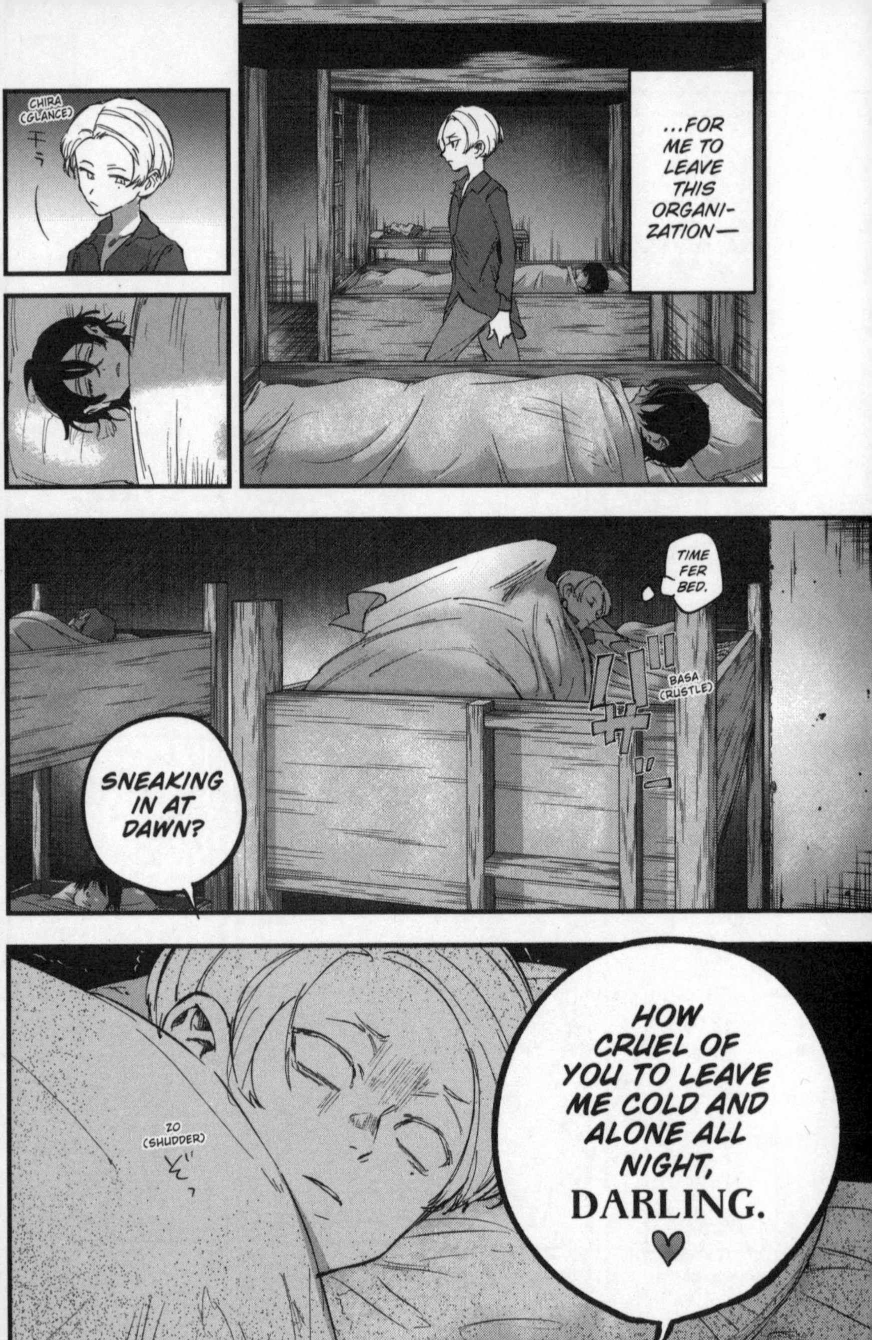
...FOR ME TO LEAVE THIS ORGANIZATION—
CHIRA (GLANCE)
TIME FER BED.
BASA (RUSTLE)
SNEAKING IN AT DAWN?
HOW CRUEL OF YOU TO LEAVE ME COLD AND ALONE ALL NIGHT, DARLING. ♥
ZO (SHUDDER)

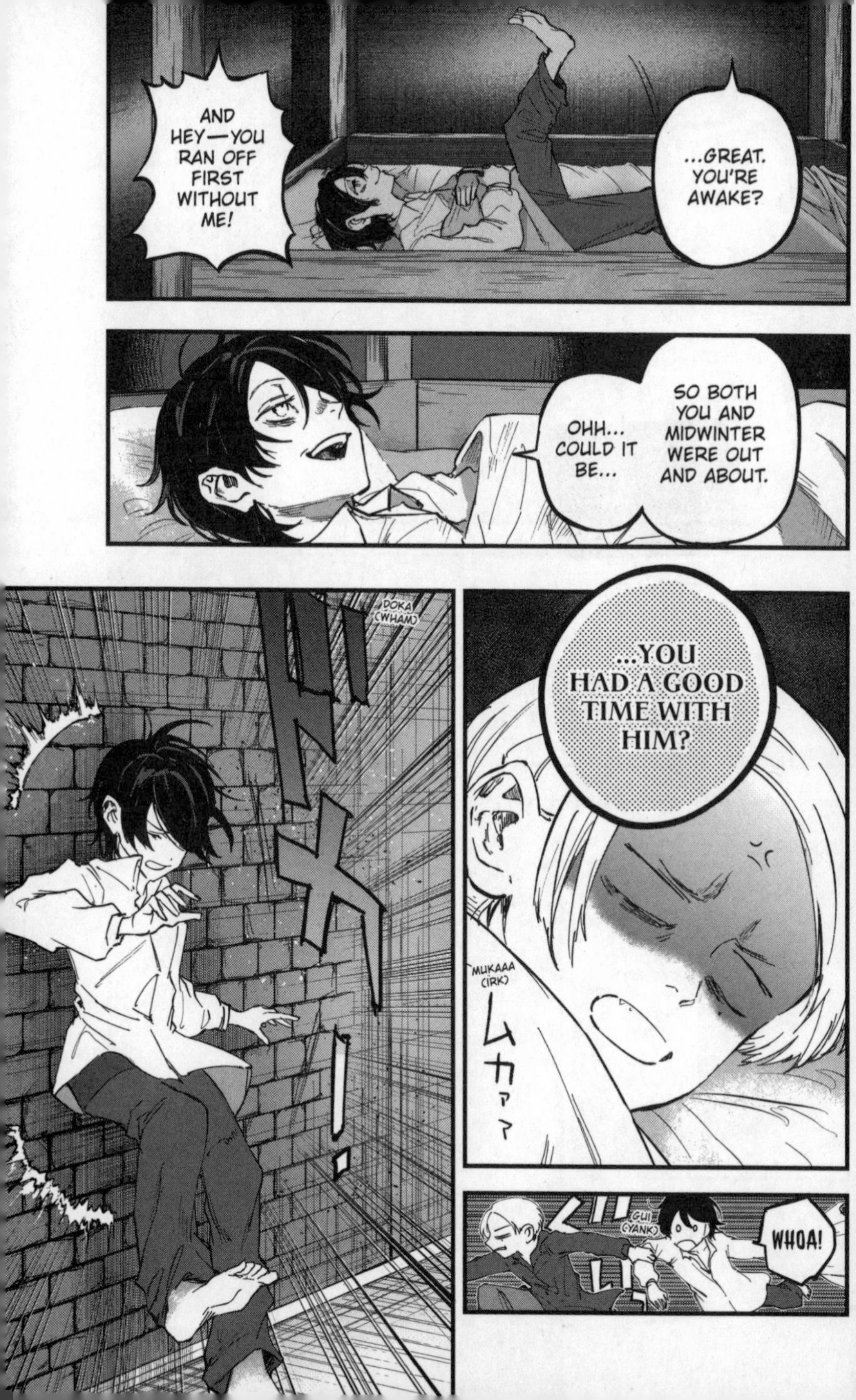
...GREAT. YOU'RE AWAKE?
AND HEY—YOU RAN OFF FIRST WITHOUT ME!
SO BOTH YOU AND MIDWINTER WERE OUT AND ABOUT.
OHH... COULD IT BE...
...YOU HAD A GOOD TIME WITH HIM?
MUKAAA (IRK)
WHOA!
GUI (YANK)
DOKA (WHAM)

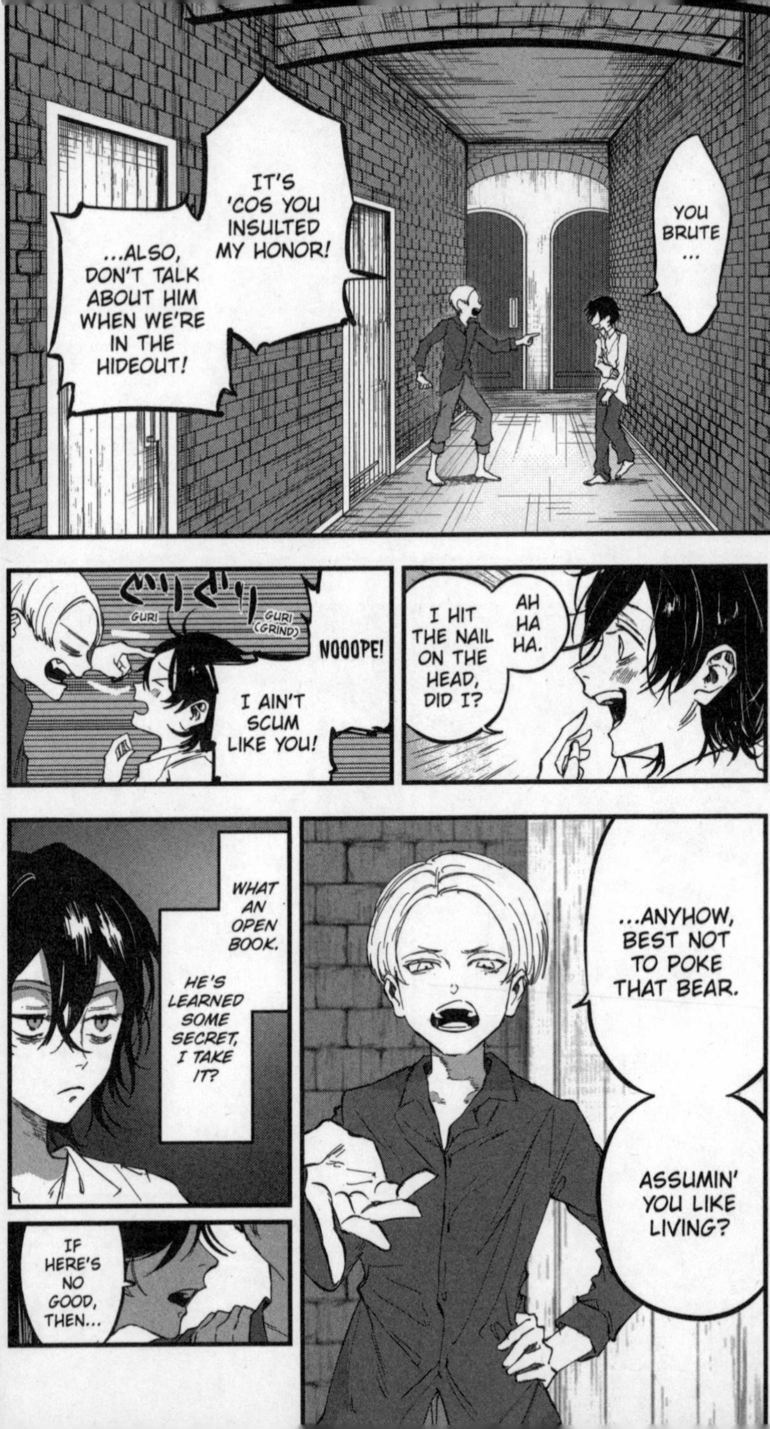
YOU BRUTE...
IT'S 'COS YOU INSULTED MY HONOR!
...ALSO, DON'T TALK ABOUT HIM WHEN WE'RE IN THE HIDEOUT!
AH HA HA.
I HIT THE NAIL ON THE HEAD, DID I?
NOOOPE!
ぐりぐり
GURI GURI (GRIND)
I AIN'T SCUM LIKE YOU!
...ANYHOW, BEST NOT TO POKE THAT BEAR.
ASSUMIN' YOU LIKE LIVING?
WHAT AN OPEN BOOK.
HE'S LEARNED SOME SECRET, I TAKE IT?
IF HERE'S NO GOOD, THEN...

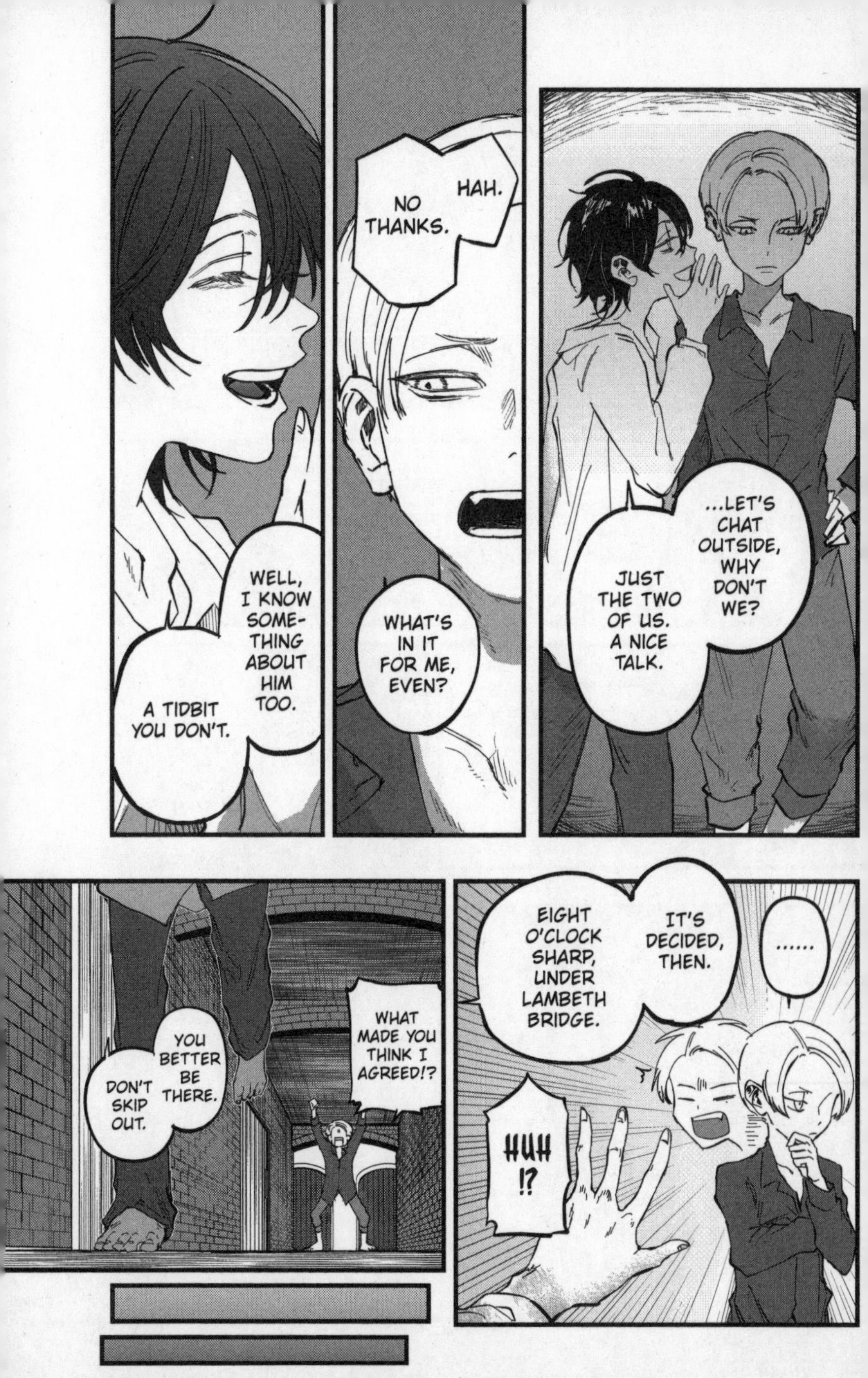
...LET'S CHAT OUTSIDE, WHY DON'T WE?
JUST THE TWO OF US. A NICE TALK.
HAH.
NO THANKS.
WHAT'S IN IT FOR ME, EVEN?
WELL, I KNOW SOME-THING ABOUT HIM TOO.
A TIDBIT YOU DON'T.
......
IT'S DECIDED, THEN.
EIGHT O'CLOCK SHARP, UNDER LAMBETH BRIDGE.
HUH!?
WHAT MADE YOU THINK I AGREED!?
YOU BETTER BE THERE.
DON'T SKIP OUT.

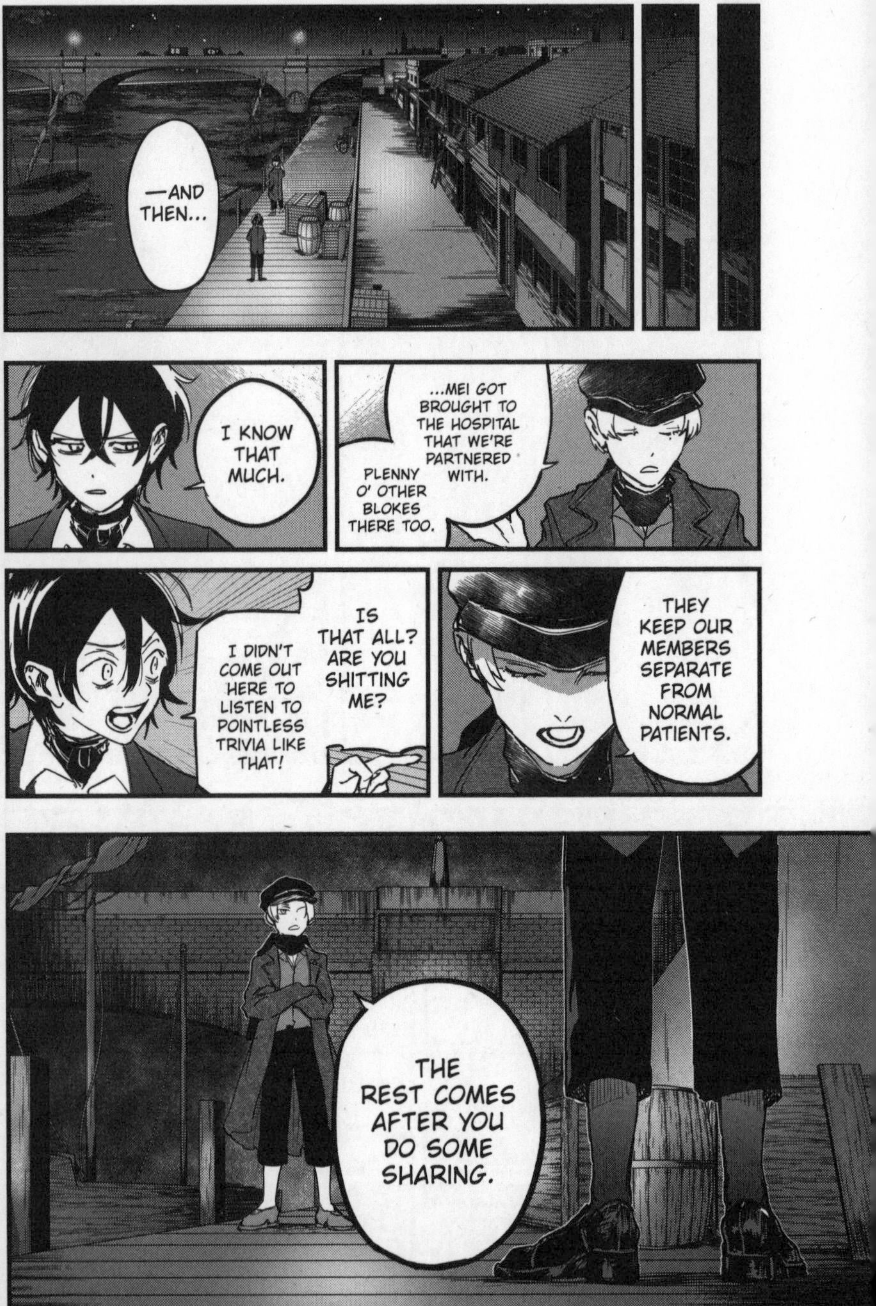
—AND THEN...
...MEI GOT BROUGHT TO THE HOSPITAL THAT WE'RE PARTNERED WITH.
PLENNY O' OTHER BLOKES THERE TOO.
I KNOW THAT MUCH.
THEY KEEP OUR MEMBERS SEPARATE FROM NORMAL PATIENTS.
IS THAT ALL? ARE YOU SHITTING ME?
I DIDN'T COME OUT HERE TO LISTEN TO POINTLESS TRIVIA LIKE THAT!
THE REST COMES AFTER YOU DO SOME SHARING.

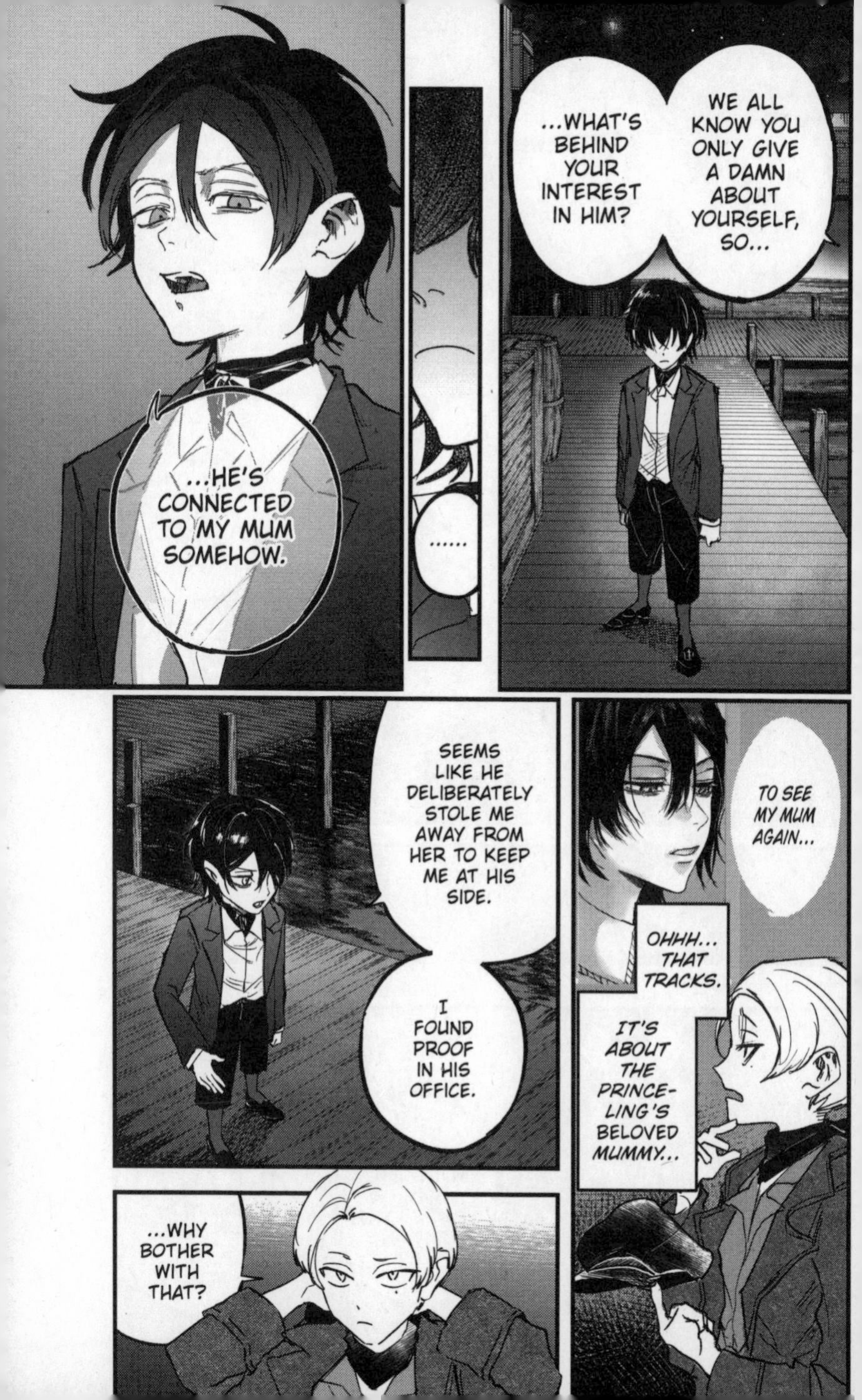
WE ALL KNOW YOU ONLY GIVE A DAMN ABOUT YOURSELF, SO...
...WHAT'S BEHIND YOUR INTEREST IN HIM?
......
...HE'S CONNECTED TO MY MUM SOMEHOW.
SEEMS LIKE HE DELIBERATELY STOLE ME AWAY FROM HER TO KEEP ME AT HIS SIDE.
I FOUND PROOF IN HIS OFFICE.
...WHY BOTHER WITH THAT?
TO SEE MY MUM AGAIN...
OHHH... THAT TRACKS.
IT'S ABOUT THE PRINCE-LING'S BELOVED MUMMY...

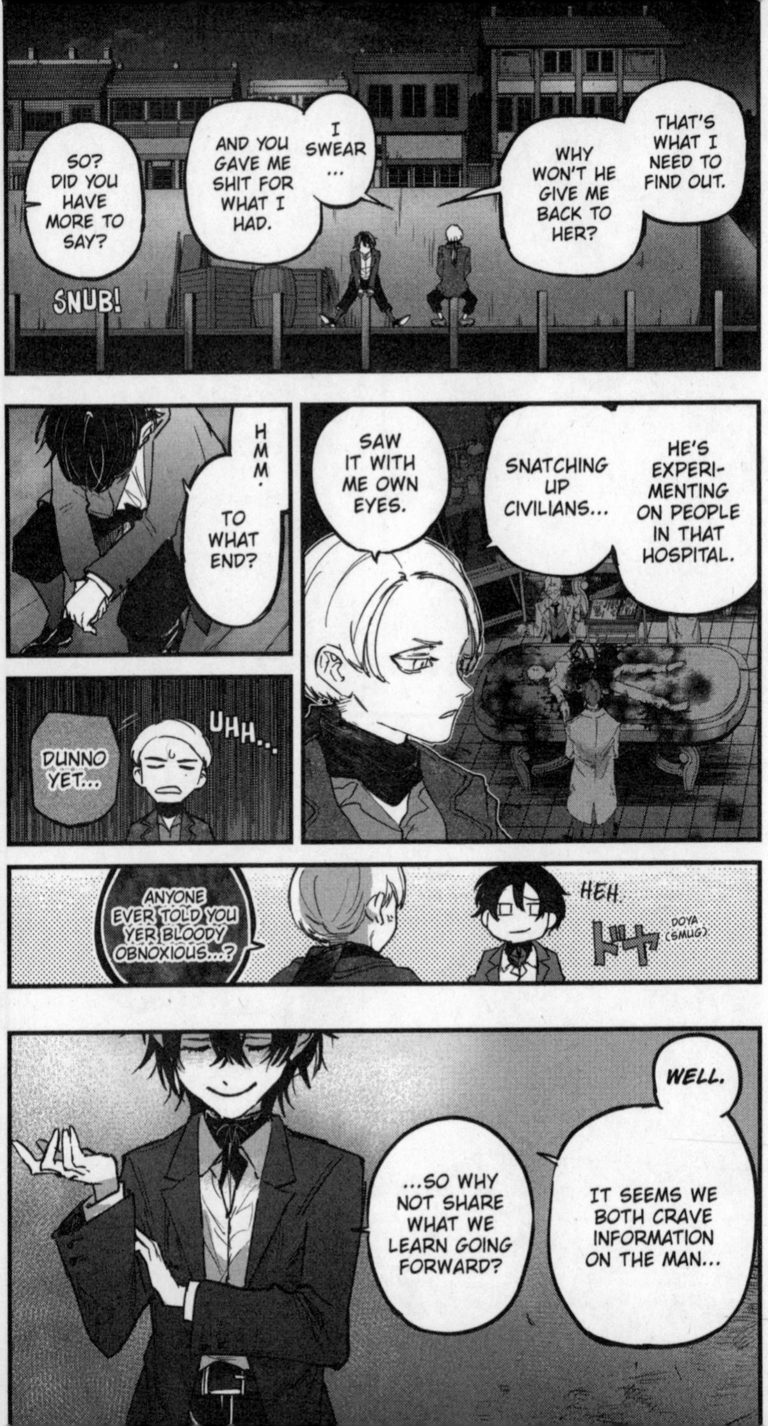
THAT'S WHAT I NEED TO FIND OUT.
WHY WON'T HE GIVE ME BACK TO HER?
I SWEAR ...
AND YOU GAVE ME SHIT FOR WHAT I HAD.
SO? DID YOU HAVE MORE TO SAY?
SNUB!
HE'S EXPERIMENTING ON PEOPLE IN THAT HOSPITAL.
SNATCHING UP CIVILIANS...
SAW IT WITH ME OWN EYES.
HMM.
TO WHAT END?
UHH...
DUNNO YET...
HEH
ドヤ
DOYA (SMUG)
ANYONE EVER TOLD YOU YER BLOODY OBNOXIOUS...?
WELL.
IT SEEMS WE BOTH CRAVE INFORMATION ON THE MAN...
...SO WHY NOT SHARE WHAT WE LEARN GOING FORWARD?

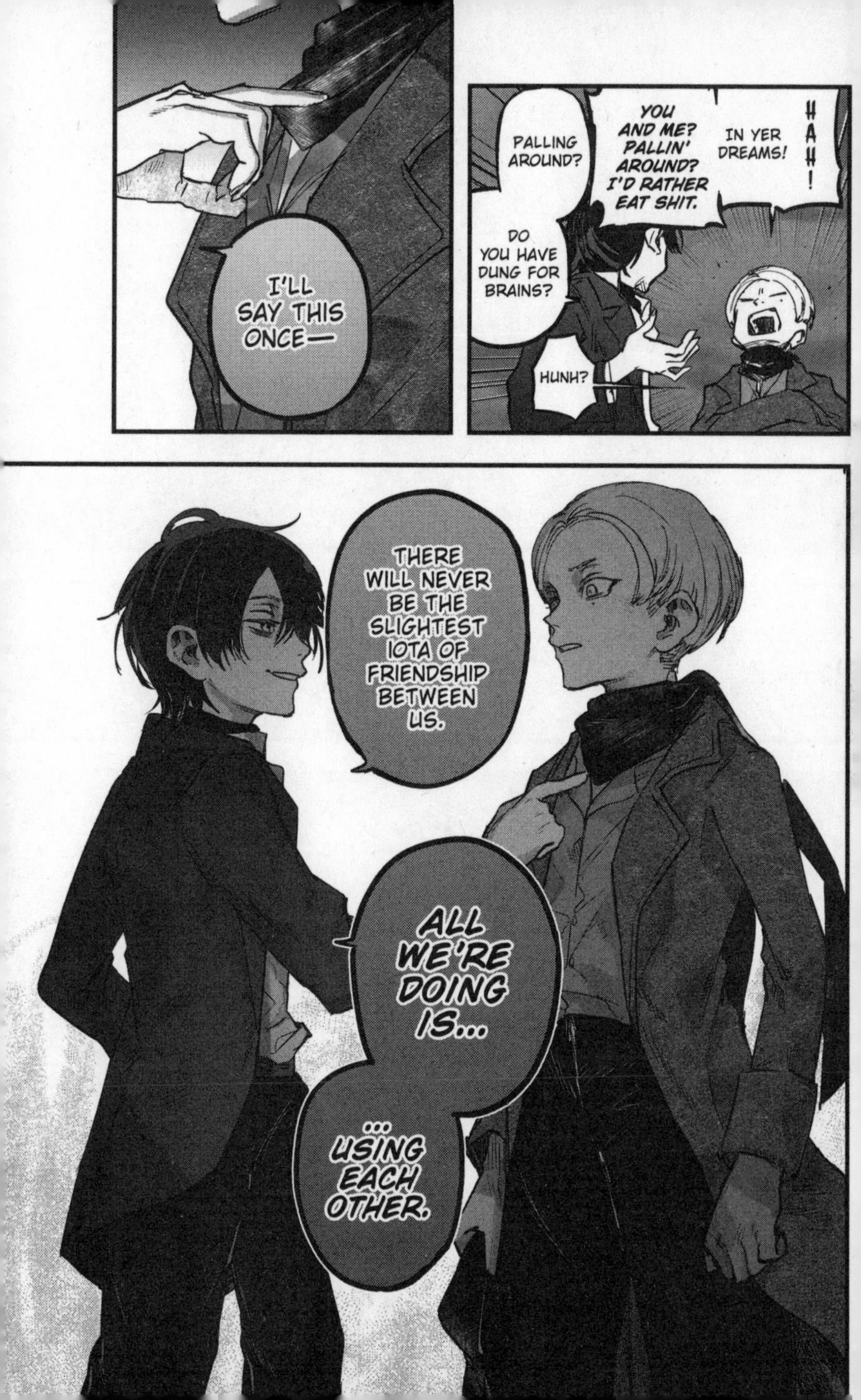
HAH!
IN YER DREAMS!
YOU AND ME? PALLIN' AROUND? I'D RATHER EAT SHIT.
PALLING AROUND?
DO YOU HAVE DUNG FOR BRAINS?
HUNH?
I'LL SAY THIS ONCE—
THERE WILL NEVER BE THE SLIGHTEST IOTA OF FRIENDSHIP BETWEEN US.
ALL WE'RE DOING IS...
...USING EACH OTHER.

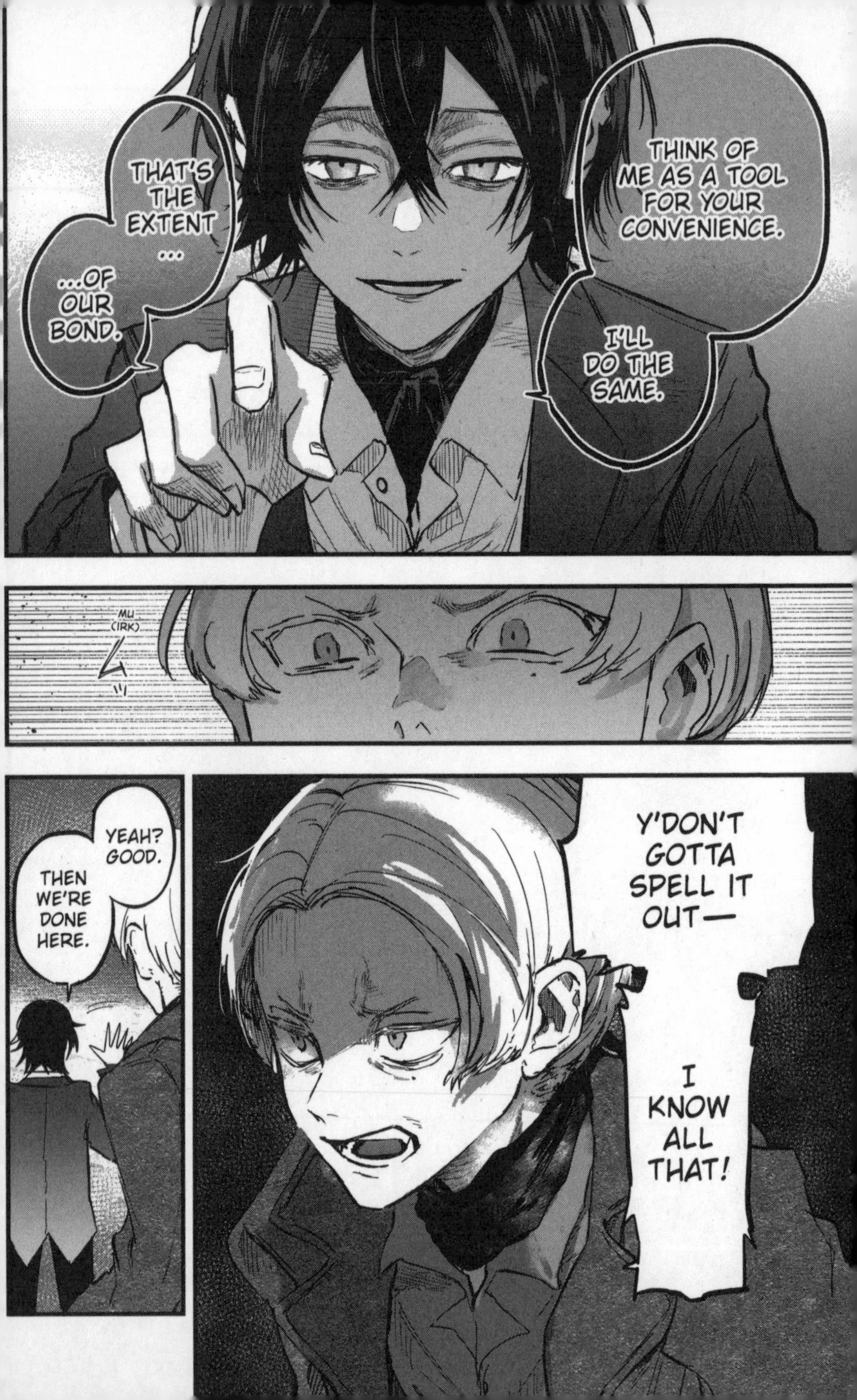
THINK OF ME AS A TOOL FOR YOUR CONVENIENCE.
I'LL DO THE SAME.
THAT'S THE EXTENT...
...OF OUR BOND.
MU (IRK)
Y'DON'T GOTTA SPELL IT OUT—
I KNOW ALL THAT!
YEAH? GOOD.
THEN WE'RE DONE HERE.

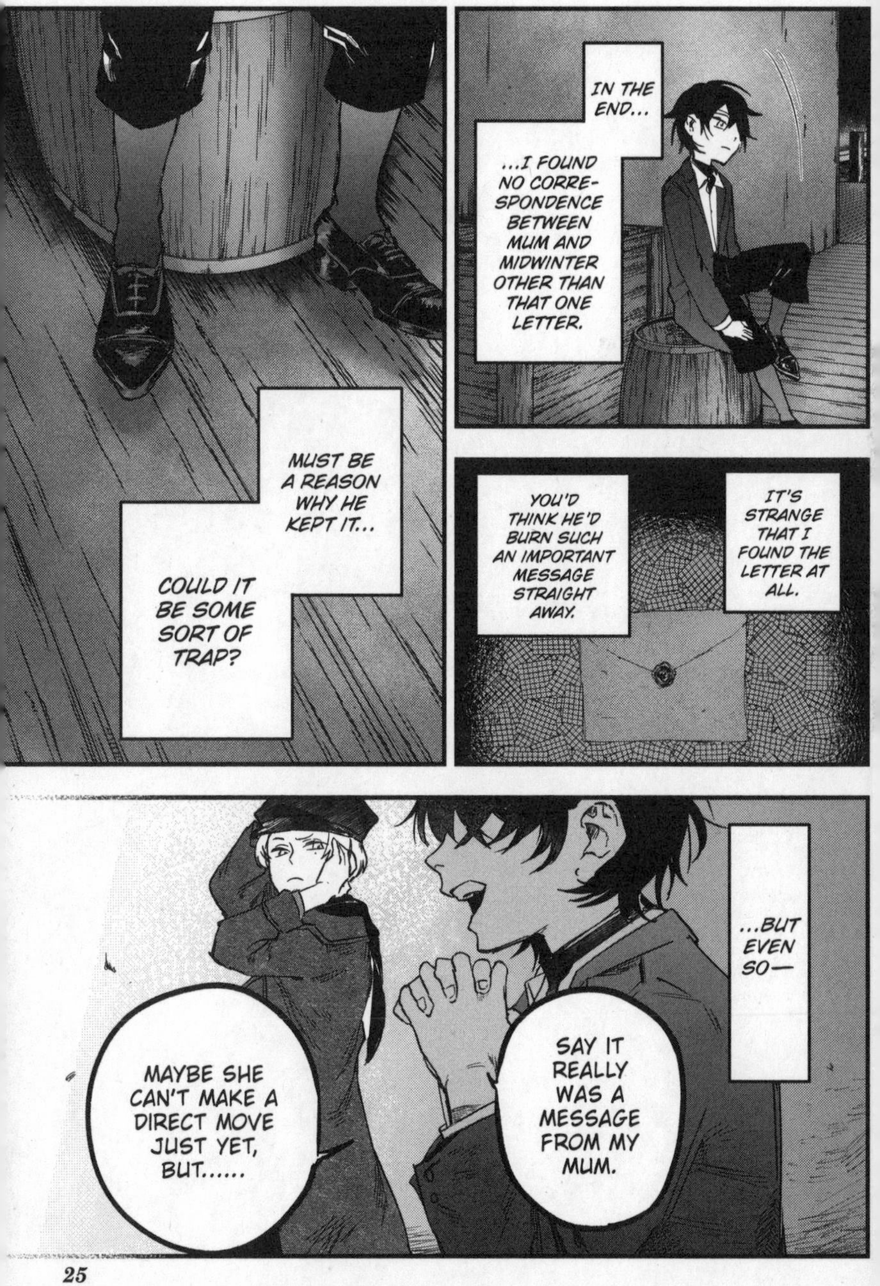
IN THE END...
...I FOUND NO CORRESPONDENCE BETWEEN MUM AND MIDWINTER OTHER THAN THAT ONE LETTER.
IT'S STRANGE THAT I FOUND THE LETTER AT ALL.
YOU'D THINK HE'D BURN SUCH AN IMPORTANT MESSAGE STRAIGHT AWAY.
MUST BE A REASON WHY HE KEPT IT...
COULD IT BE SOME SORT OF TRAP?
...BUT EVEN SO—
SAY IT REALLY WAS A MESSAGE FROM MY MUM.
MAYBE SHE CAN'T MAKE A DIRECT MOVE JUST YET, BUT......

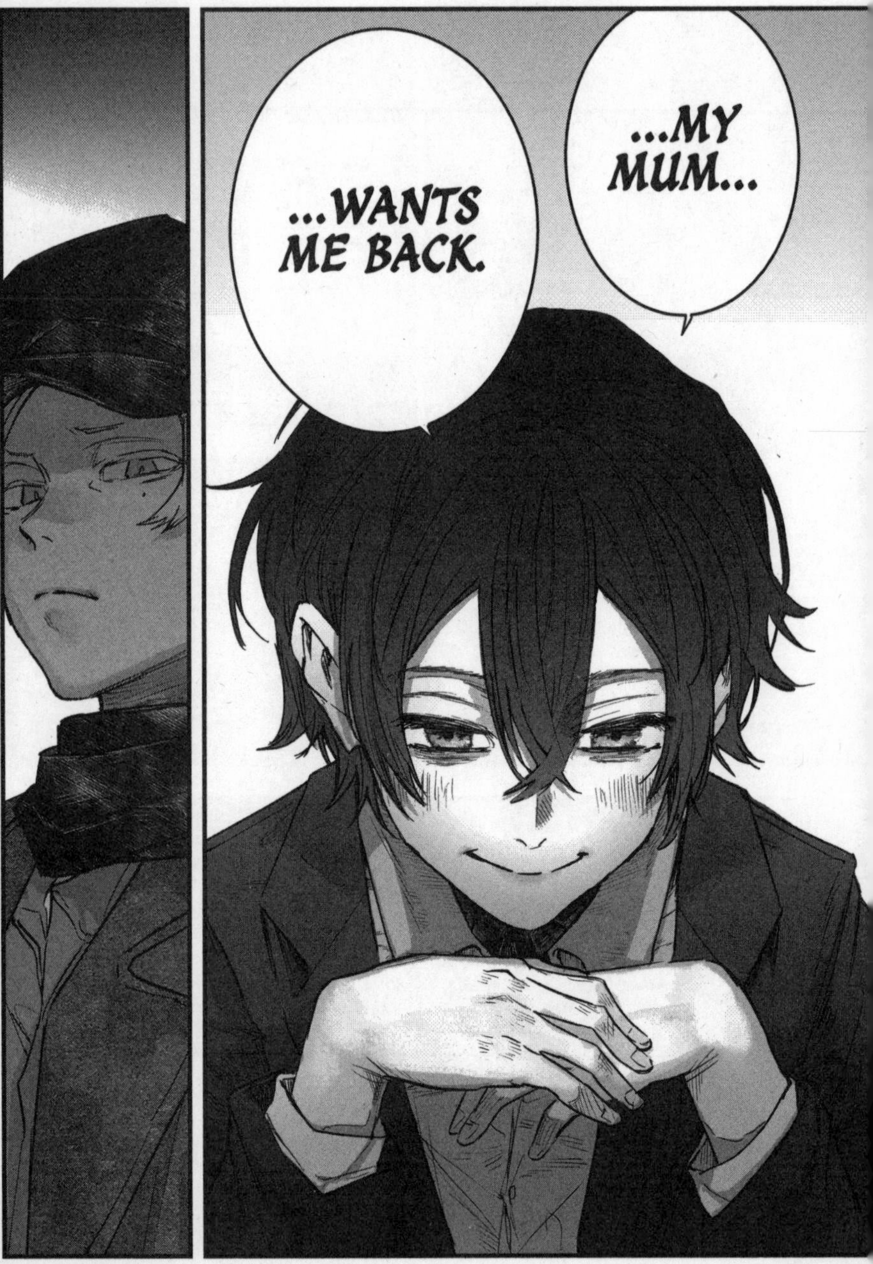
...MY MUM...
...WANTS ME BACK.

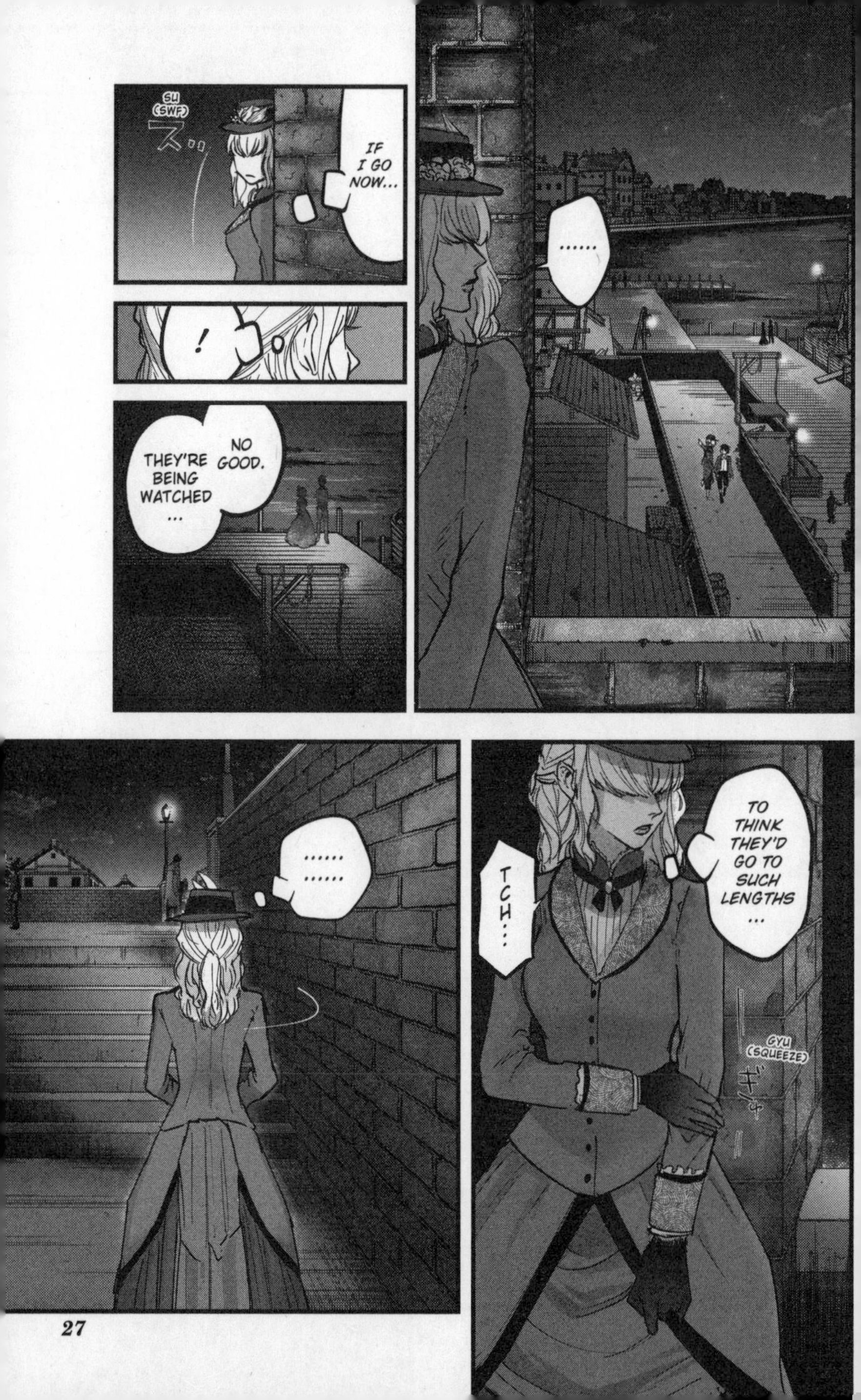
......
IF I GO NOW...
SU (SWF)
ス
!
NO GOOD.
THEY'RE BEING WATCHED ...
TO THINK THEY'D GO TO SUCH LENGTHS ...
TCH...
GYU (SQUEEZE)
ギュ
....

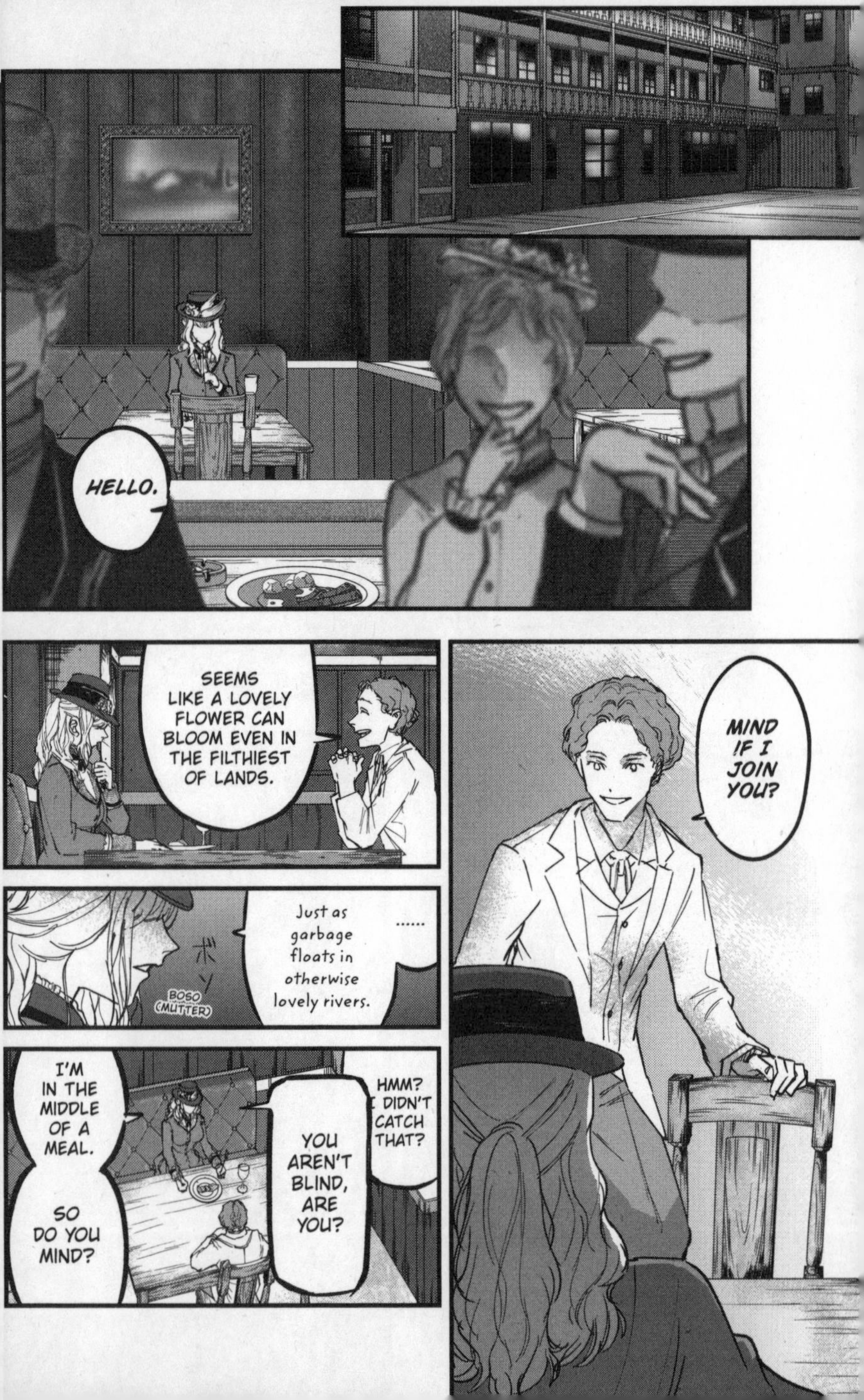
HELLO.
MIND IF I JOIN YOU?
SEEMS LIKE A LOVELY FLOWER CAN BLOOM EVEN IN THE FILTHIEST OF LANDS.
......
Just as garbage floats in otherwise lovely rivers.
ボソ
BOSO (MUTTER)
HMM? I DIDN'T CATCH THAT?
YOU AREN'T BLIND, ARE YOU?
I'M IN THE MIDDLE OF A MEAL.
SO DO YOU MIND?

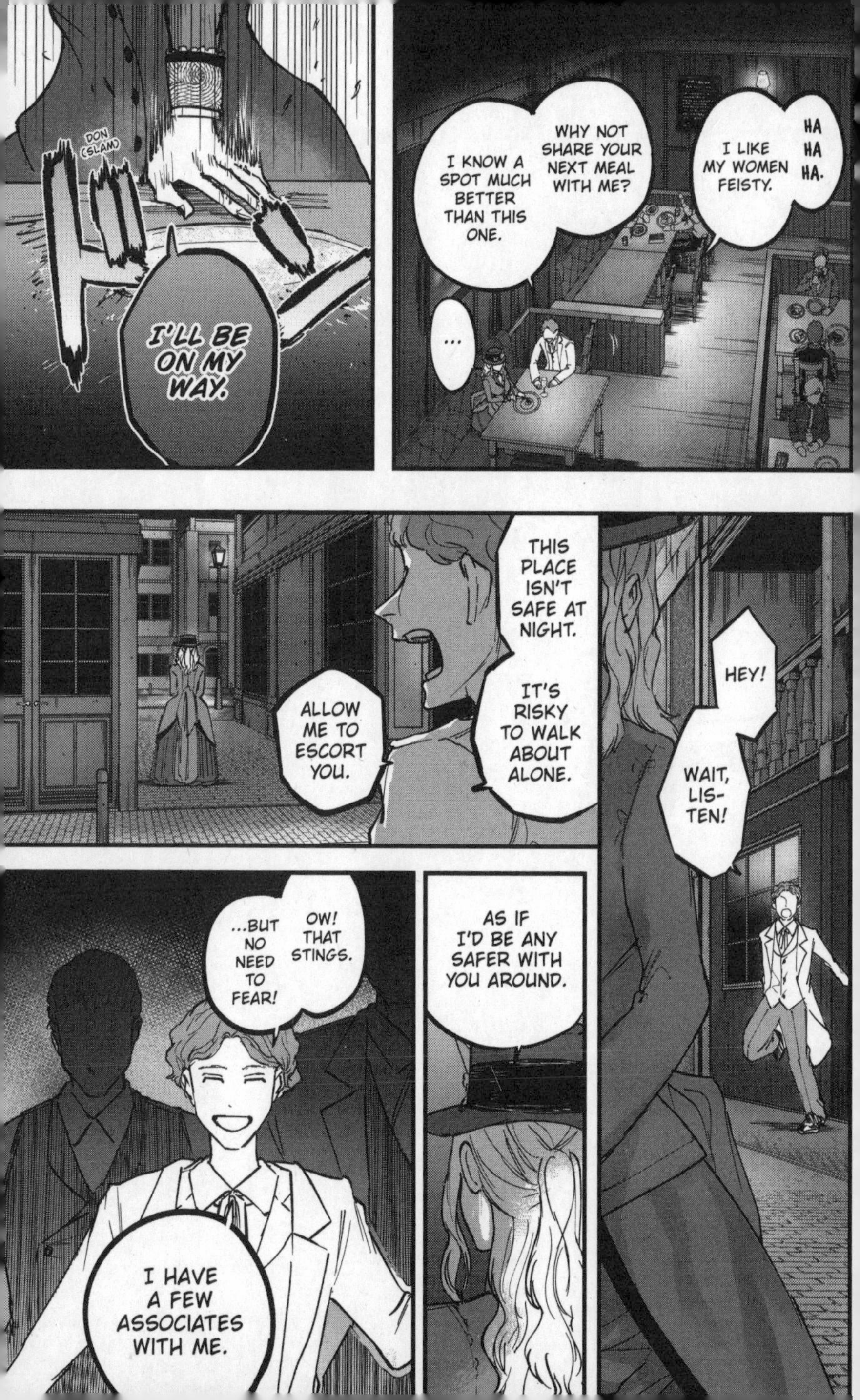
HA HA HA.
I LIKE MY WOMEN FEISTY.
WHY NOT SHARE YOUR NEXT MEAL WITH ME?
I KNOW A SPOT MUCH BETTER THAN THIS ONE.
...
DON (SLAM)
I'LL BE ON MY WAY.
HEY!
WAIT, LIS- TEN!
THIS PLACE ISN'T SAFE AT NIGHT.
IT'S RISKY TO WALK ABOUT ALONE.
ALLOW ME TO ESCORT YOU.
AS IF I'D BE ANY SAFER WITH YOU AROUND.
OW! THAT STINGS.
...BUT NO NEED TO FEAR!
I HAVE A FEW ASSOCIATES WITH ME.

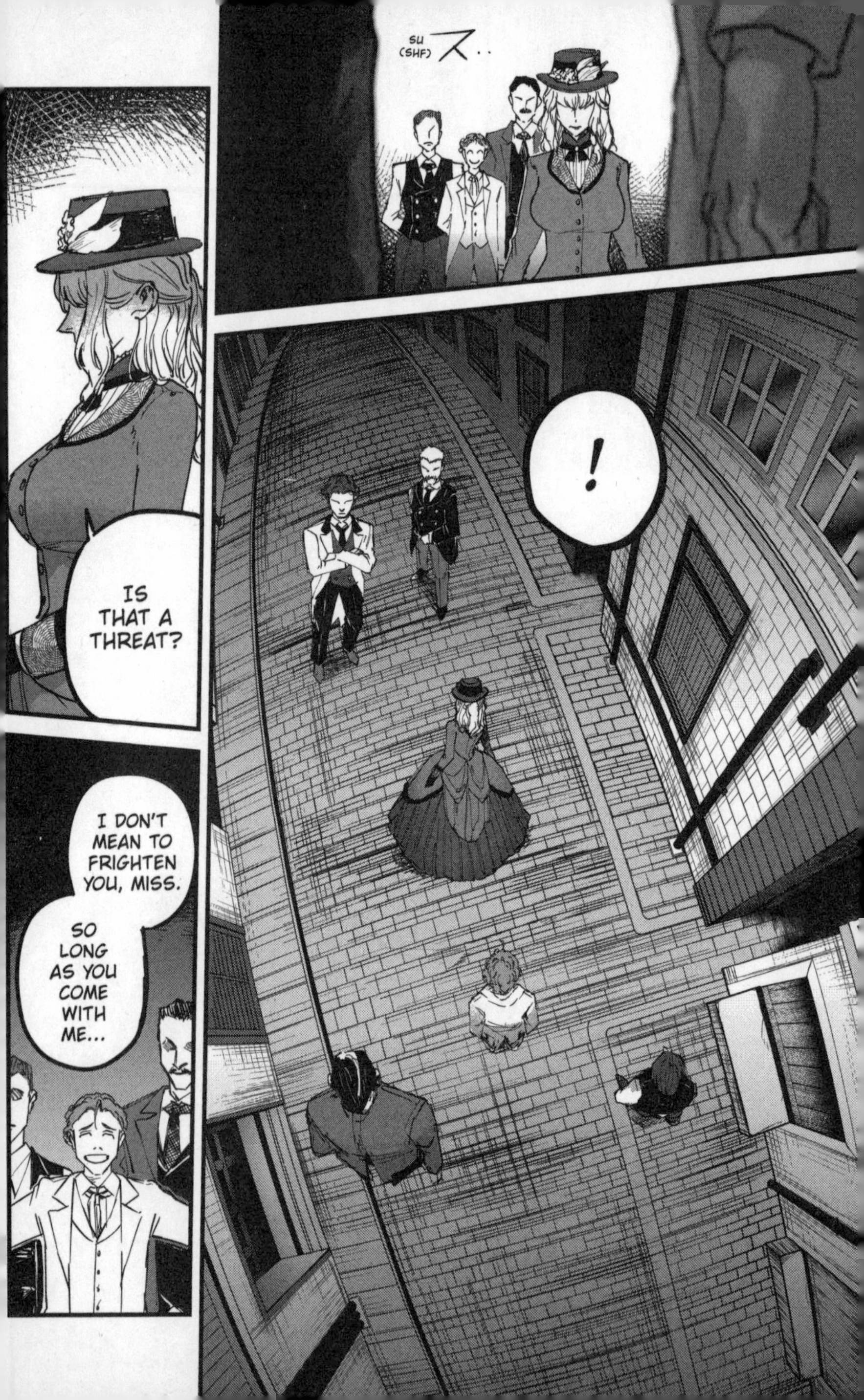
SU (SHF) ス..
!
IS THAT A THREAT?
I DON'T MEAN TO FRIGHTEN YOU, MISS.
SO LONG AS YOU COME WITH ME...

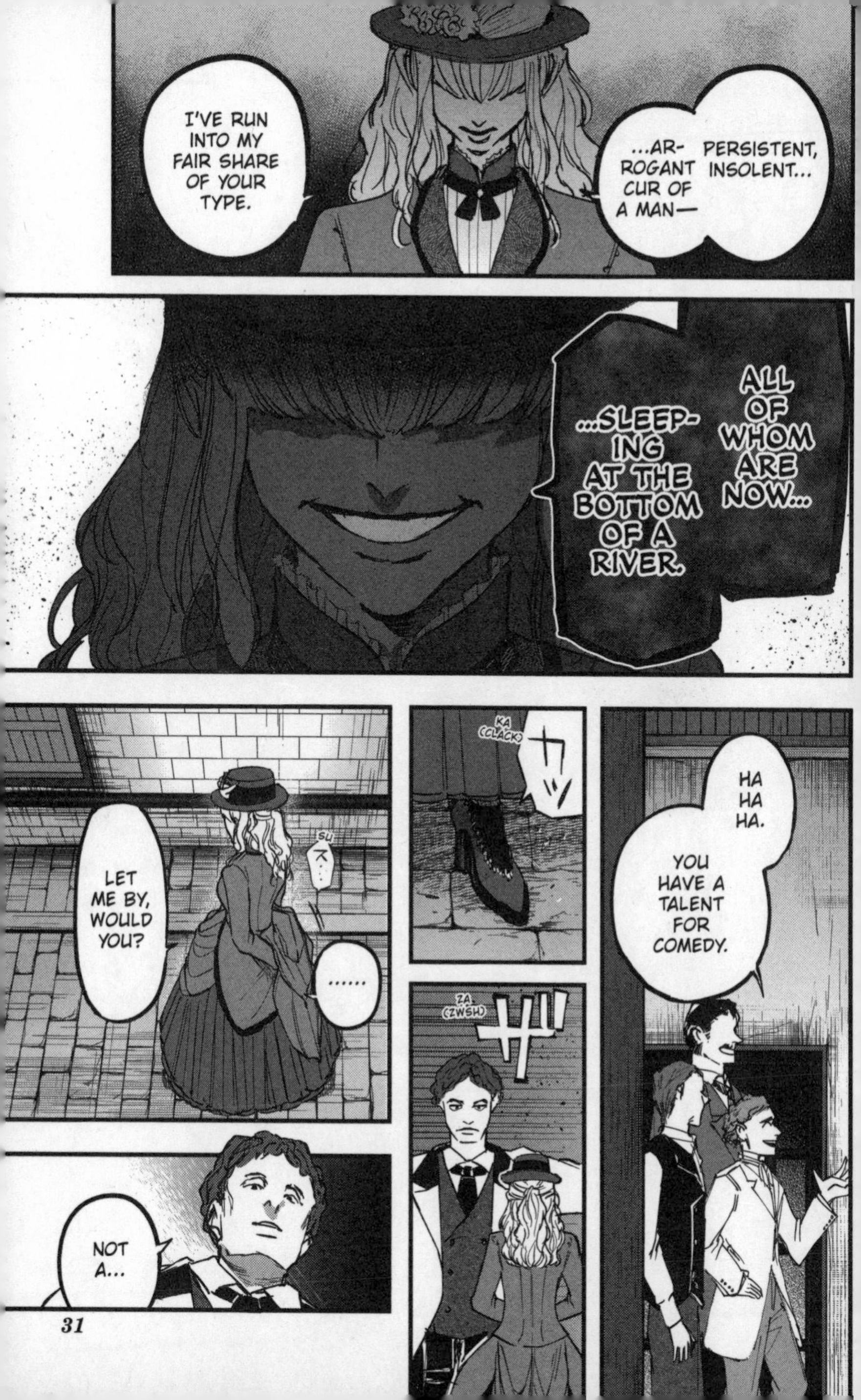
PERSISTENT, INSOLENT...
...AR-ROGANT CUR OF A MAN—
I'VE RUN INTO MY FAIR SHARE OF YOUR TYPE.
ALL OF WHOM ARE NOW...
...SLEEP-ING AT THE BOTTOM OF A RIVER.
HA HA HA.
YOU HAVE A TALENT FOR COMEDY.
KA (CLACK)
カッ
ZA (ZWSH)
ザッ
LET ME BY, WOULD YOU?
SU
ス…
......
NOT A...

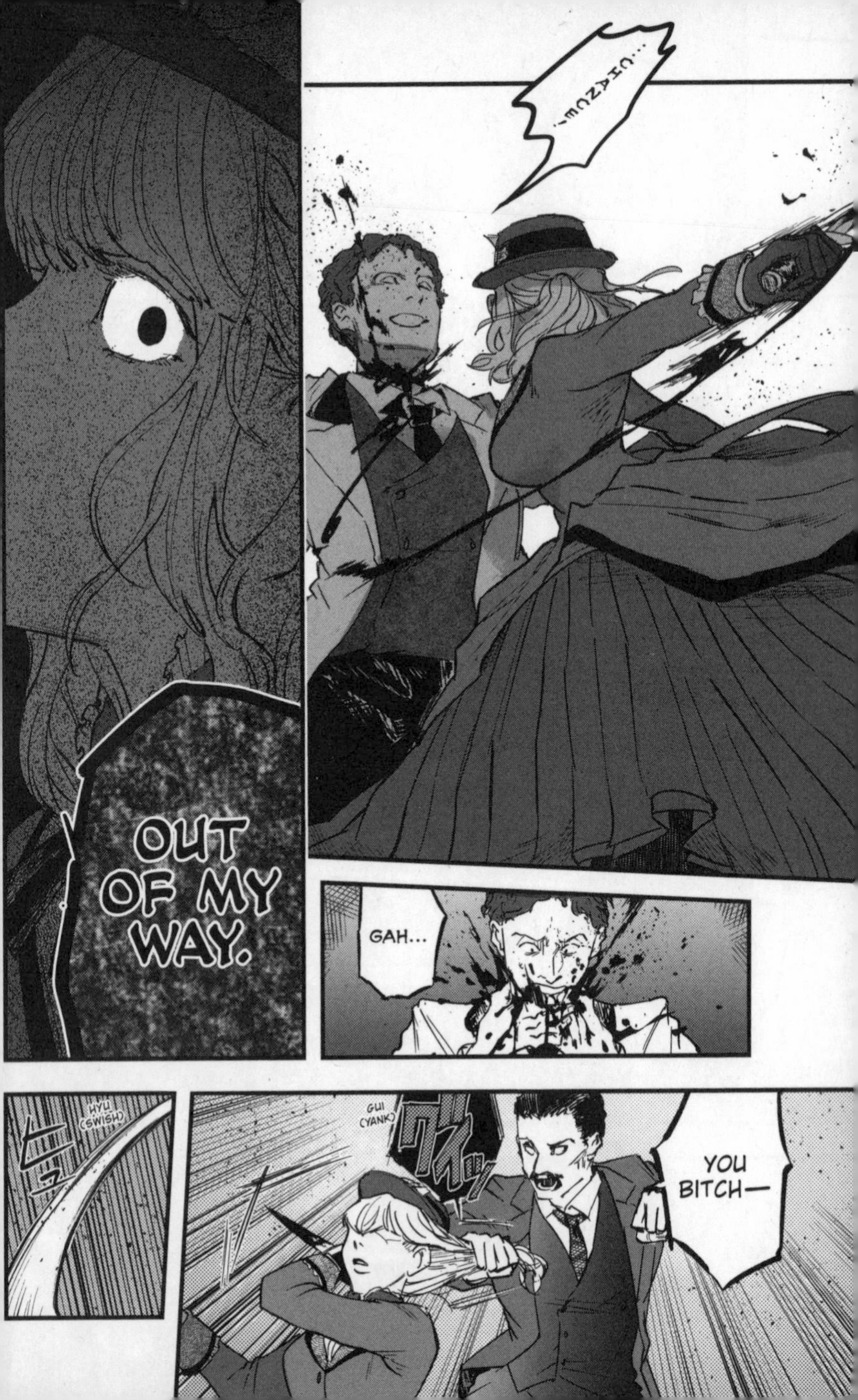
...UHAZUE!
GAH...
OUT OF MY WAY.
GUI (YANK)
YOU BITCH—
HYU (SWISH)

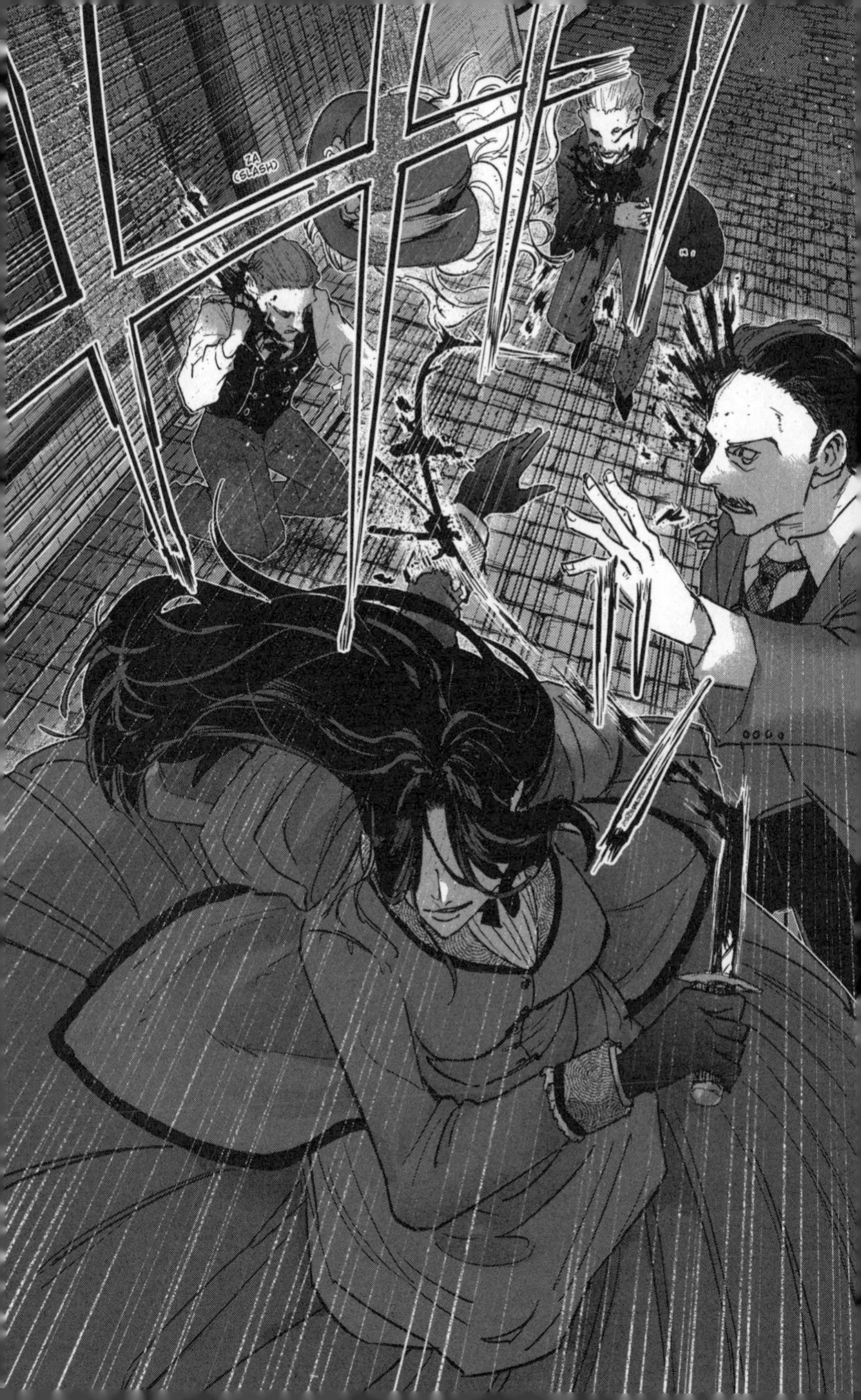
ZA (SLASH)

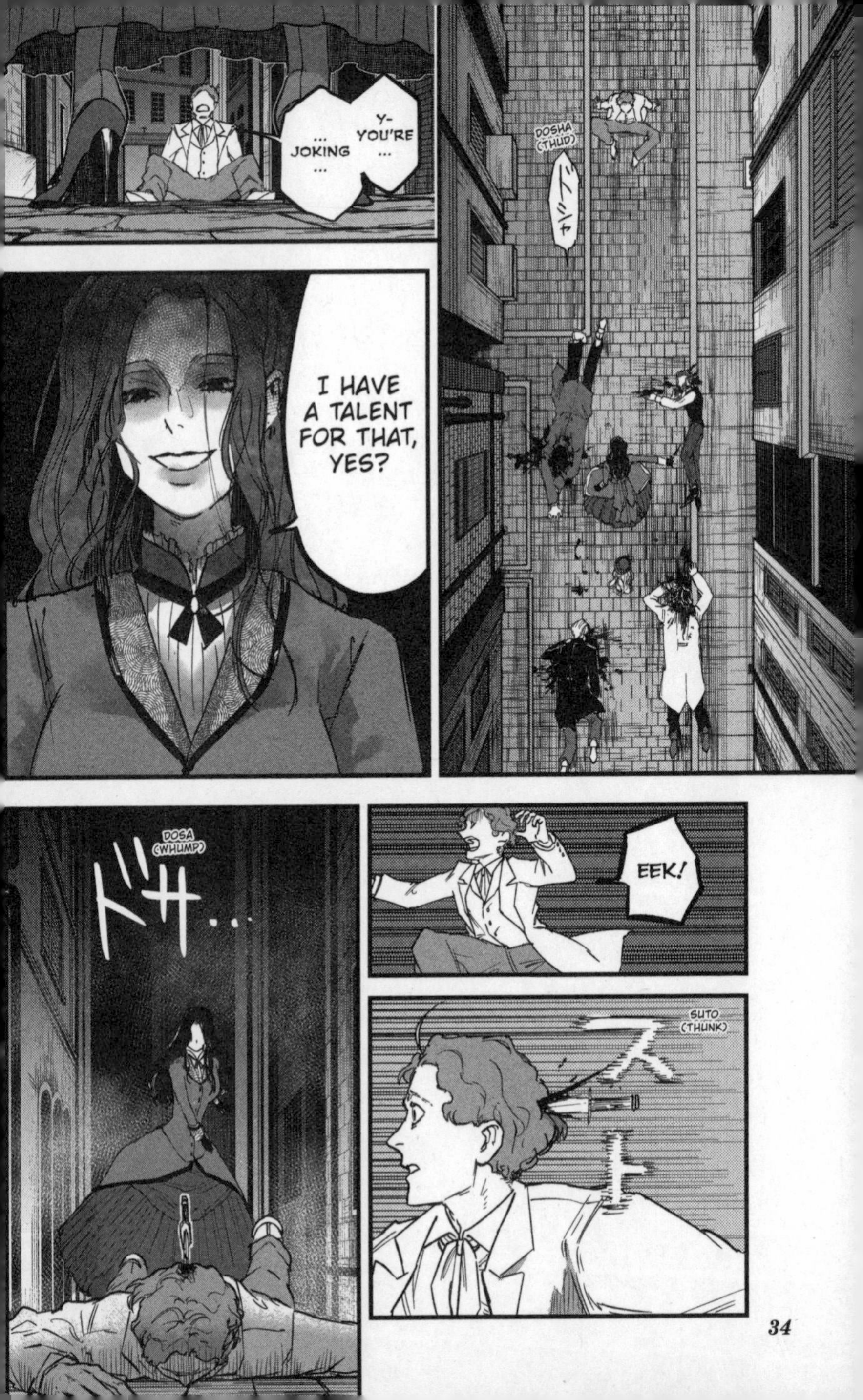
DOSHA (THUD)
Y- YOU'RE ... ... JOKING ...
I HAVE A TALENT FOR THAT, YES?
EEK!
SUTO (THUNK)
DOSA (WHUMP)

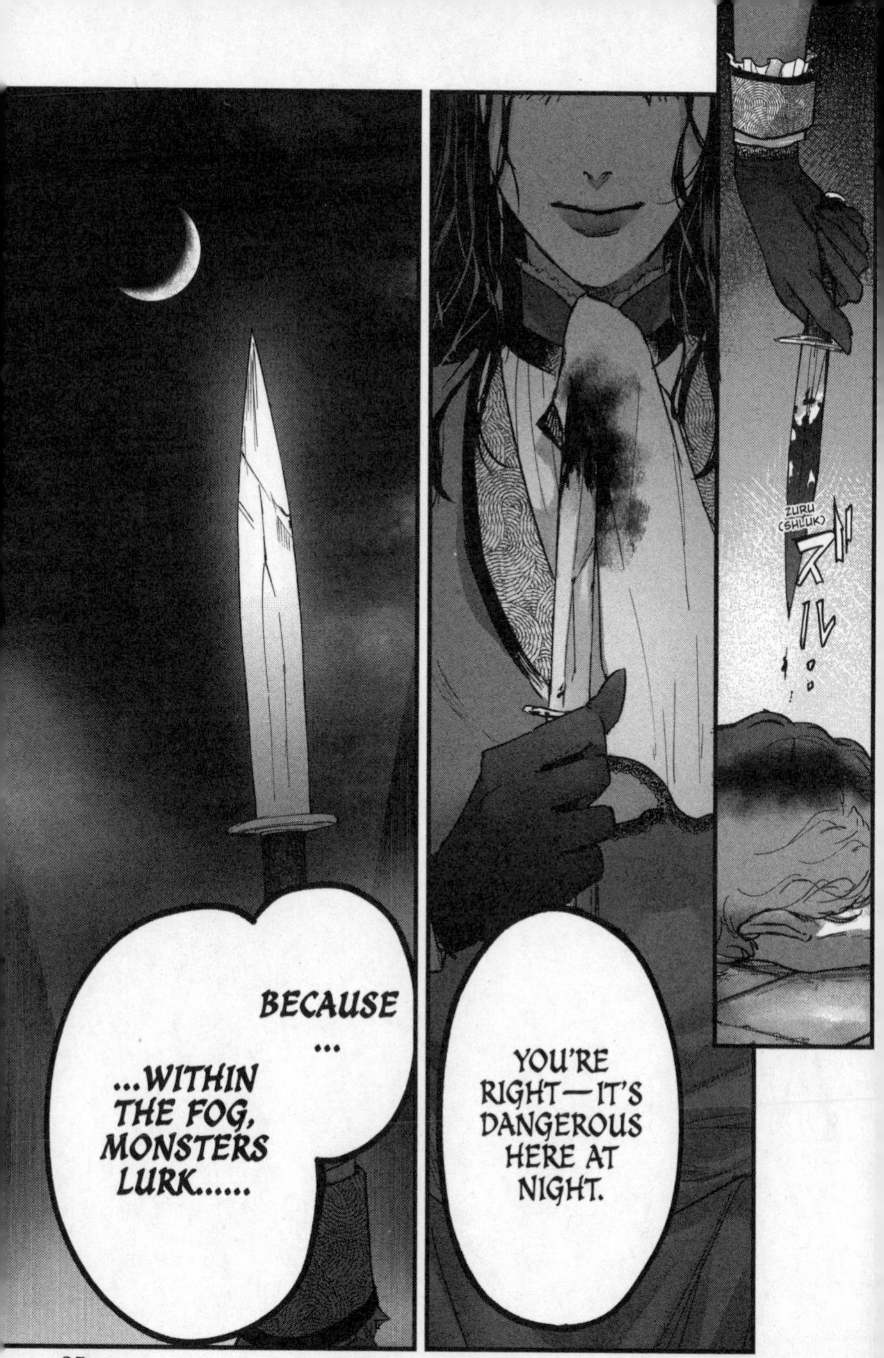
ZURU (SHLUK)
ズル
YOU'RE RIGHT—IT'S DANGEROUS HERE AT NIGHT.
BECAUSE ...
...WITHIN THE FOG, MONSTERS LURK......

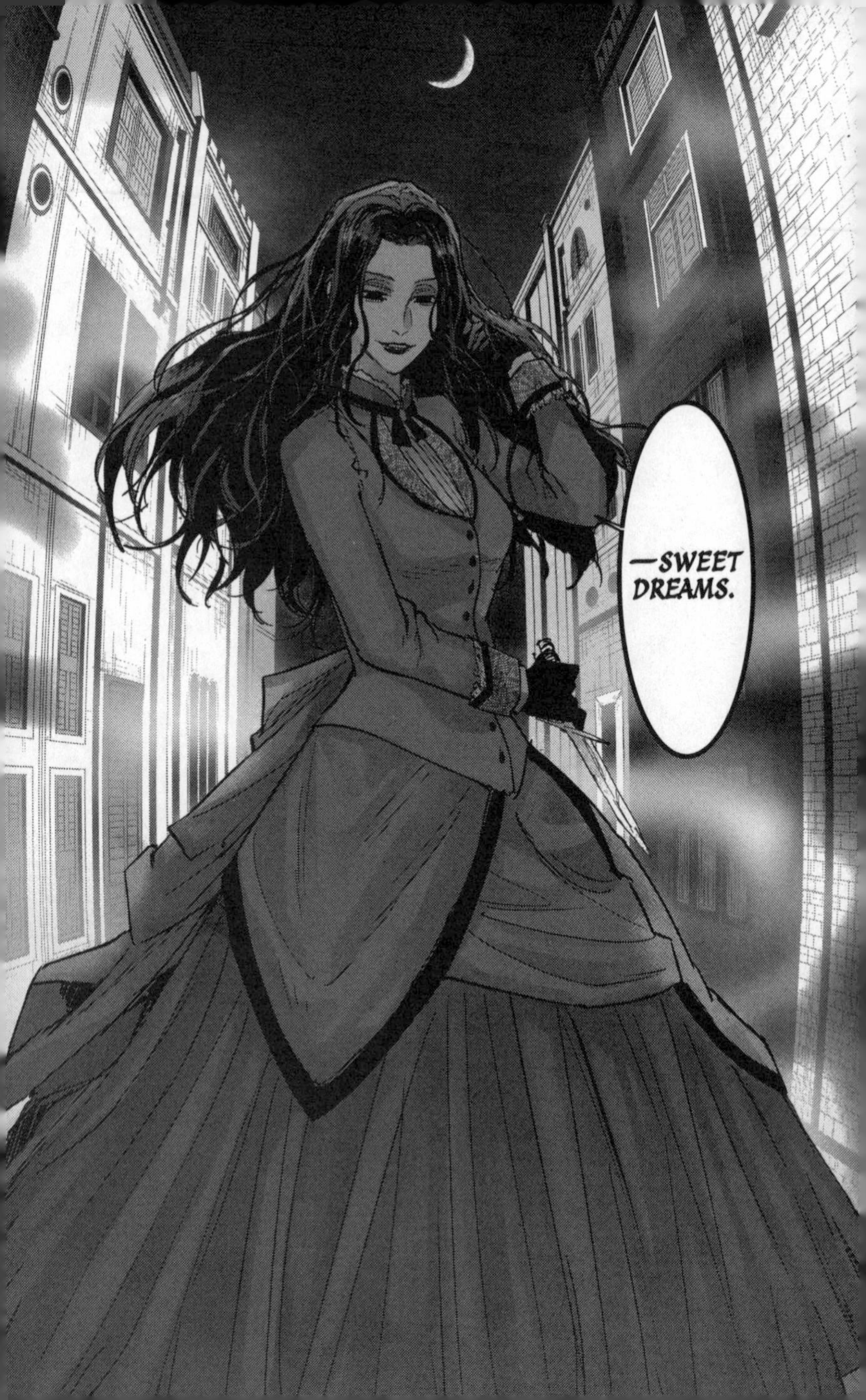
—SWEET DREAMS.

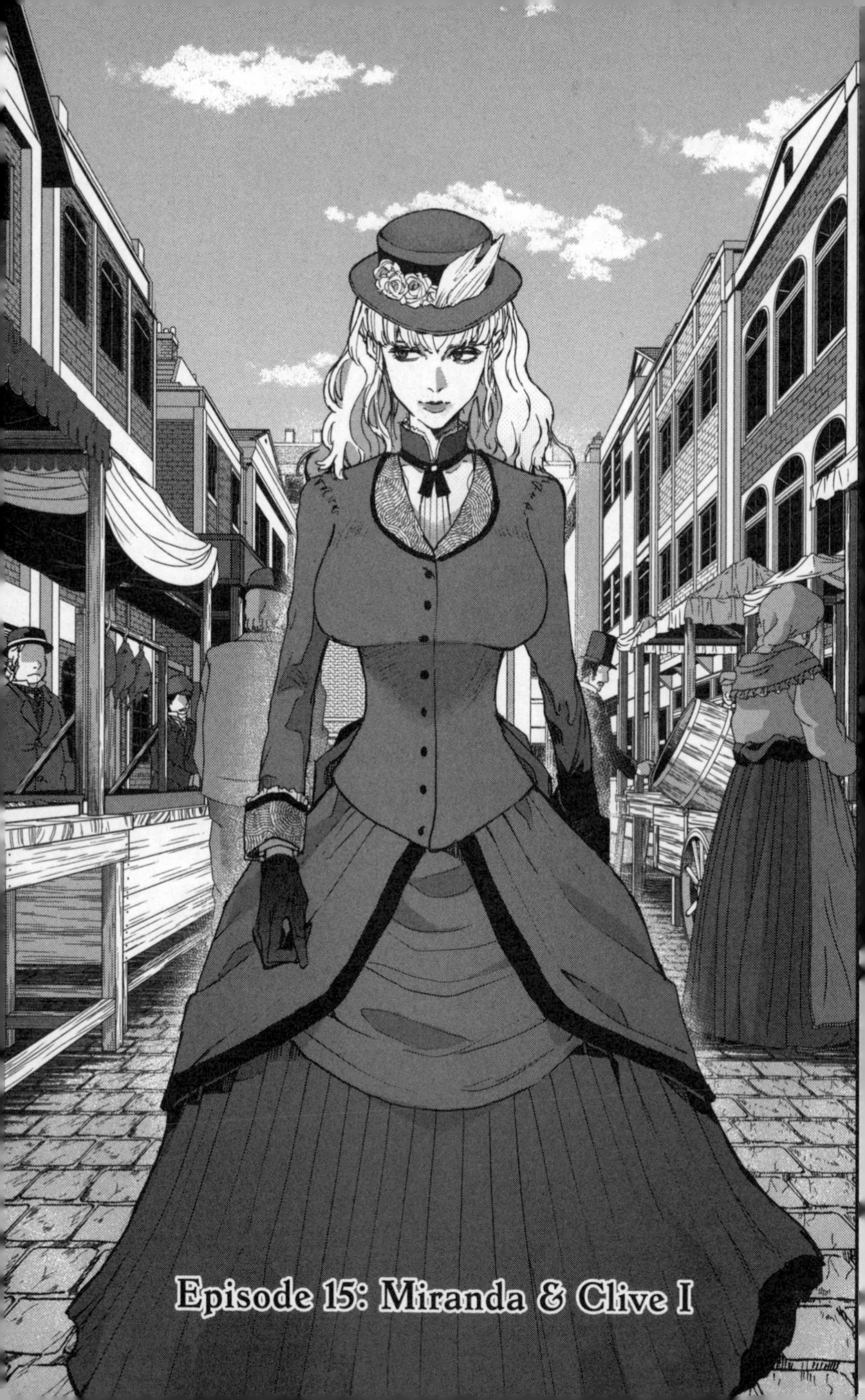
Episode 15: Miranda & Clive I

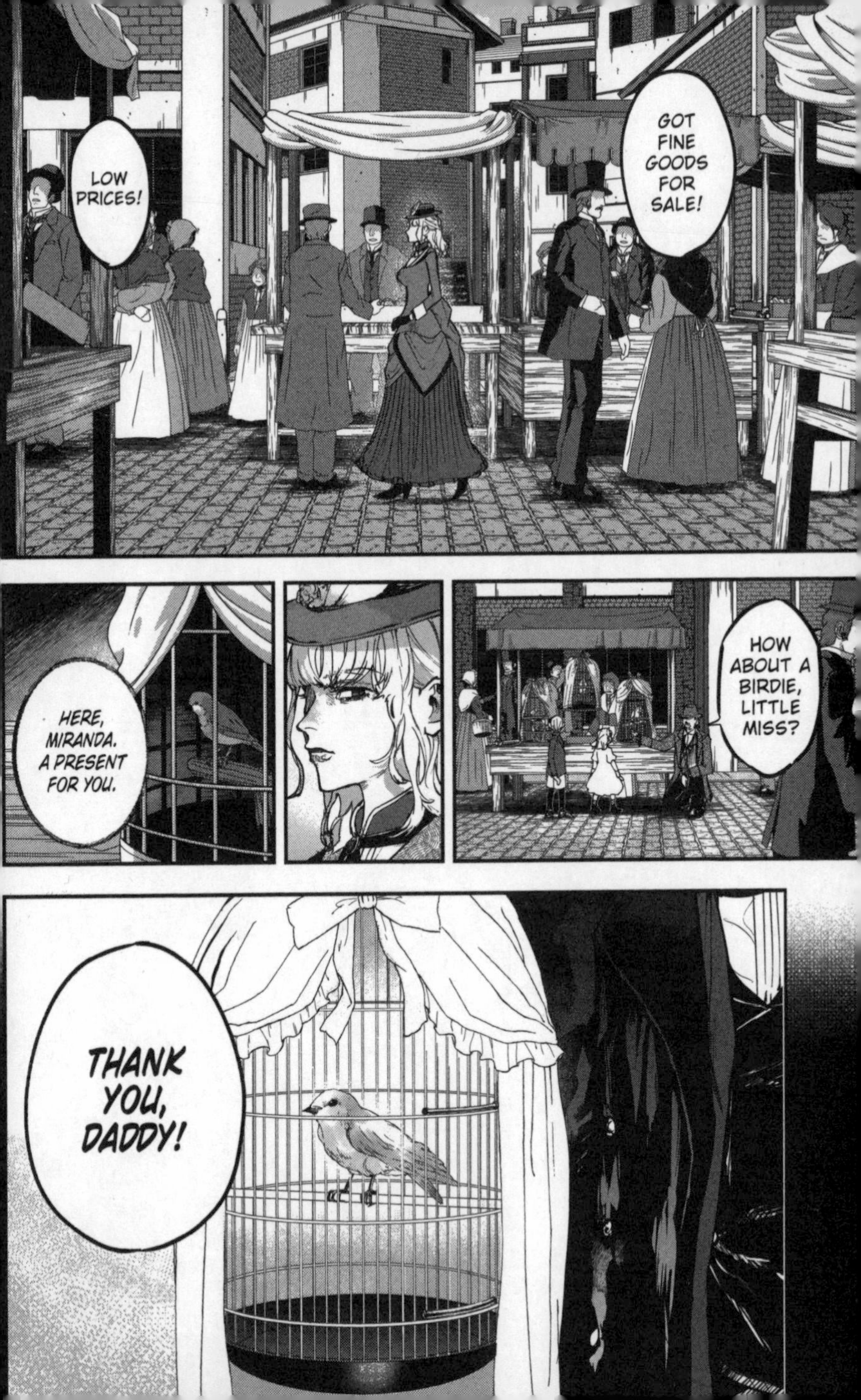
GOT FINE GOODS FOR SALE!
LOW PRICES!
HOW ABOUT A BIRDIE, LITTLE MISS?
HERE, MIRANDA. A PRESENT FOR YOU.
THANK YOU, DADDY!

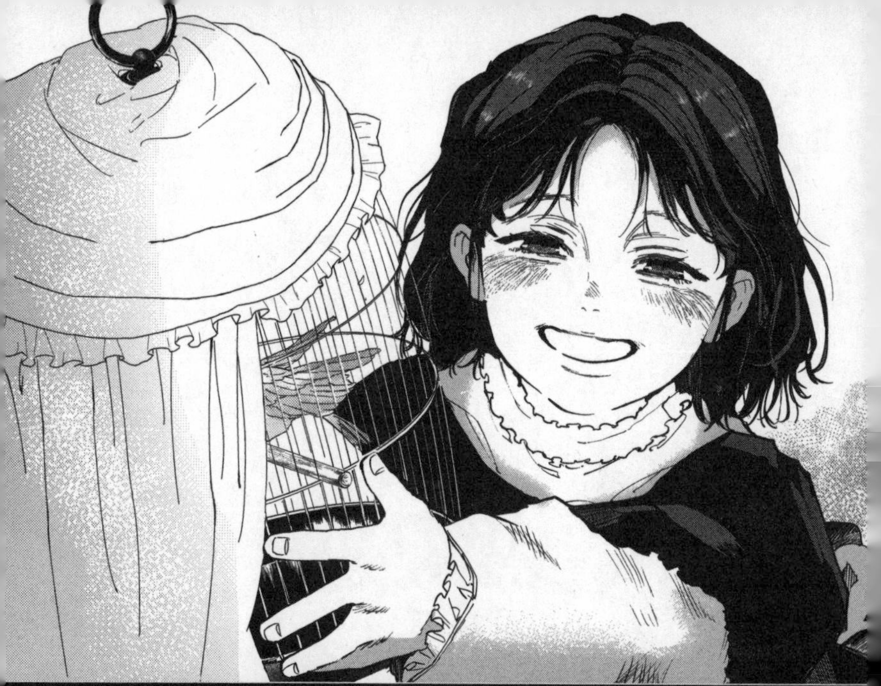
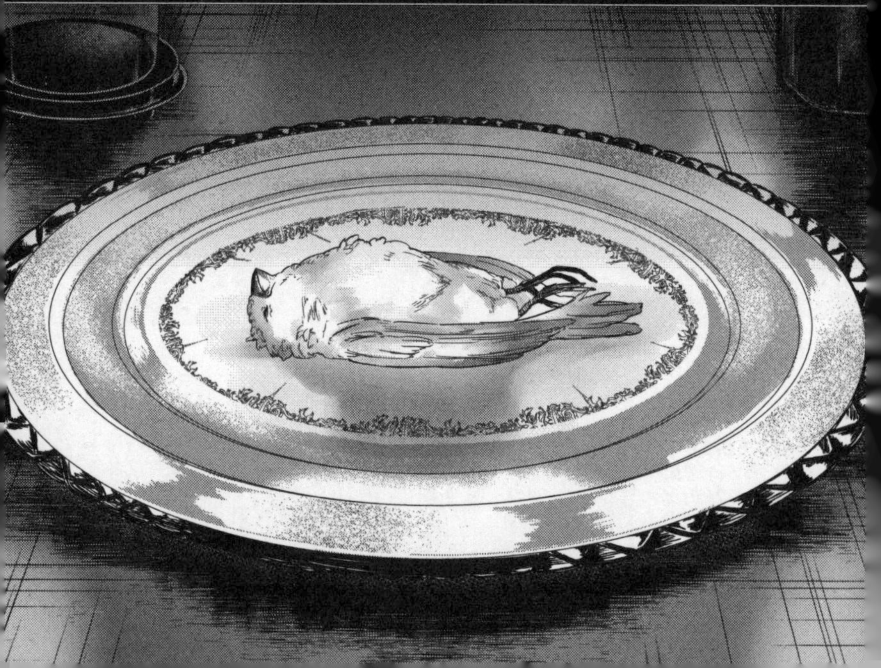

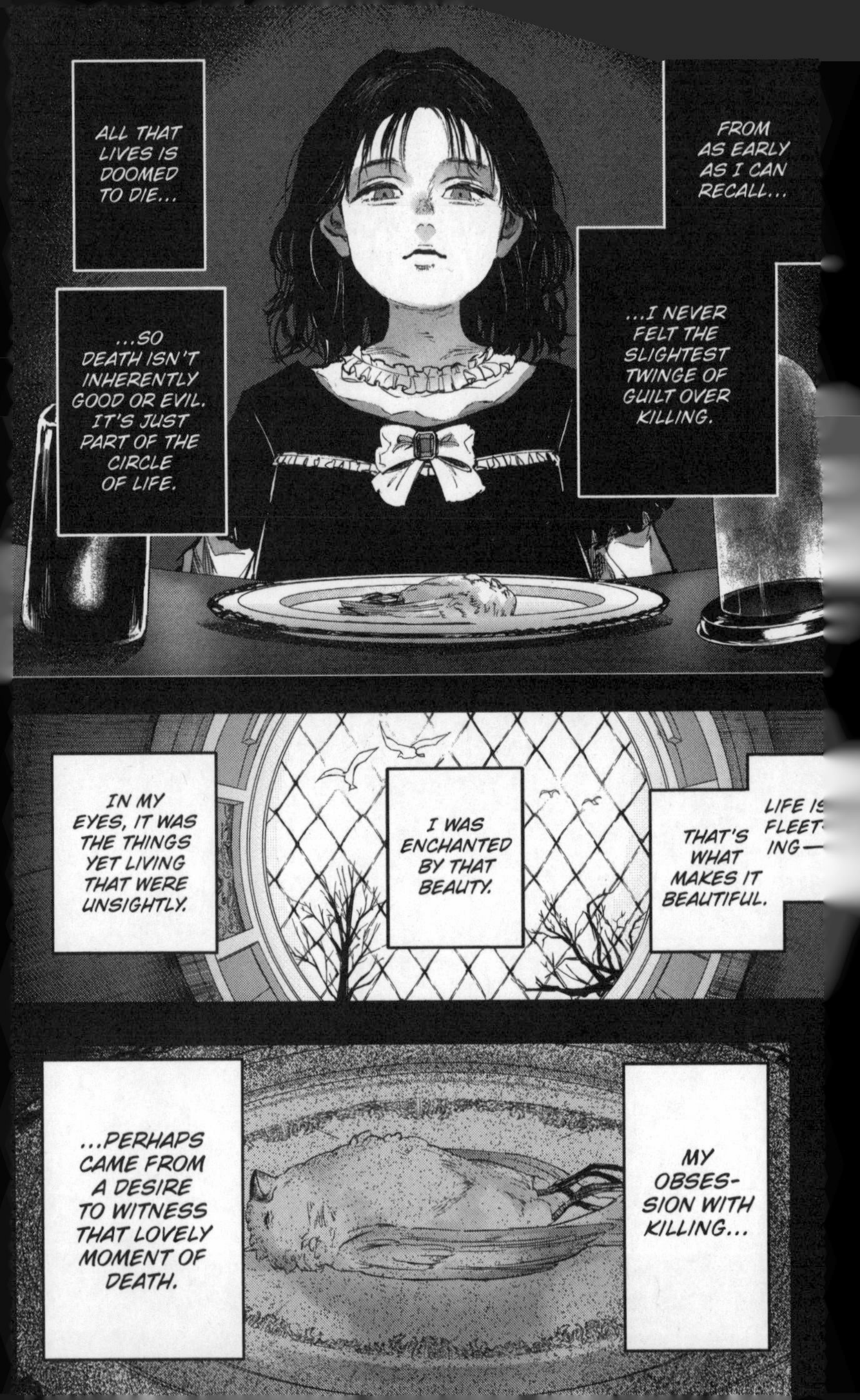
FROM AS EARLY AS I CAN RECALL...
...I NEVER FELT THE SLIGHTEST TWINGE OF GUILT OVER KILLING.
ALL THAT LIVES IS DOOMED TO DIE...
...SO DEATH ISN'T INHERENTLY GOOD OR EVIL. IT'S JUST PART OF THE CIRCLE OF LIFE.
LIFE IS FLEETING—
THAT'S WHAT MAKES IT BEAUTIFUL.
I WAS ENCHANTED BY THAT BEAUTY.
IN MY EYES, IT WAS THE THINGS YET LIVING THAT WERE UNSIGHTLY.
MY OBSESSION WITH KILLING...
...PERHAPS CAME FROM A DESIRE TO WITNESS THAT LOVELY MOMENT OF DEATH.

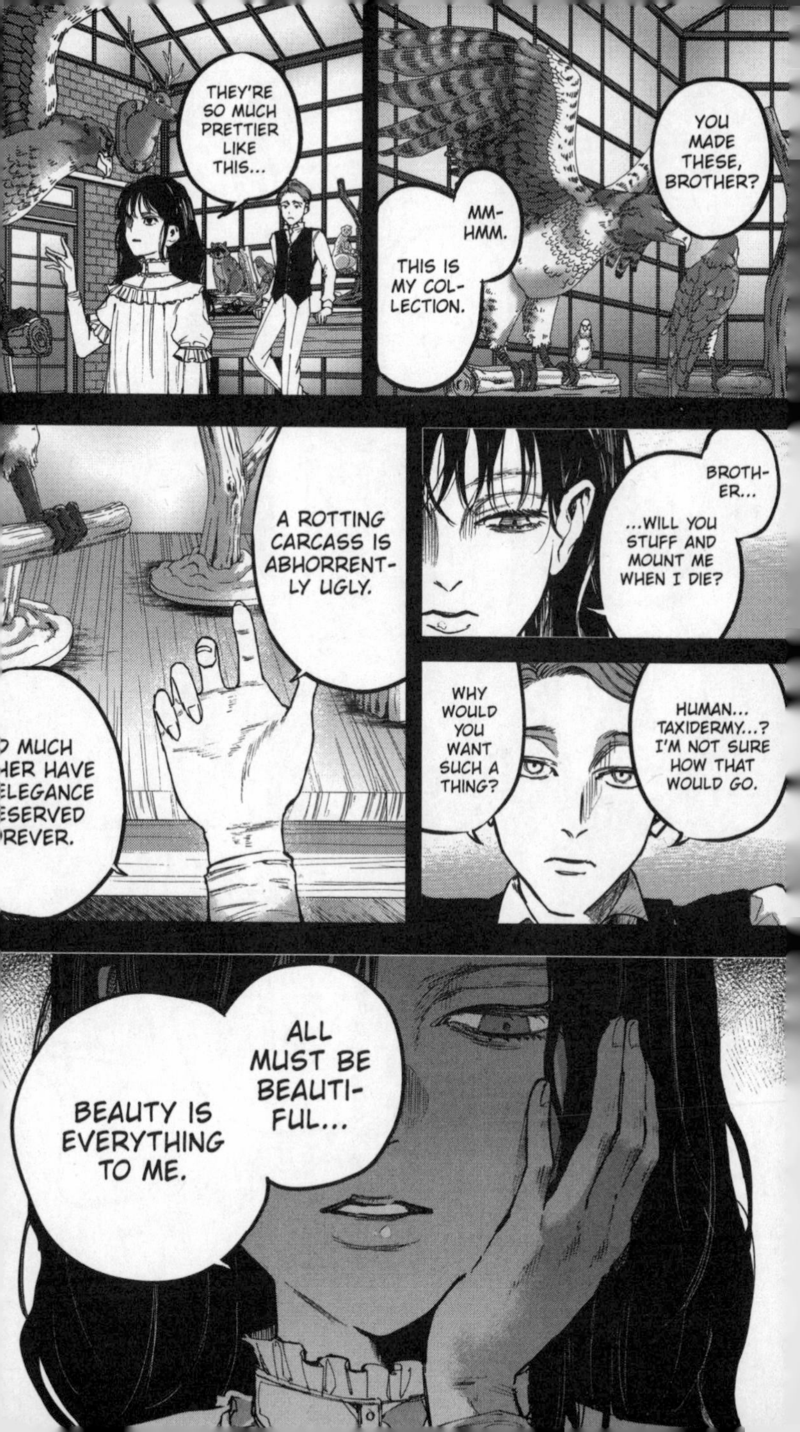
YOU MADE THESE, BROTHER?
MM-HMM.
THIS IS MY COLLECTION.
THEY'RE SO MUCH PRETTIER LIKE THIS...
BROTHER...
...WILL YOU STUFF AND MOUNT ME WHEN I DIE?
HUMAN... TAXIDERMY...? I'M NOT SURE HOW THAT WOULD GO.
WHY WOULD YOU WANT SUCH A THING?
A ROTTING CARCASS IS ABHORRENTLY UGLY.
D MUCH HER HAVE ELEGANCE ESERVED REVER.
ALL MUST BE BEAUTIFUL...
BEAUTY IS EVERYTHING TO ME.

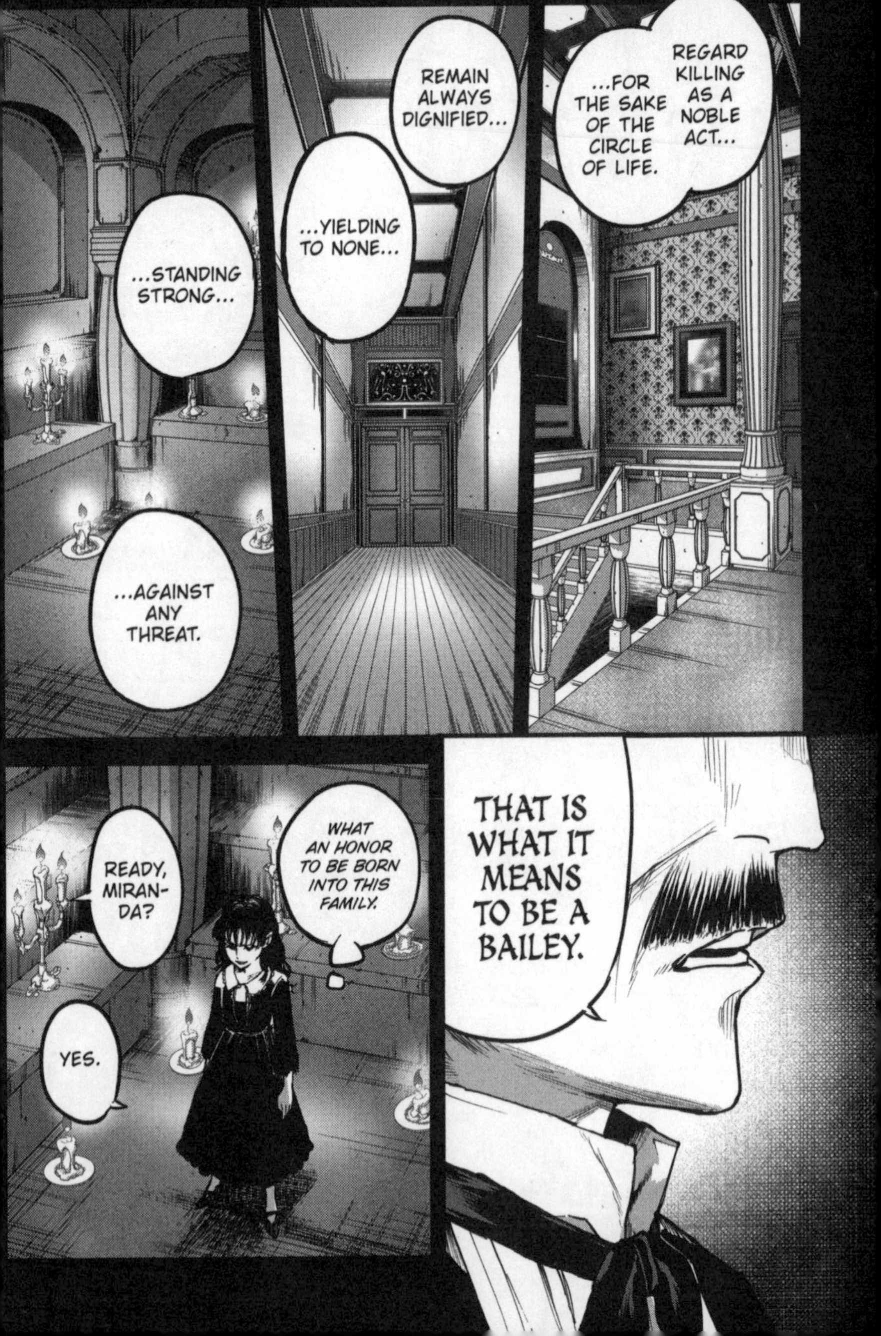
REGARD KILLING AS A NOBLE ACT...
...FOR THE SAKE OF THE CIRCLE OF LIFE.
REMAIN ALWAYS DIGNIFIED...
...YIELDING TO NONE...
...STANDING STRONG...
...AGAINST ANY THREAT.
THAT IS WHAT IT MEANS TO BE A BAILEY.
WHAT AN HONOR TO BE BORN INTO THIS FAMILY.
READY, MIRAN-DA?
YES.

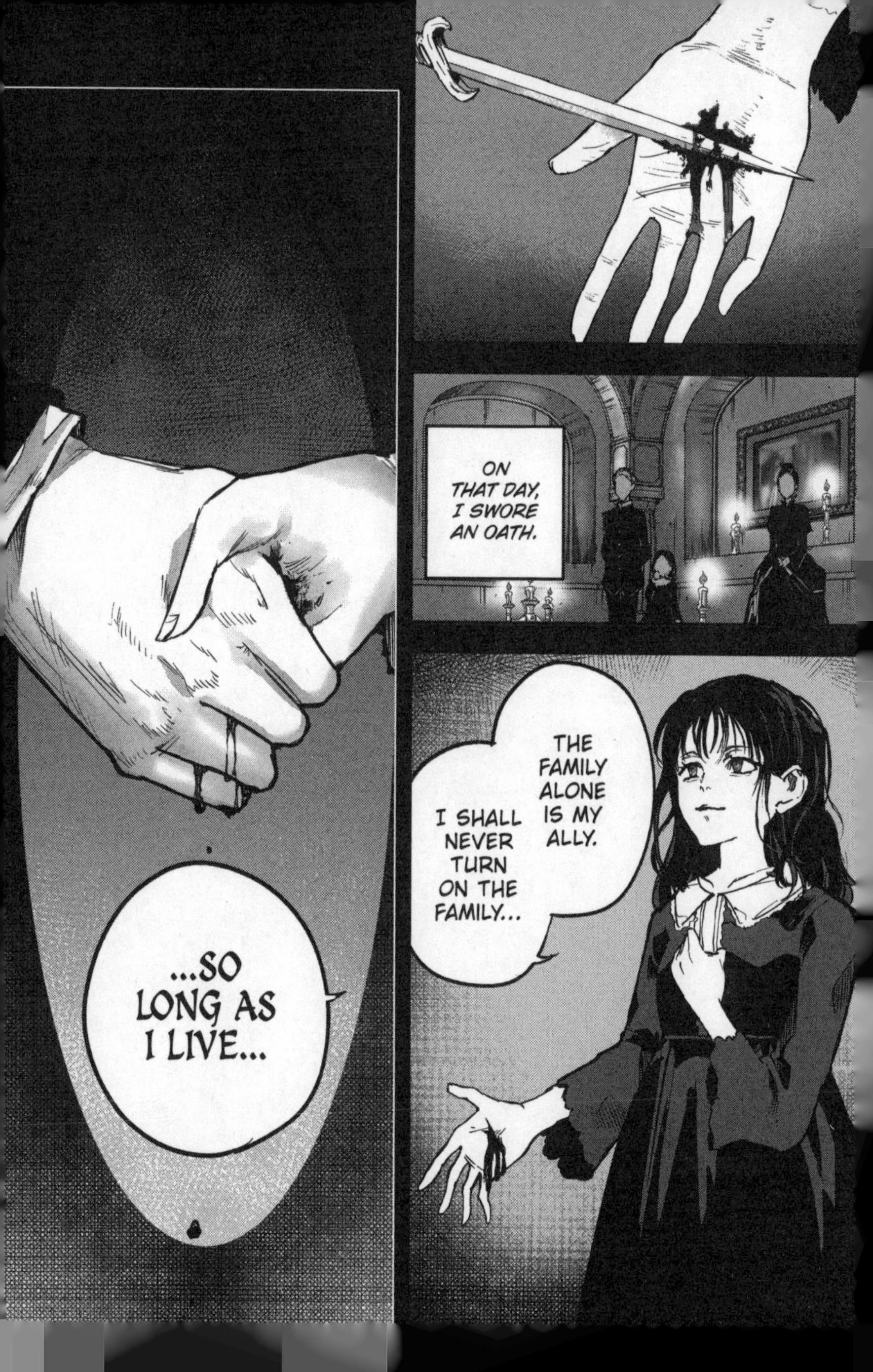
ON THAT DAY, I SWORE AN OATH.
I SHALL NEVER TURN ON THE FAMILY... THE FAMILY ALONE IS MY ALLY.
...SO LONG AS I LIVE...

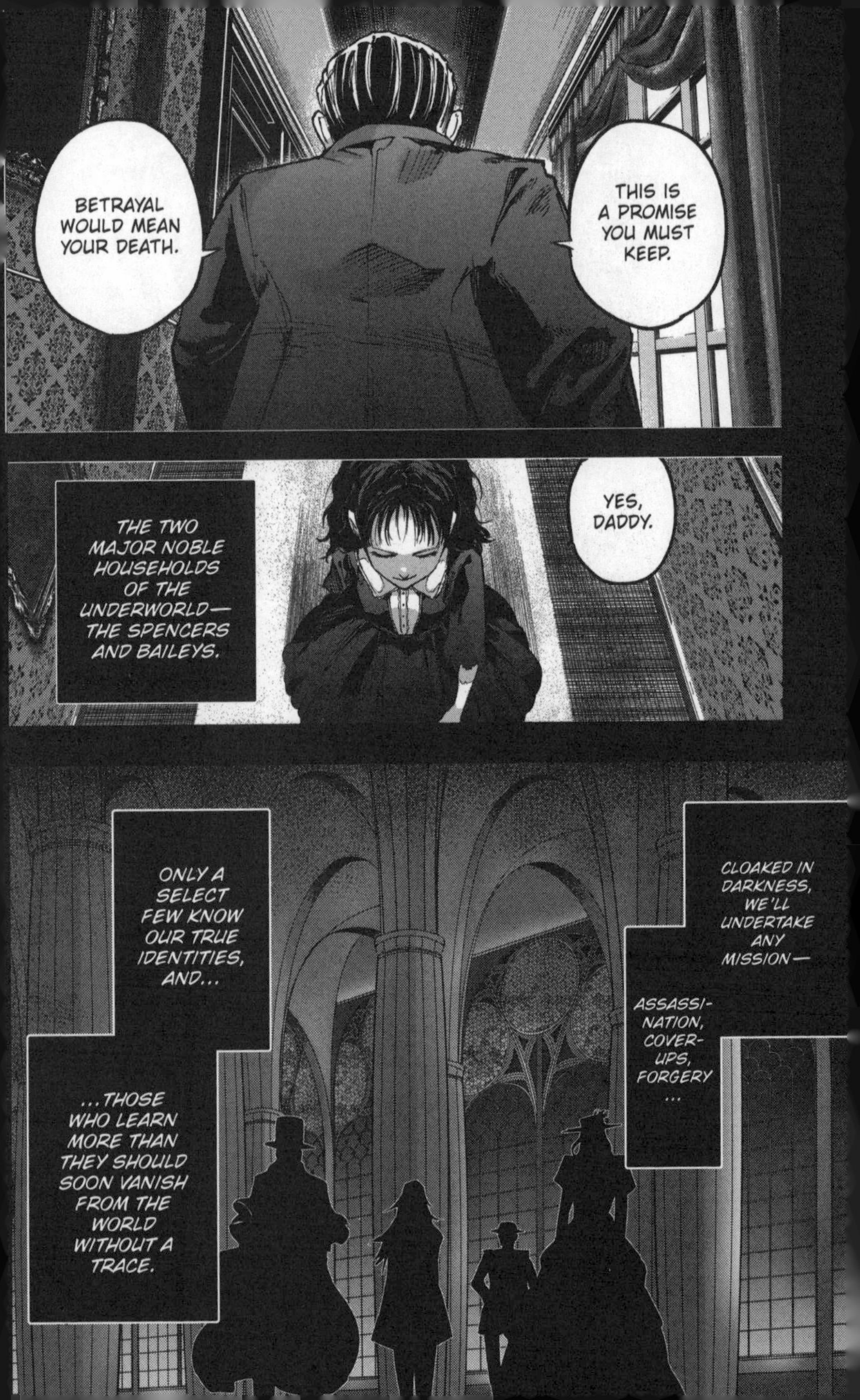
THIS IS A PROMISE YOU MUST KEEP.
BETRAYAL WOULD MEAN YOUR DEATH.
YES, DADDY.
THE TWO MAJOR NOBLE HOUSEHOLDS OF THE UNDERWORLD—THE SPENCERS AND BAILEYS.
CLOAKED IN DARKNESS, WE'LL UNDERTAKE ANY MISSION—
ASSASSI-NATION, COVER-UPS, FORGERY...
ONLY A SELECT FEW KNOW OUR TRUE IDENTITIES, AND...
...THOSE WHO LEARN MORE THAN THEY SHOULD SOON VANISH FROM THE WORLD WITHOUT A TRACE.

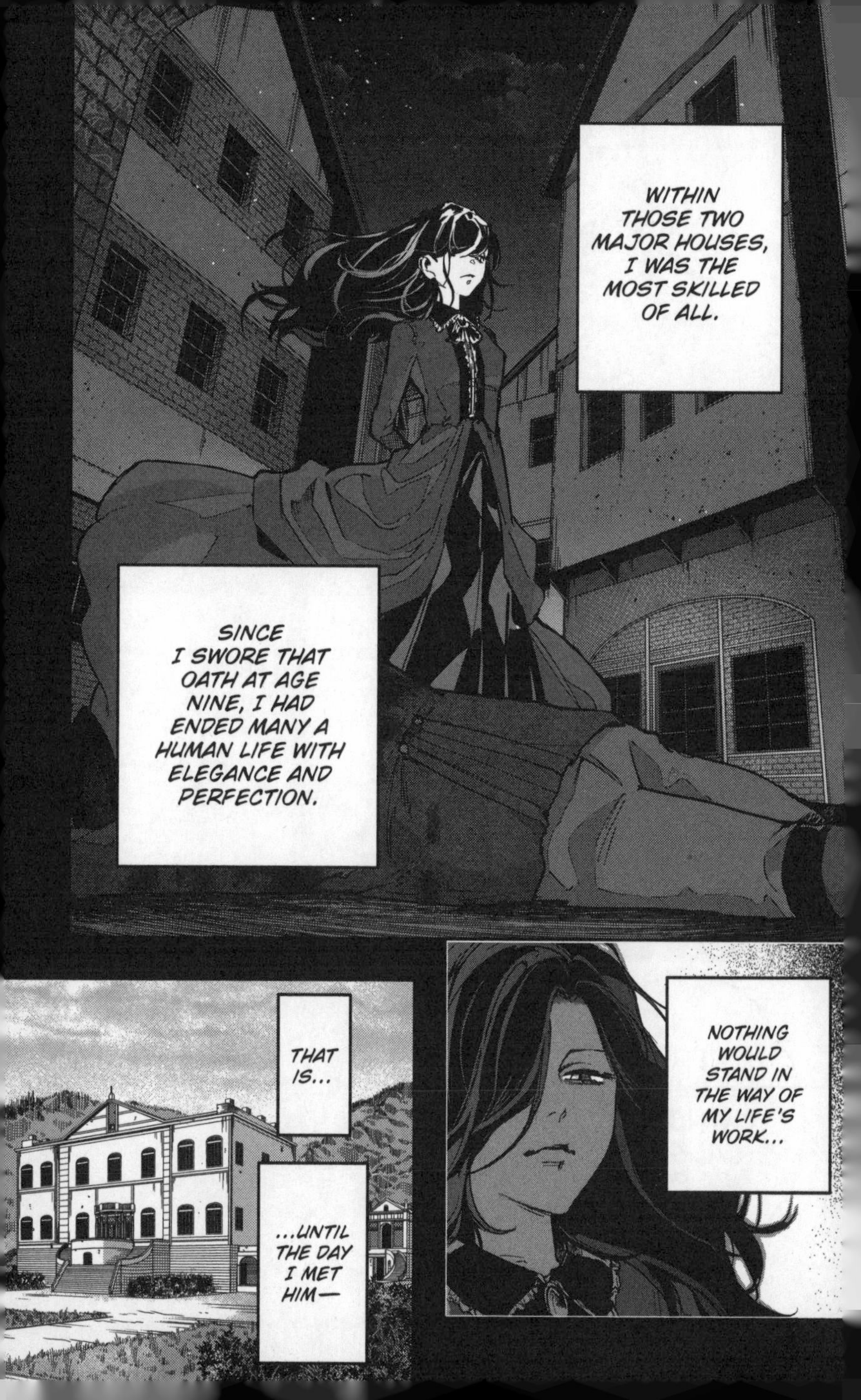
WITHIN THOSE TWO MAJOR HOUSES, I WAS THE MOST SKILLED OF ALL.
SINCE I SWORE THAT OATH AT AGE NINE, I HAD ENDED MANY A HUMAN LIFE WITH ELEGANCE AND PERFECTION.
NOTHING WOULD STAND IN THE WAY OF MY LIFE'S WORK...
THAT IS...
...UNTIL THE DAY I MET HIM—

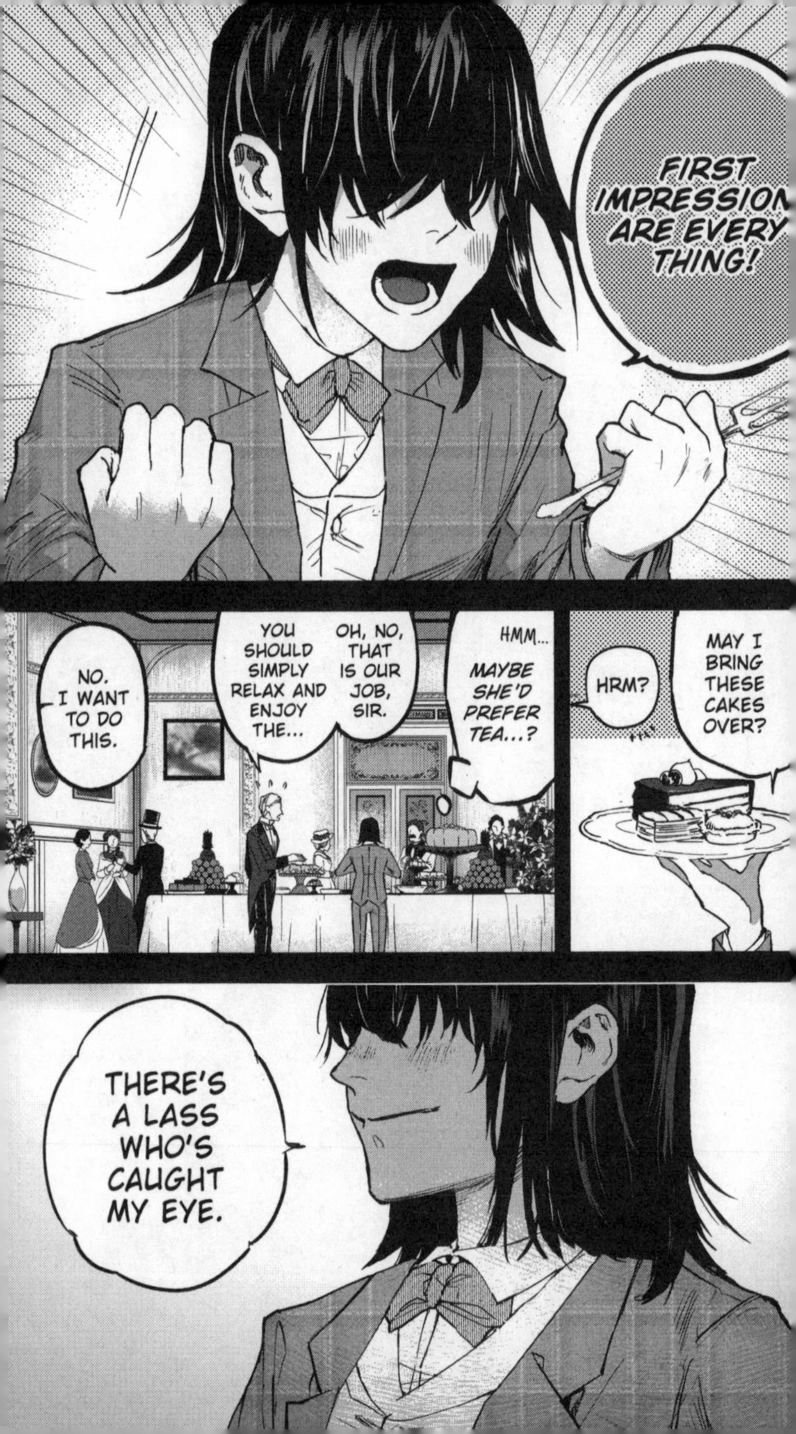
FIRST IMPRESSION ARE EVERY THING!
MAY I BRING THESE CAKES OVER?
HRM?
HMM...
MAYBE SHE'D PREFER TEA...?
OH, NO, THAT IS OUR JOB, SIR.
YOU SHOULD SIMPLY RELAX AND ENJOY THE...
NO. I WANT TO DO THIS.
THERE'S A LASS WHO'S CAUGHT MY EYE.

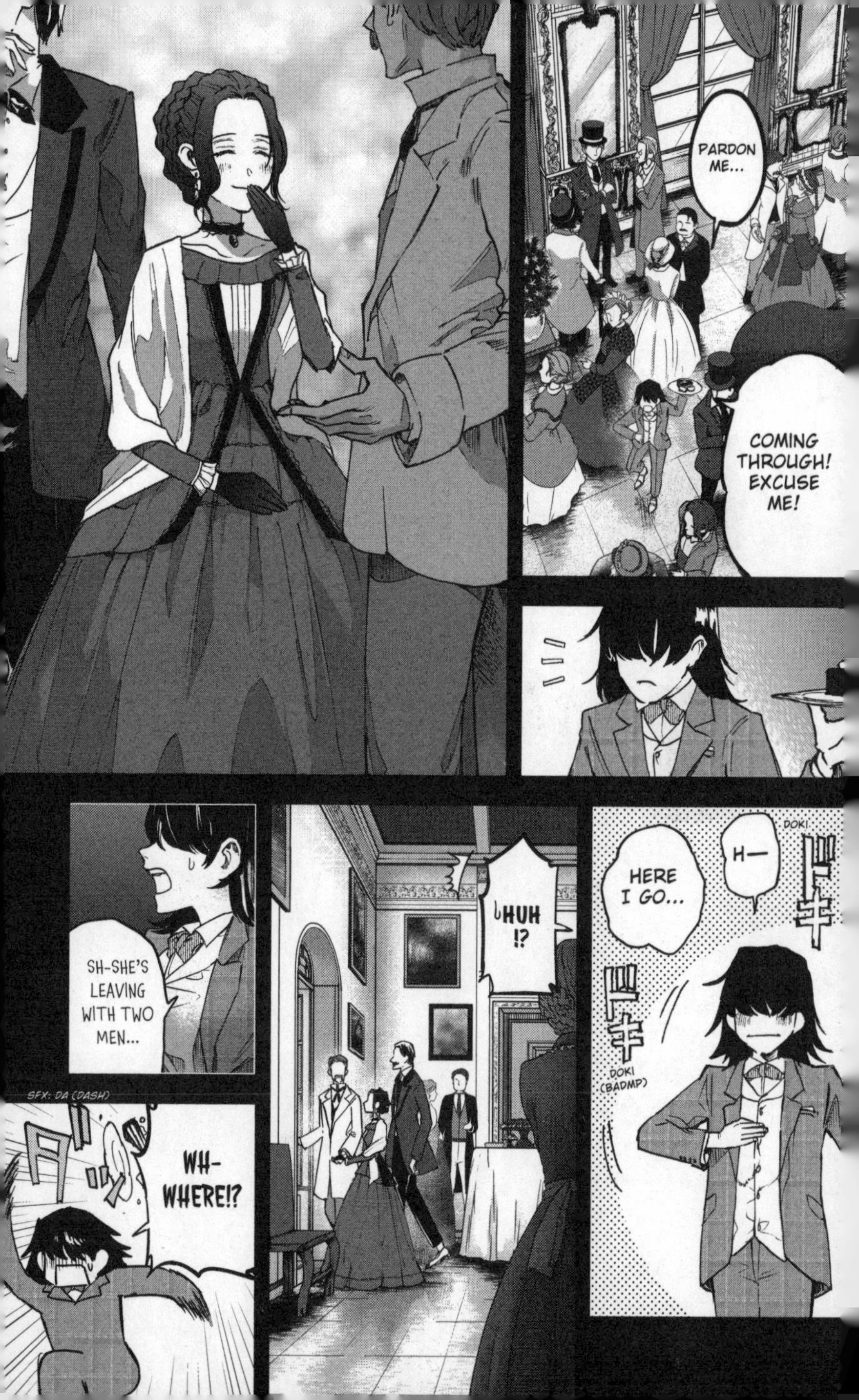
PARDON ME...
COMING THROUGH! EXCUSE ME!
DOKI
H—
HERE I GO...
DOKI (BADMP)
HUH !?
SH-SHE'S LEAVING WITH TWO MEN...
SFX: DA (DASH)
WH-WHERE!?

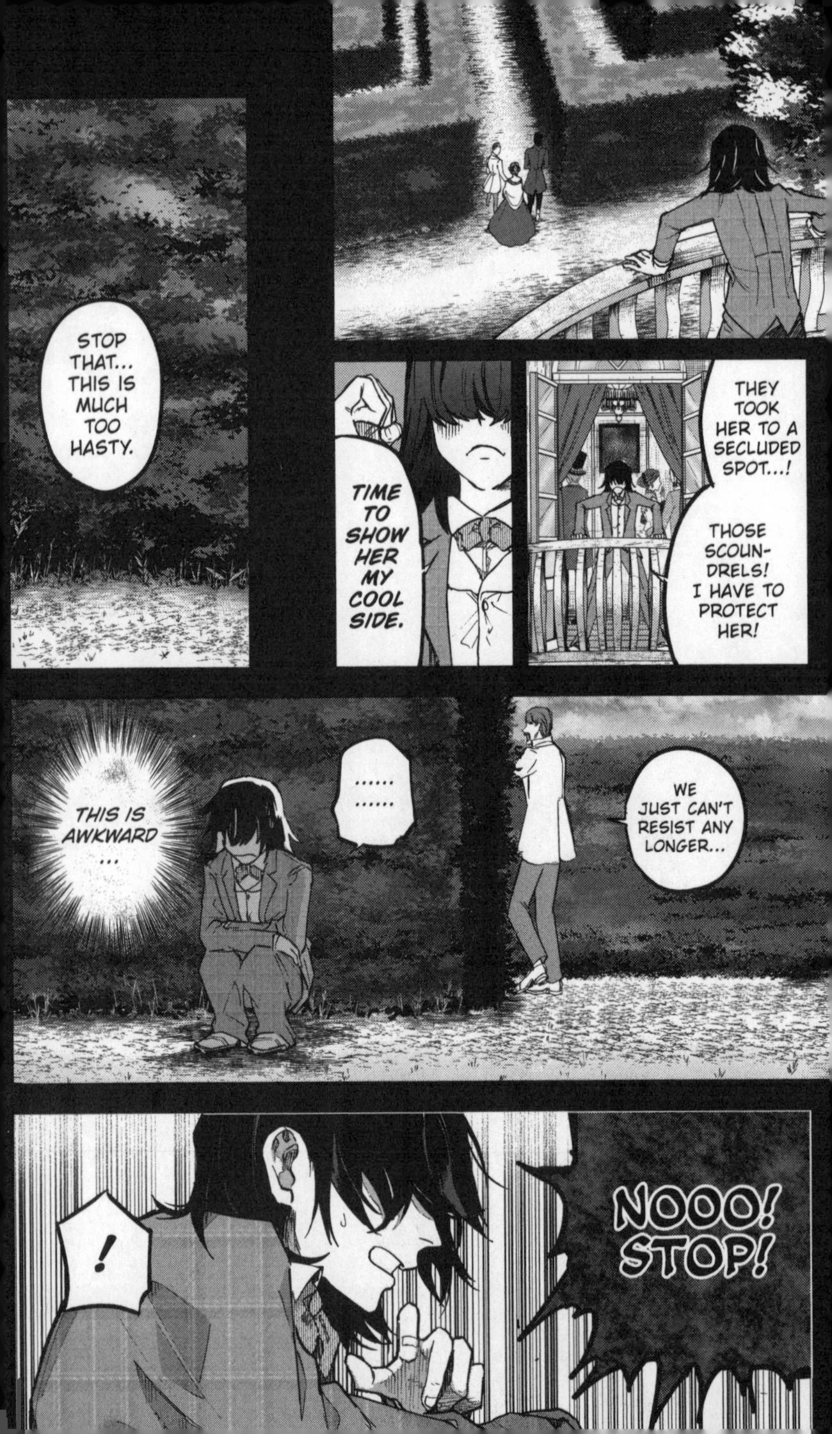
THEY TOOK HER TO A SECLUDED SPOT...!
THOSE SCOUN-DRELS! I HAVE TO PROTECT HER!
TIME TO SHOW HER MY COOL SIDE.
STOP THAT... THIS IS MUCH TOO HASTY.
WE JUST CAN'T RESIST ANY LONGER...
....
THIS IS AWKWARD ...
NOOO! STOP!
!

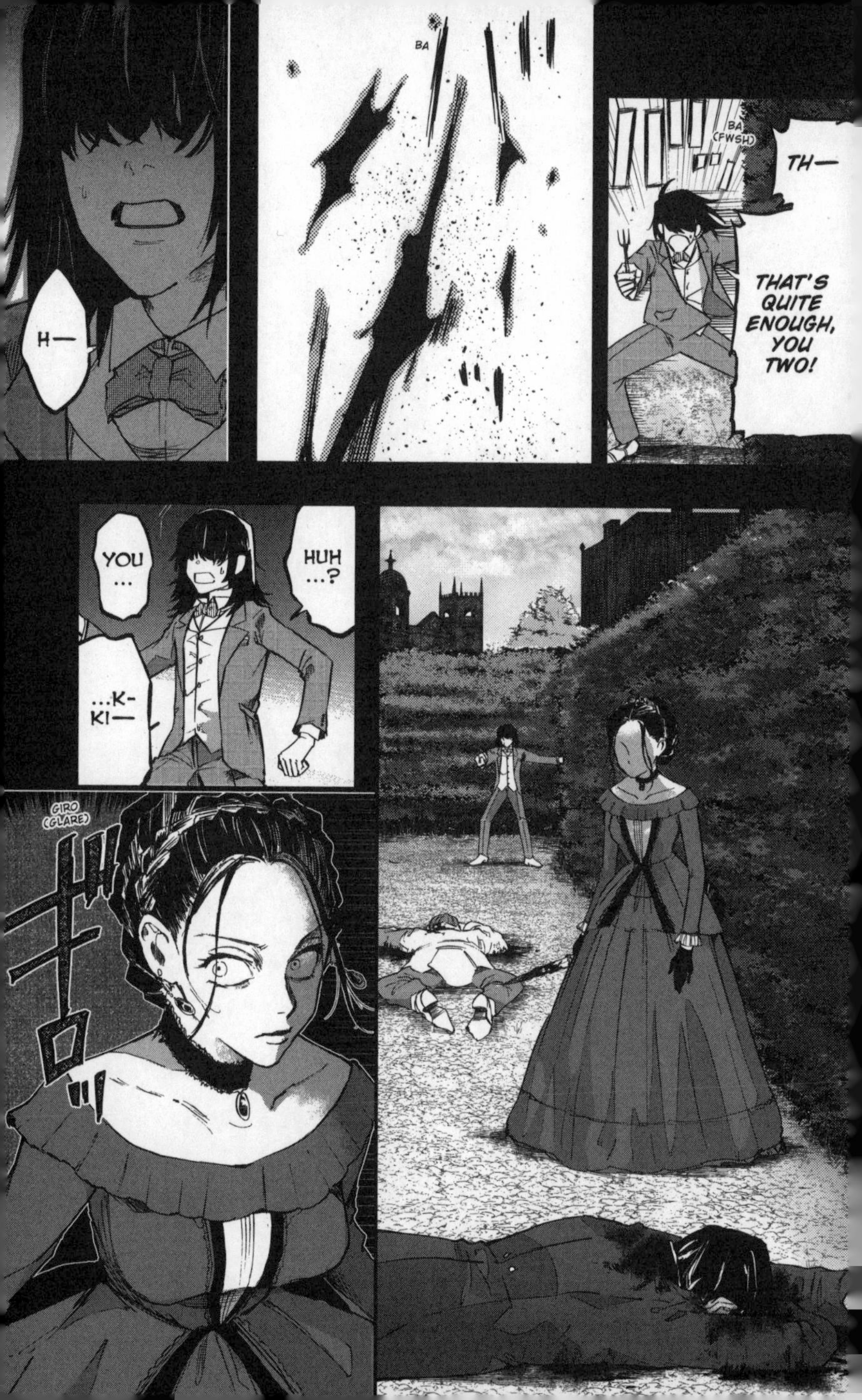
BA
(FWSH)
TH—
THAT'S QUITE ENOUGH, YOU TWO!
BA
H—
HUH ...?
YOU ...
...K-KI—
GIRO
(GLARE)

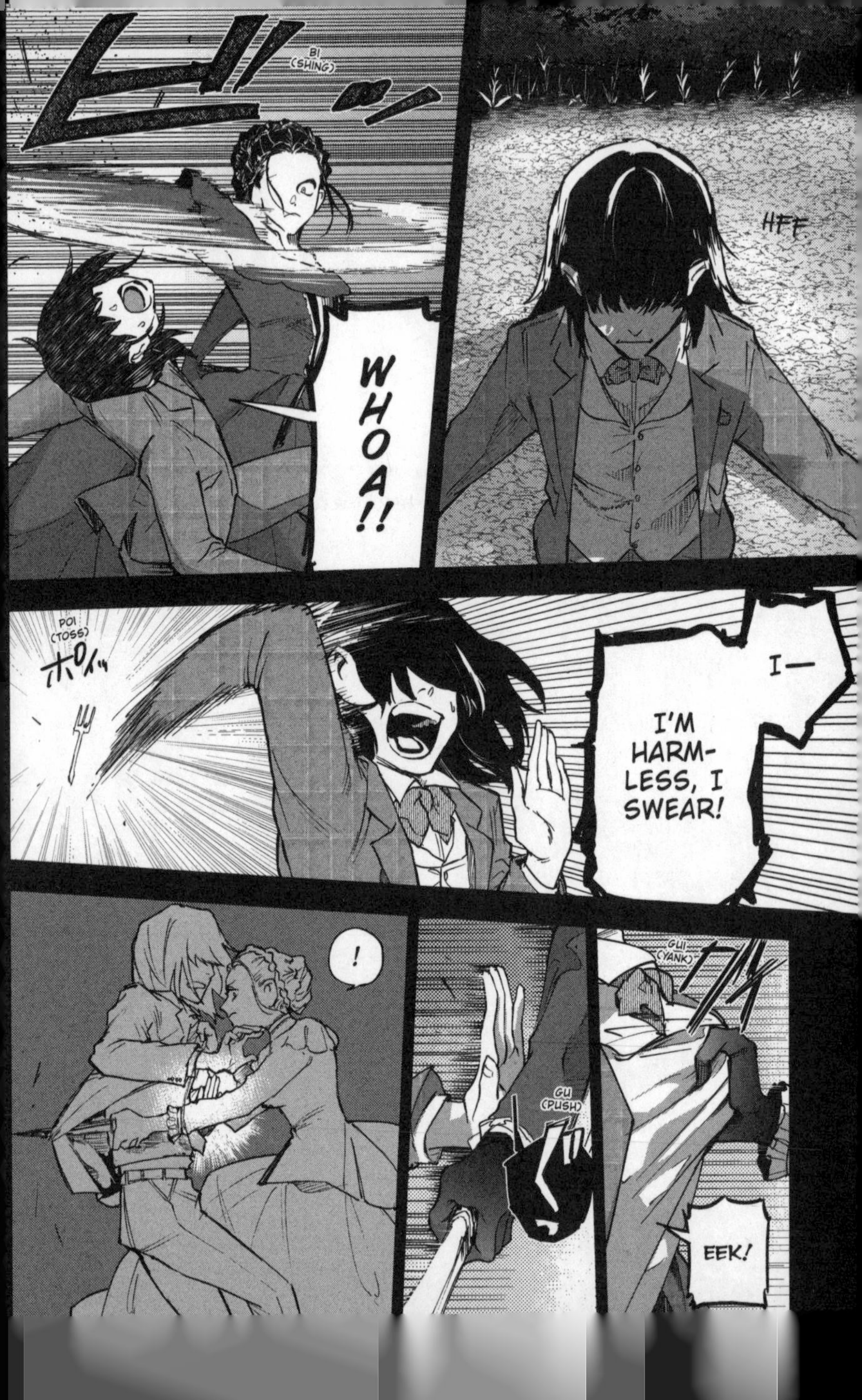
HFF
BI (SHING)
WHOA!!
I—
I'M HARMLESS, I SWEAR!
POI (TOSS)
GUI (YANK)
EEK!
GU (PUSH)
!

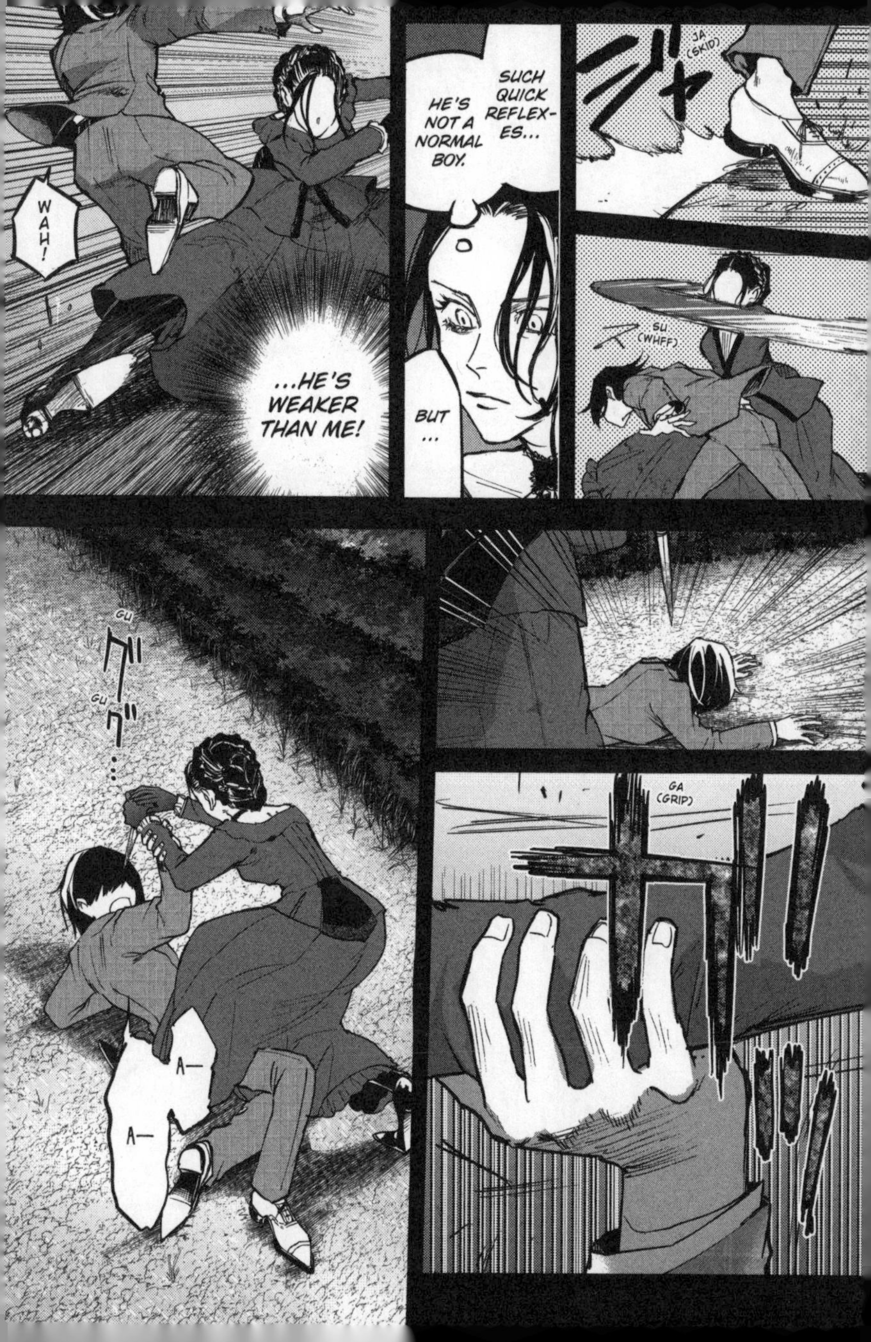
JA (SKID)
SU (WHFF)
SUCH QUICK REFLEXES...
HE'S NOT A NORMAL BOY.
BUT...
WAH!
...HE'S WEAKER THAN ME!
GA (GRIP)
GU
GU
...
A—
A—

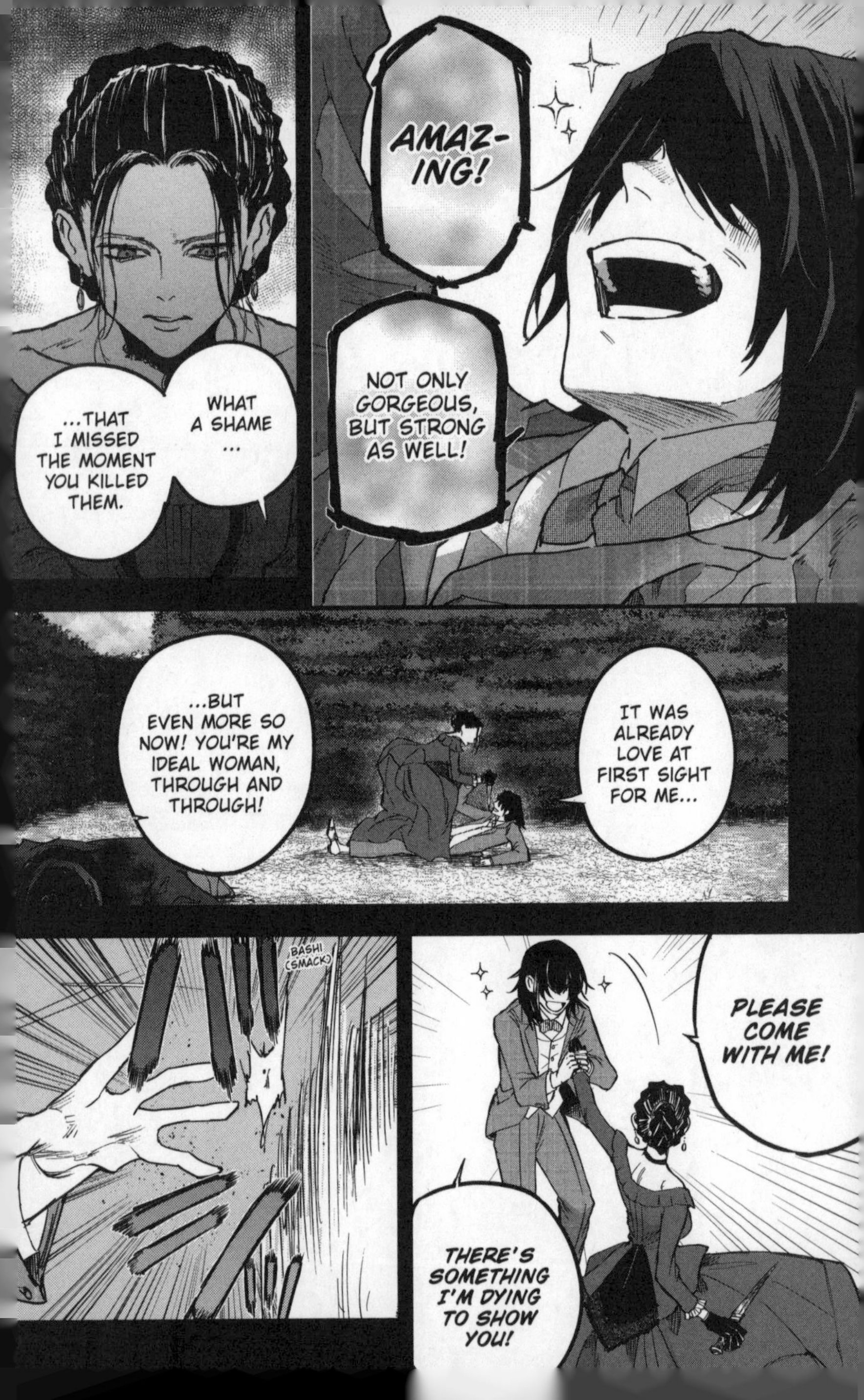
AMAZ-ING!
NOT ONLY GORGEOUS, BUT STRONG AS WELL!
WHAT A SHAME...
...THAT I MISSED THE MOMENT YOU KILLED THEM.
IT WAS ALREADY LOVE AT FIRST SIGHT FOR ME...
...BUT EVEN MORE SO NOW! YOU'RE MY IDEAL WOMAN, THROUGH AND THROUGH!
PLEASE COME WITH ME!
THERE'S SOMETHING I'M DYING TO SHOW YOU!
BASHI (SMACK)

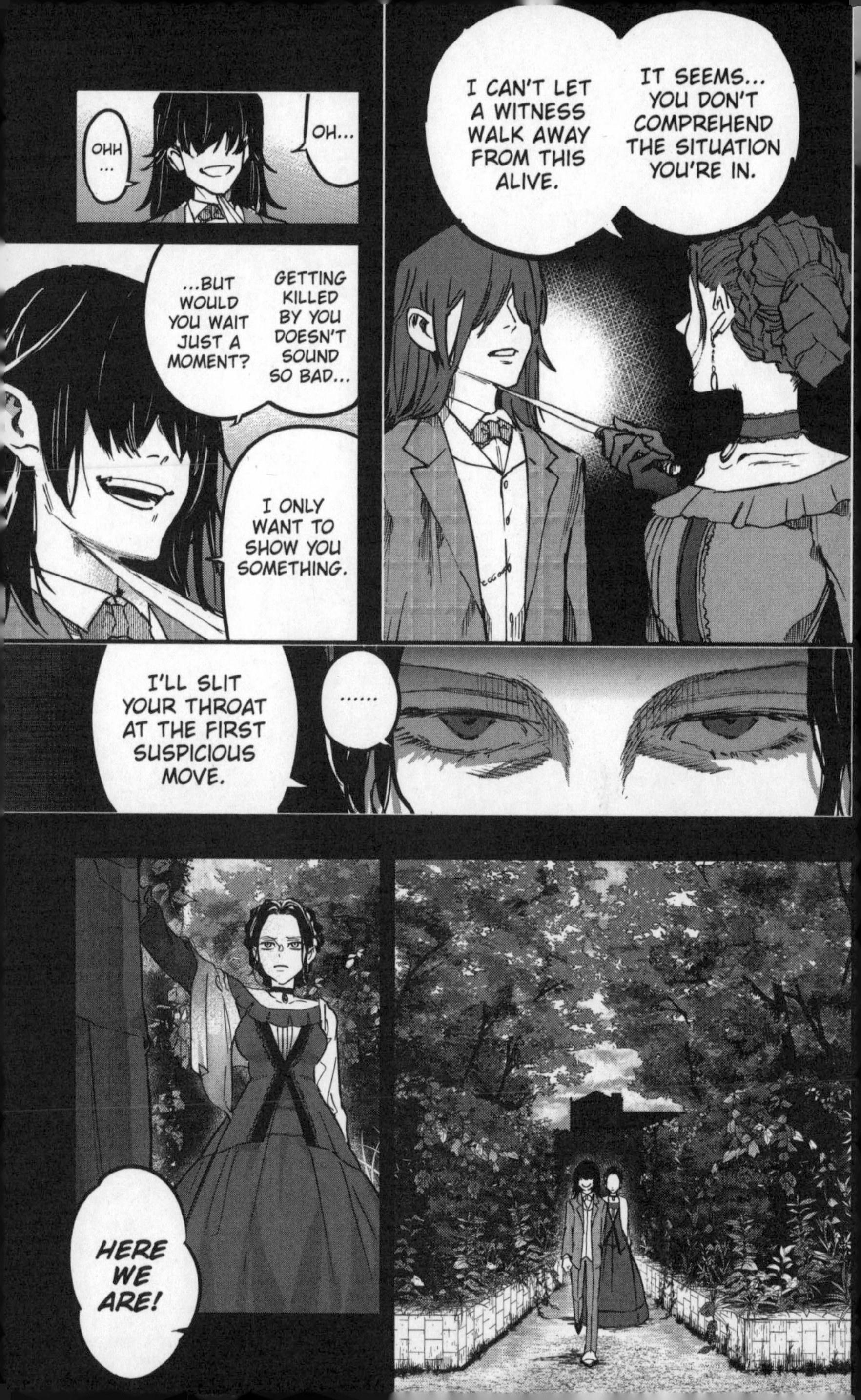
IT SEEMS... YOU DON'T COMPREHEND THE SITUATION YOU'RE IN.
I CAN'T LET A WITNESS WALK AWAY FROM THIS ALIVE.
OH...
OHH ...
GETTING KILLED BY YOU DOESN'T SOUND SO BAD...
...BUT WOULD YOU WAIT JUST A MOMENT?
I ONLY WANT TO SHOW YOU SOMETHING.
......
I'LL SLIT YOUR THROAT AT THE FIRST SUSPICIOUS MOVE.
HERE WE ARE!

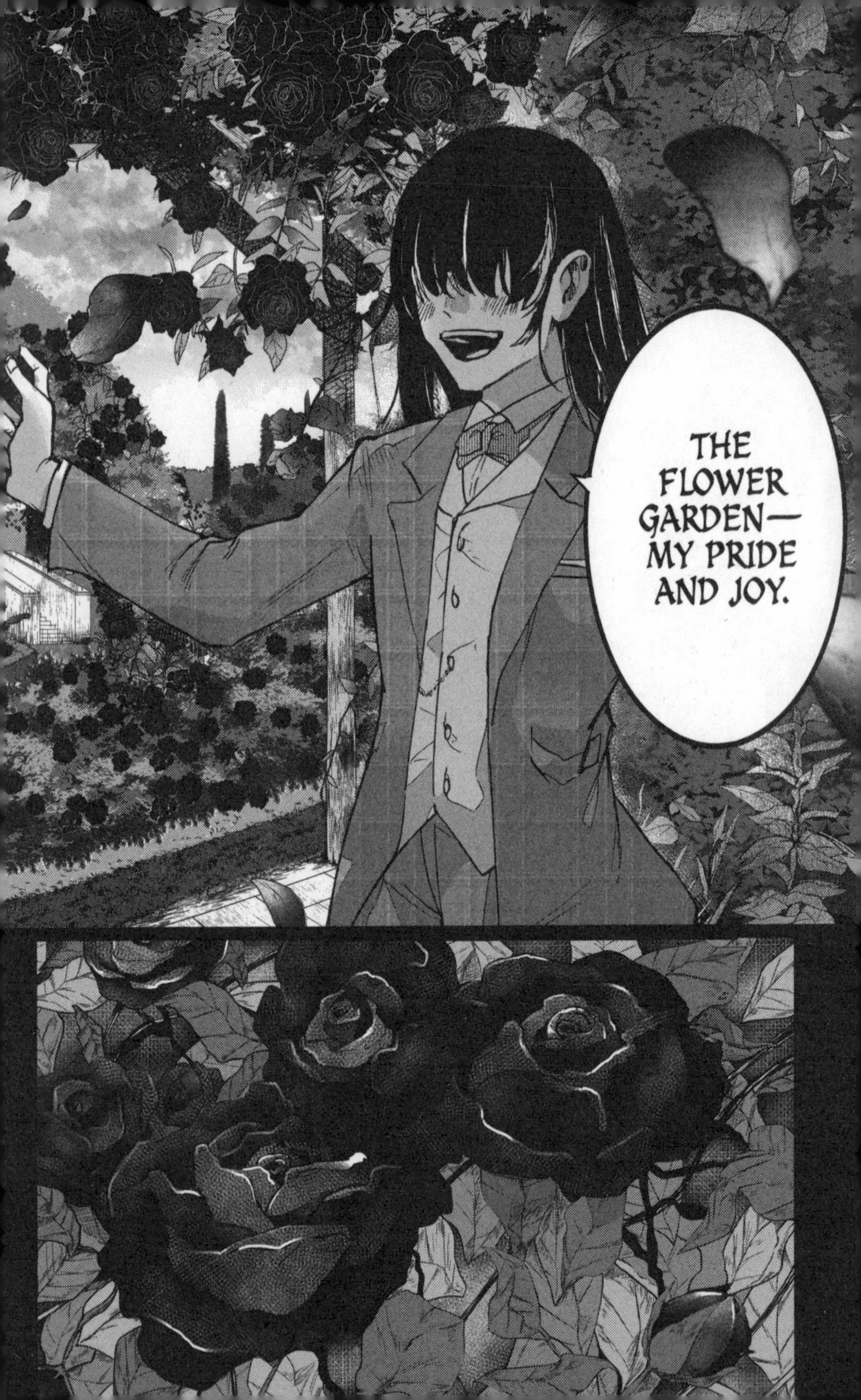
THE FLOWER GARDEN—MY PRIDE AND JOY.

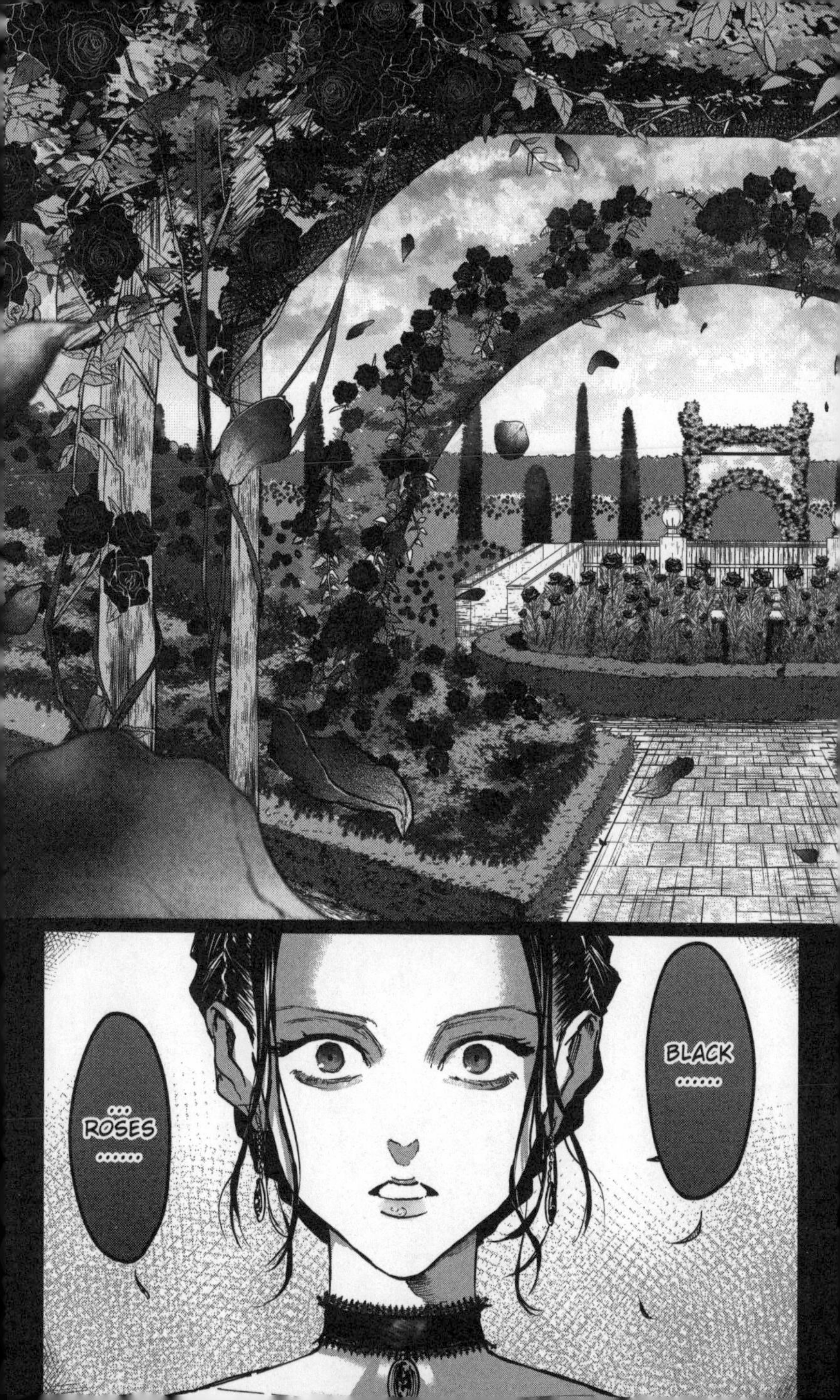
BLACK ......
...ROSES ......

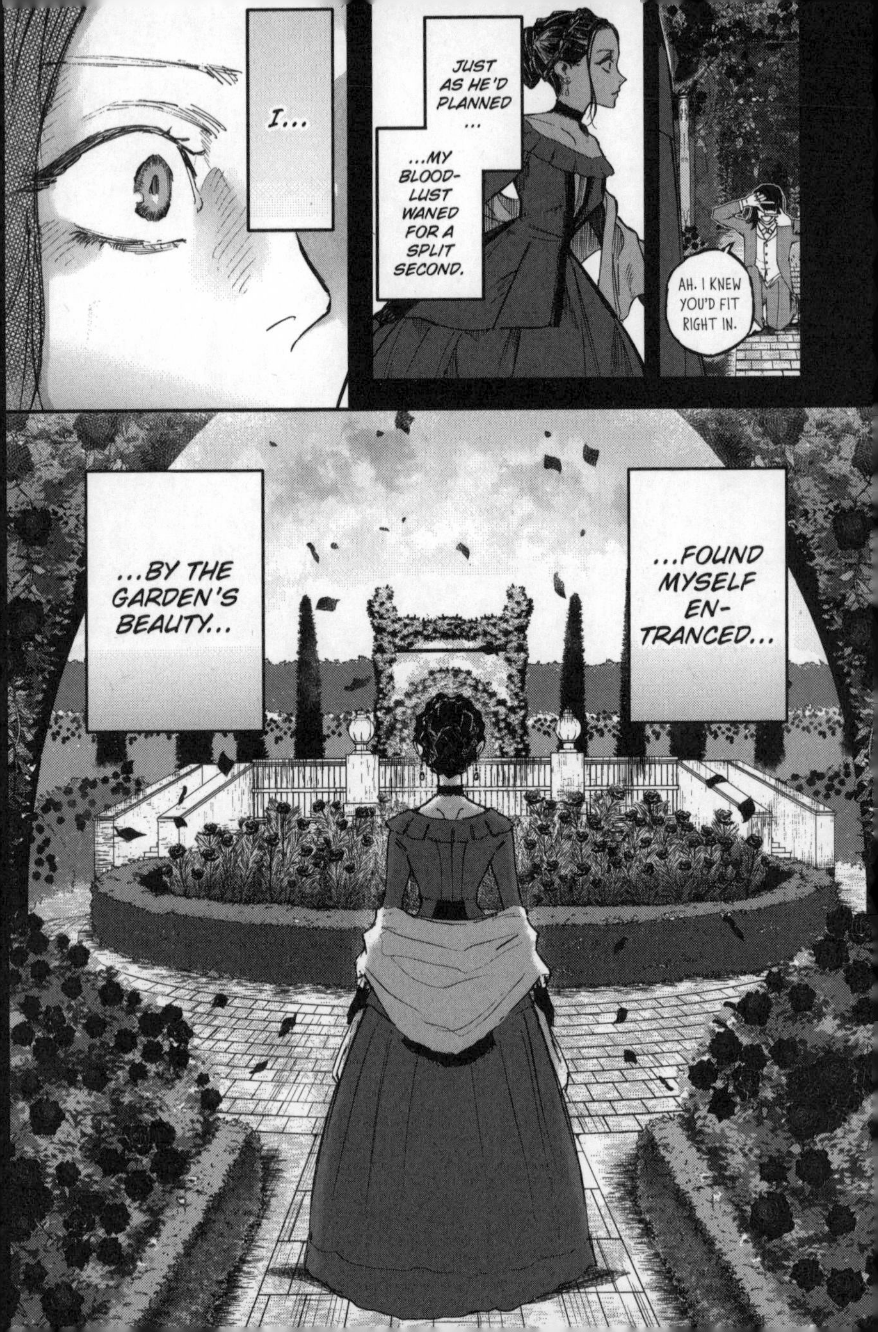
AH. I KNEW YOU'D FIT RIGHT IN.
JUST AS HE'D PLANNED...
...MY BLOOD-LUST WANED FOR A SPLIT SECOND.
I...
...FOUND MYSELF EN-TRANCED...
...BY THE GARDEN'S BEAUTY...

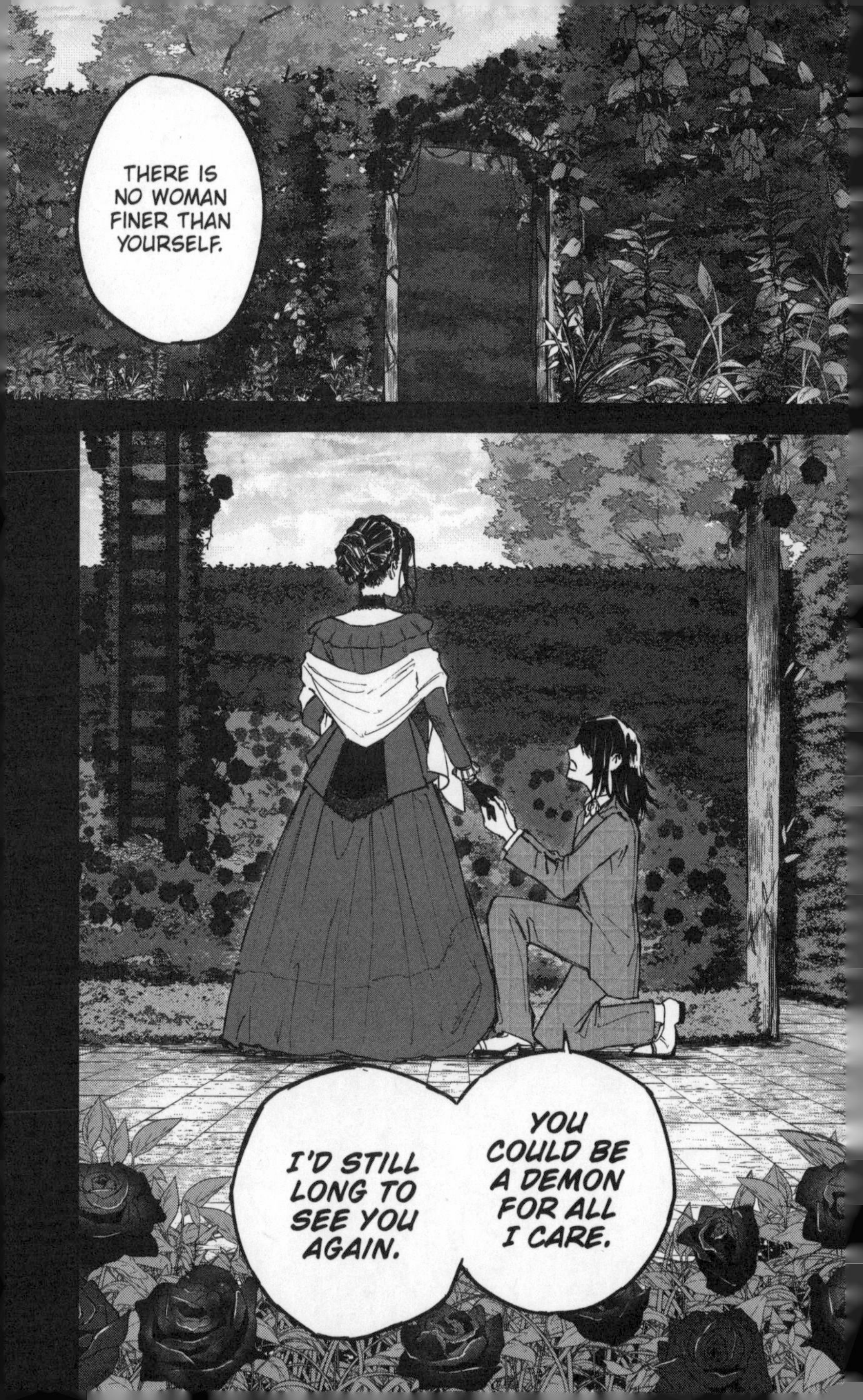
THERE IS NO WOMAN FINER THAN YOURSELF.
YOU COULD BE A DEMON FOR ALL I CARE.
I'D STILL LONG TO SEE YOU AGAIN.

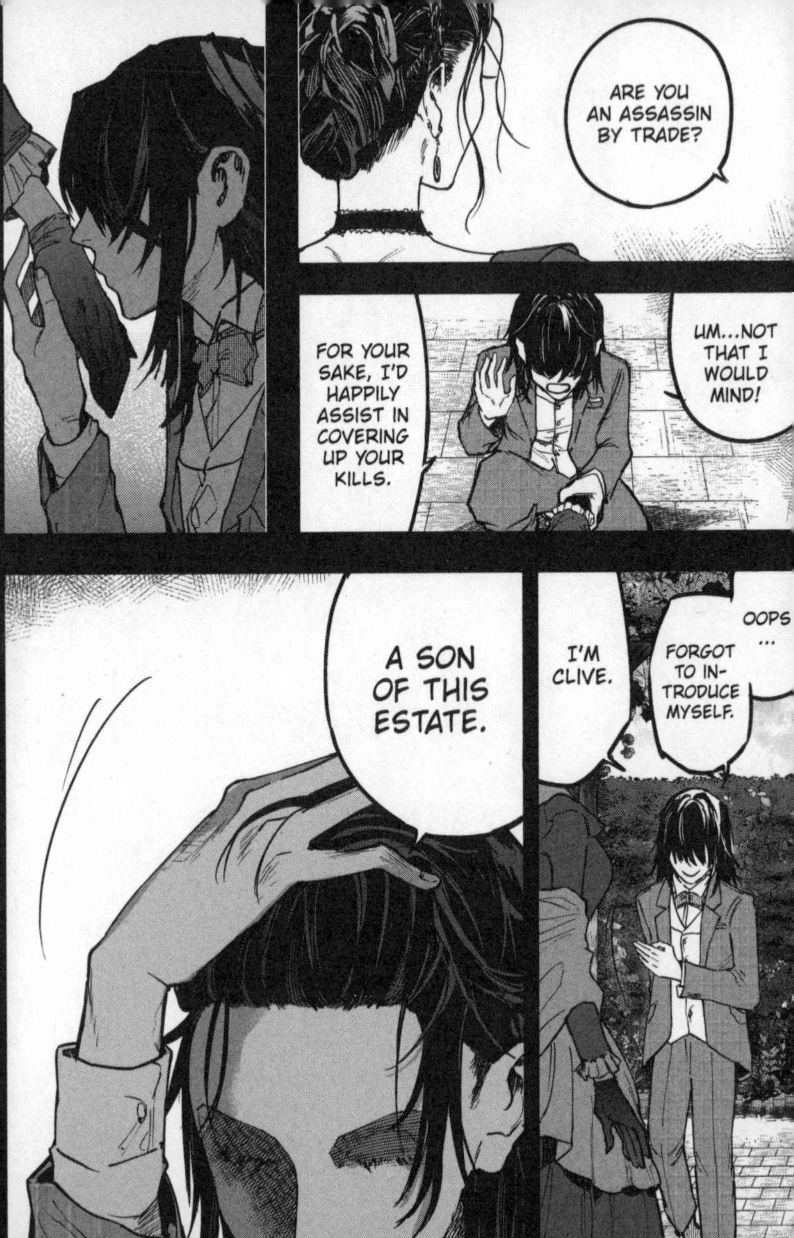
ARE YOU AN ASSASSIN BY TRADE?
UM...NOT THAT I WOULD MIND!
FOR YOUR SAKE, I'D HAPPILY ASSIST IN COVERING UP YOUR KILLS.
OOPS...
FORGOT TO IN-TRODUCE MYSELF.
I'M CLIVE.
A SON OF THIS ESTATE.

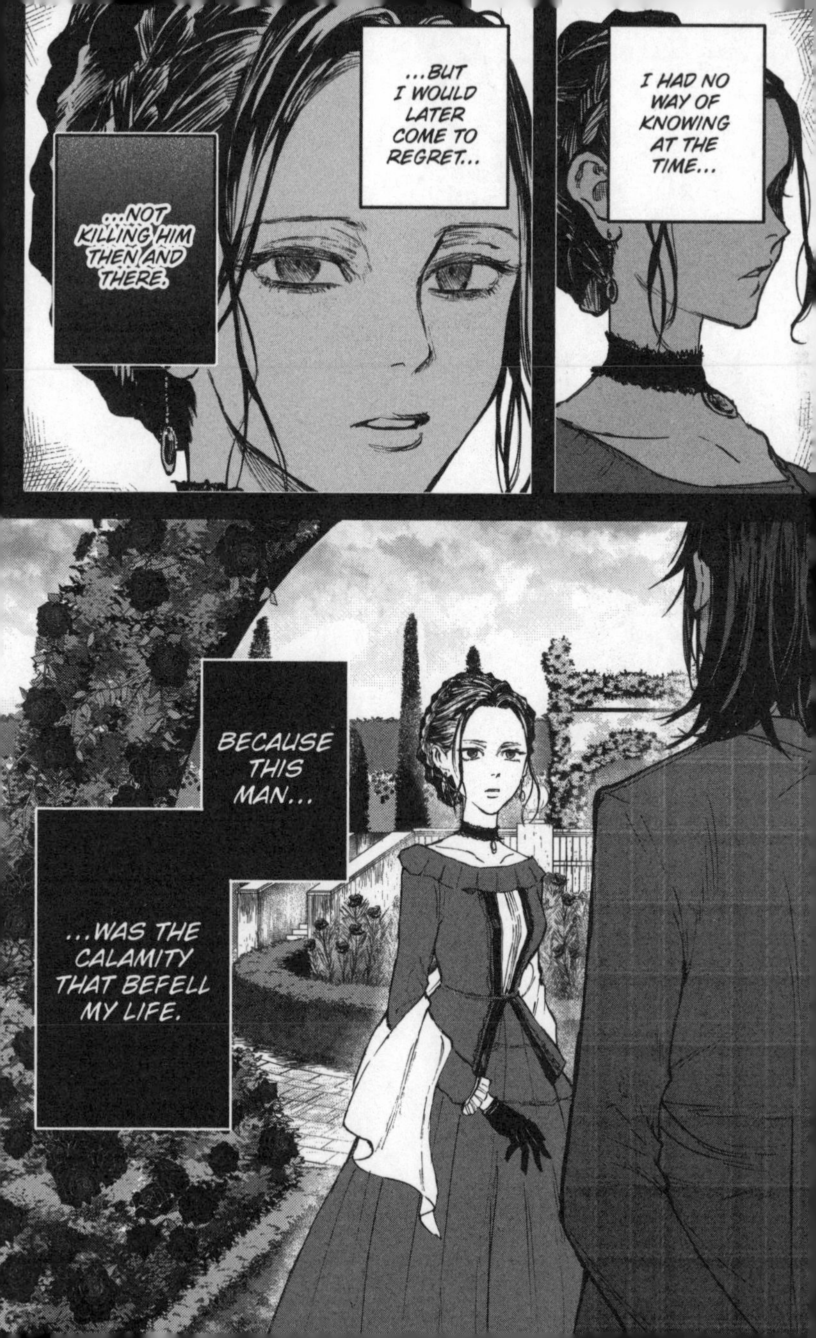
I HAD NO WAY OF KNOWING AT THE TIME...
...BUT I WOULD LATER COME TO REGRET...
...NOT KILLING HIM THEN AND THERE.
BECAUSE THIS MAN...
...WAS THE CALAMITY THAT BEFELL MY LIFE.

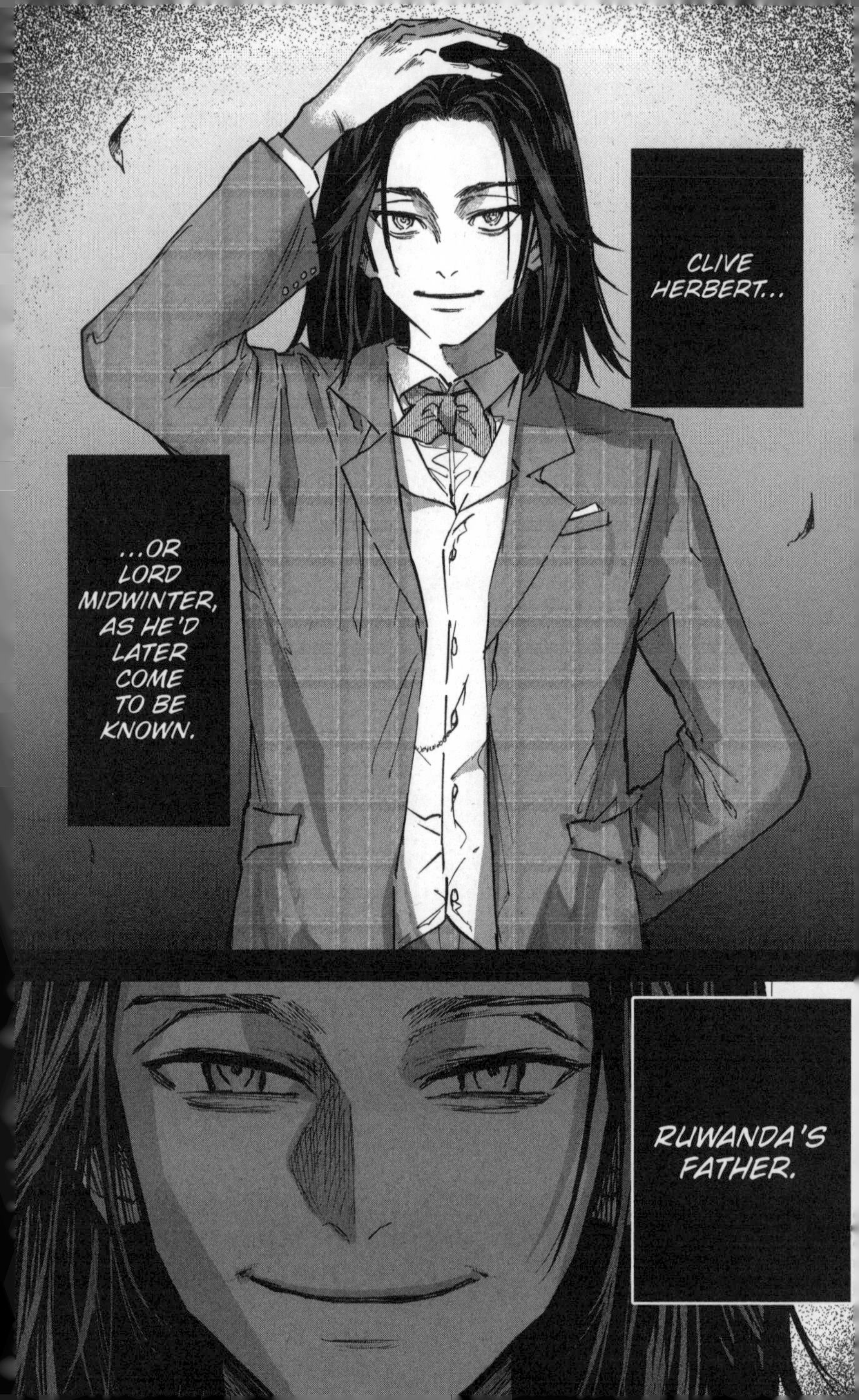
CLIVE HERBERT...
...OR LORD MIDWINTER, AS HE'D LATER COME TO BE KNOWN.
RUWANDA'S FATHER.

Episode 16: Miranda & Clive II

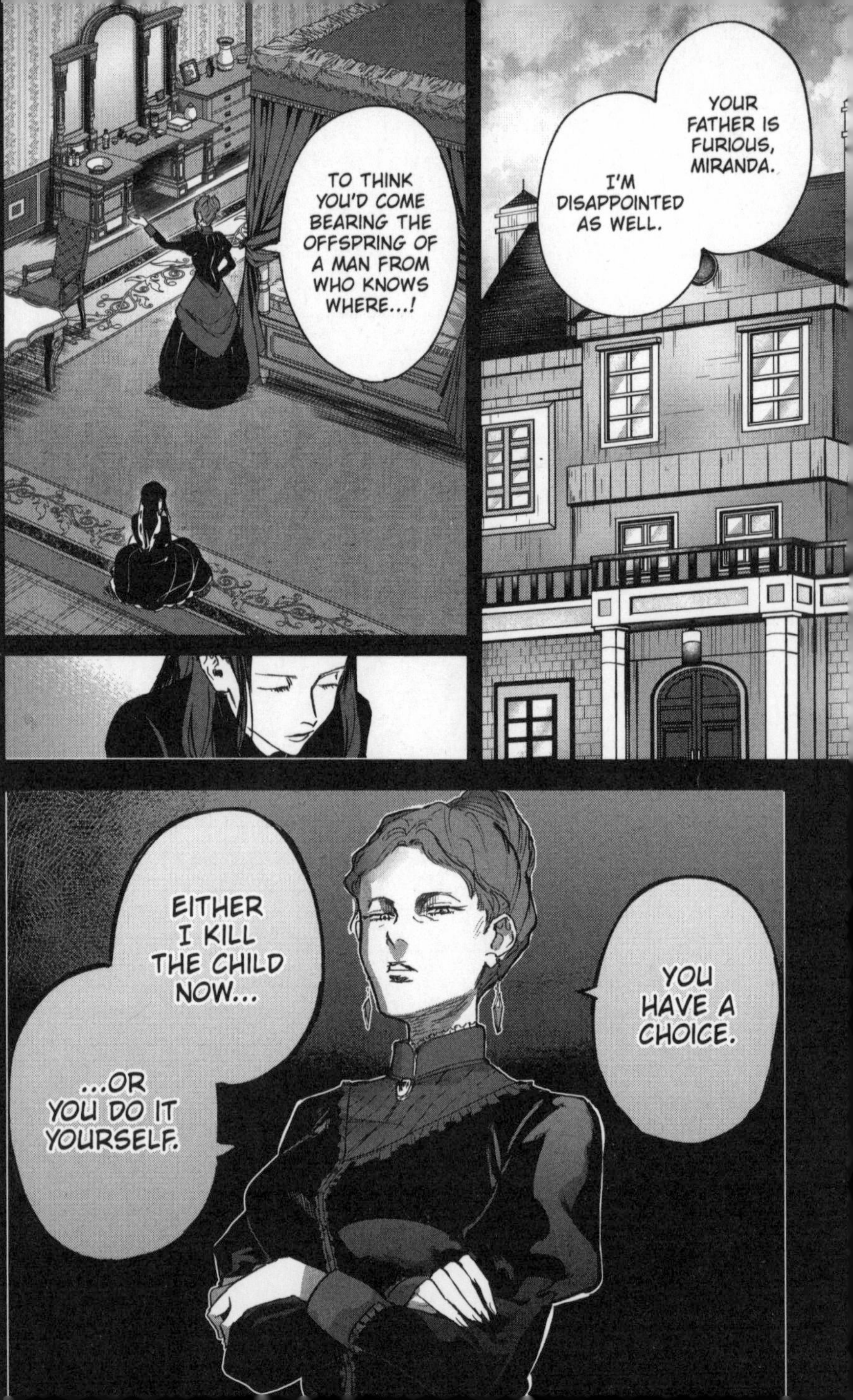
YOUR FATHER IS FURIOUS, MIRANDA.
I'M DISAPPOINTED AS WELL.
TO THINK YOU'D COME BEARING THE OFFSPRING OF A MAN FROM WHO KNOWS WHERE...!
YOU HAVE A CHOICE.
EITHER I KILL THE CHILD NOW...
...OR YOU DO IT YOURSELF.

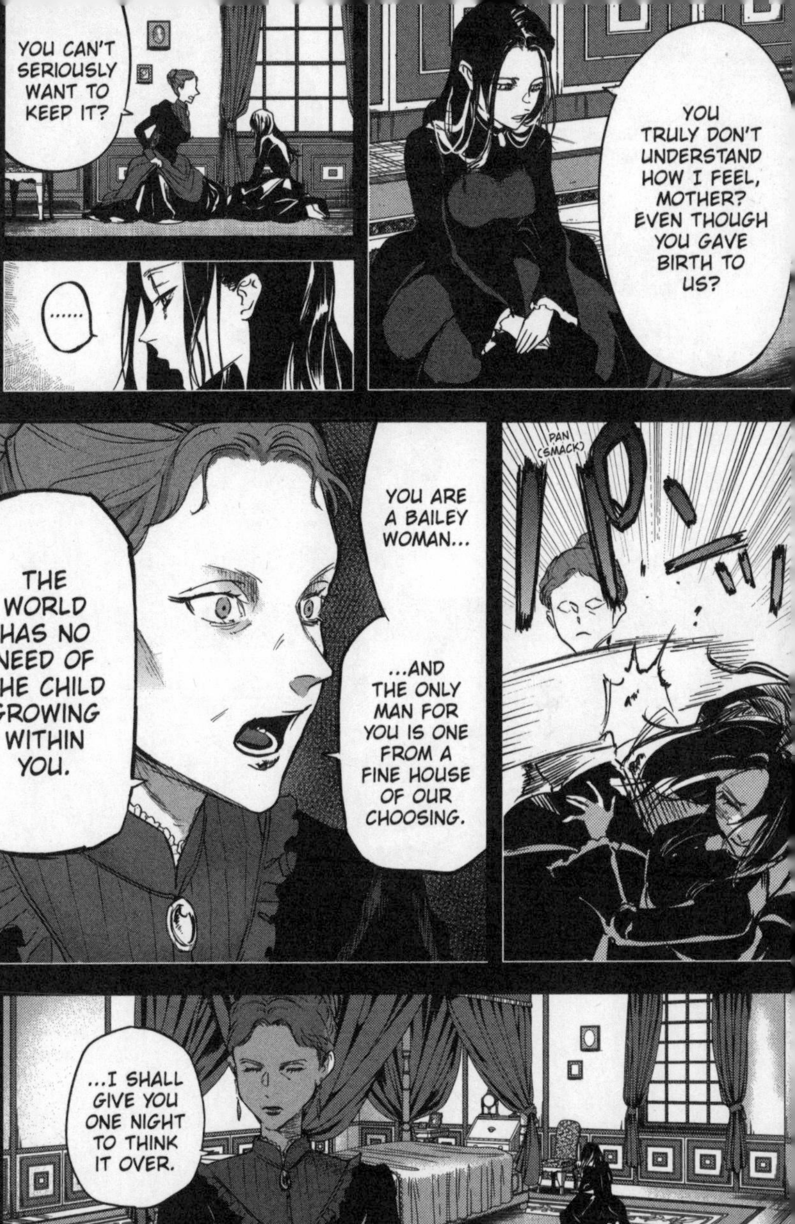
YOU TRULY DON'T UNDERSTAND HOW I FEEL, MOTHER? EVEN THOUGH YOU GAVE BIRTH TO US?
YOU CAN'T SERIOUSLY WANT TO KEEP IT?
......
PAN (SMACK)
YOU ARE A BAILEY WOMAN...
...AND THE ONLY MAN FOR YOU IS ONE FROM A FINE HOUSE OF OUR CHOOSING.
THE WORLD HAS NO NEED OF THE CHILD GROWING WITHIN YOU.
...I SHALL GIVE YOU ONE NIGHT TO THINK IT OVER.

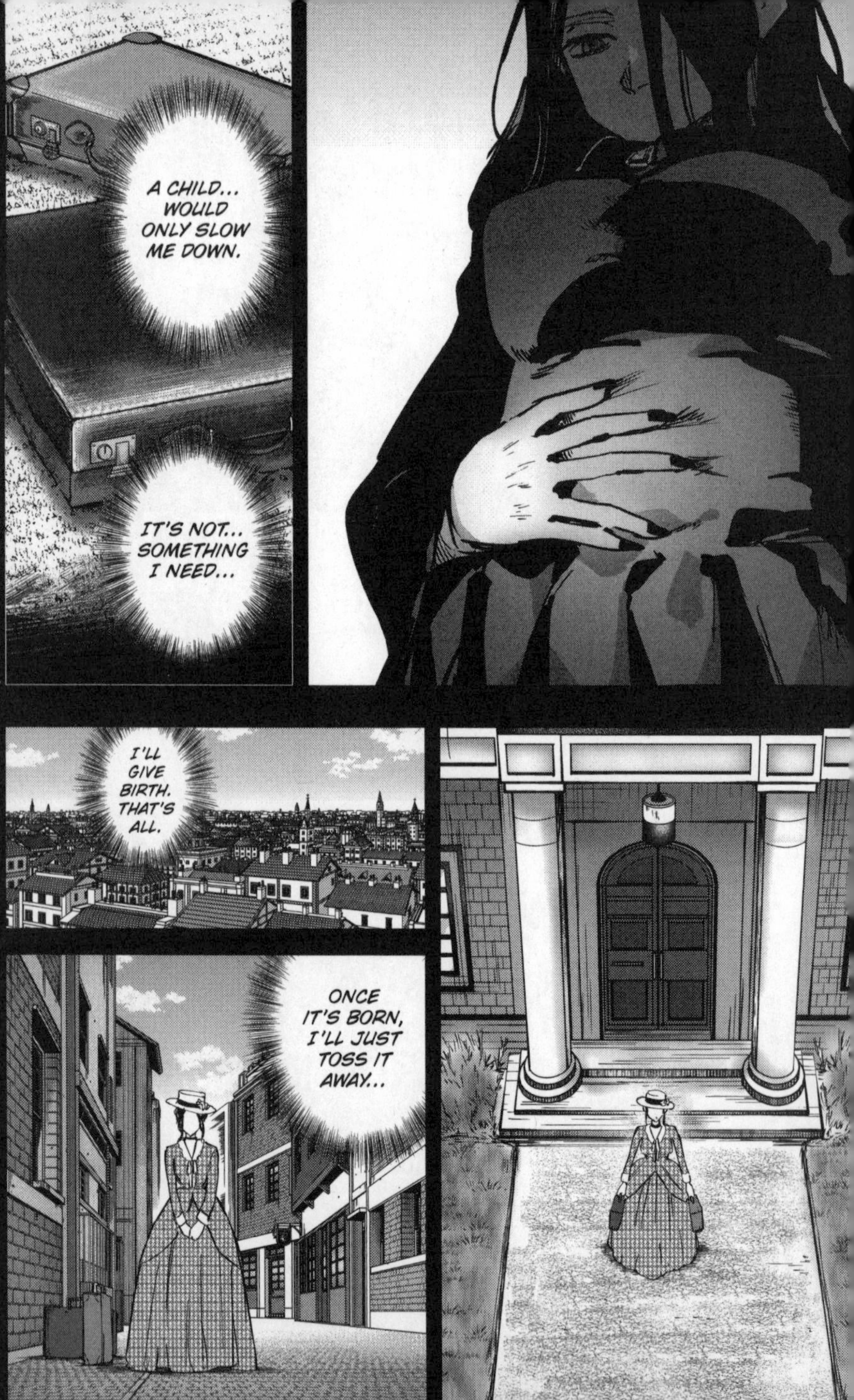
A CHILD... WOULD ONLY SLOW ME DOWN.
IT'S NOT... SOMETHING I NEED...
I'LL GIVE BIRTH. THAT'S ALL.
ONCE IT'S BORN, I'LL JUST TOSS IT AWAY...

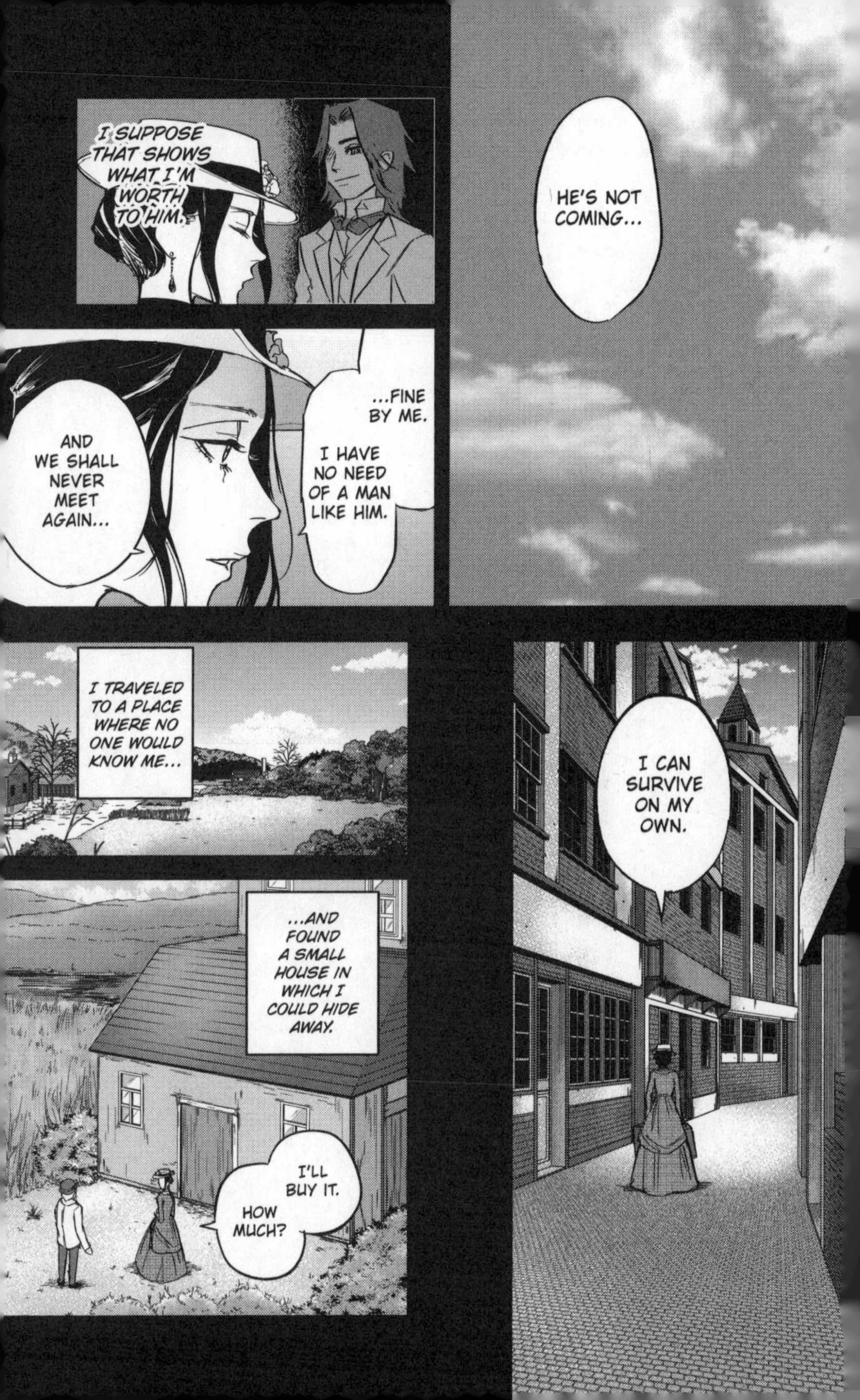
HE'S NOT COMING...
I SUPPOSE THAT SHOWS WHAT I'M WORTH TO HIM.
...FINE BY ME.
I HAVE NO NEED OF A MAN LIKE HIM.
AND WE SHALL NEVER MEET AGAIN...
I CAN SURVIVE ON MY OWN.
I TRAVELED TO A PLACE WHERE NO ONE WOULD KNOW ME...
...AND FOUND A SMALL HOUSE IN WHICH I COULD HIDE AWAY.
I'LL BUY IT.
HOW MUCH?

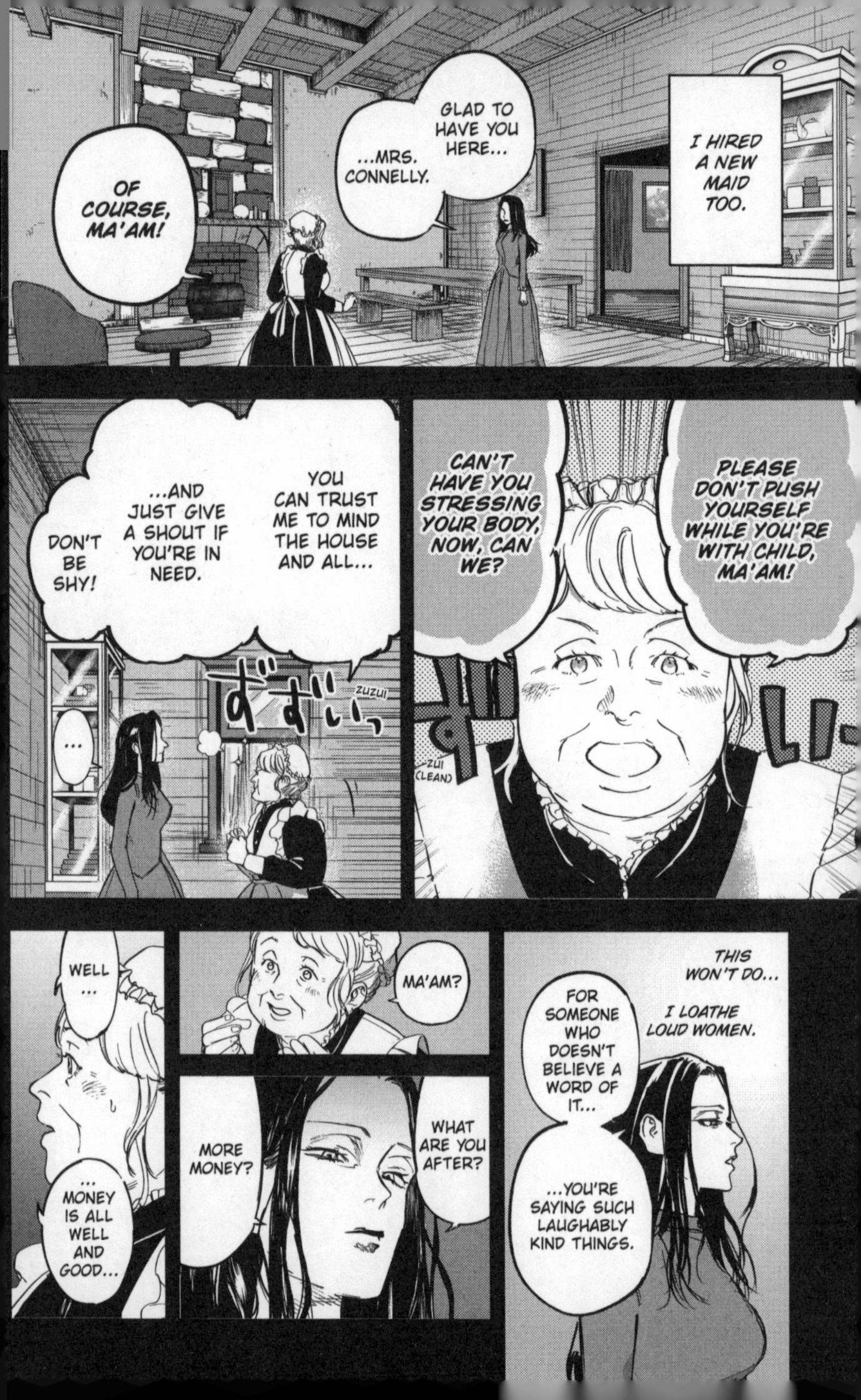
I HIRED A NEW MAID TOO.
GLAD TO HAVE YOU HERE...
...MRS. CONNELLY.
OF COURSE, MA'AM!
PLEASE DON'T PUSH YOURSELF WHILE YOU'RE WITH CHILD, MA'AM!
CAN'T HAVE YOU STRESSING YOUR BODY, NOW, CAN WE?
ZUI (LEAN)
YOU CAN TRUST ME TO MIND THE HOUSE AND ALL...
...AND JUST GIVE A SHOUT IF YOU'RE IN NEED.
DON'T BE SHY!
ZUZUI
...
THIS WON'T DO...
I LOATHE LOUD WOMEN.
FOR SOMEONE WHO DOESN'T BELIEVE A WORD OF IT...
...YOU'RE SAYING SUCH LAUGHABLY KIND THINGS.
MA'AM?
WHAT ARE YOU AFTER?
MORE MONEY?
WELL...
...MONEY IS ALL WELL AND GOOD...

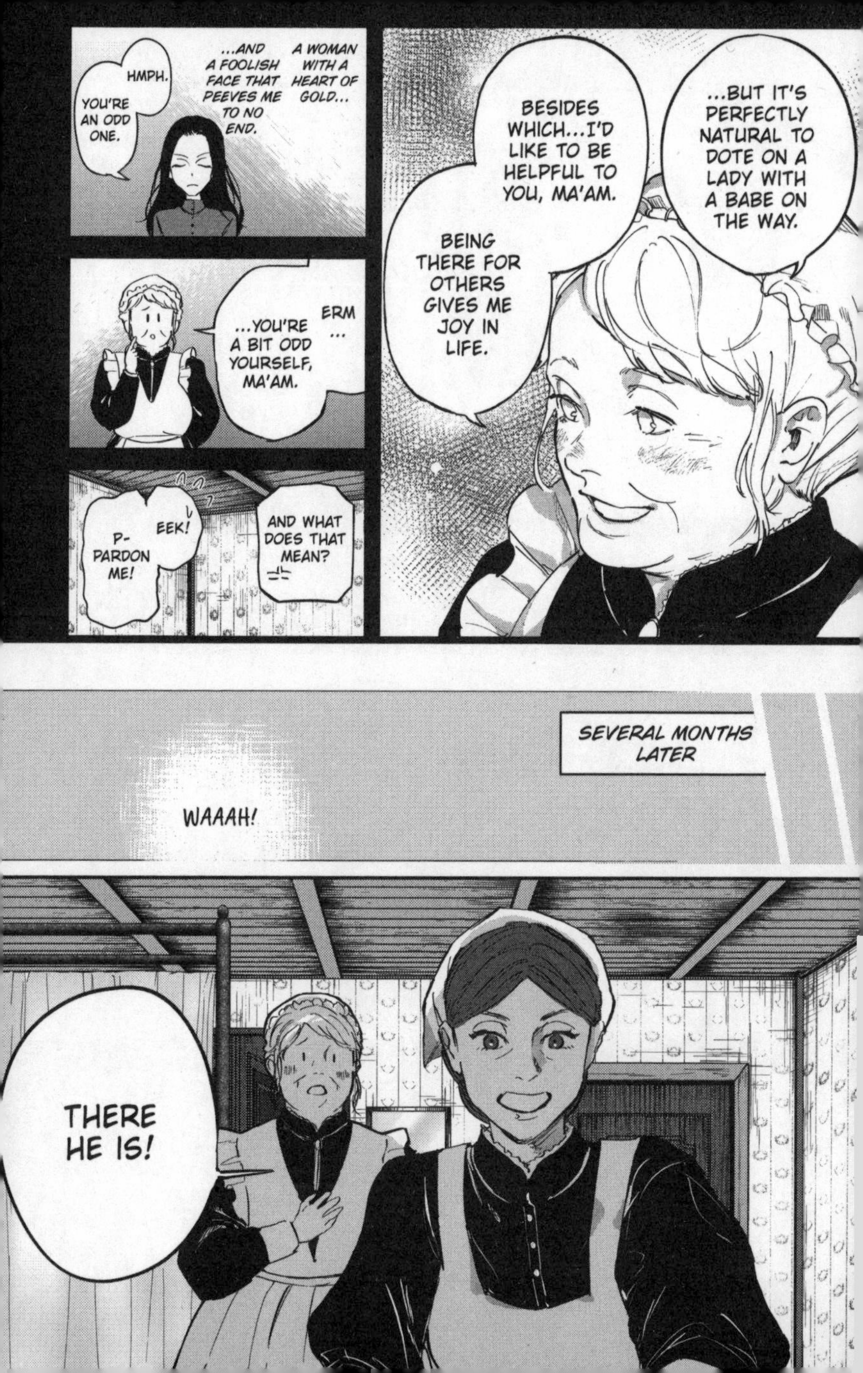
...BUT IT'S PERFECTLY NATURAL TO DOTE ON A LADY WITH A BABE ON THE WAY.
BESIDES WHICH...I'D LIKE TO BE HELPFUL TO YOU, MA'AM.
BEING THERE FOR OTHERS GIVES ME JOY IN LIFE.
A WOMAN WITH A HEART OF GOLD...
...AND A FOOLISH FACE THAT PEEVES ME TO NO END.
HMPH.
YOU'RE AN ODD ONE.
ERM...
...YOU'RE A BIT ODD YOURSELF, MA'AM.
AND WHAT DOES THAT MEAN?
EEK!
P-PARDON ME!
SEVERAL MONTHS LATER
WAAAH!
THERE HE IS!

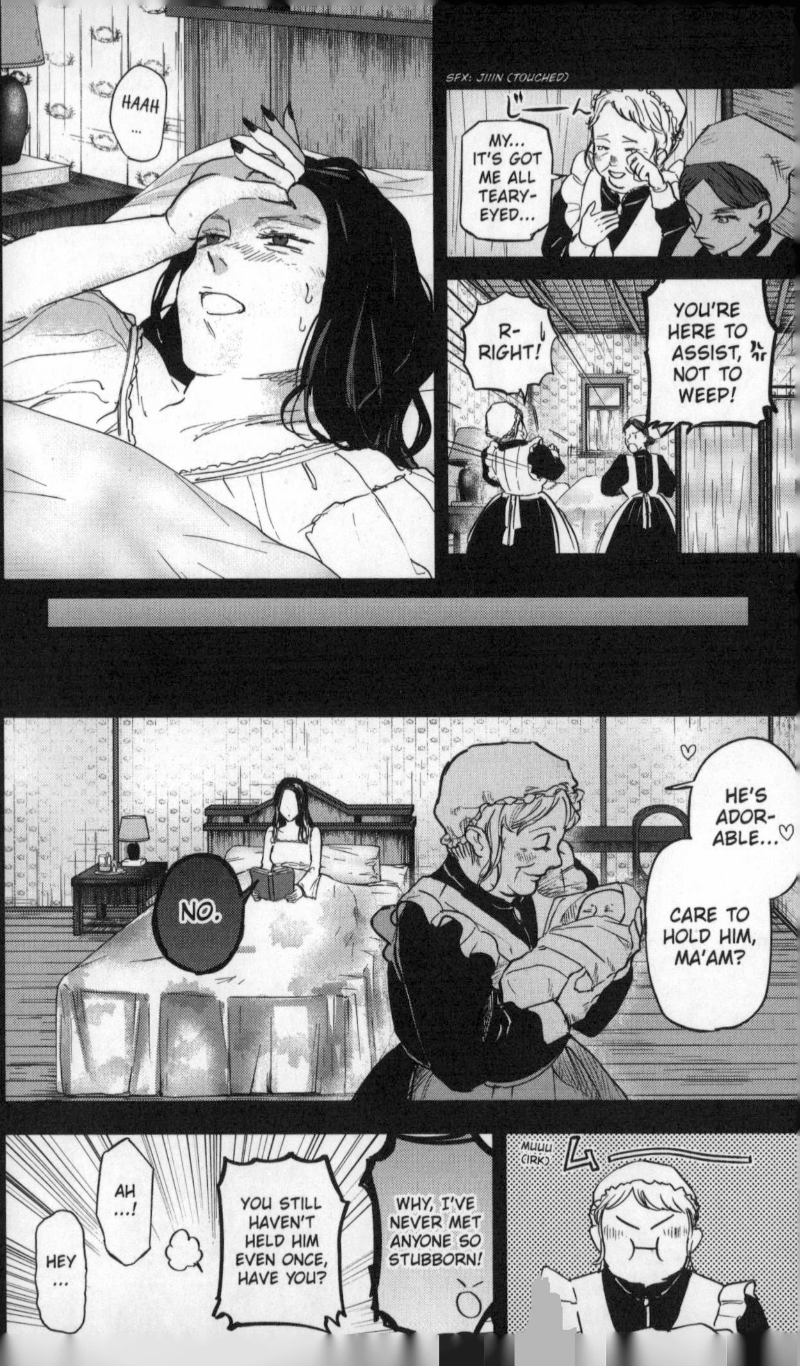
SFX: JIIIN (TOUCHED)
じーん
MY... IT'S GOT ME ALL TEARY-EYED...
YOU'RE HERE TO ASSIST, NOT TO WEEP!
R-RIGHT!
HAAH ...
HE'S ADORABLE...♡
CARE TO HOLD HIM, MA'AM?
NO.
MUUU (IRK)
WHY, I'VE NEVER MET ANYONE SO STUBBORN!
YOU STILL HAVEN'T HELD HIM EVEN ONCE, HAVE YOU?
AH ...!
HEY ...

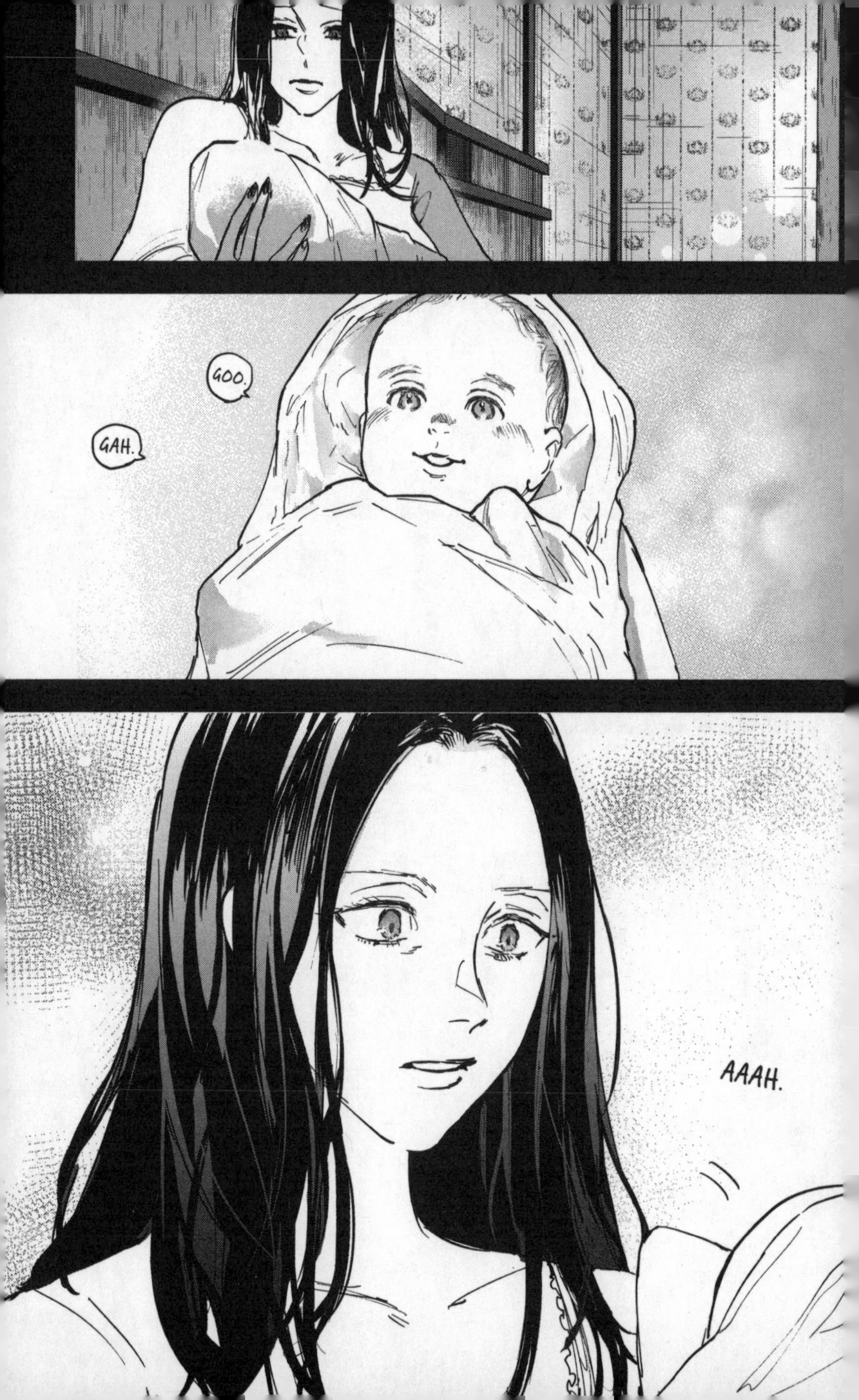
GOO.
GAH.
AAAH.

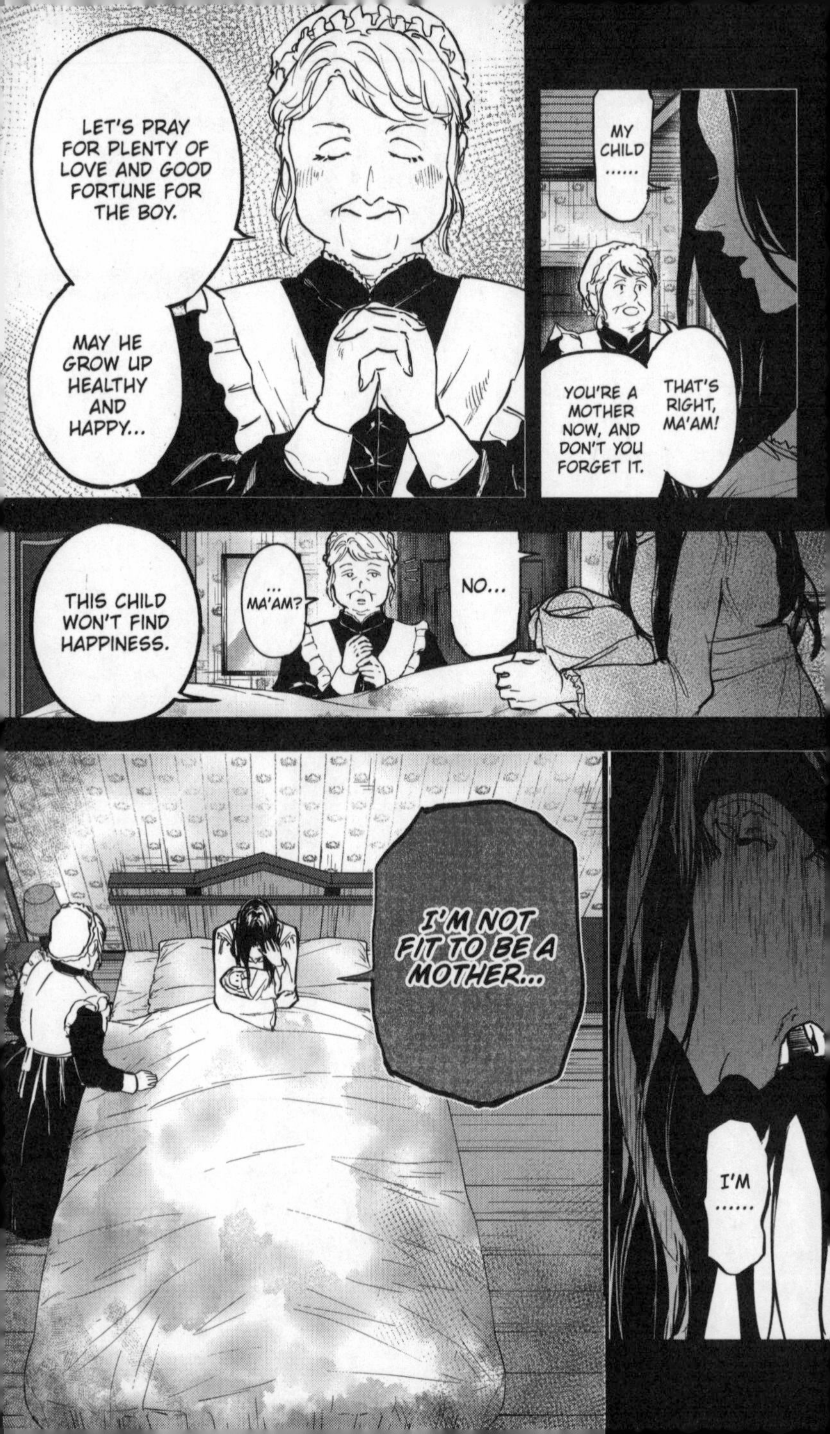
MY CHILD ......
THAT'S RIGHT, MA'AM!
YOU'RE A MOTHER NOW, AND DON'T YOU FORGET IT.
LET'S PRAY FOR PLENTY OF LOVE AND GOOD FORTUNE FOR THE BOY.
MAY HE GROW UP HEALTHY AND HAPPY...
NO...
... MA'AM?
THIS CHILD WON'T FIND HAPPINESS.
I'M ......
I'M NOT FIT TO BE A MOTHER...

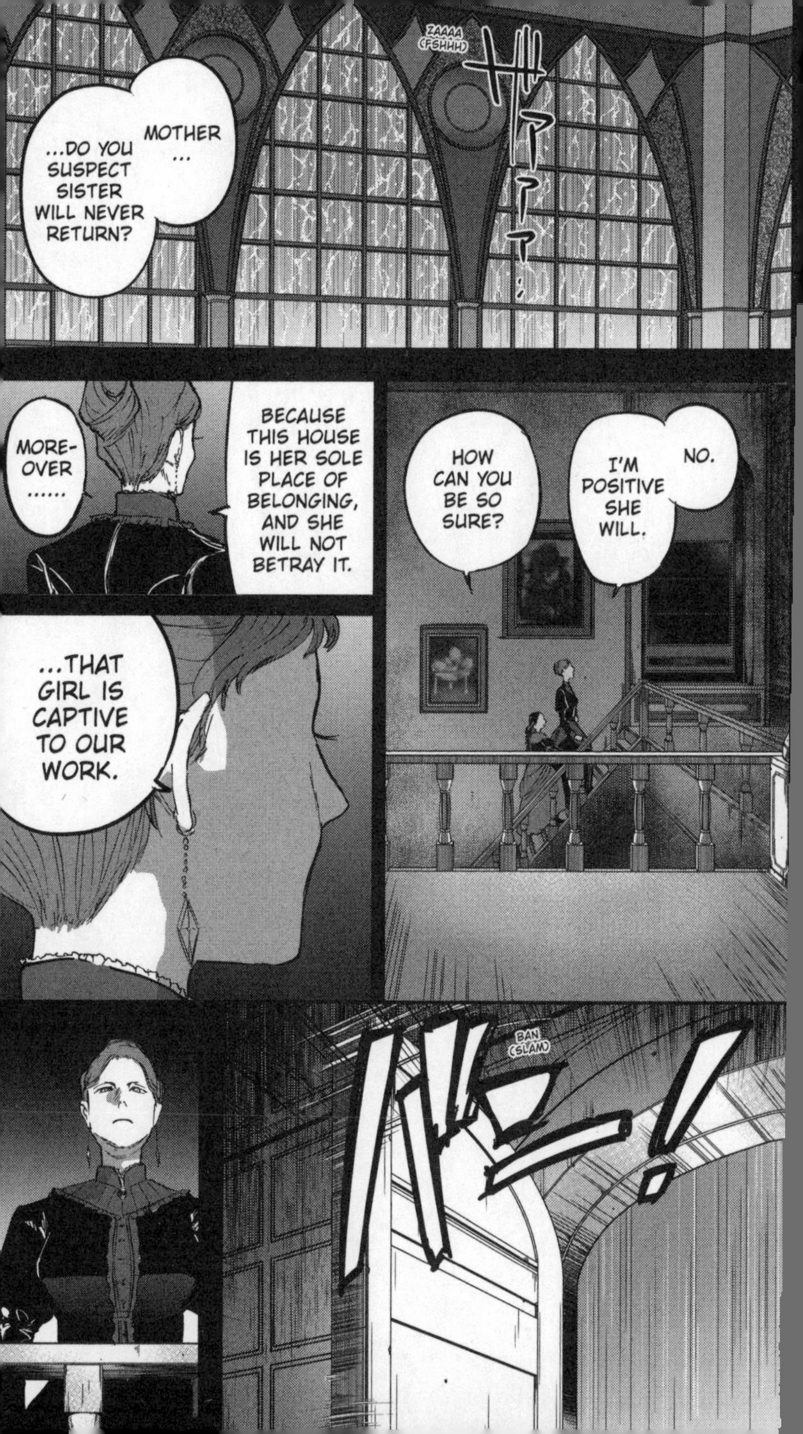
ZAAAA (FSHHH)
MOTHER ...
...DO YOU SUSPECT SISTER WILL NEVER RETURN?
NO.
I'M POSITIVE SHE WILL.
HOW CAN YOU BE SO SURE?
BECAUSE THIS HOUSE IS HER SOLE PLACE OF BELONGING, AND SHE WILL NOT BETRAY IT.
MORE-OVER ......
...THAT GIRL IS CAPTIVE TO OUR WORK.
BAN (SLAM)

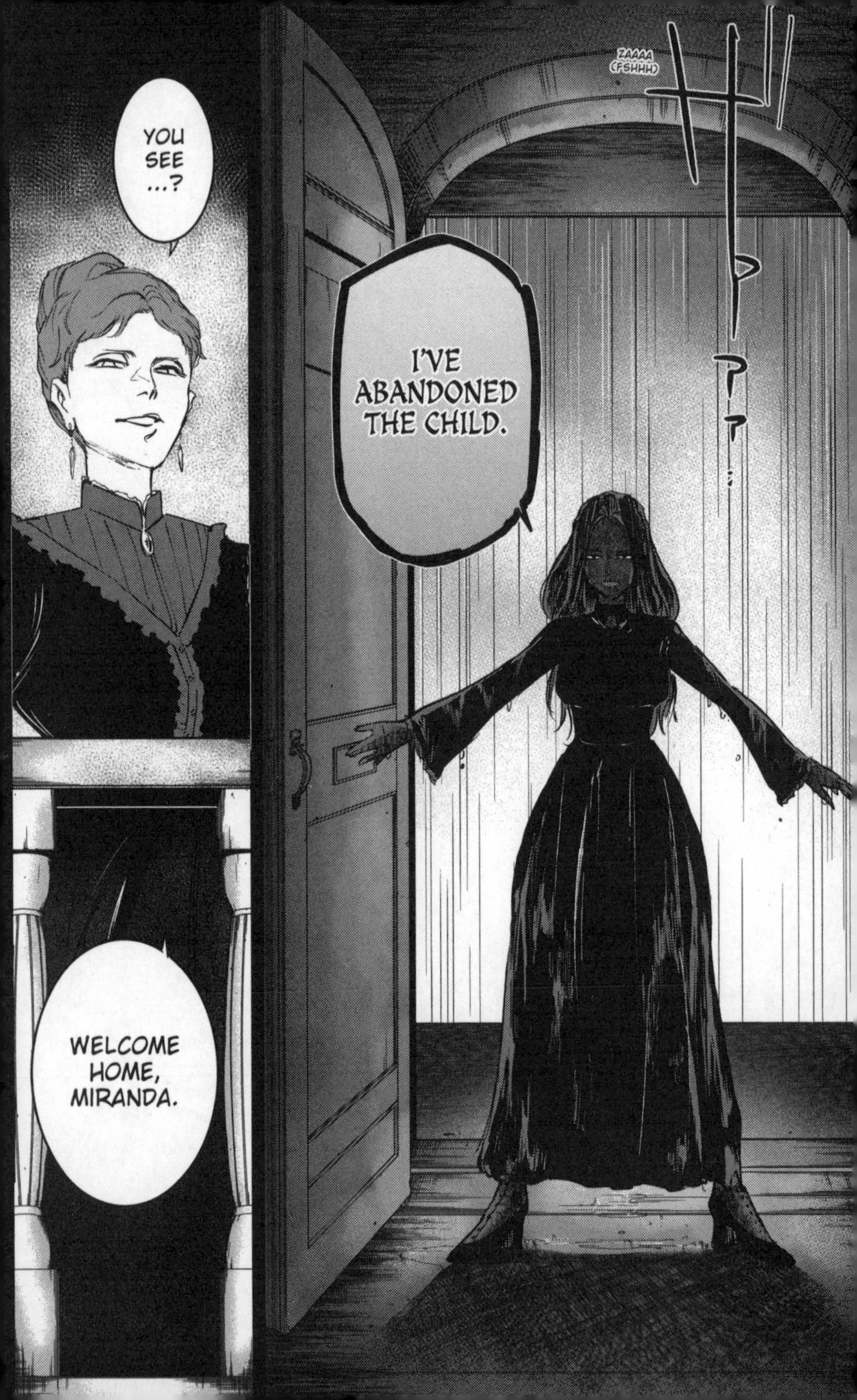
ZAAAA (FSHHH)
I'VE ABANDONED THE CHILD.
YOU SEE ...?
WELCOME HOME, MIRANDA.

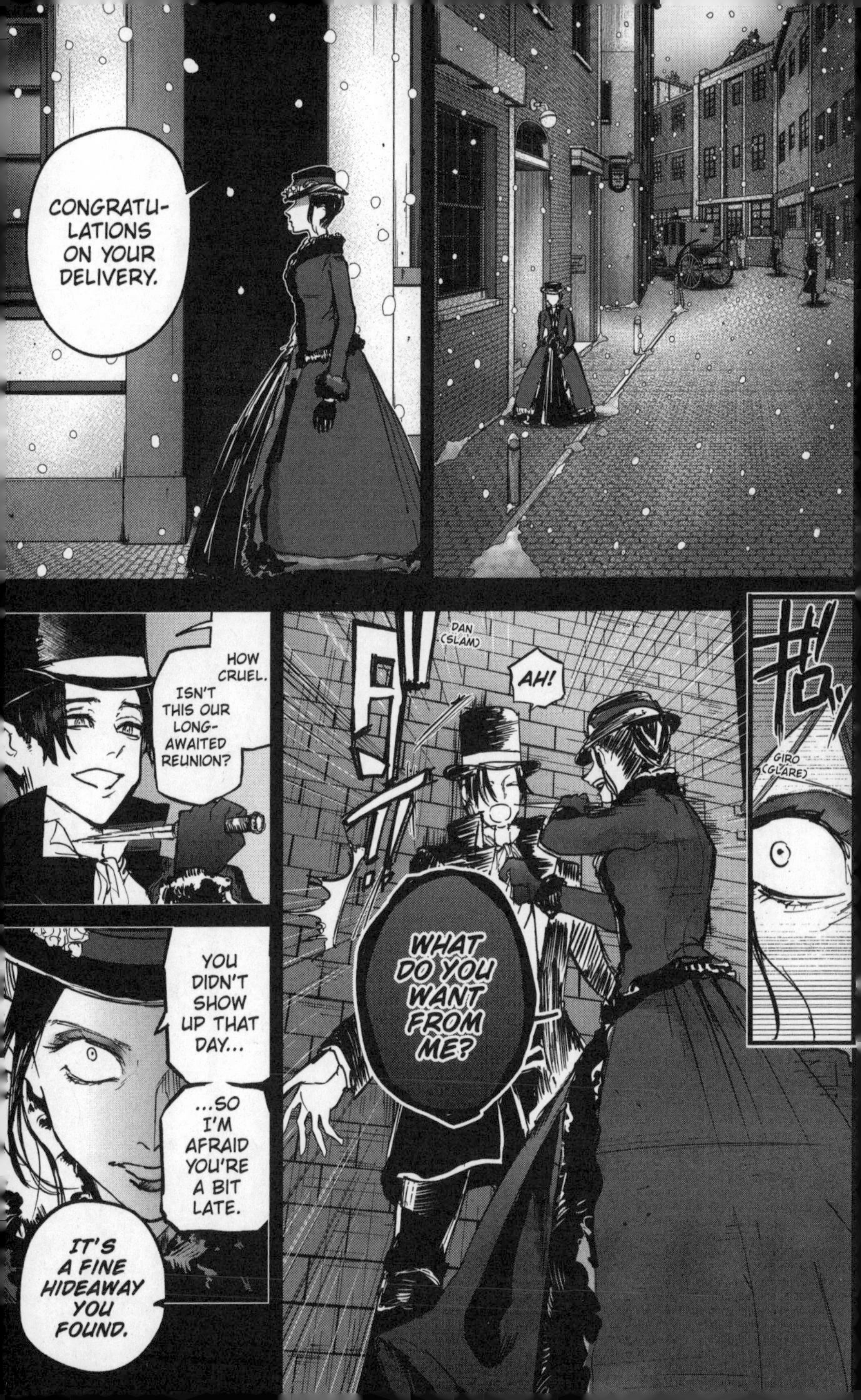
CONGRATULATIONS ON YOUR DELIVERY.
GIRO (GLARE)
DAN (SLAM)
AH!
WHAT DO YOU WANT FROM ME?
HOW CRUEL. ISN'T THIS OUR LONG-AWAITED REUNION?
YOU DIDN'T SHOW UP THAT DAY...
...SO I'M AFRAID YOU'RE A BIT LATE.
IT'S A FINE HIDEAWAY YOU FOUND.

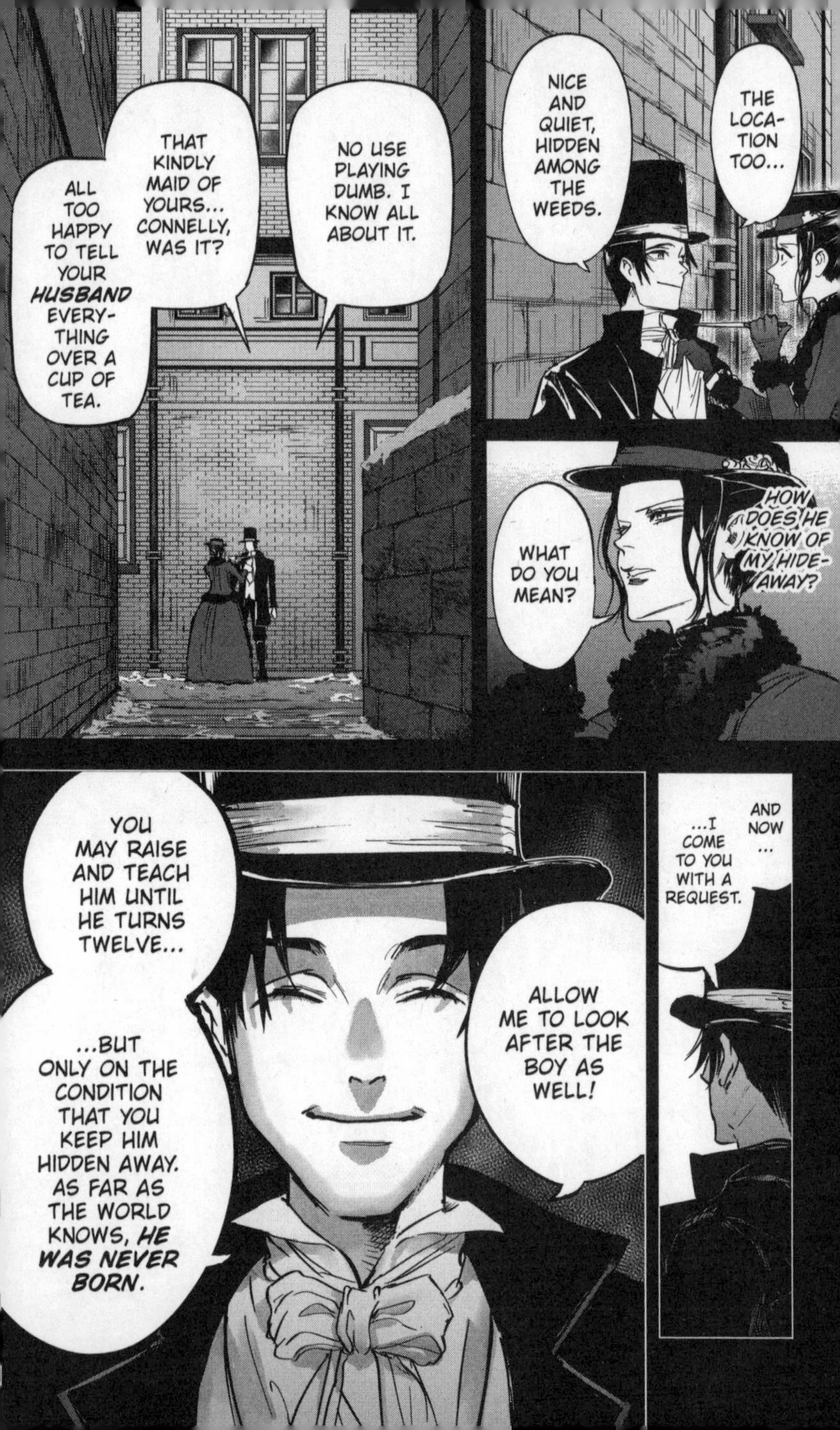
THE LOCATION TOO...
NICE AND QUIET, HIDDEN AMONG THE WEEDS.
HOW DOES HE KNOW OF MY HIDEAWAY?
WHAT DO YOU MEAN?
NO USE PLAYING DUMB. I KNOW ALL ABOUT IT.
THAT KINDLY MAID OF YOURS... CONNELLY, WAS IT?
ALL TOO HAPPY TO TELL YOUR *HUSBAND* EVERYTHING OVER A CUP OF TEA.
AND NOW...
...I COME TO YOU WITH A REQUEST.
ALLOW ME TO LOOK AFTER THE BOY AS WELL!
YOU MAY RAISE AND TEACH HIM UNTIL HE TURNS TWELVE...
...BUT ONLY ON THE CONDITION THAT YOU KEEP HIM HIDDEN AWAY. AS FAR AS THE WORLD KNOWS, ***HE WAS NEVER BORN***.

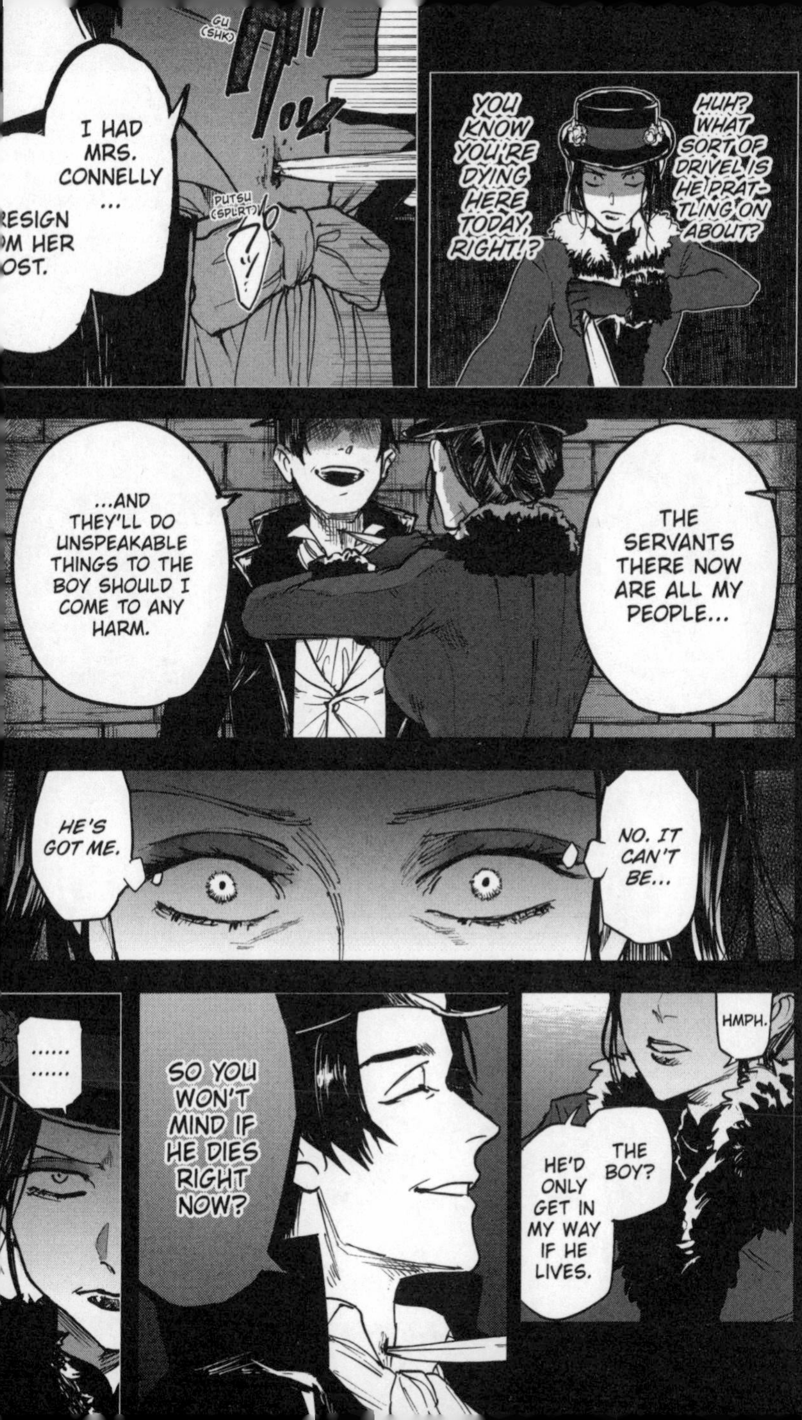
HUH? WHAT SORT OF DRIVEL IS HE PRATTLING ON ABOUT?
YOU KNOW YOU'RE DYING HERE TODAY, RIGHT!?
GU (SHK)
PUTSU (SPLRT)
I HAD MRS. CONNELLY ... RESIGN OM HER OST.
THE SERVANTS THERE NOW ARE ALL MY PEOPLE...
...AND THEY'LL DO UNSPEAKABLE THINGS TO THE BOY SHOULD I COME TO ANY HARM.
NO. IT CAN'T BE...
HE'S GOT ME.
HMPH.
THE BOY?
HE'D ONLY GET IN MY WAY IF HE LIVES.
SO YOU WON'T MIND IF HE DIES RIGHT NOW?
....

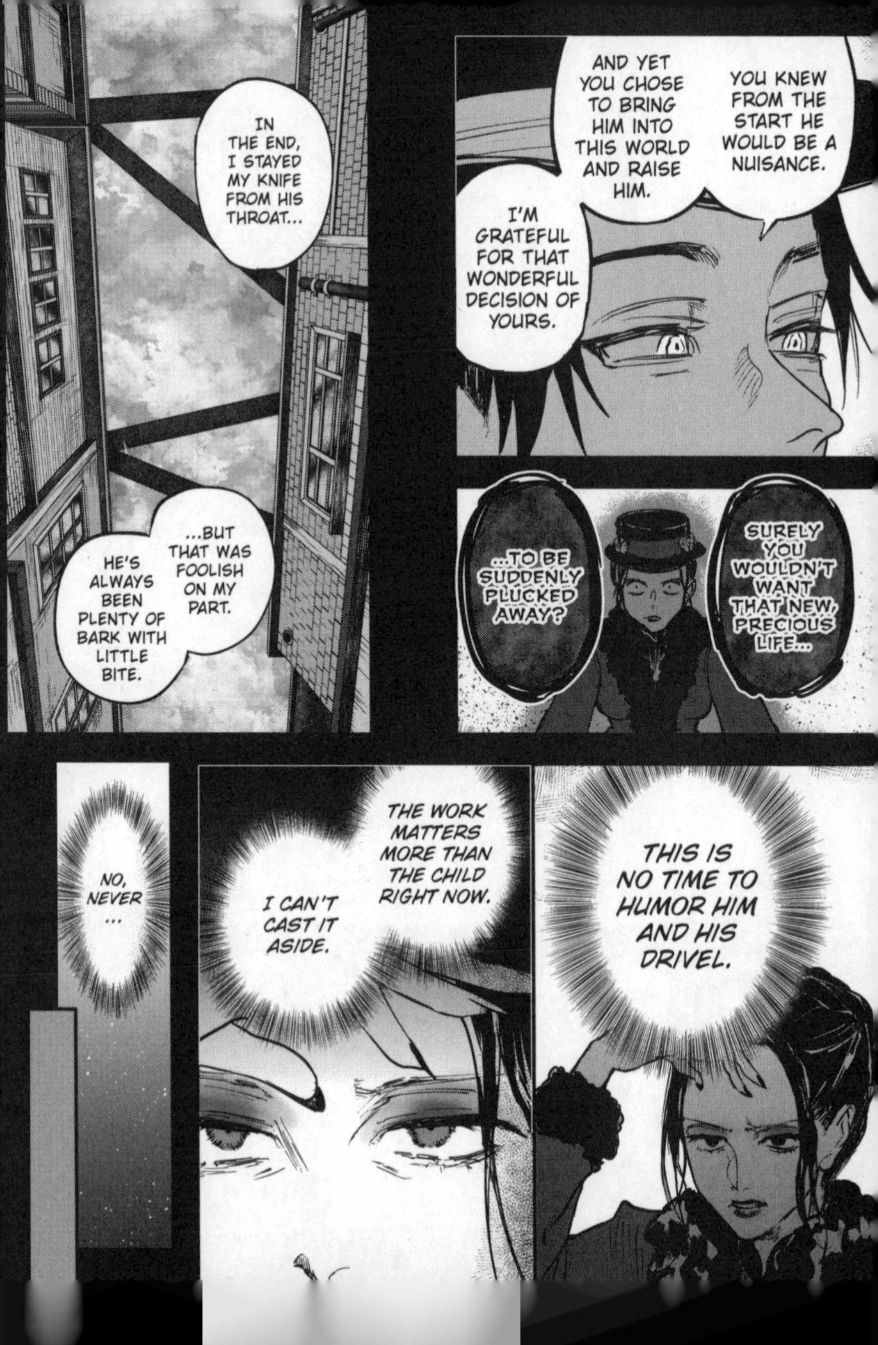
YOU KNEW FROM THE START HE WOULD BE A NUISANCE.
AND YET YOU CHOSE TO BRING HIM INTO THIS WORLD AND RAISE HIM.
I'M GRATEFUL FOR THAT WONDERFUL DECISION OF YOURS.
SURELY YOU WOULDN'T WANT THAT NEW, PRECIOUS LIFE...
...TO BE SUDDENLY PLUCKED AWAY?
IN THE END, I STAYED MY KNIFE FROM HIS THROAT...
...BUT THAT WAS FOOLISH ON MY PART.
HE'S ALWAYS BEEN PLENTY OF BARK WITH LITTLE BITE.
THIS IS NO TIME TO HUMOR HIM AND HIS DRIVEL.
THE WORK MATTERS MORE THAN THE CHILD RIGHT NOW.
I CAN'T CAST IT ASIDE.
NO, NEVER...

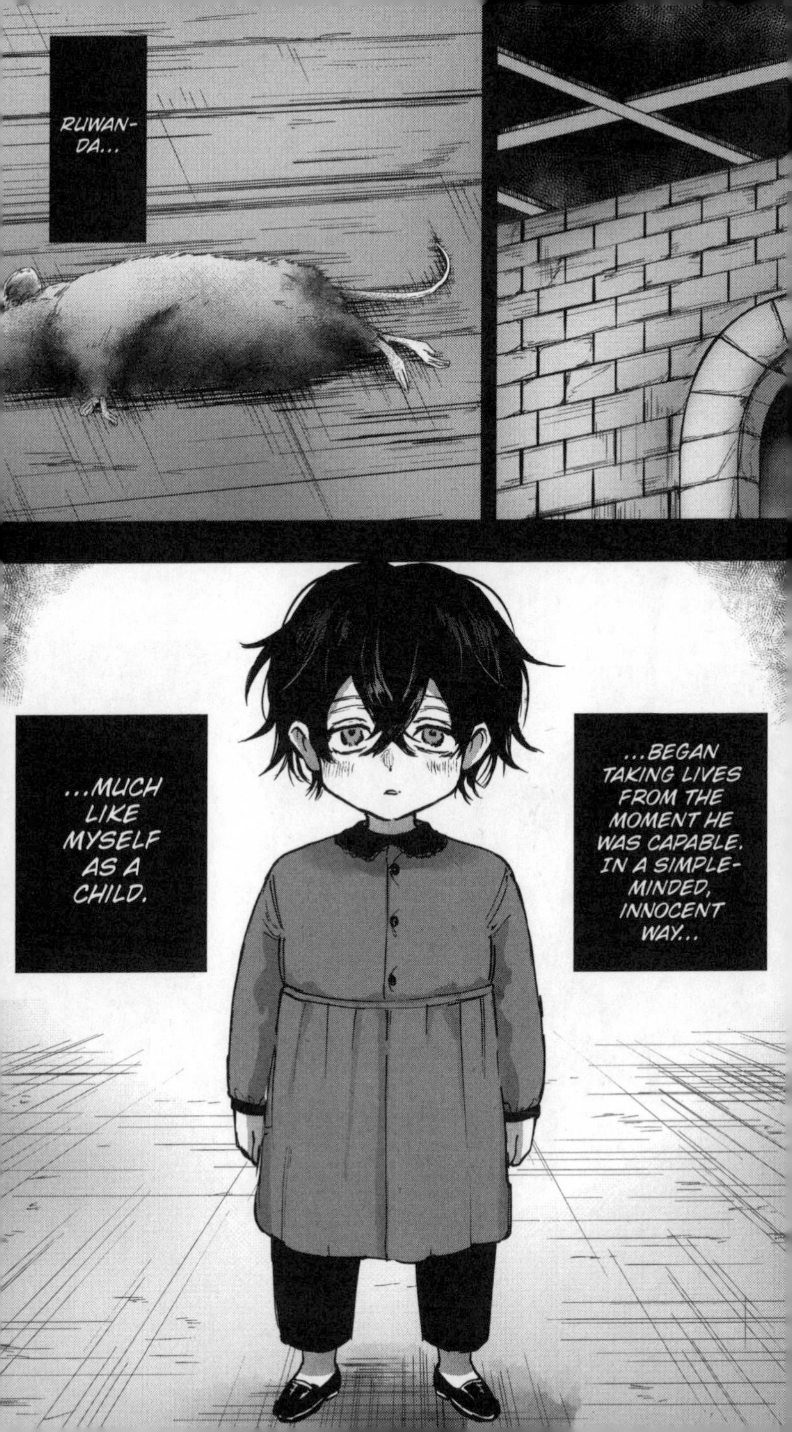
RUWAN-DA...
...BEGAN TAKING LIVES FROM THE MOMENT HE WAS CAPABLE. IN A SIMPLE-MINDED, INNOCENT WAY...
...MUCH LIKE MYSELF AS A CHILD.

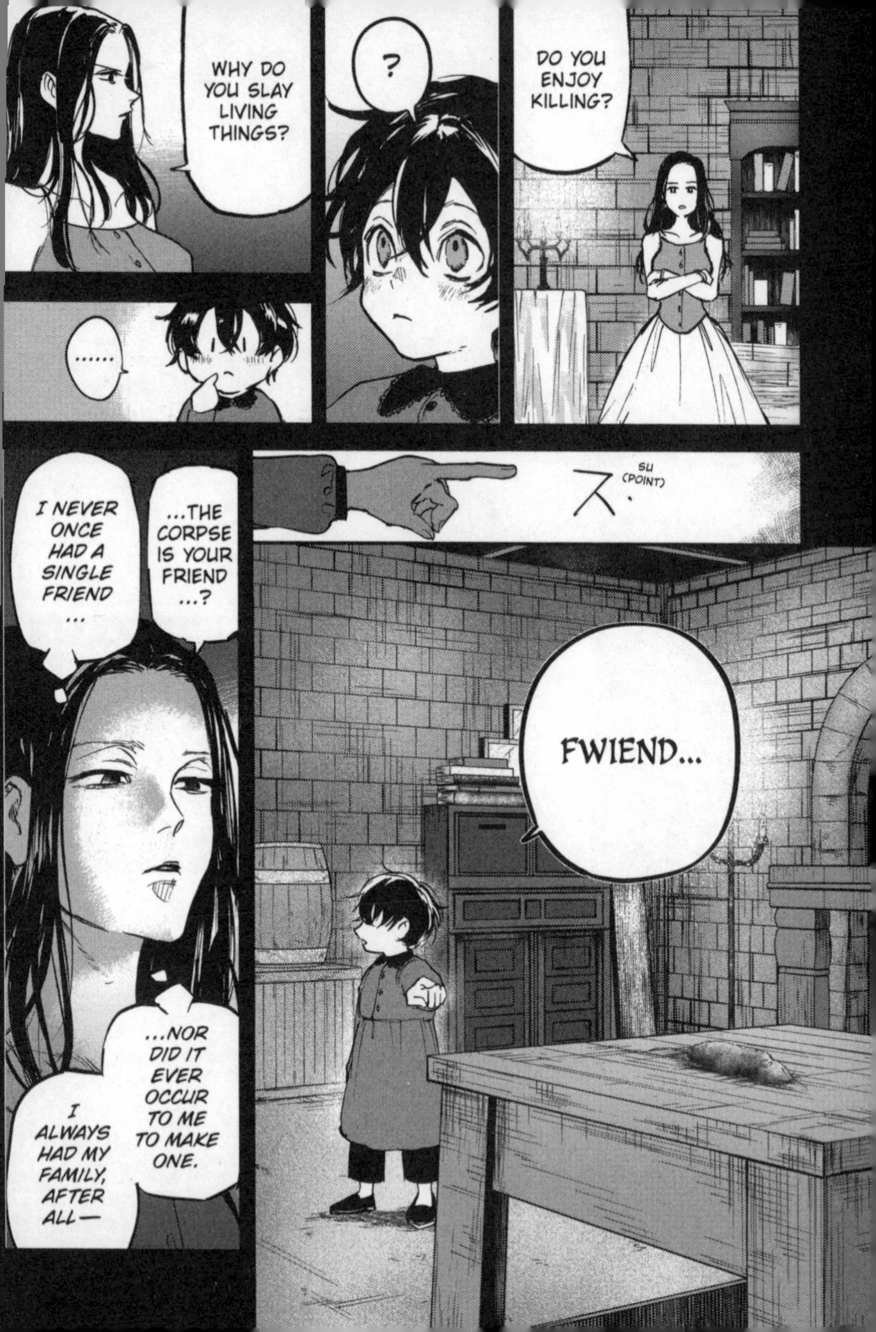
DO YOU ENJOY KILLING?
?
WHY DO YOU SLAY LIVING THINGS?
......
ス
SU (POINT)
FWIEND...
...THE CORPSE IS YOUR FRIEND ...?
I NEVER ONCE HAD A SINGLE FRIEND ...
...NOR DID IT EVER OCCUR TO ME TO MAKE ONE.
I ALWAYS HAD MY FAMILY, AFTER ALL—

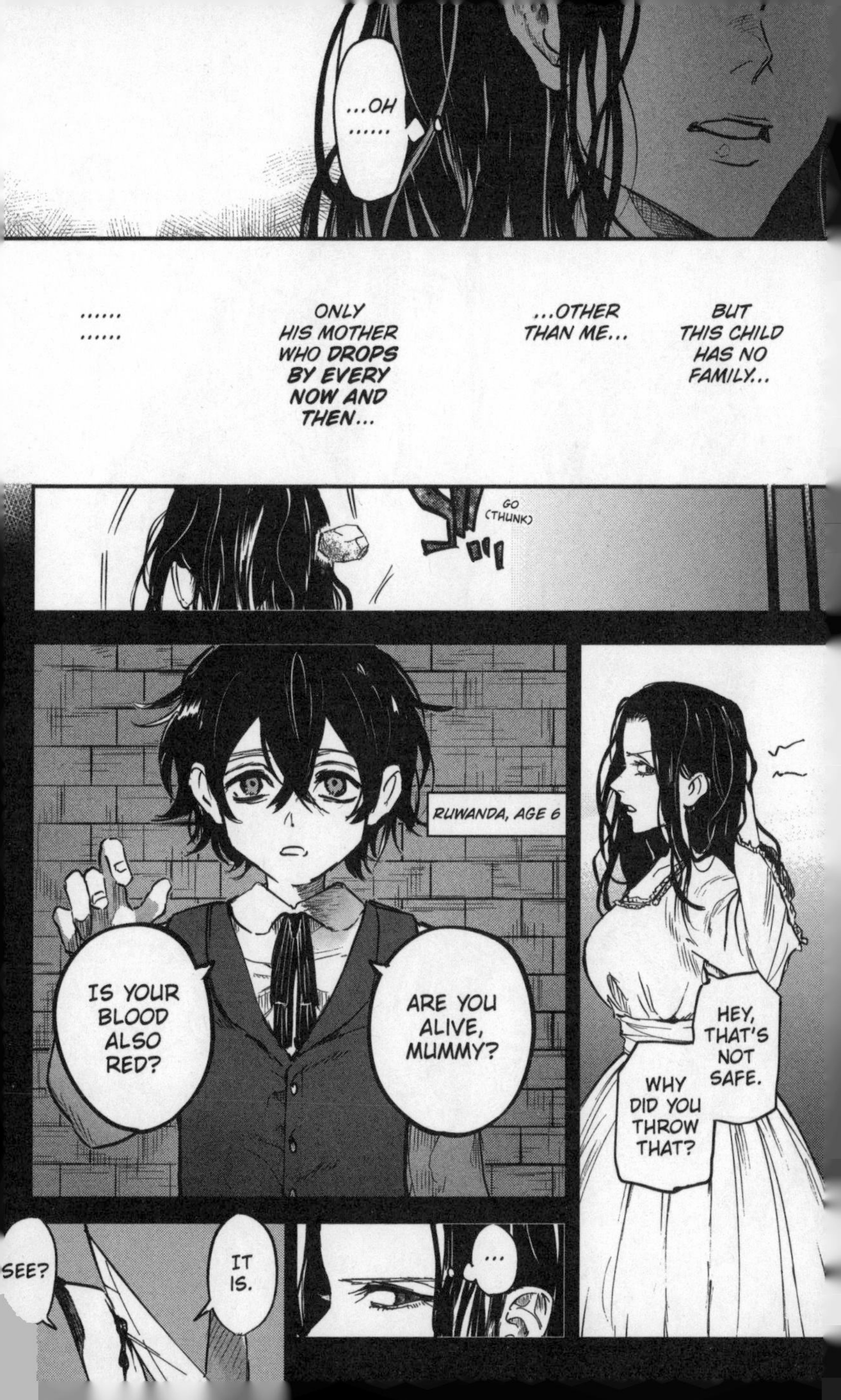
...OH ......
BUT THIS CHILD HAS NO FAMILY...
...OTHER THAN ME...
ONLY HIS MOTHER WHO DROPS BY EVERY NOW AND THEN...
....
GO (THUNK)
HEY, THAT'S NOT SAFE.
WHY DID YOU THROW THAT?
RUWANDA, AGE 6
ARE YOU ALIVE, MUMMY?
IS YOUR BLOOD ALSO RED?
...
IT IS.
SEE?

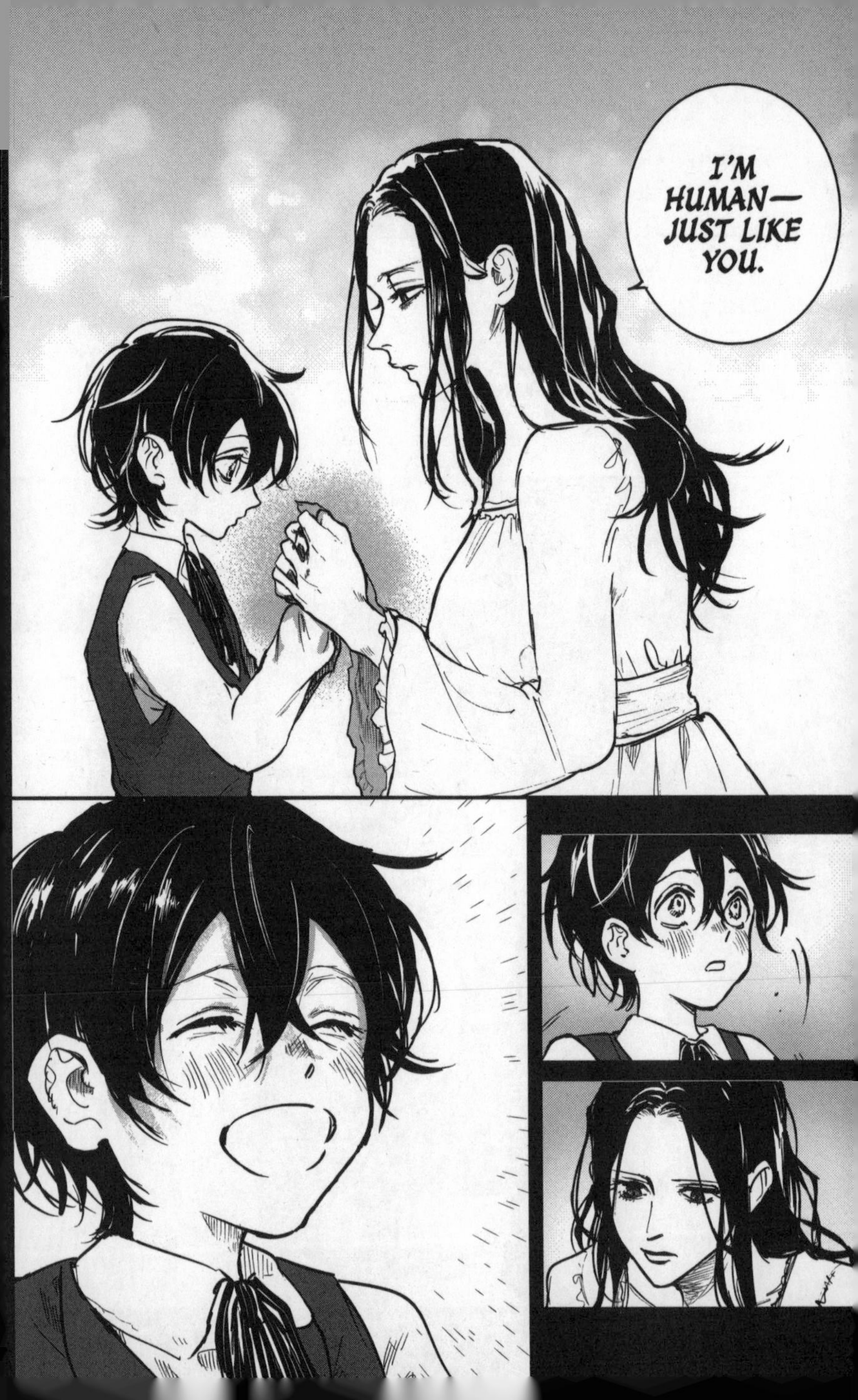
I'M HUMAN— JUST LIKE YOU.

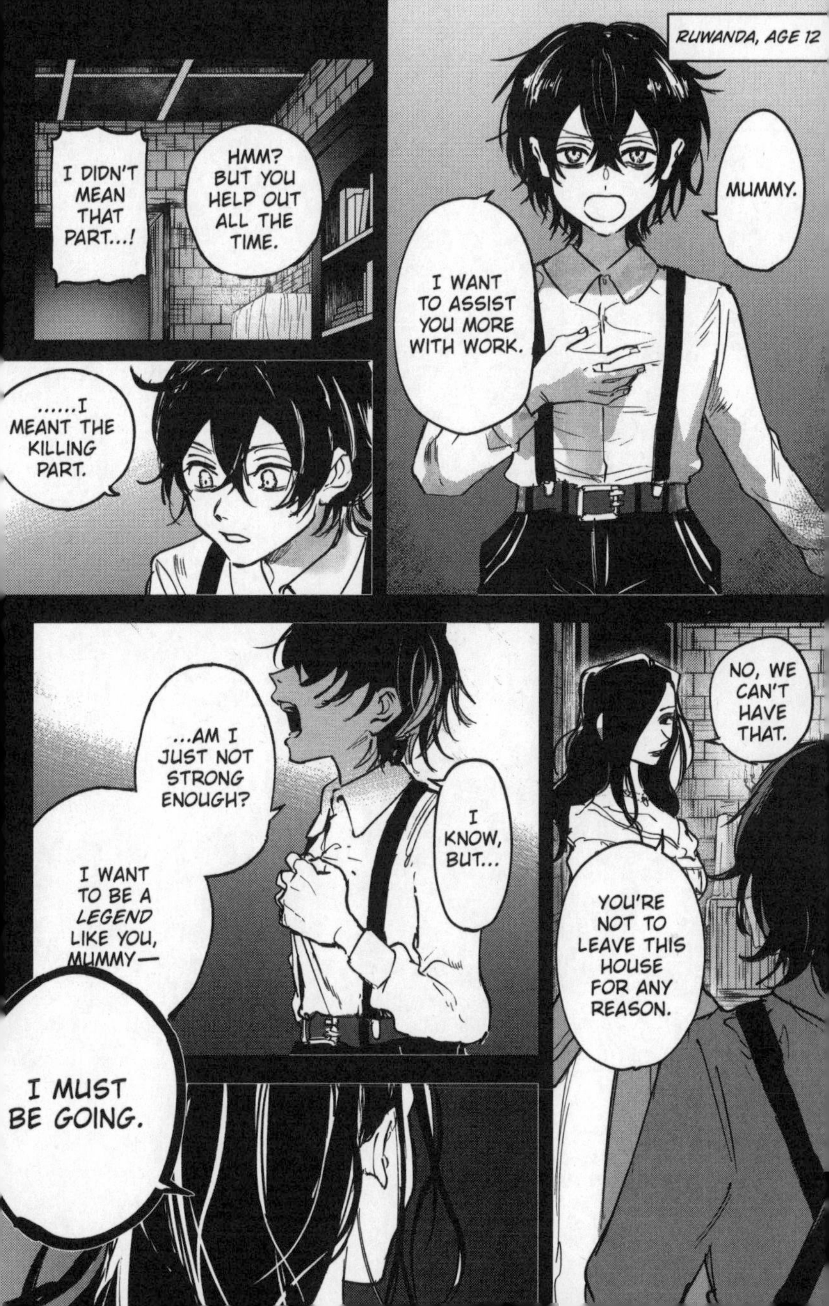
RUWANDA, AGE 12
MUMMY.
I WANT TO ASSIST YOU MORE WITH WORK.
HMM? BUT YOU HELP OUT ALL THE TIME.
I DIDN'T MEAN THAT PART...!
......I MEANT THE KILLING PART.
NO, WE CAN'T HAVE THAT.
YOU'RE NOT TO LEAVE THIS HOUSE FOR ANY REASON.
I KNOW, BUT...
...AM I JUST NOT STRONG ENOUGH?
I WANT TO BE A *LEGEND* LIKE YOU, MUMMY—
I MUST BE GOING.

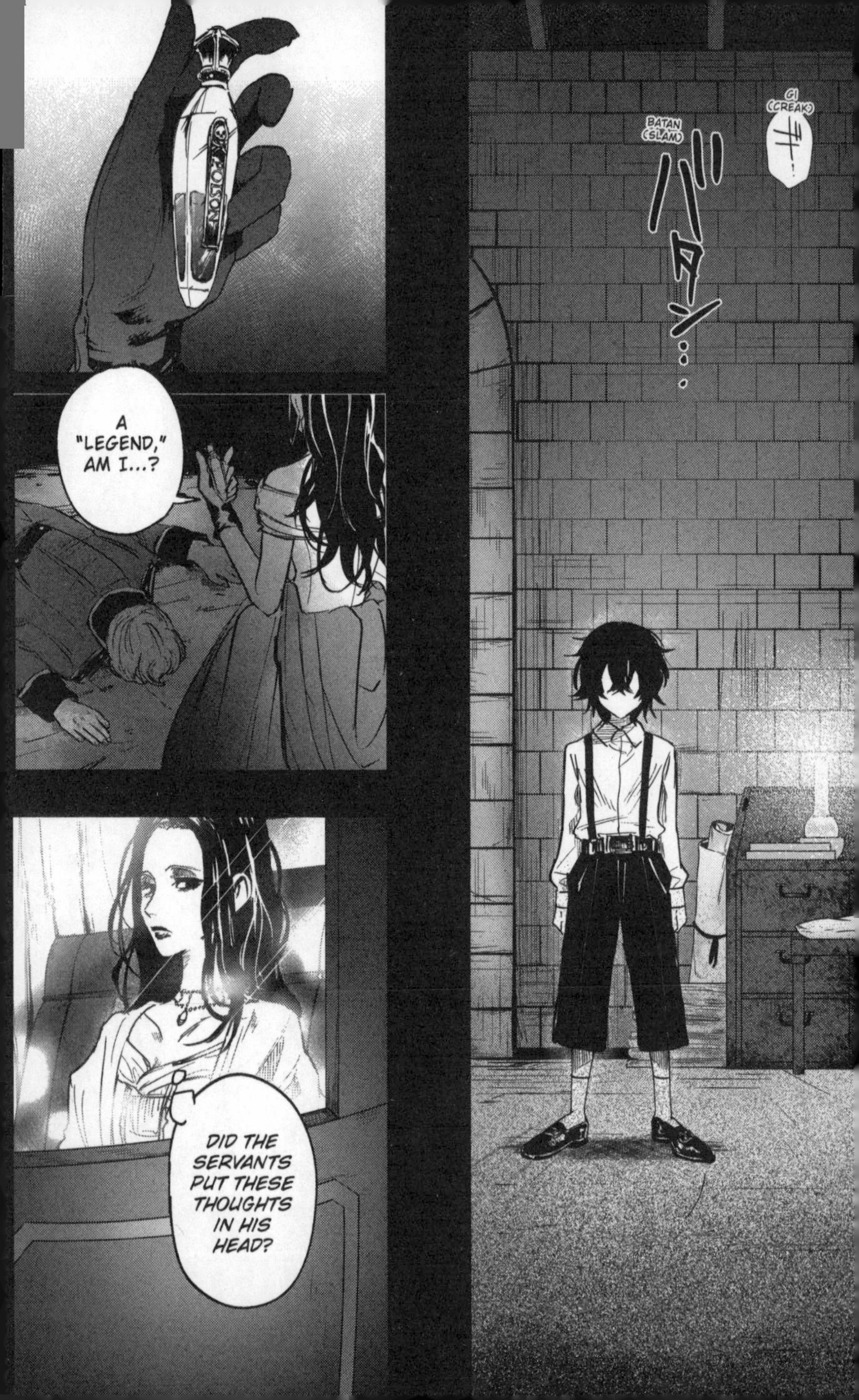
GI (CREAK)
ギ！
BATAN (SLAM)
バタン…
POISON
A "LEGEND," AM I...?
DID THE SERVANTS PUT THESE THOUGHTS IN HIS HEAD?

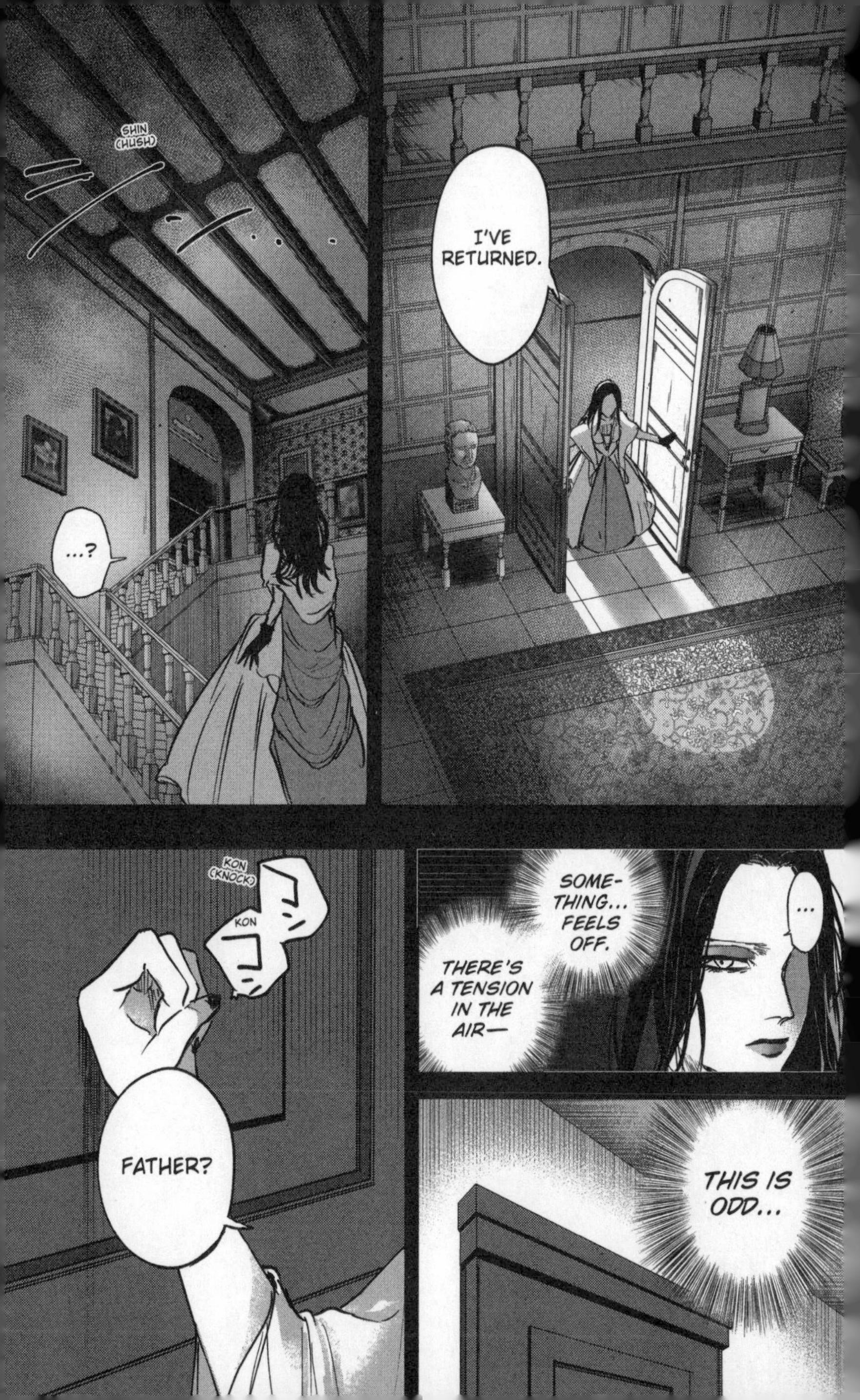
I'VE RETURNED.
SHIN (HUSH)
...?
...
SOME-THING... FEELS OFF.
THERE'S A TENSION IN THE AIR—
THIS IS ODD...
KON (KNOCK)
KON
FATHER?

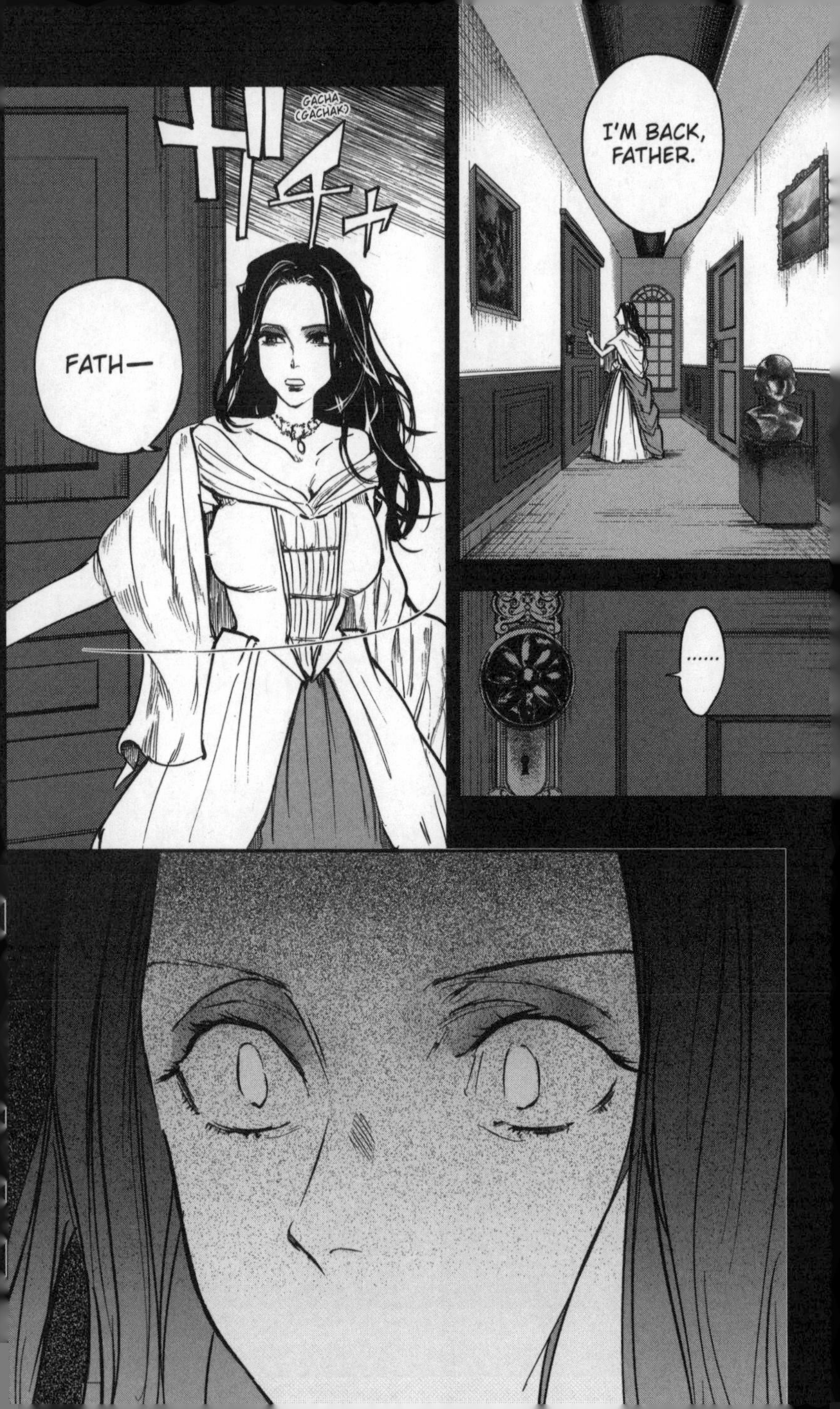
I'M BACK, FATHER.
......
GACHA (GACHAK)
FATH—

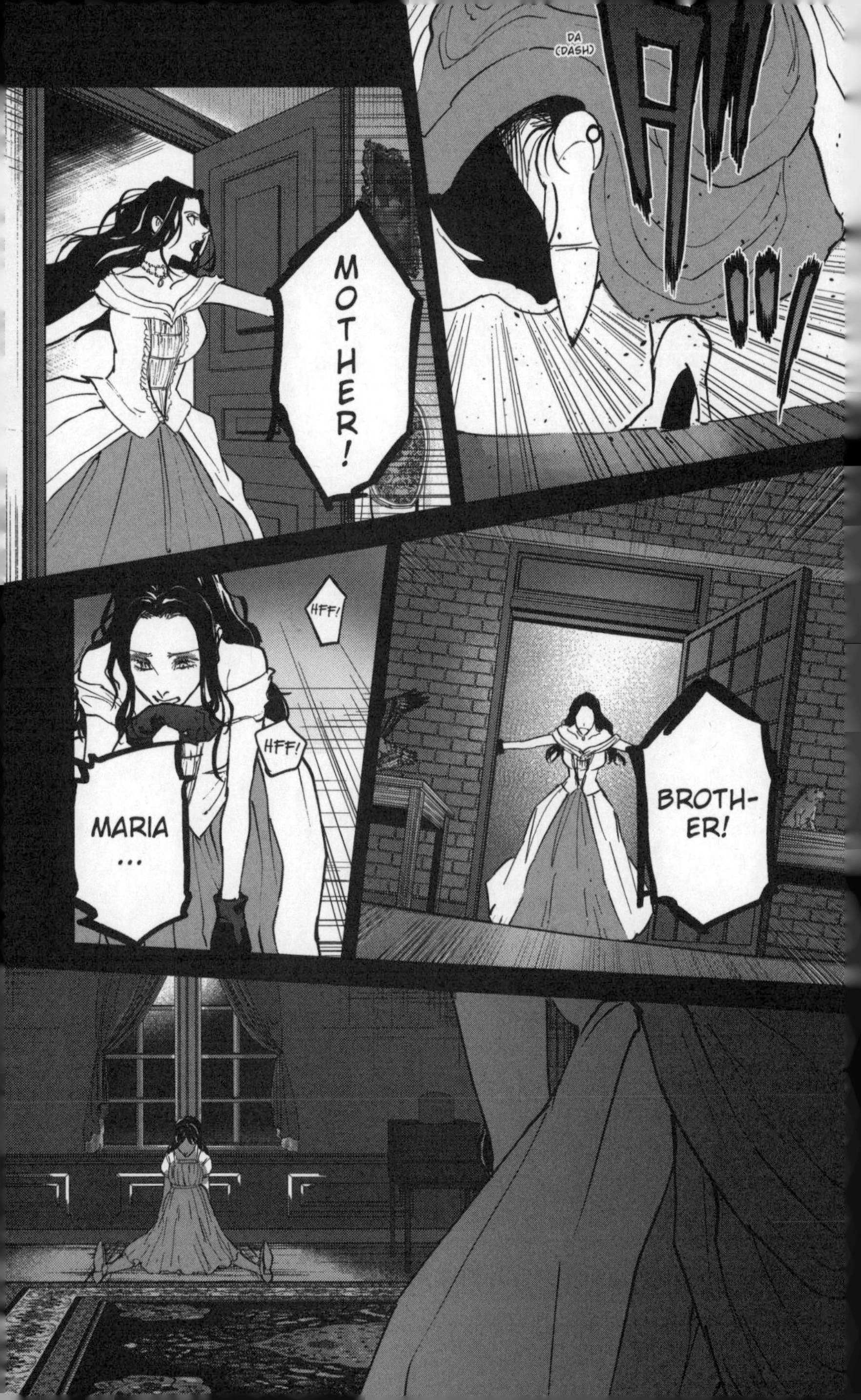
DA (DASH)
MOTHER!
BROTH-ER!
HFF!
HFF!
MARIA ...

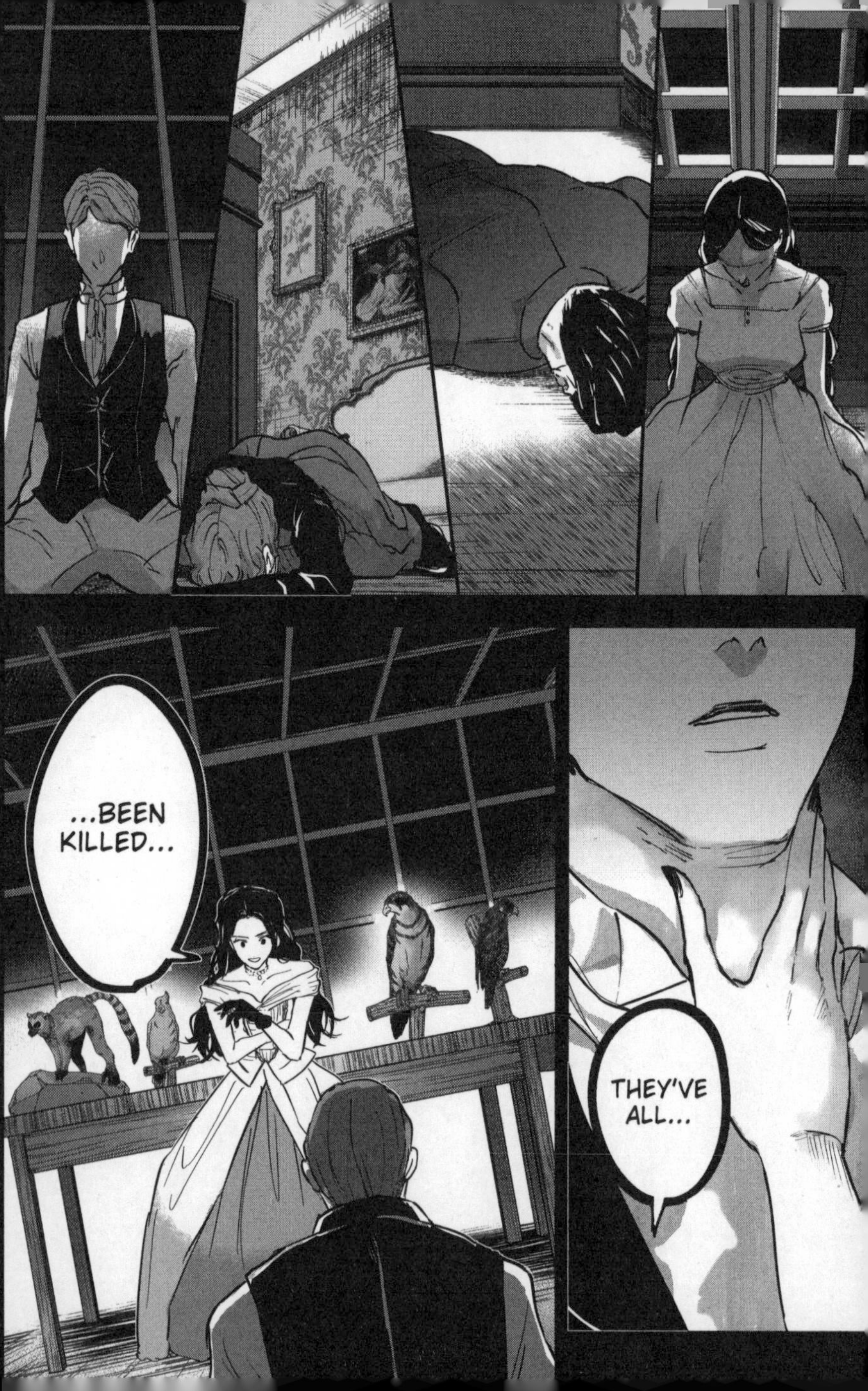
THEY'VE ALL...
...BEEN KILLED...

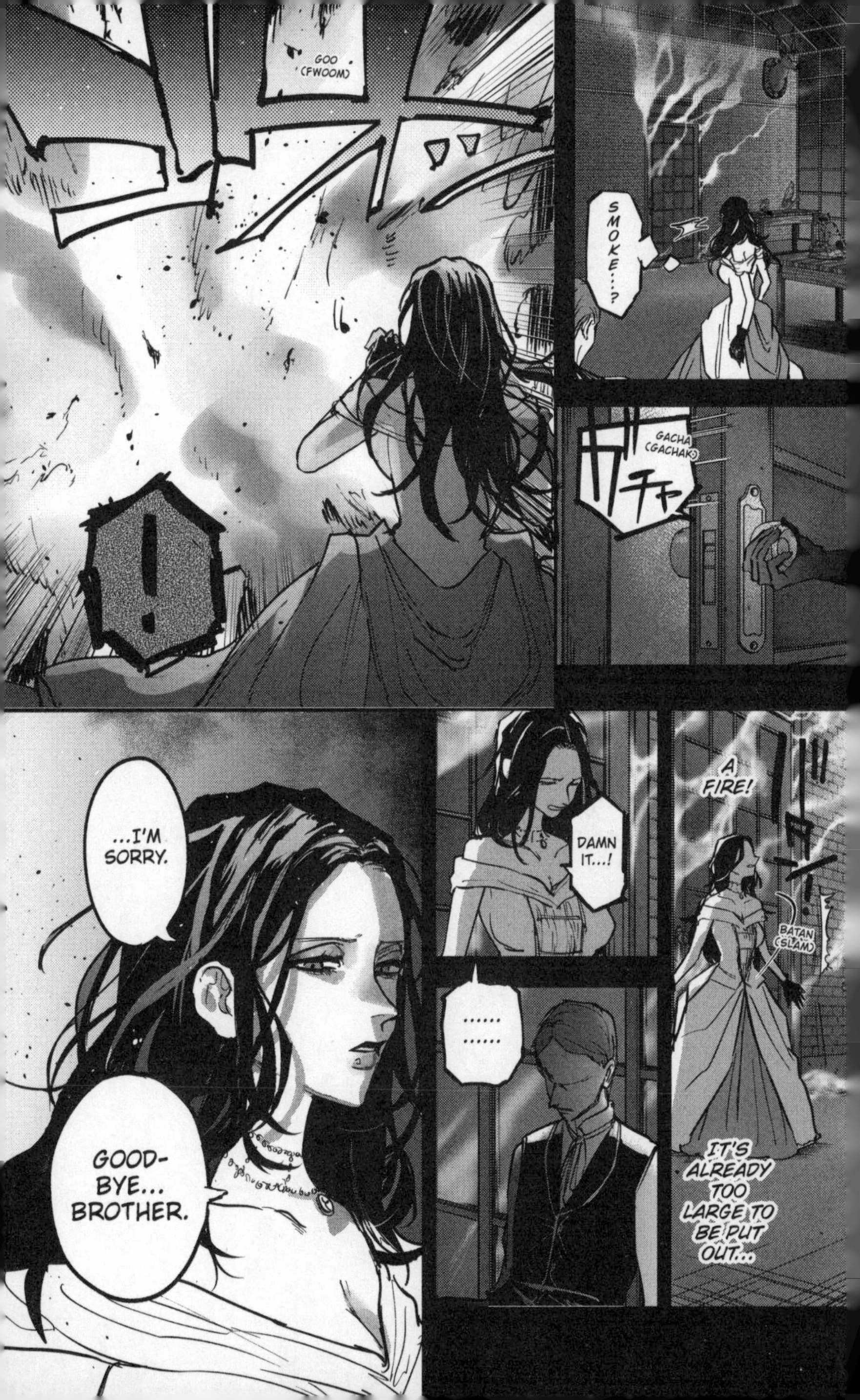
SMOKE...?
GACHA (GACHAK)
GOO (FWOOM)
!
A FIRE!
BATAN (SLAM)
IT'S ALREADY TOO LARGE TO BE PUT OUT...
DAMN IT...!
....
...I'M SORRY.
GOOD-BYE... BROTHER.

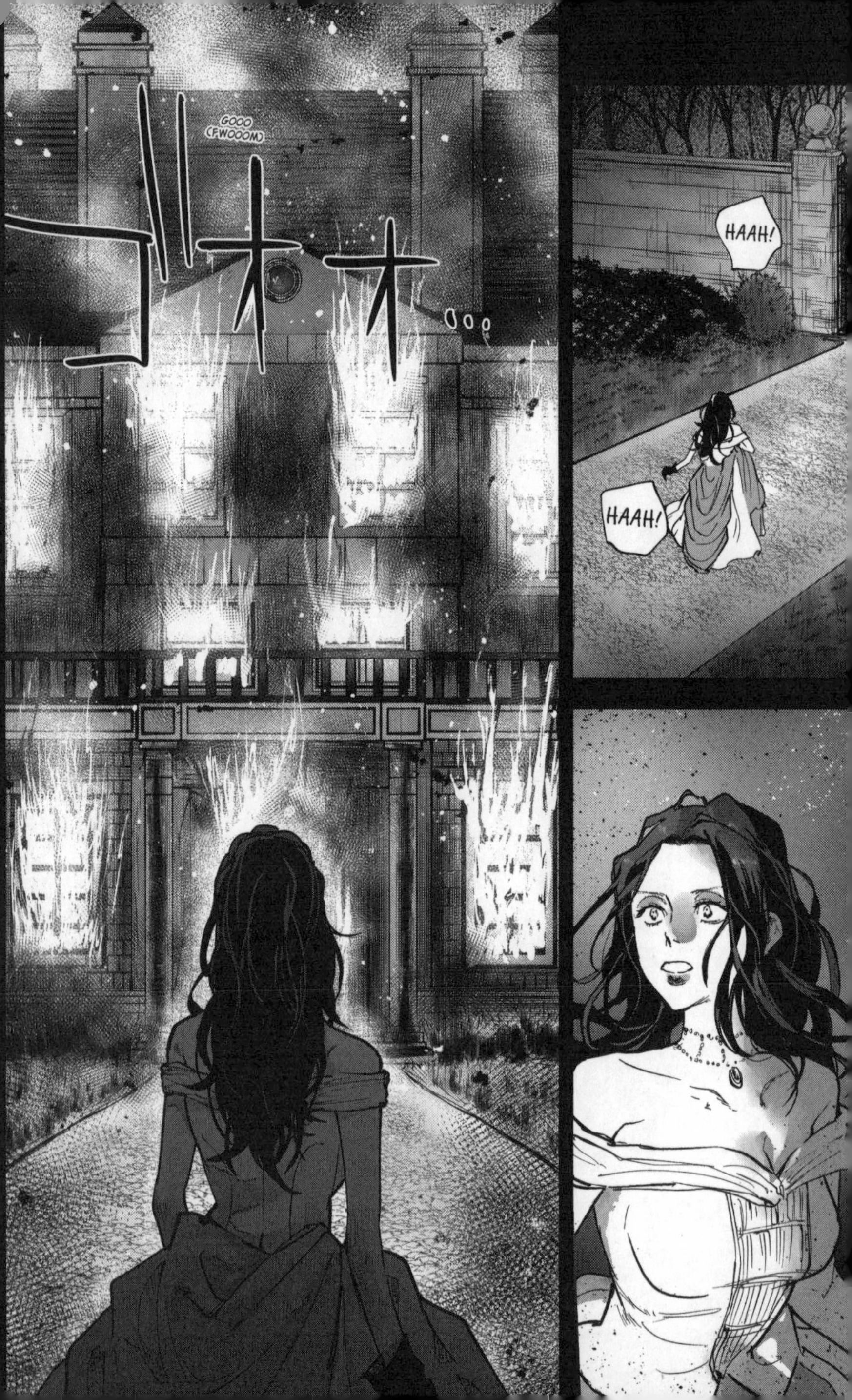
HAAH!
HAAH!
GOOO (FWOOOM)

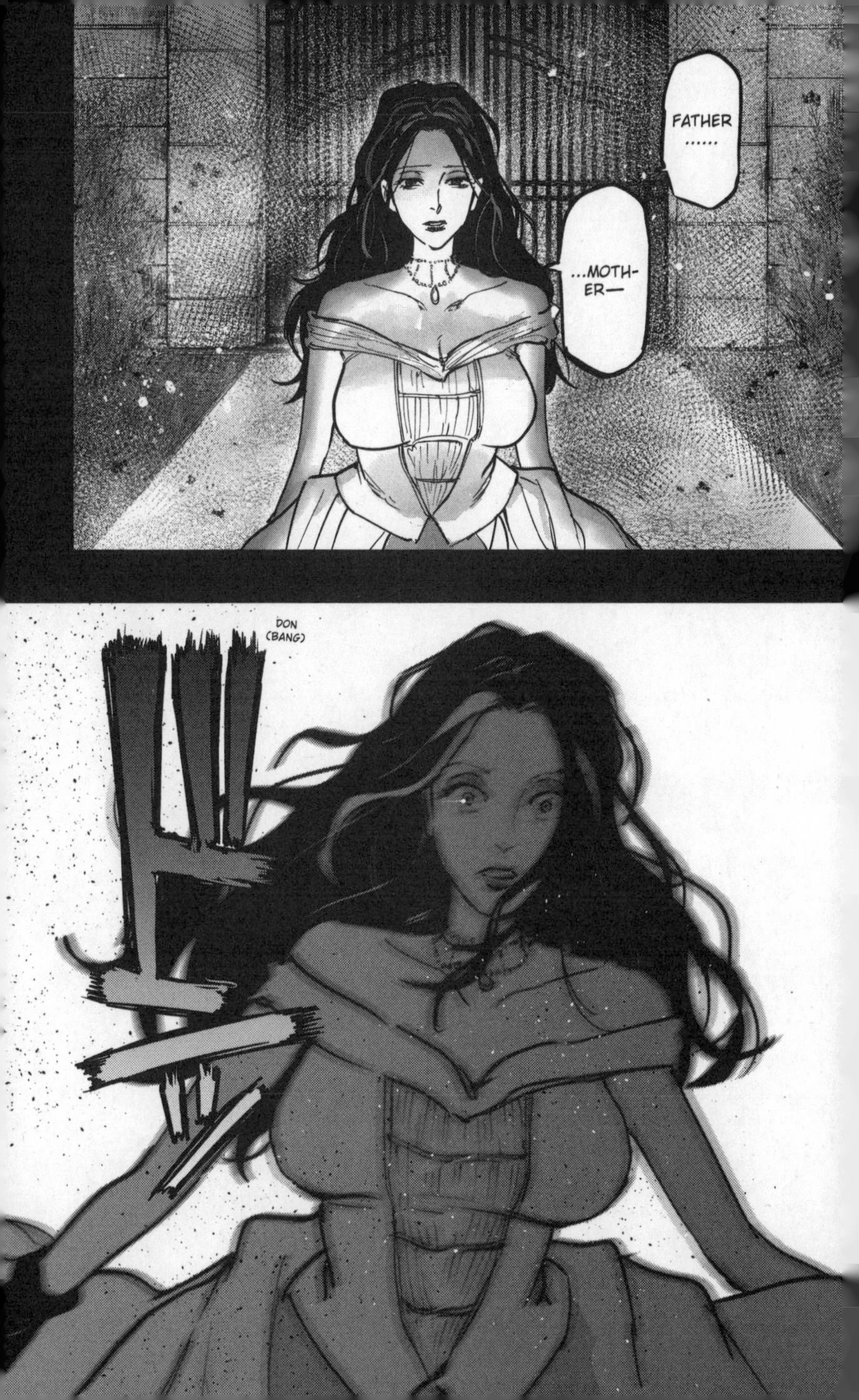
FATHER ......
...MOTH-ER—
DON (BANG)

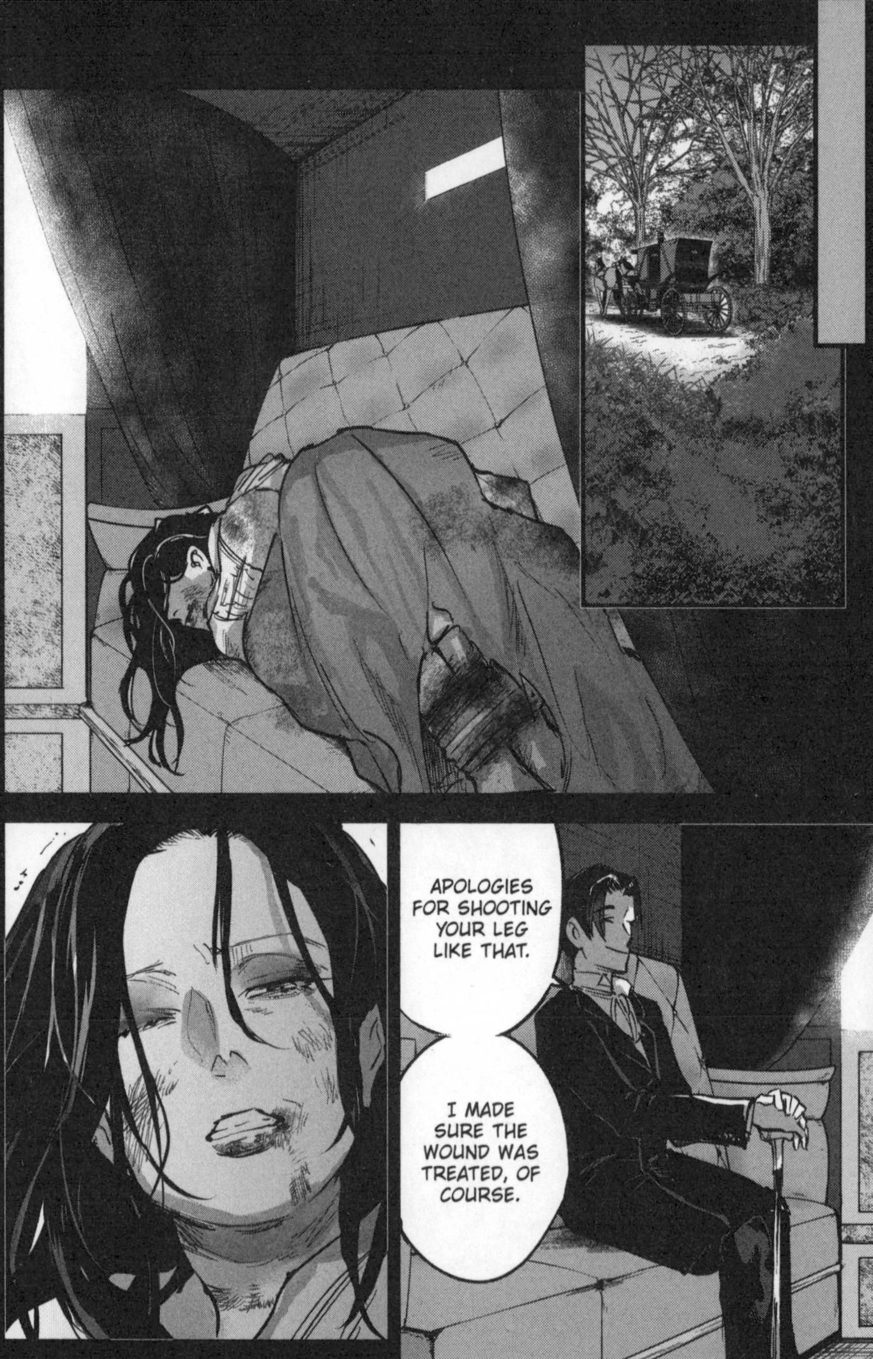
APOLOGIES FOR SHOOTING YOUR LEG LIKE THAT.
I MADE SURE THE WOUND WAS TREATED, OF COURSE.

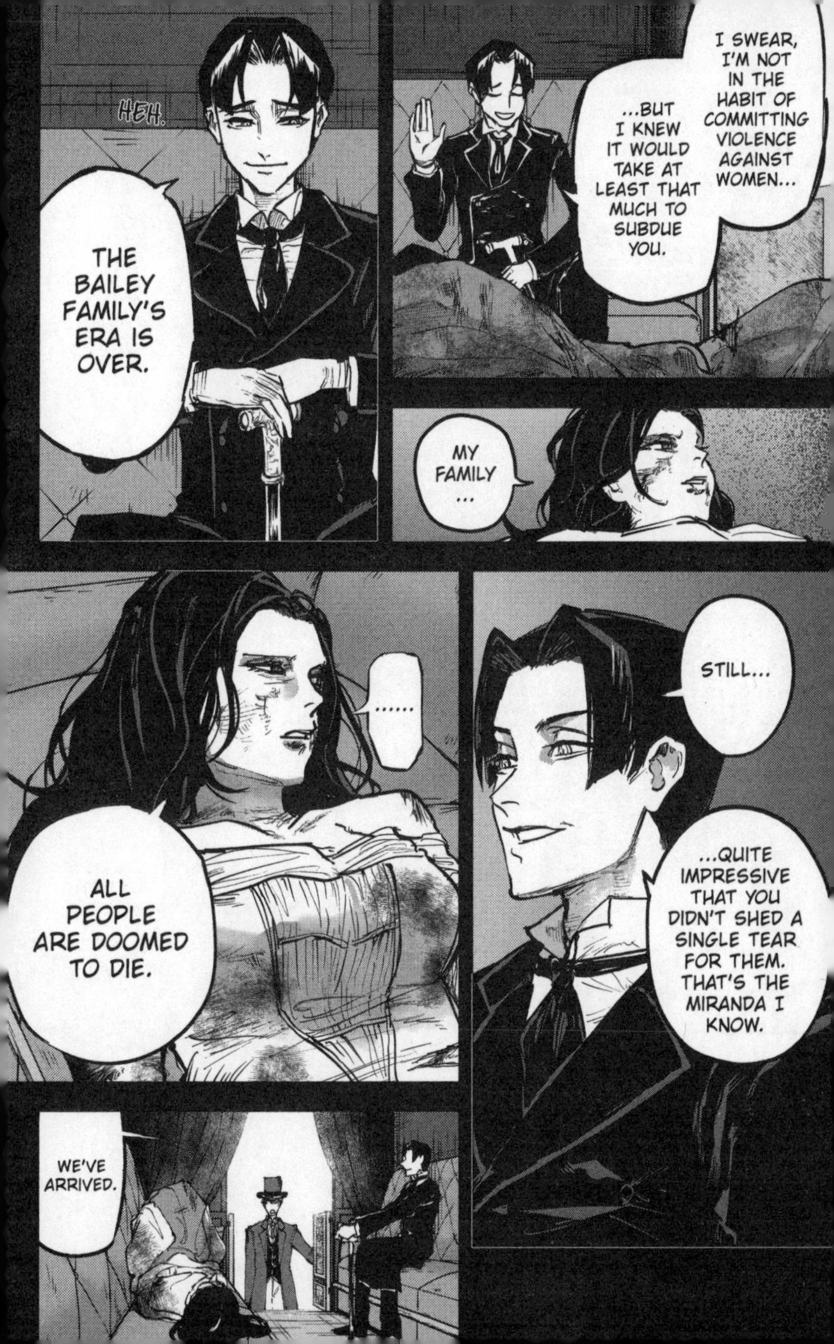

I SWEAR, I'M NOT IN THE HABIT OF COMMITTING VIOLENCE AGAINST WOMEN...
...BUT I KNEW IT WOULD TAKE AT LEAST THAT MUCH TO SUBDUE YOU.
MY FAMILY...
HEH.
THE BAILEY FAMILY'S ERA IS OVER.
STILL...
...QUITE IMPRESSIVE THAT YOU DIDN'T SHED A SINGLE TEAR FOR THEM. THAT'S THE MIRANDA I KNOW.
......
ALL PEOPLE ARE DOOMED TO DIE.
WE'VE ARRIVED.

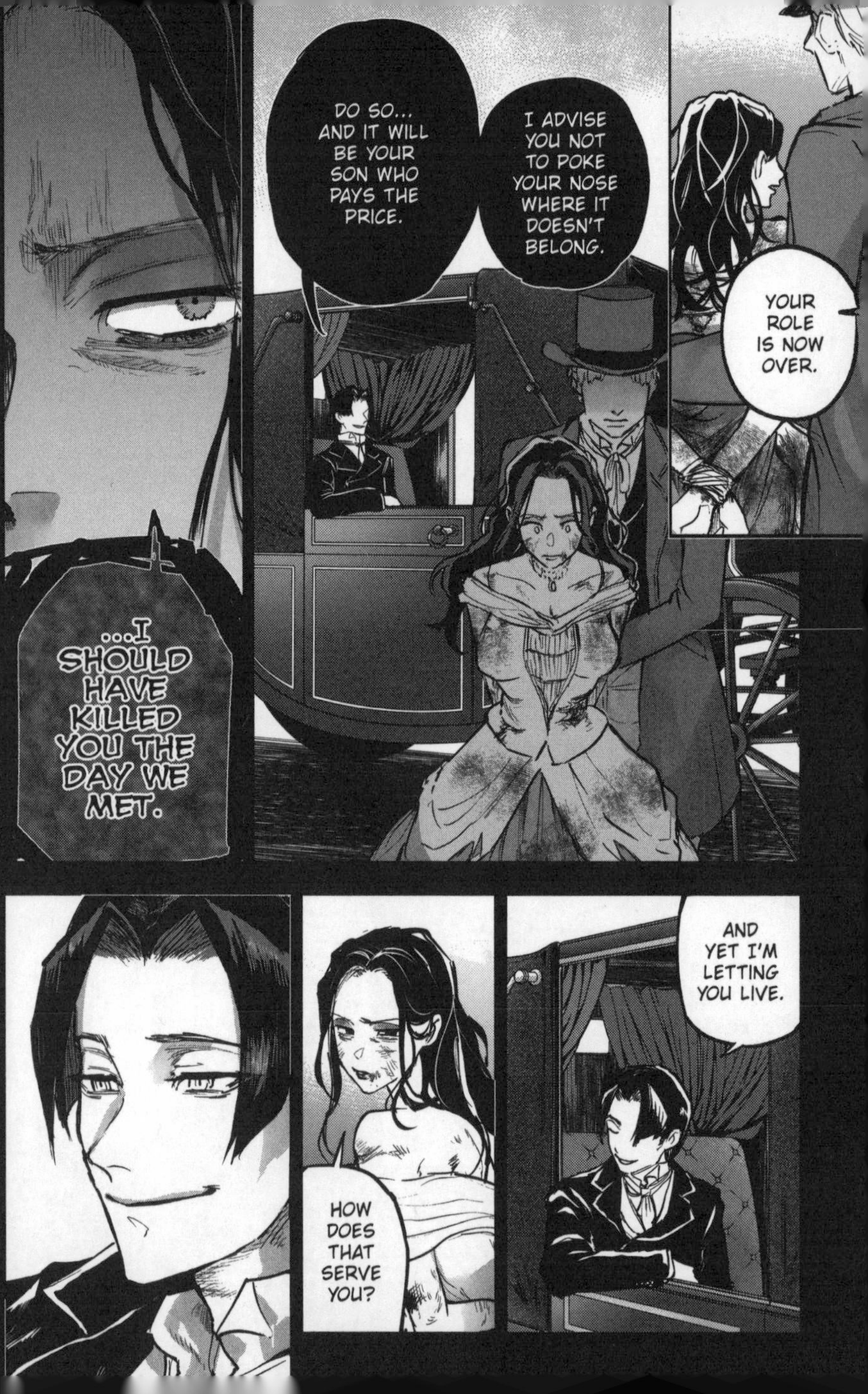
YOUR ROLE IS NOW OVER.
I ADVISE YOU NOT TO POKE YOUR NOSE WHERE IT DOESN'T BELONG.
DO SO... AND IT WILL BE YOUR SON WHO PAYS THE PRICE.
...I SHOULD HAVE KILLED YOU THE DAY WE MET.
AND YET I'M LETTING YOU LIVE.
HOW DOES THAT SERVE YOU?

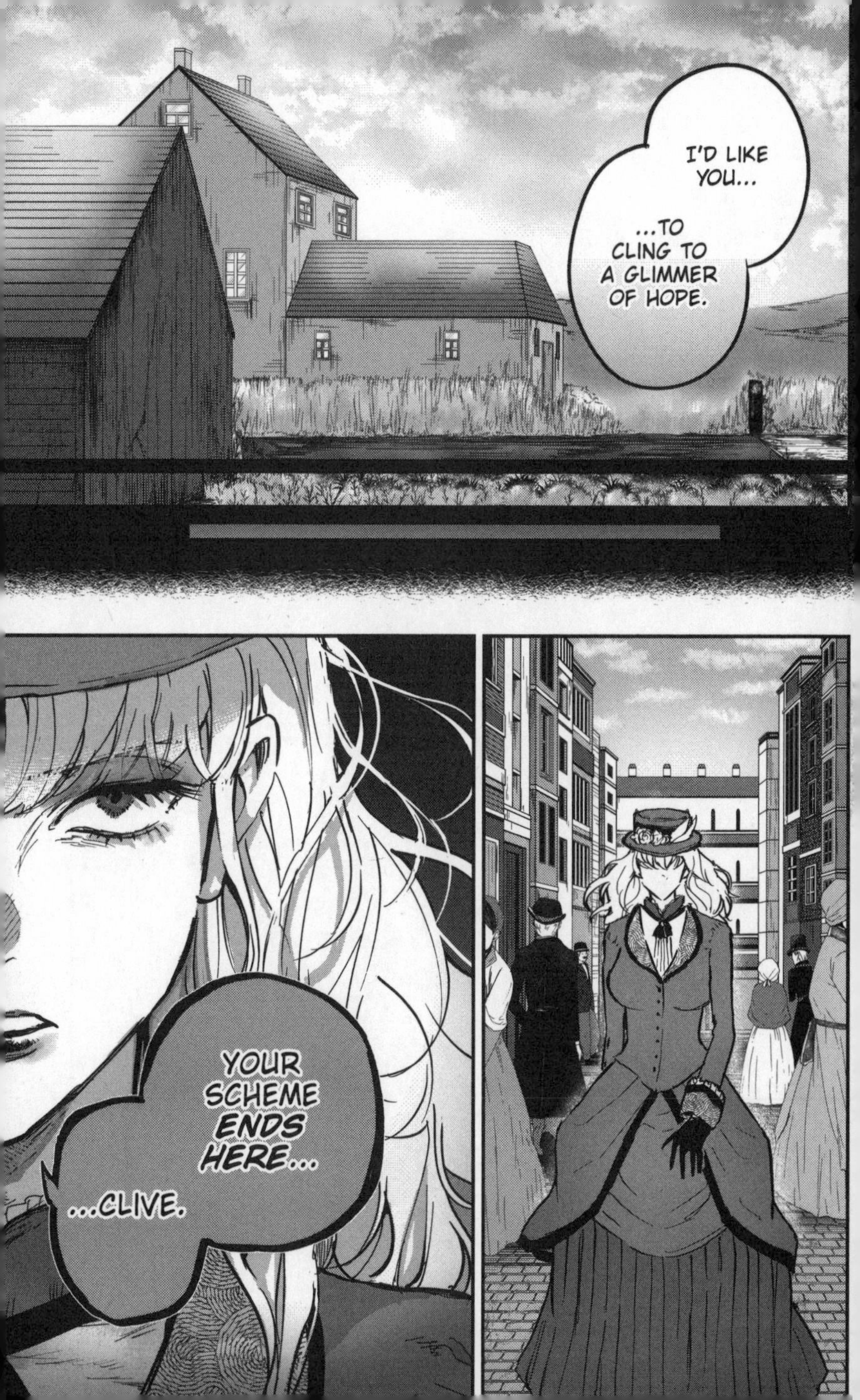
I'D LIKE YOU...
...TO CLING TO A GLIMMER OF HOPE.
YOUR SCHEME ENDS HERE...
...CLIVE.

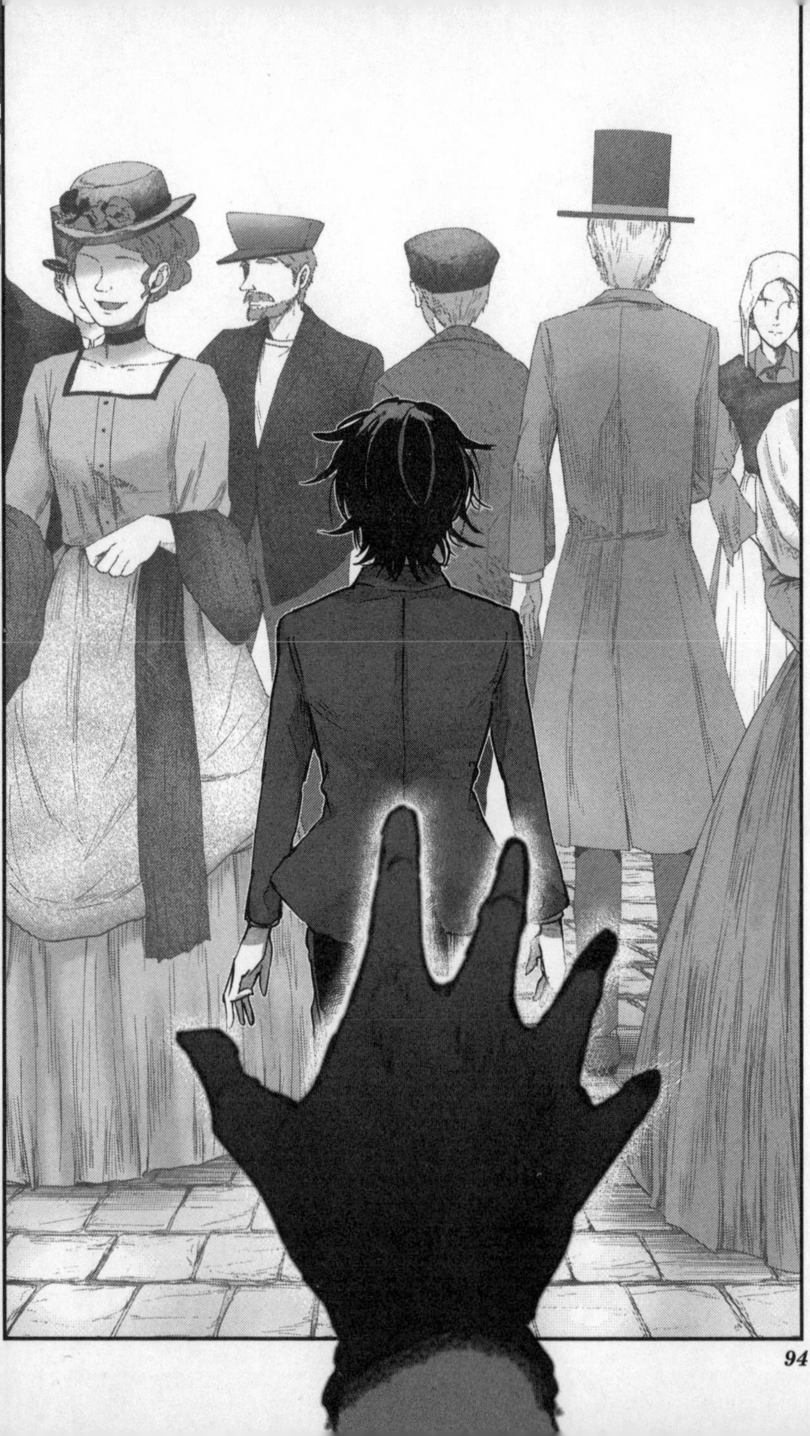

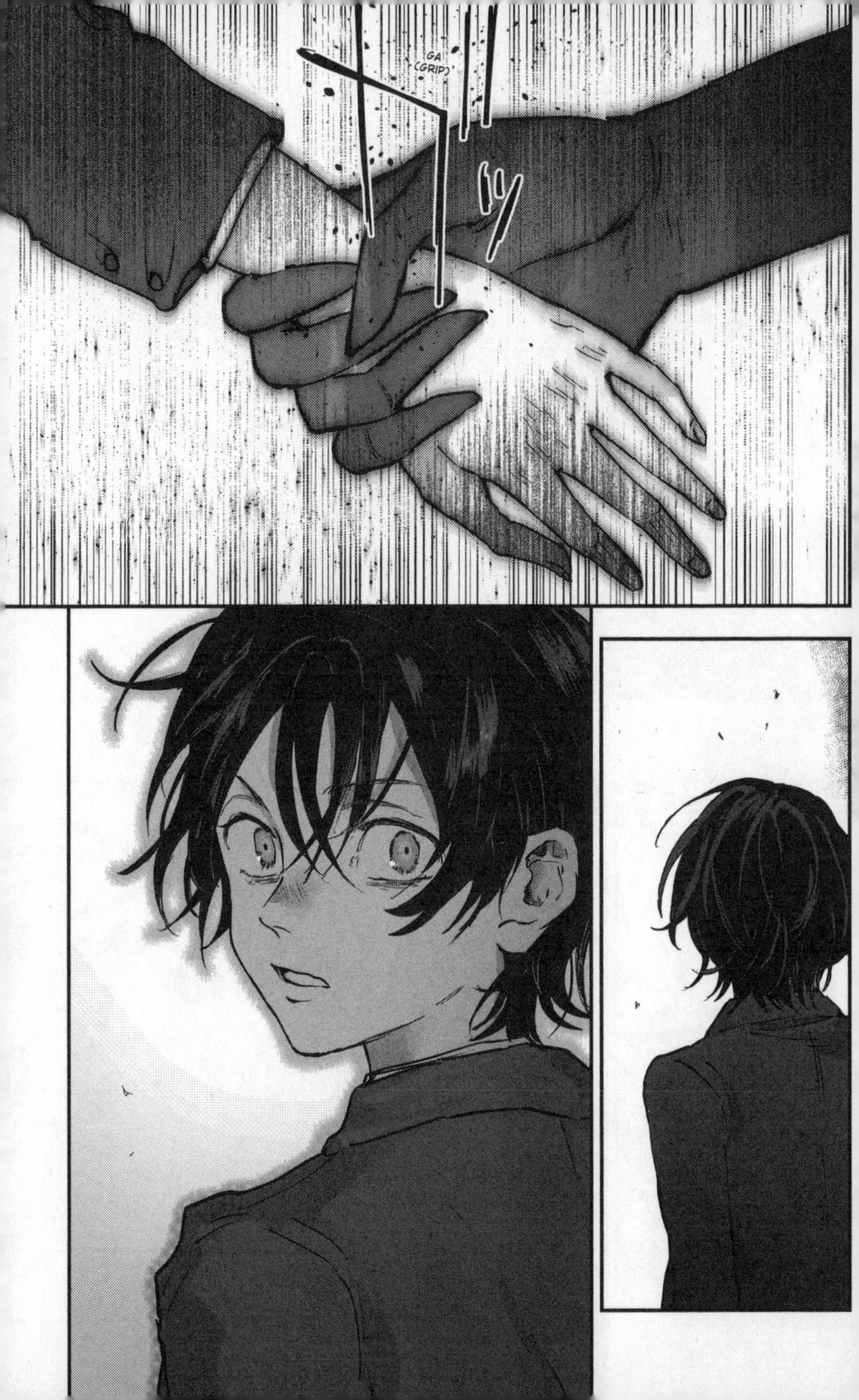
GA
(GRIP)

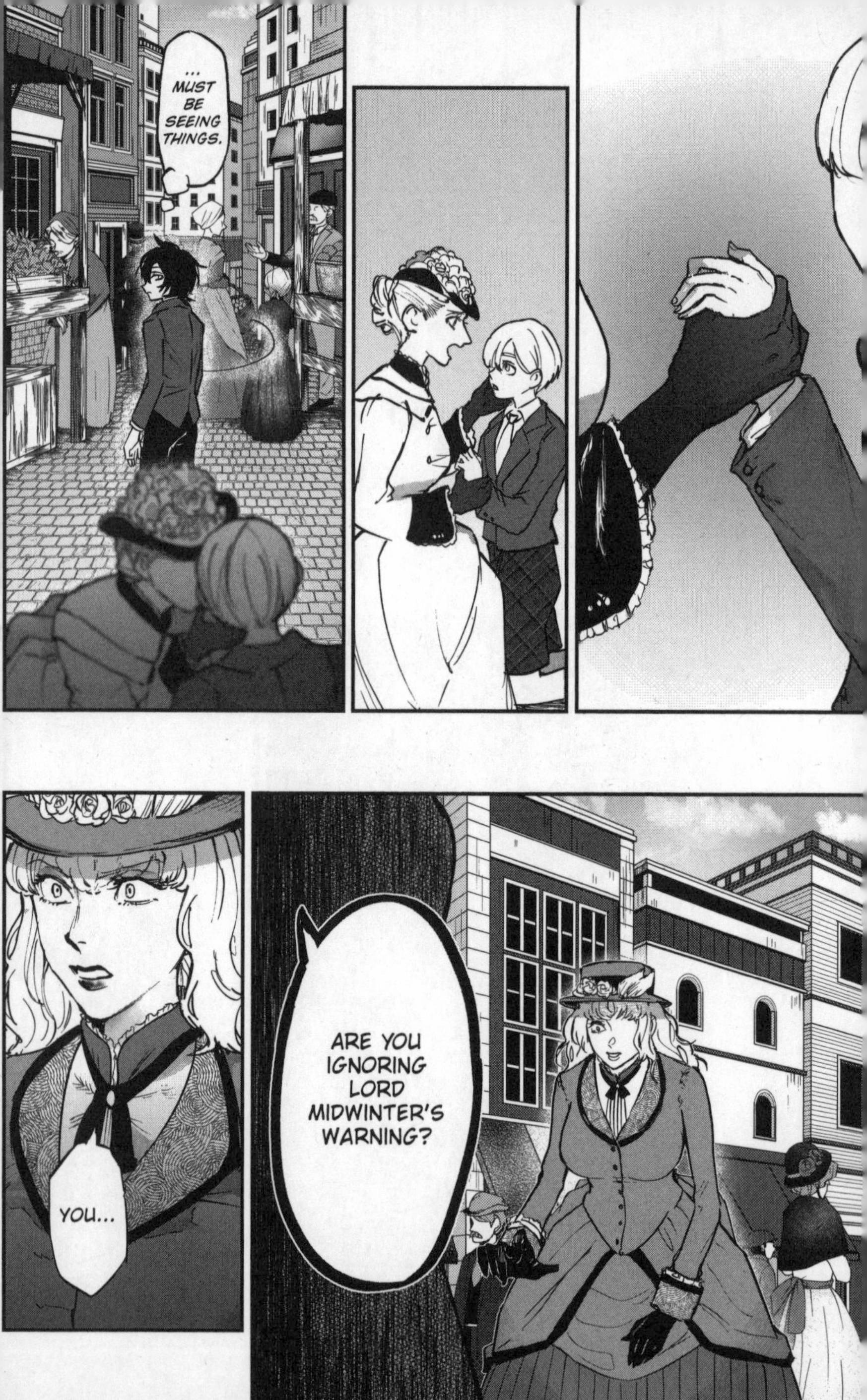
... MUST BE SEEING THINGS.
ARE YOU IGNORING LORD MIDWINTER'S WARNING?
YOU...

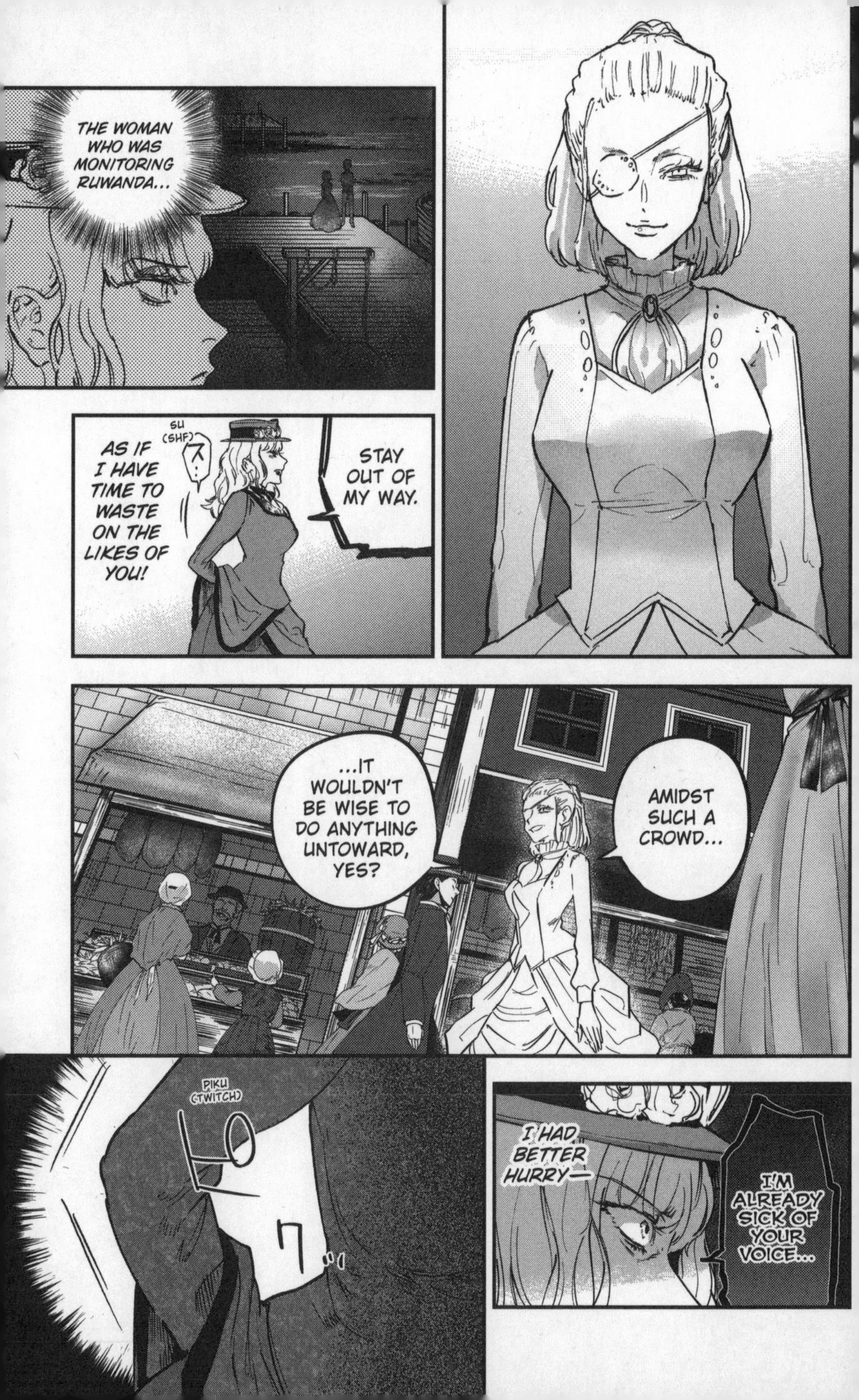
THE WOMAN WHO WAS MONITORING RUWANDA...
STAY OUT OF MY WAY.
SU (SHF)
AS IF I HAVE TIME TO WASTE ON THE LIKES OF YOU!
AMIDST SUCH A CROWD...
...IT WOULDN'T BE WISE TO DO ANYTHING UNTOWARD, YES?
I'M ALREADY SICK OF YOUR VOICE...
I HAD BETTER HURRY—
PIKU (TWITCH)

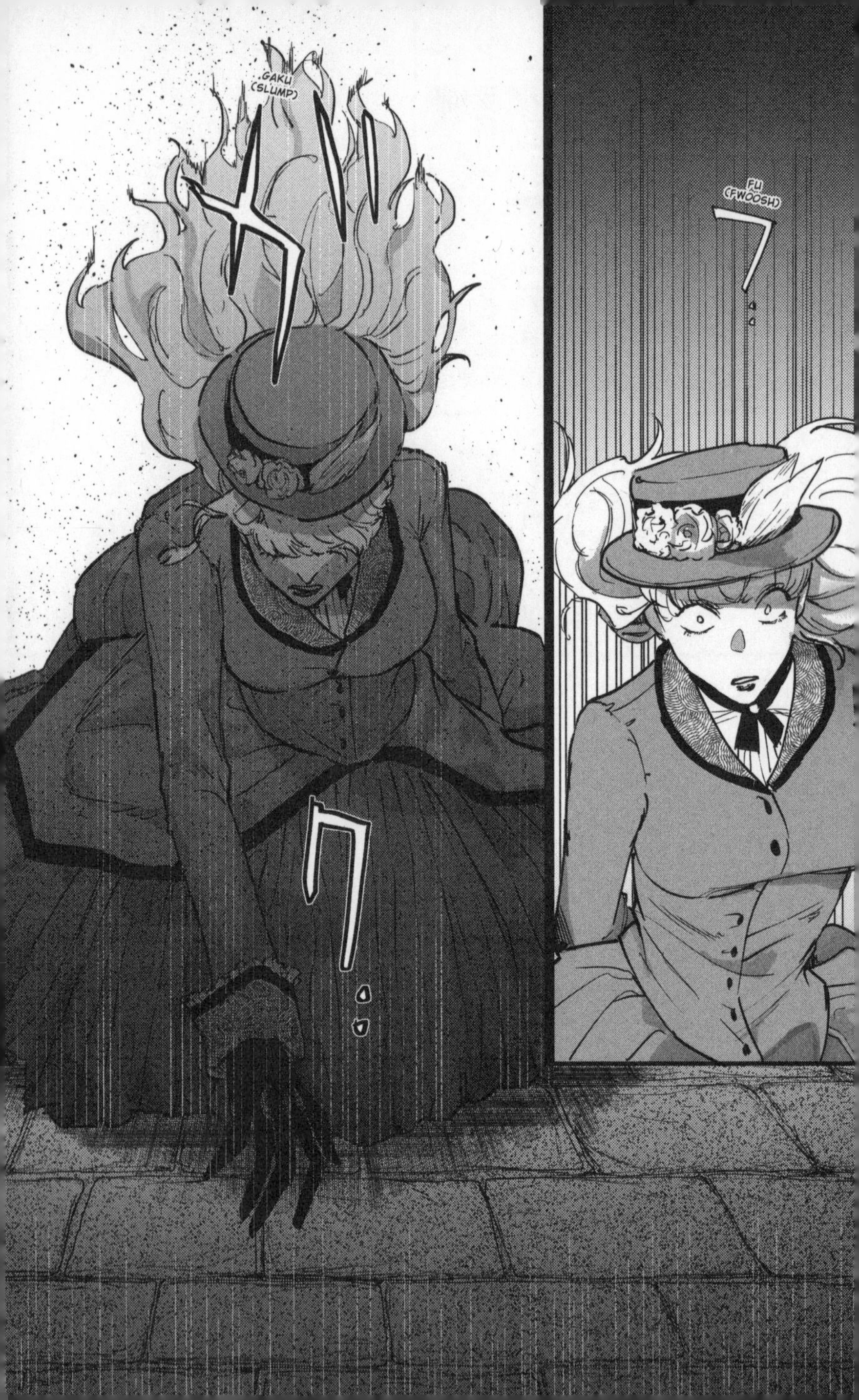
FU (FWOOSH)
GAKU (SLUMP)

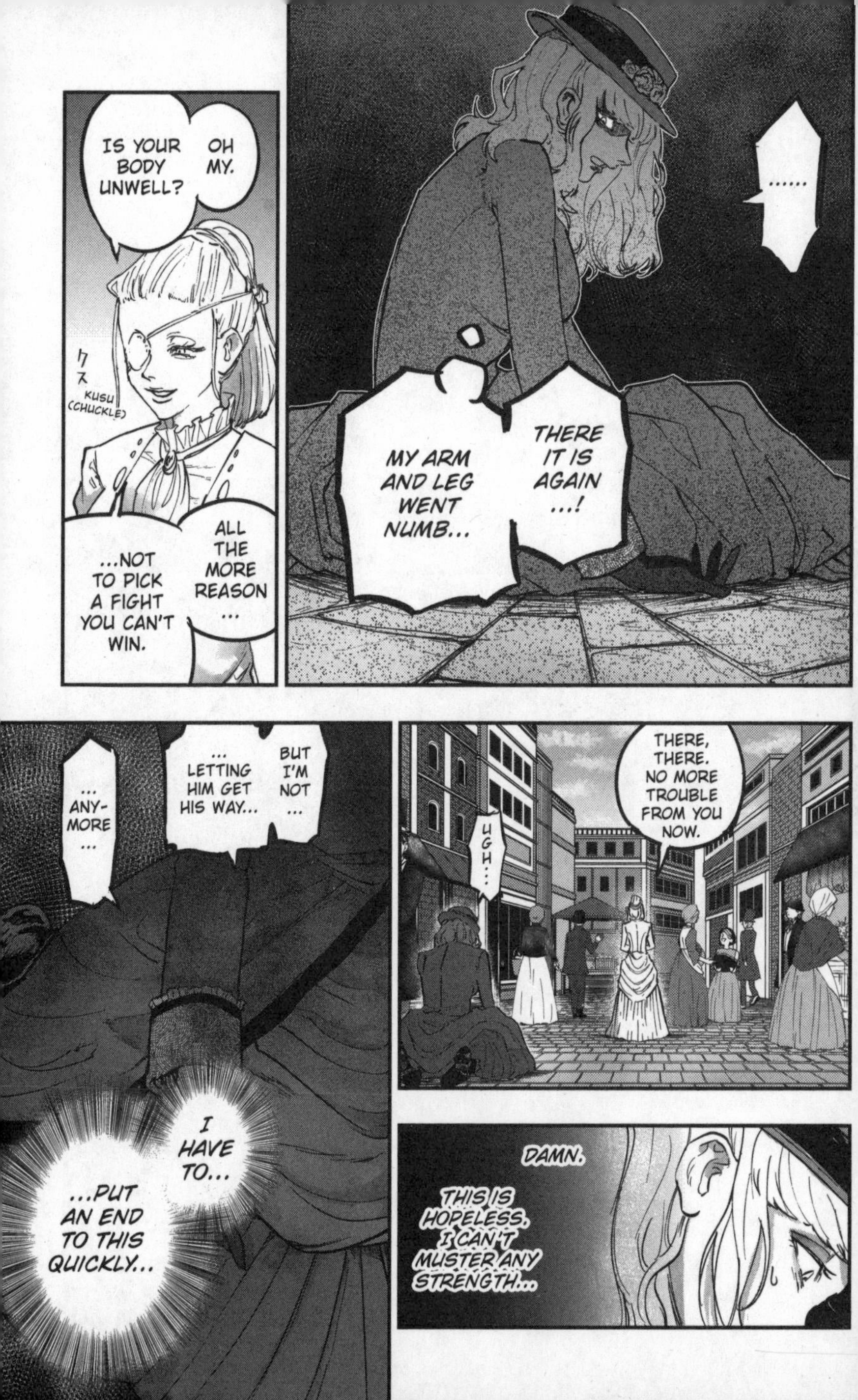
......
THERE IT IS AGAIN ...!
MY ARM AND LEG WENT NUMB...
OH MY.
IS YOUR BODY UNWELL?
クス
KUSU (CHUCKLE)
ALL THE MORE REASON ...
...NOT TO PICK A FIGHT YOU CAN'T WIN.
THERE, THERE. NO MORE TROUBLE FROM YOU NOW.
UGH...
DAMN.
THIS IS HOPELESS. I CAN'T MUSTER ANY STRENGTH...
BUT I'M NOT ...
... LETTING HIM GET HIS WAY...
... ANY-MORE ...
I HAVE TO...
...PUT AN END TO THIS QUICKLY...

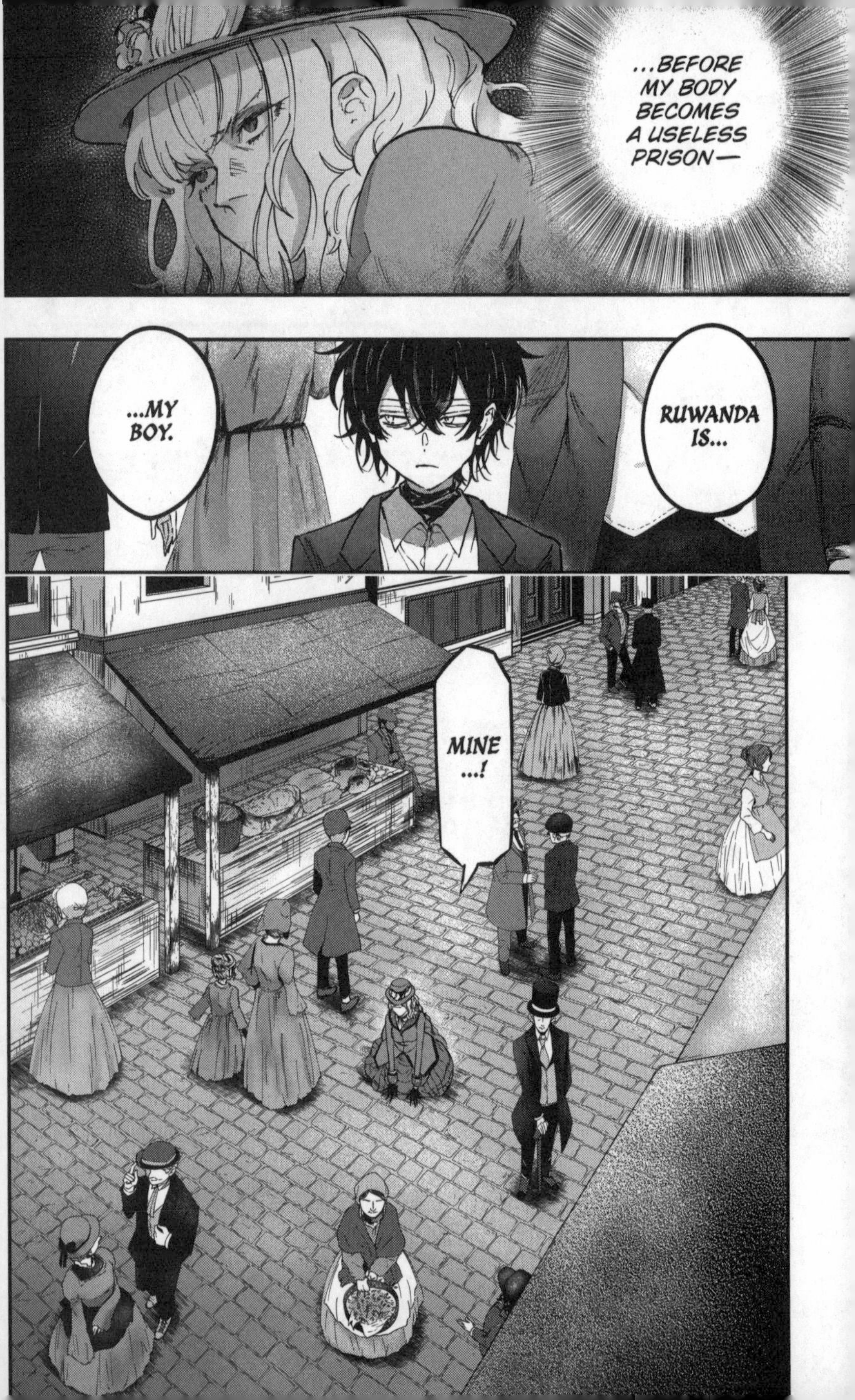
...BEFORE MY BODY BECOMES A USELESS PRISON—
RUWANDA IS...
...MY BOY.
MINE ...!

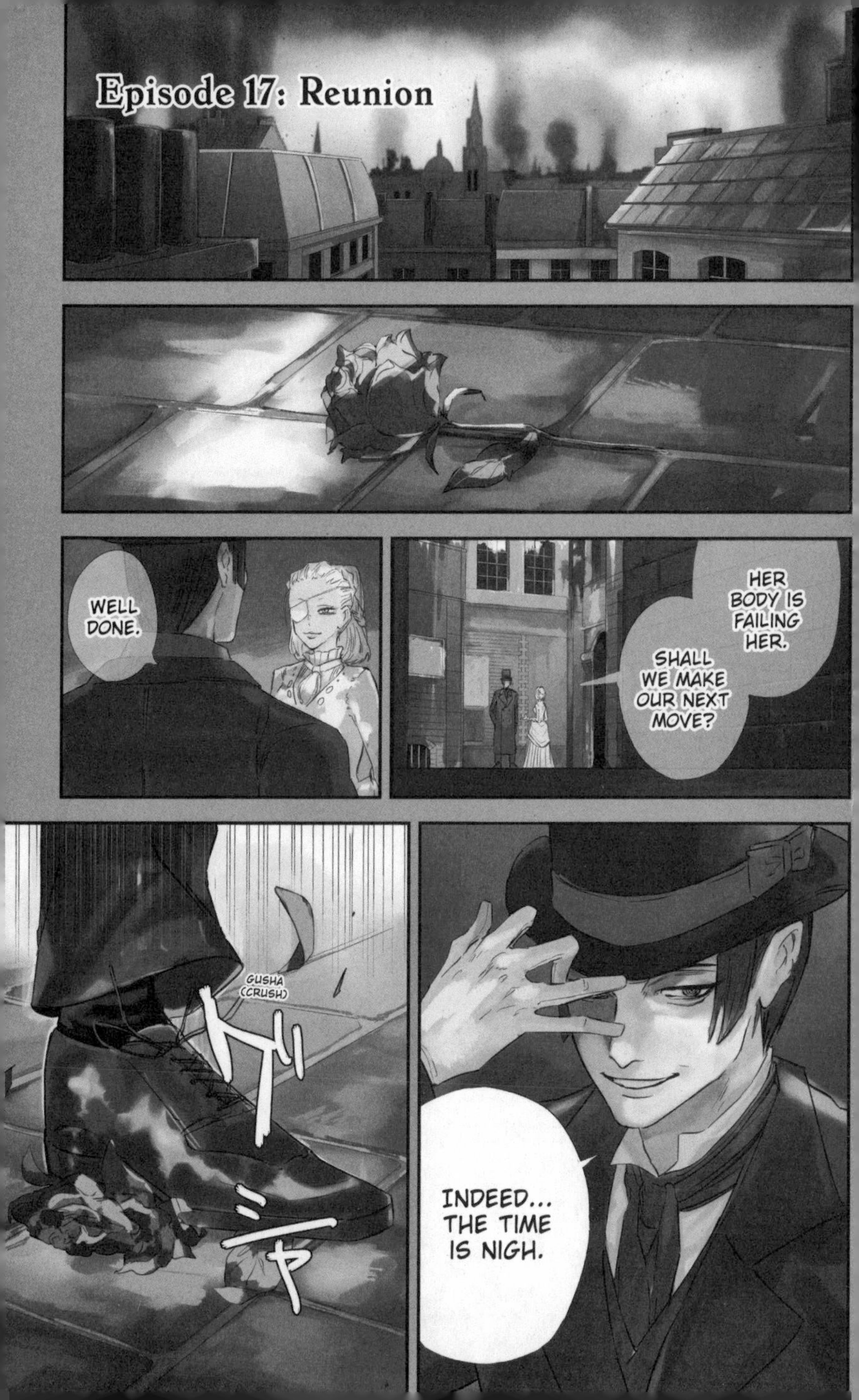
Episode 17: Reunion
HER BODY IS FAILING HER.
SHALL WE MAKE OUR NEXT MOVE?
WELL DONE.
INDEED... THE TIME IS NIGH.
グシャ
GUSHA (CRUSH)

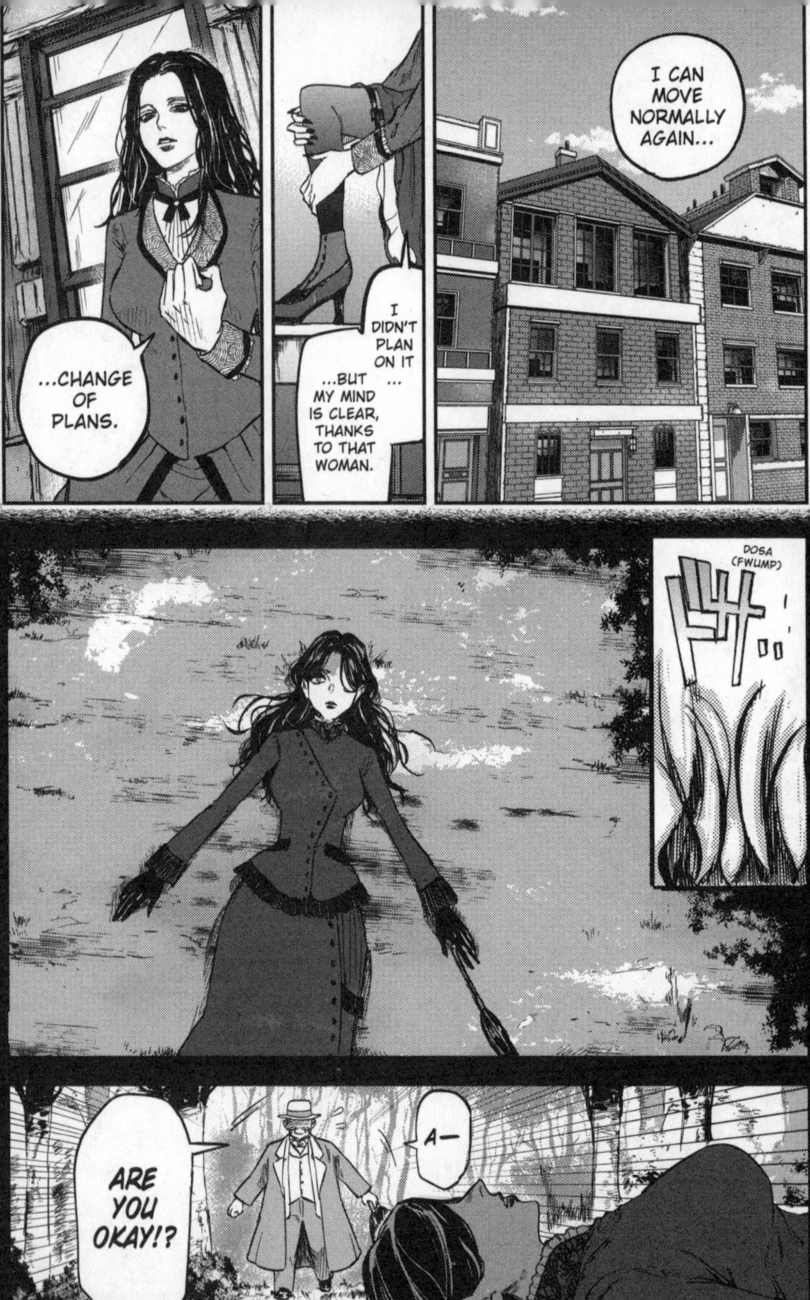
I CAN MOVE NORMALLY AGAIN...
I DIDN'T PLAN ON IT ...
...BUT MY MIND IS CLEAR, THANKS TO THAT WOMAN.
...CHANGE OF PLANS.
DOSA (FWUMP)
A—
ARE YOU OKAY!?

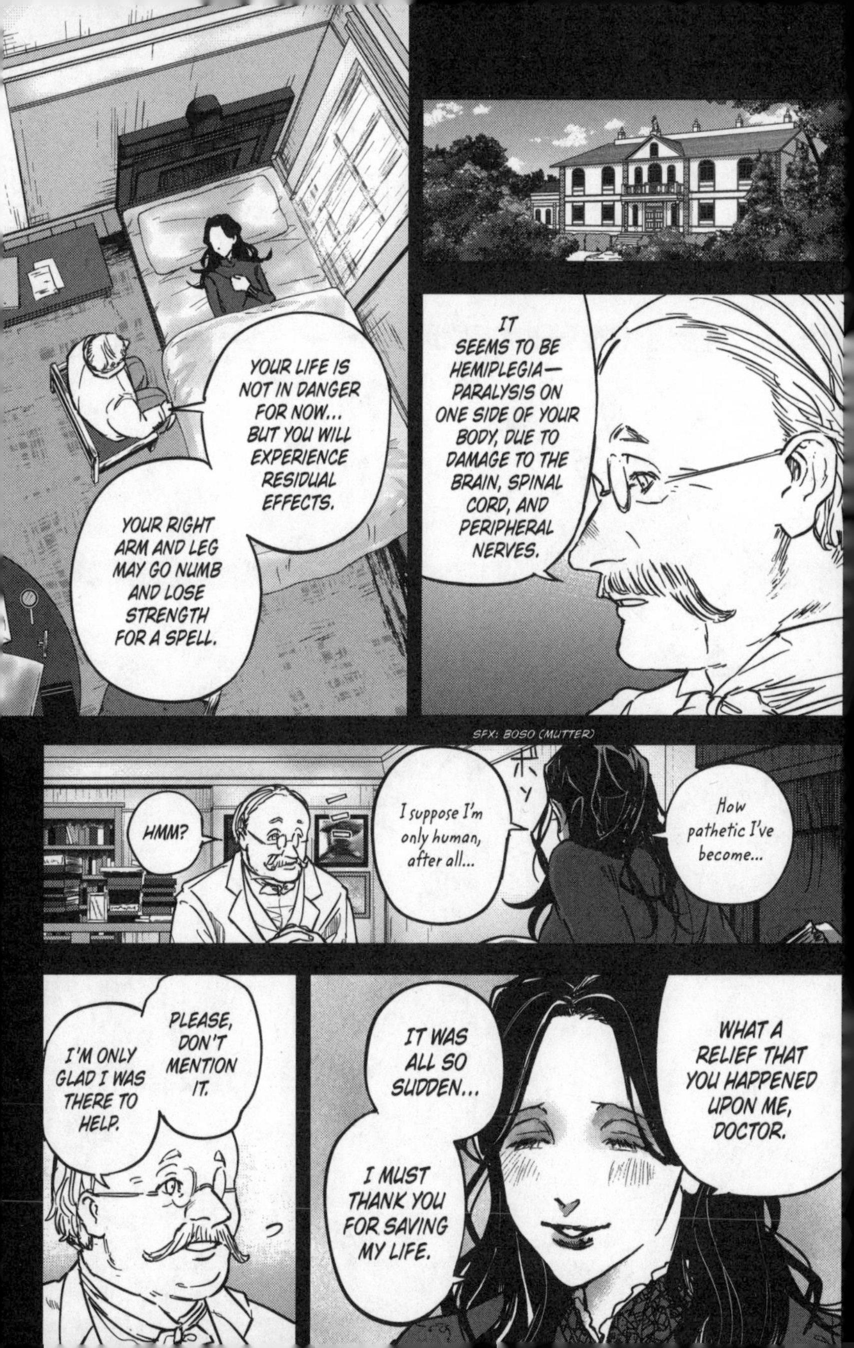
IT SEEMS TO BE HEMIPLEGIA— PARALYSIS ON ONE SIDE OF YOUR BODY, DUE TO DAMAGE TO THE BRAIN, SPINAL CORD, AND PERIPHERAL NERVES.
YOUR LIFE IS NOT IN DANGER FOR NOW... BUT YOU WILL EXPERIENCE RESIDUAL EFFECTS.
YOUR RIGHT ARM AND LEG MAY GO NUMB AND LOSE STRENGTH FOR A SPELL.
SFX: BOSO (MUTTER)
How pathetic I've become...
I suppose I'm only human, after all...
HMM?
WHAT A RELIEF THAT YOU HAPPENED UPON ME, DOCTOR.
IT WAS ALL SO SUDDEN...
I MUST THANK YOU FOR SAVING MY LIFE.
PLEASE, DON'T MENTION IT.
I'M ONLY GLAD I WAS THERE TO HELP.

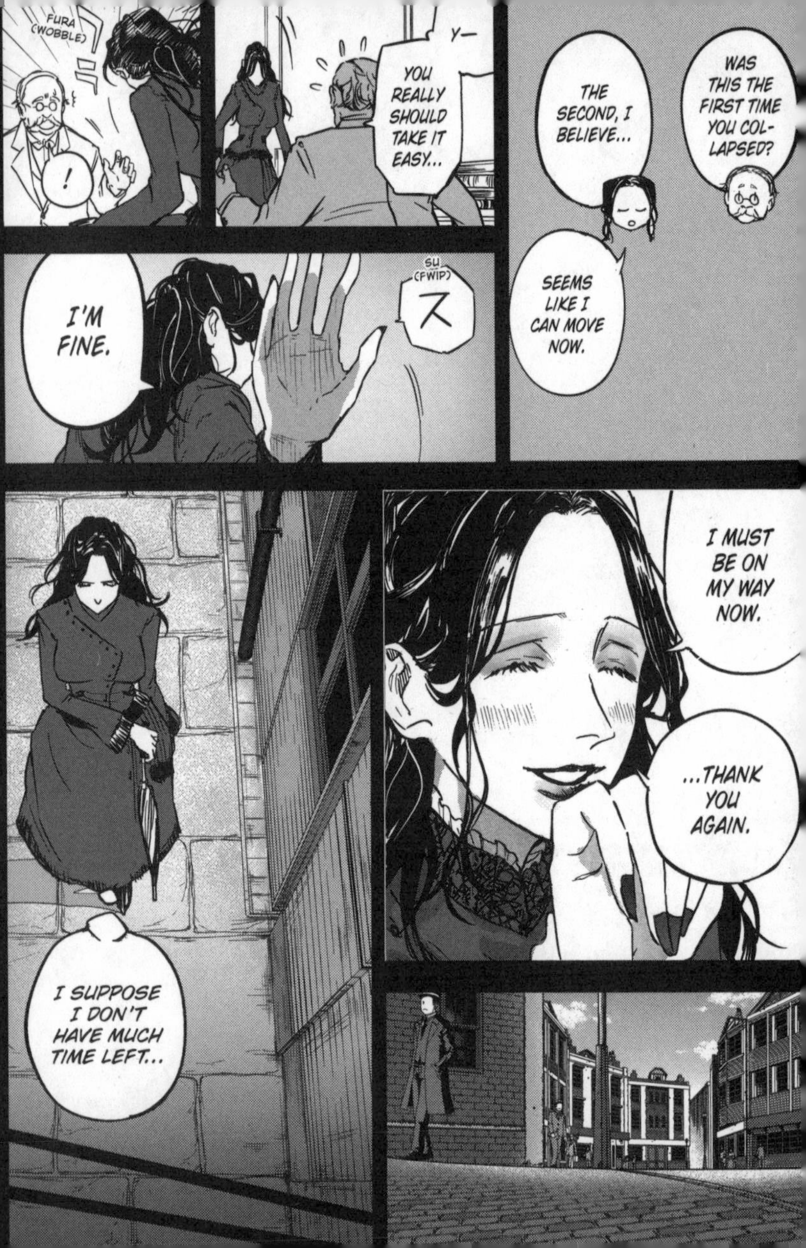
WAS THIS THE FIRST TIME YOU COL-LAPSED?
THE SECOND, I BELIEVE...
SEEMS LIKE I CAN MOVE NOW.
Y—
YOU REALLY SHOULD TAKE IT EASY...
FURA (WOBBLE)
!
SU (FWIP)
ス
I'M FINE.
I MUST BE ON MY WAY NOW.
...THANK YOU AGAIN.
I SUPPOSE I DON'T HAVE MUCH TIME LEFT...

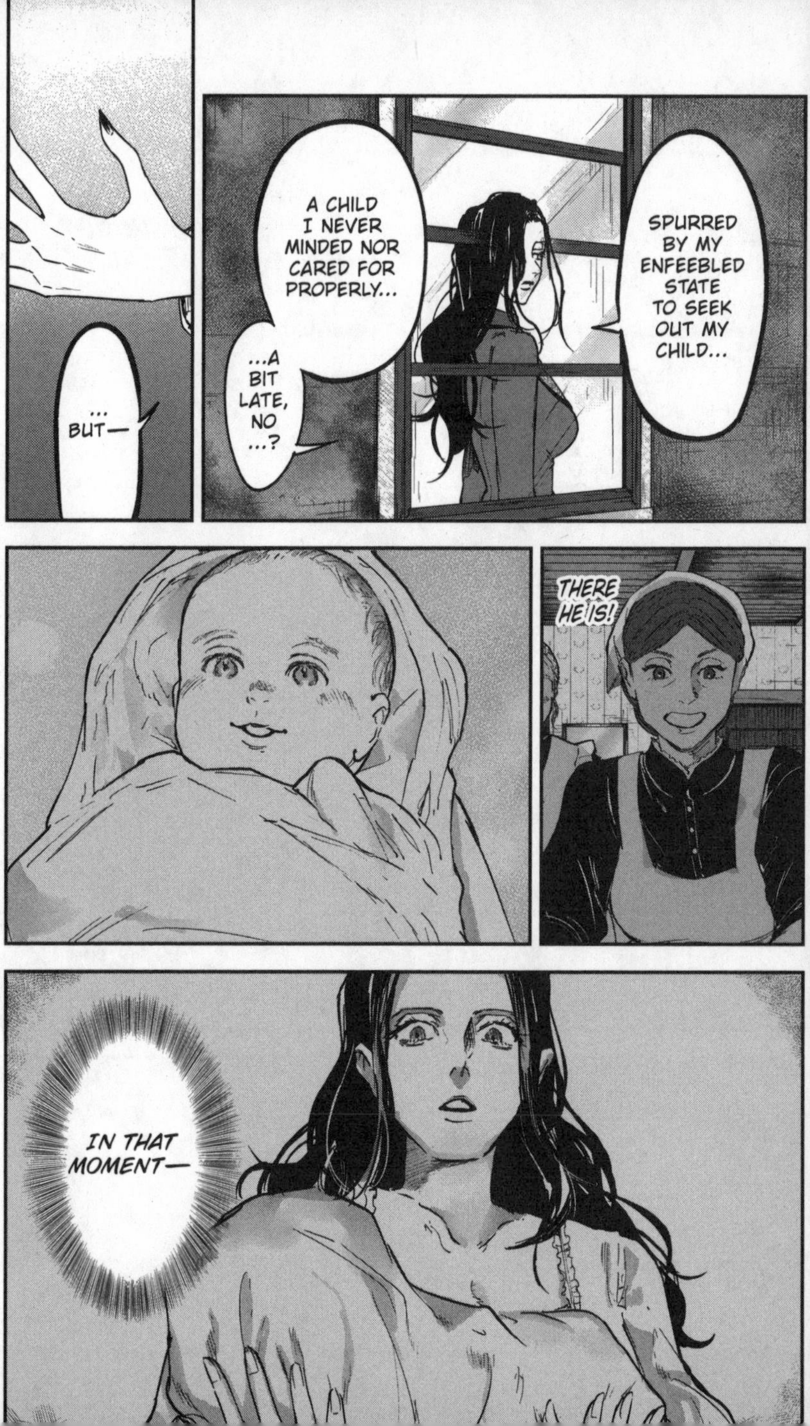
SPURRED BY MY ENFEEBLED STATE TO SEEK OUT MY CHILD...
A CHILD I NEVER MINDED NOR CARED FOR PROPERLY...
...A BIT LATE, NO ...?
... BUT—
THERE HE IS!
IN THAT MOMENT—

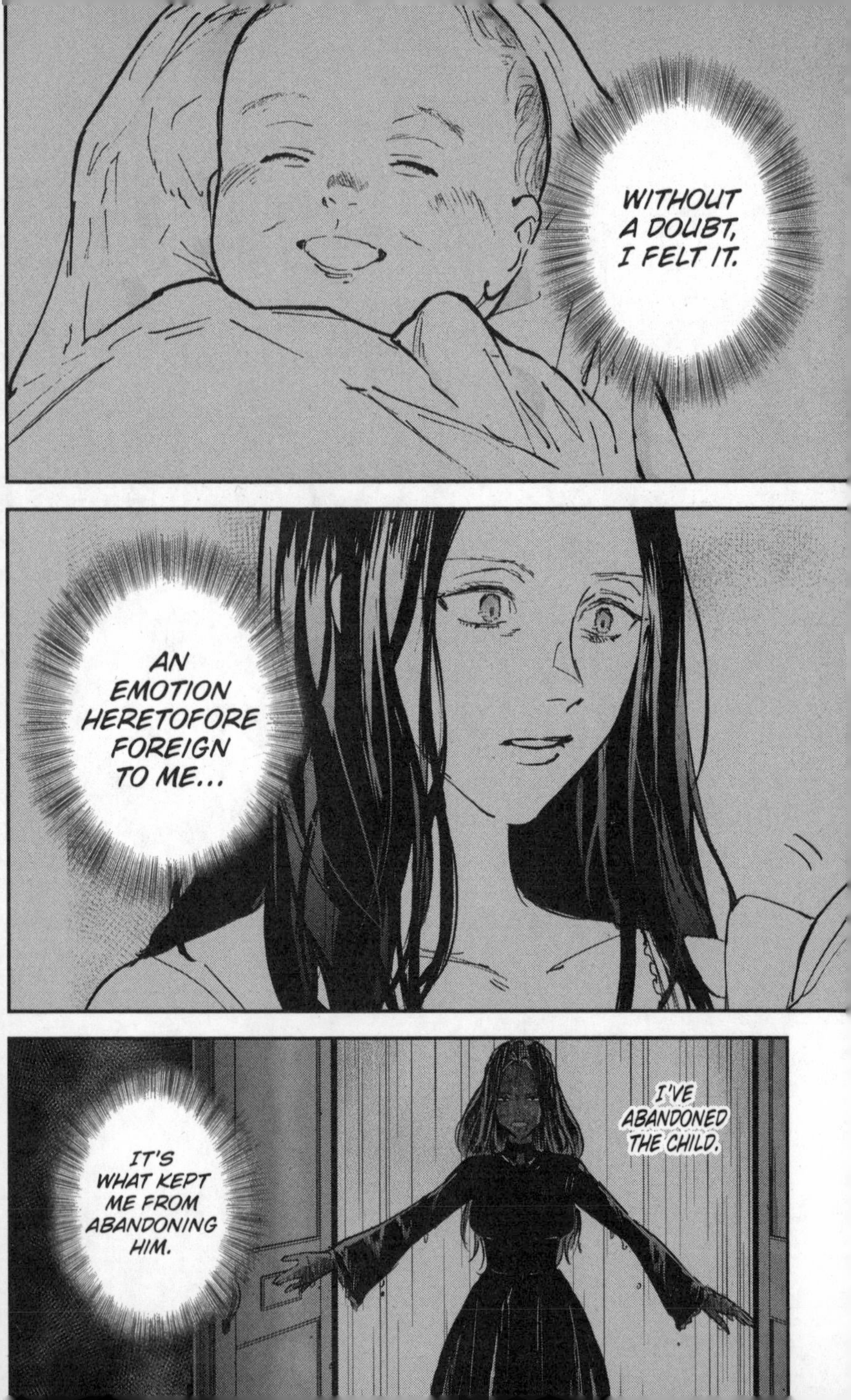
WITHOUT A DOUBT, I FELT IT.
AN EMOTION HERETOFORE FOREIGN TO ME...
I'VE ABANDONED THE CHILD.
IT'S WHAT KEPT ME FROM ABANDONING HIM.

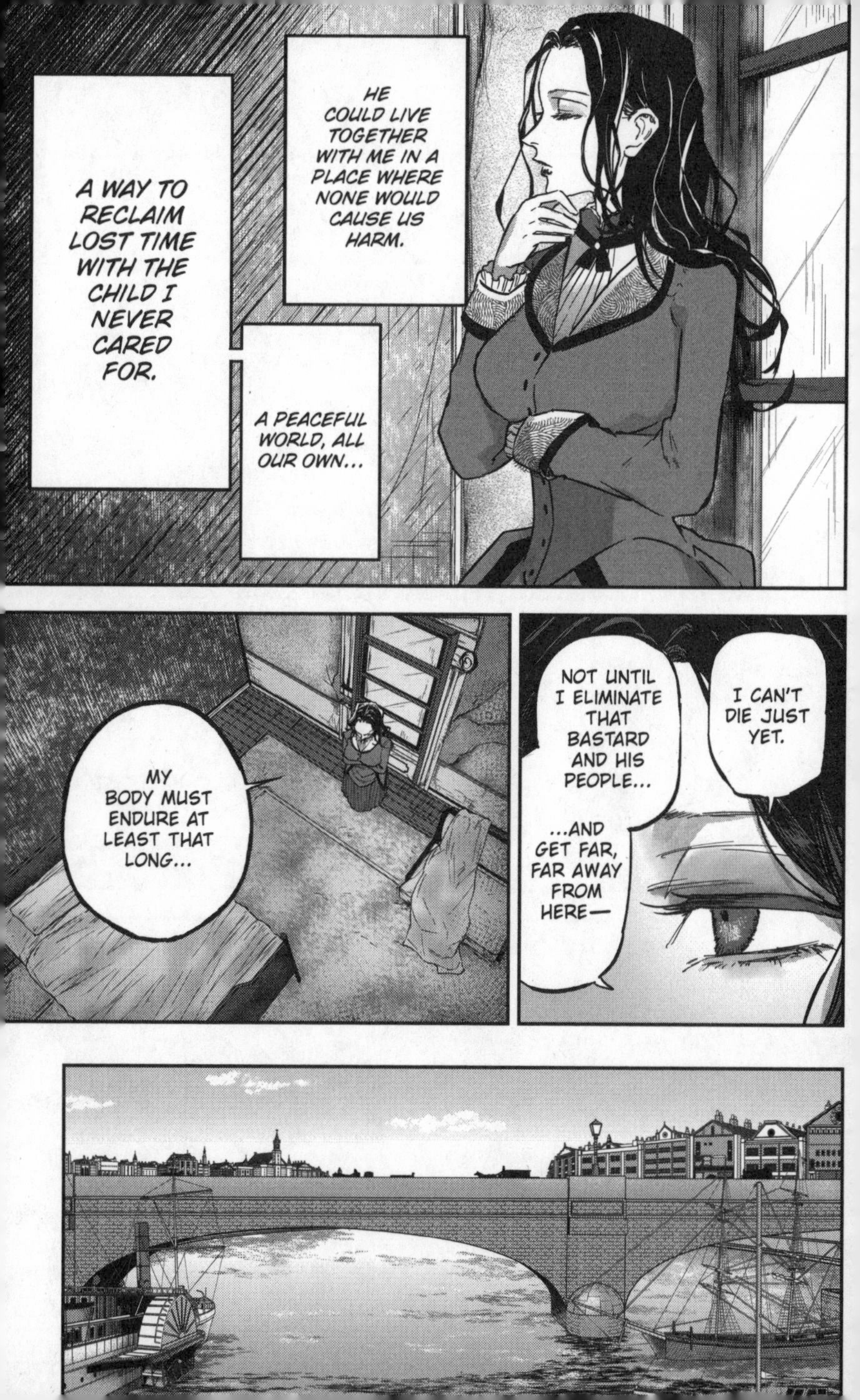
HE COULD LIVE TOGETHER WITH ME IN A PLACE WHERE NONE WOULD CAUSE US HARM.
A WAY TO RECLAIM LOST TIME WITH THE CHILD I NEVER CARED FOR.
A PEACEFUL WORLD, ALL OUR OWN...
I CAN'T DIE JUST YET.
NOT UNTIL I ELIMINATE THAT BASTARD AND HIS PEOPLE...
...AND GET FAR, FAR AWAY FROM HERE—
MY BODY MUST ENDURE AT LEAST THAT LONG...

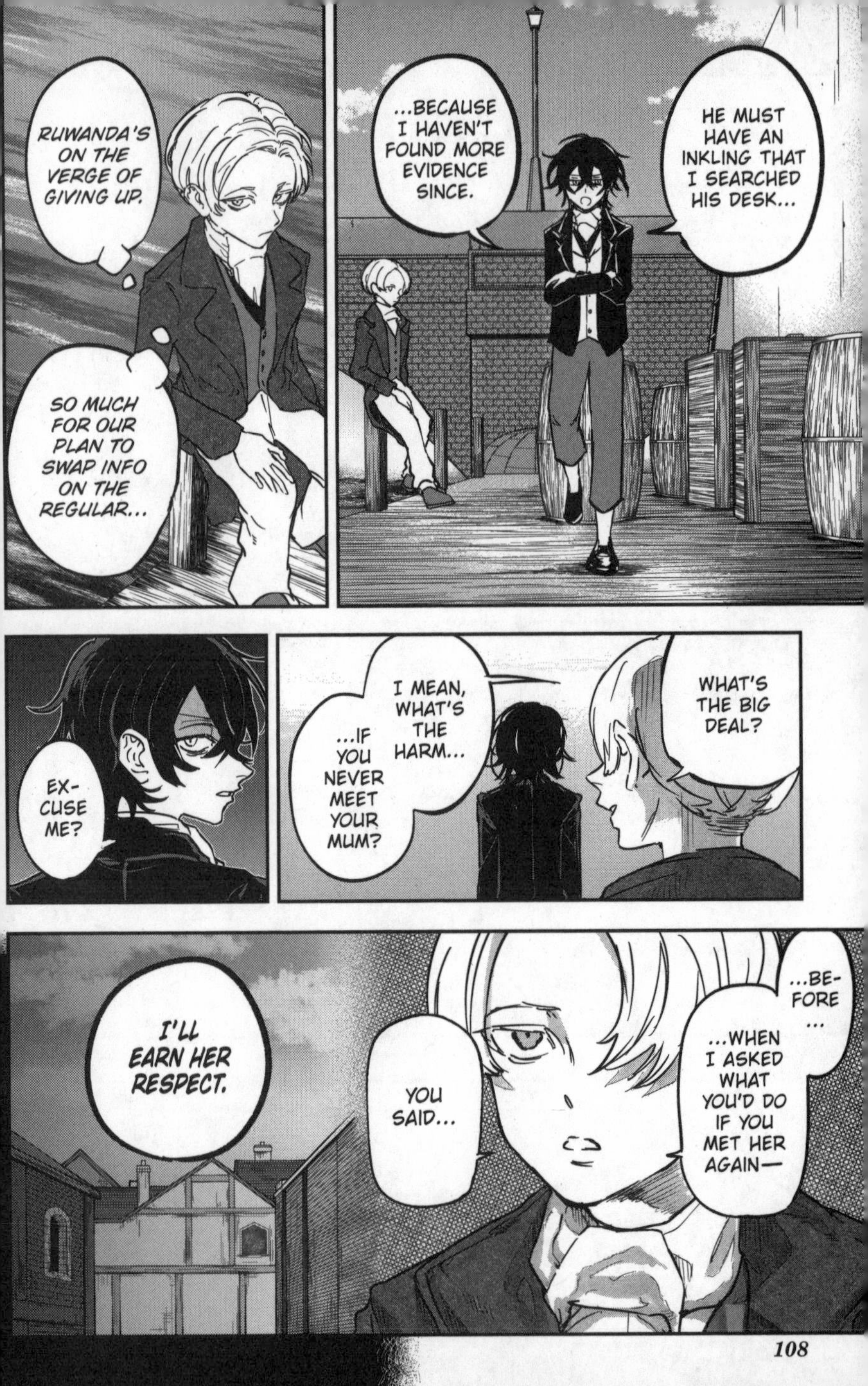
HE MUST HAVE AN INKLING THAT I SEARCHED HIS DESK...
...BECAUSE I HAVEN'T FOUND MORE EVIDENCE SINCE.
RUWANDA'S ON THE VERGE OF GIVING UP.
SO MUCH FOR OUR PLAN TO SWAP INFO ON THE REGULAR...
WHAT'S THE BIG DEAL?
I MEAN, WHAT'S THE HARM...
...IF YOU NEVER MEET YOUR MUM?
EX-CUSE ME?
...BE-FORE...
...WHEN I ASKED WHAT YOU'D DO IF YOU MET HER AGAIN—
YOU SAID...
I'LL EARN HER RESPECT.

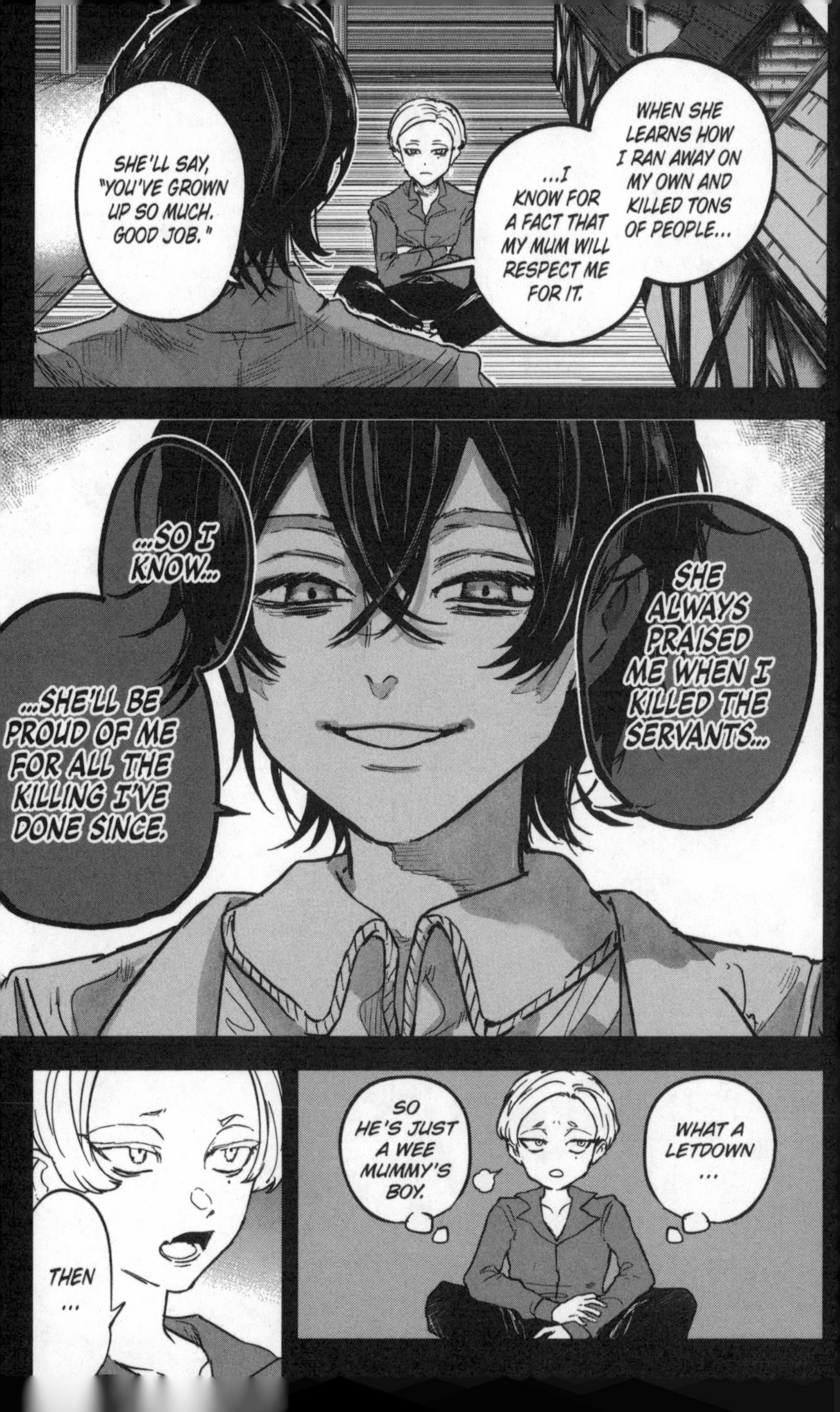
WHEN SHE LEARNS HOW I RAN AWAY ON MY OWN AND KILLED TONS OF PEOPLE...
...I KNOW FOR A FACT THAT MY MUM WILL RESPECT ME FOR IT.
SHE'LL SAY, "YOU'VE GROWN UP SO MUCH. GOOD JOB."
SHE ALWAYS PRAISED ME WHEN I KILLED THE SERVANTS...
...SO I KNOW...
...SHE'LL BE PROUD OF ME FOR ALL THE KILLING I'VE DONE SINCE.
WHAT A LETDOWN ...
SO HE'S JUST A WEE MUMMY'S BOY.
THEN ...

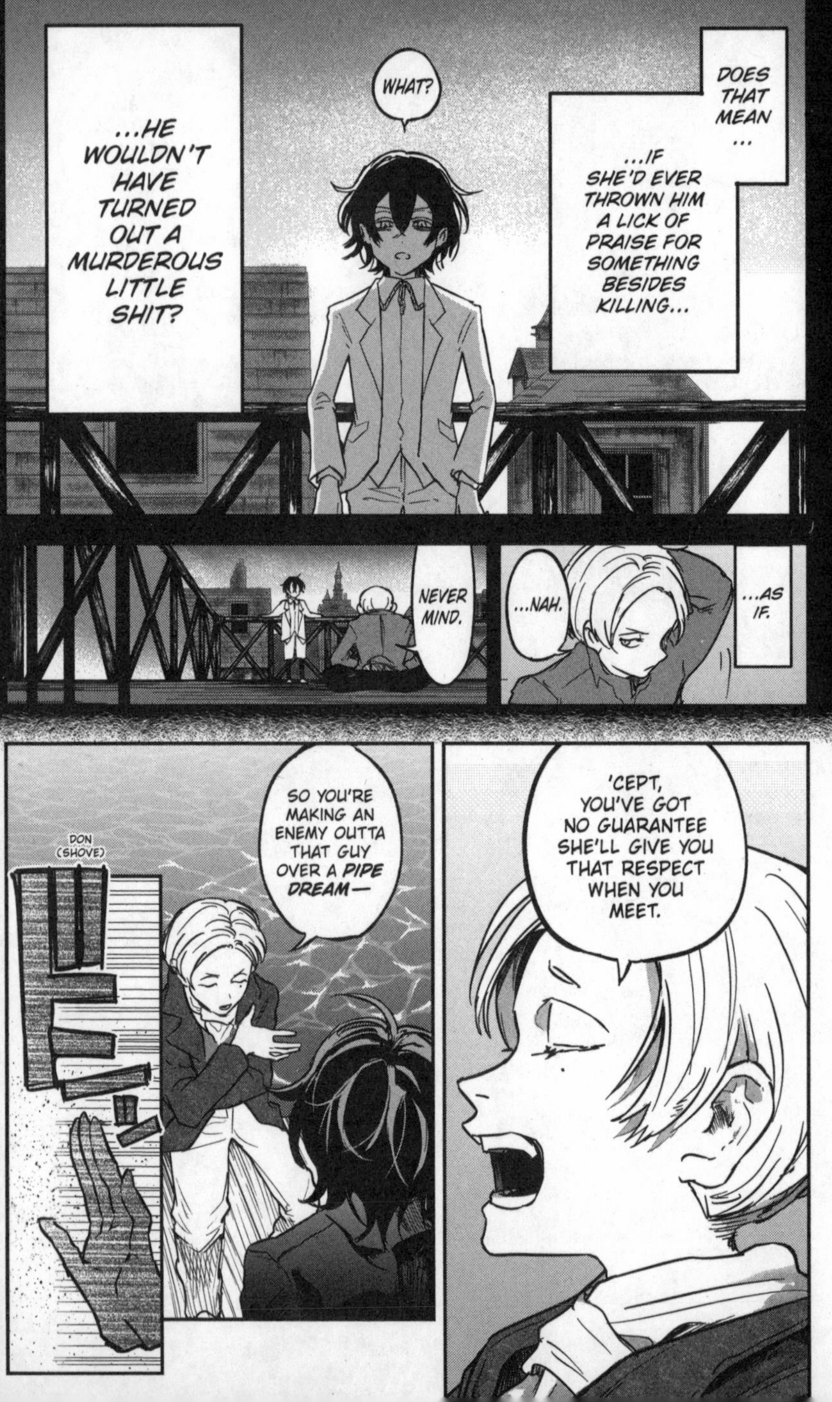
DOES THAT MEAN...
...IF SHE'D EVER THROWN HIM A LICK OF PRAISE FOR SOMETHING BESIDES KILLING...
...HE WOULDN'T HAVE TURNED OUT A MURDEROUS LITTLE SHIT?
WHAT?
...AS IF.
...NAH.
NEVER MIND.
'CEPT, YOU'VE GOT NO GUARANTEE SHE'LL GIVE YOU THAT RESPECT WHEN YOU MEET.
SO YOU'RE MAKING AN ENEMY OUTTA THAT GUY OVER A *PIPE DREAM*—
DON (SHOVE)

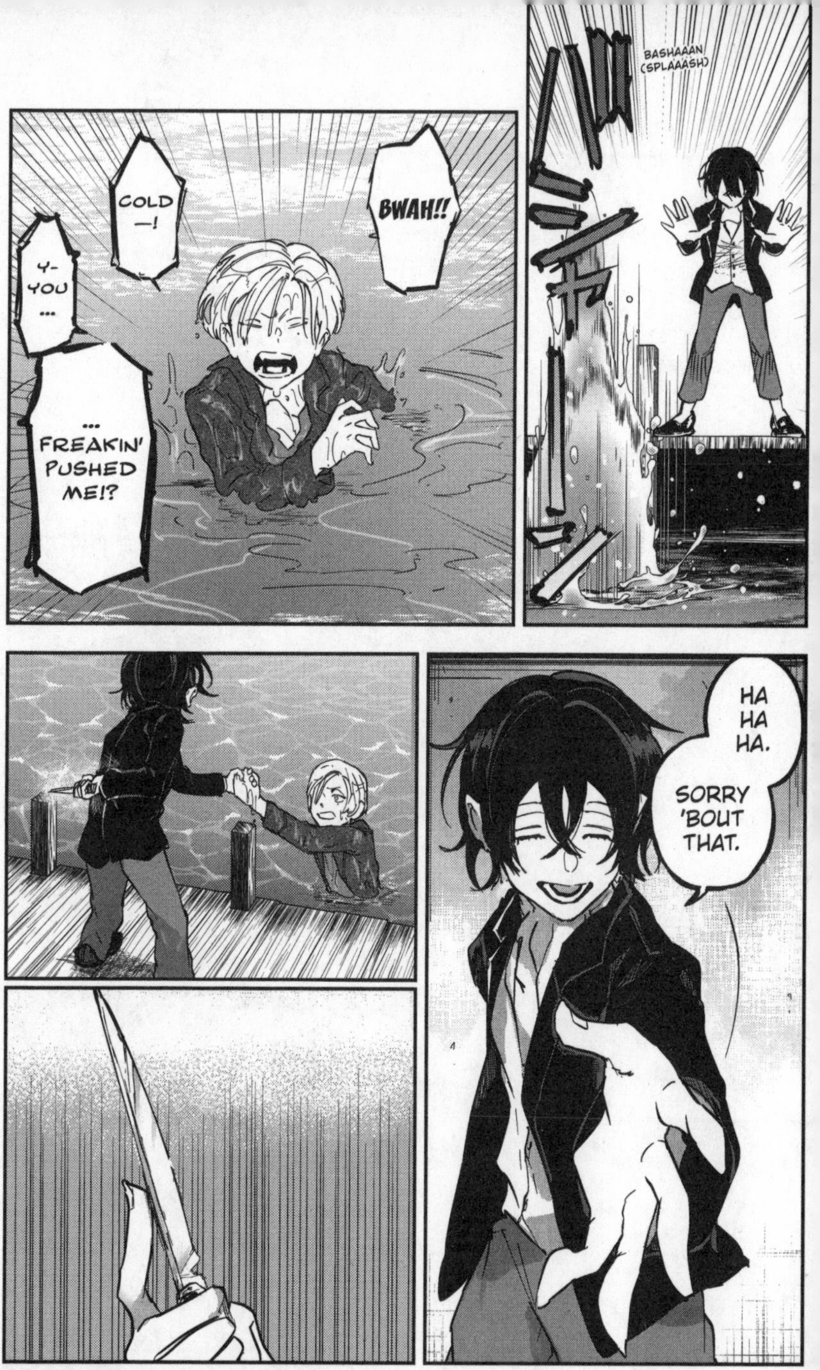
BASHAAAN (SPLAAASH)
BWAH!!
COLD—!
Y-YOU...
...FREAKIN' PUSHED ME!?
HA HA HA.
SORRY 'BOUT THAT.

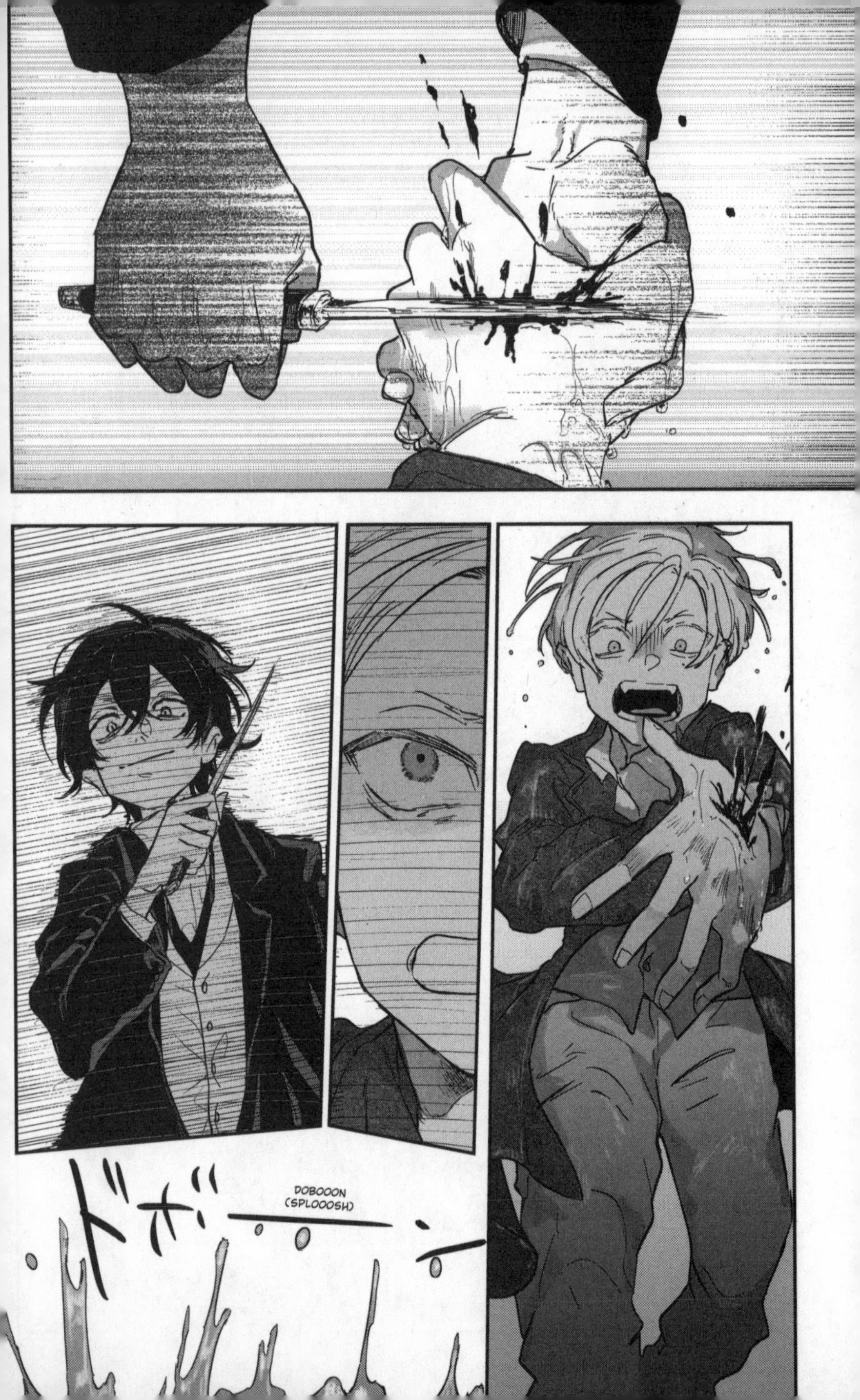
DOBOOON
(SPLOOOSH)

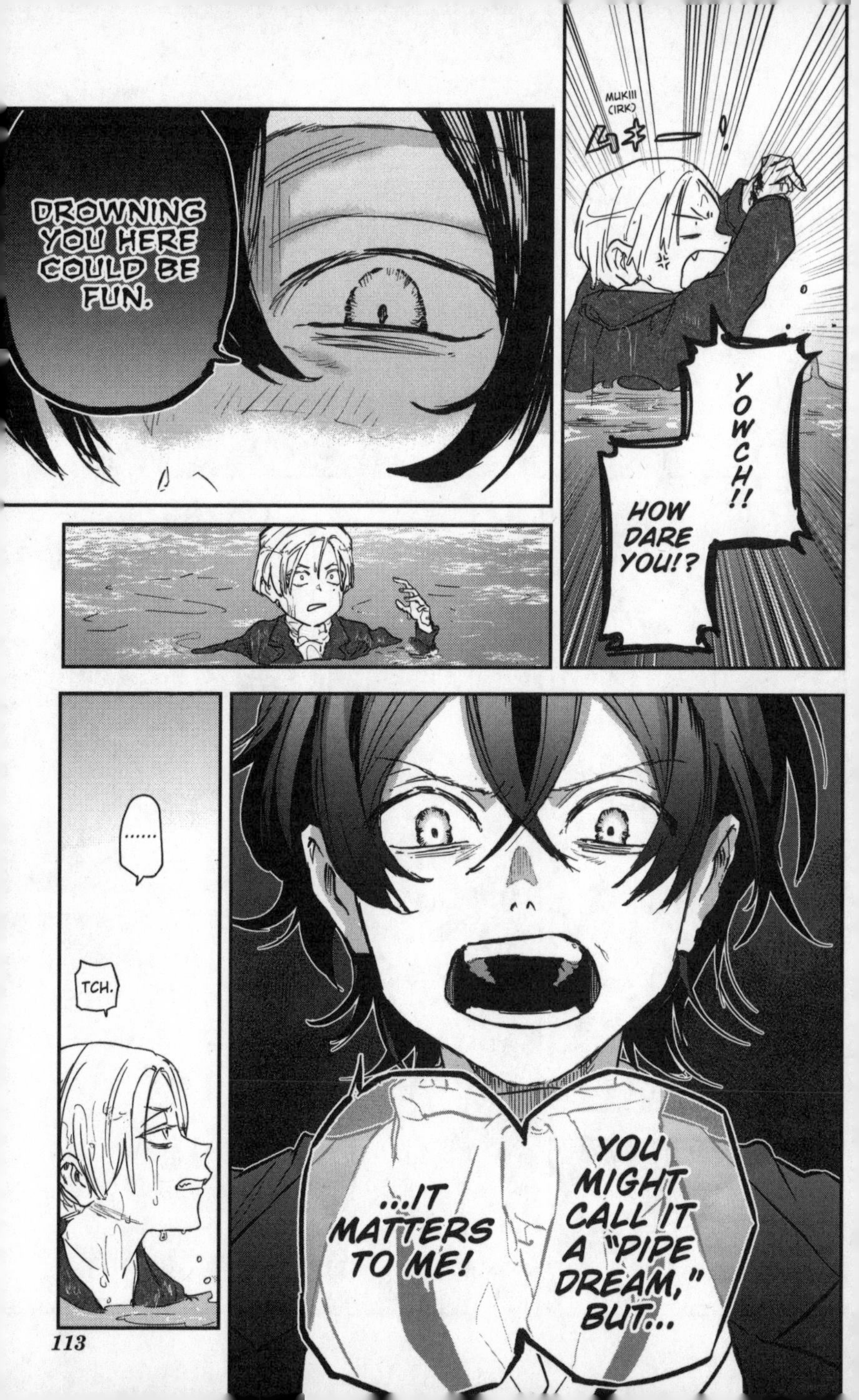
MUKIII (IRK)
YOWCH!!
HOW DARE YOU!?
DROWNING YOU HERE COULD BE FUN.
YOU MIGHT CALL IT A "PIPE DREAM," BUT...
...IT MATTERS TO ME!
......
TCH.

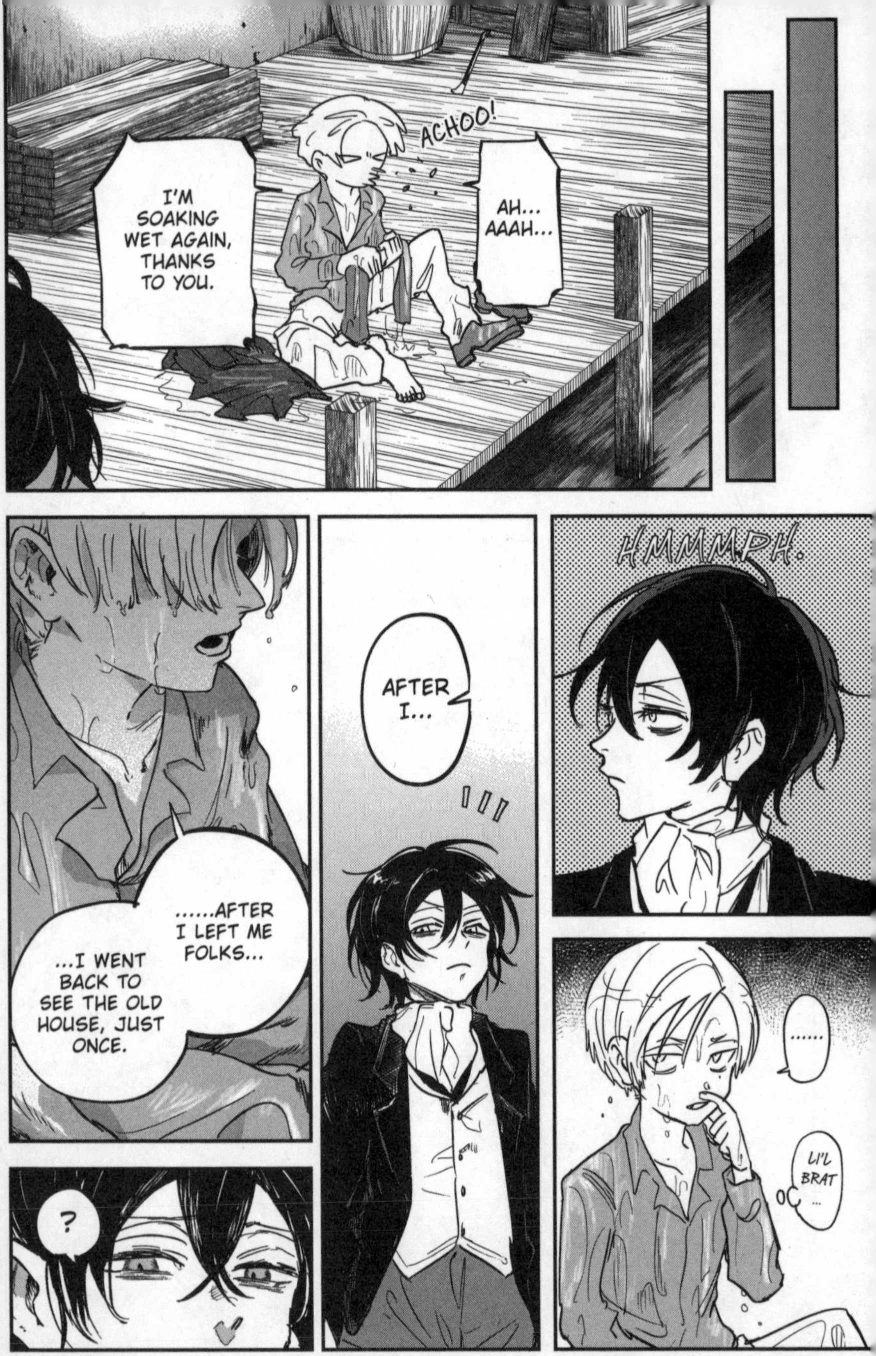
AH... AAAH...
ACHOO!
I'M SOAKING WET AGAIN, THANKS TO YOU.
HMMMPH.
......
LI'L BRAT ...
AFTER I...
......AFTER I LEFT ME FOLKS...
...I WENT BACK TO SEE THE OLD HOUSE, JUST ONCE.
?

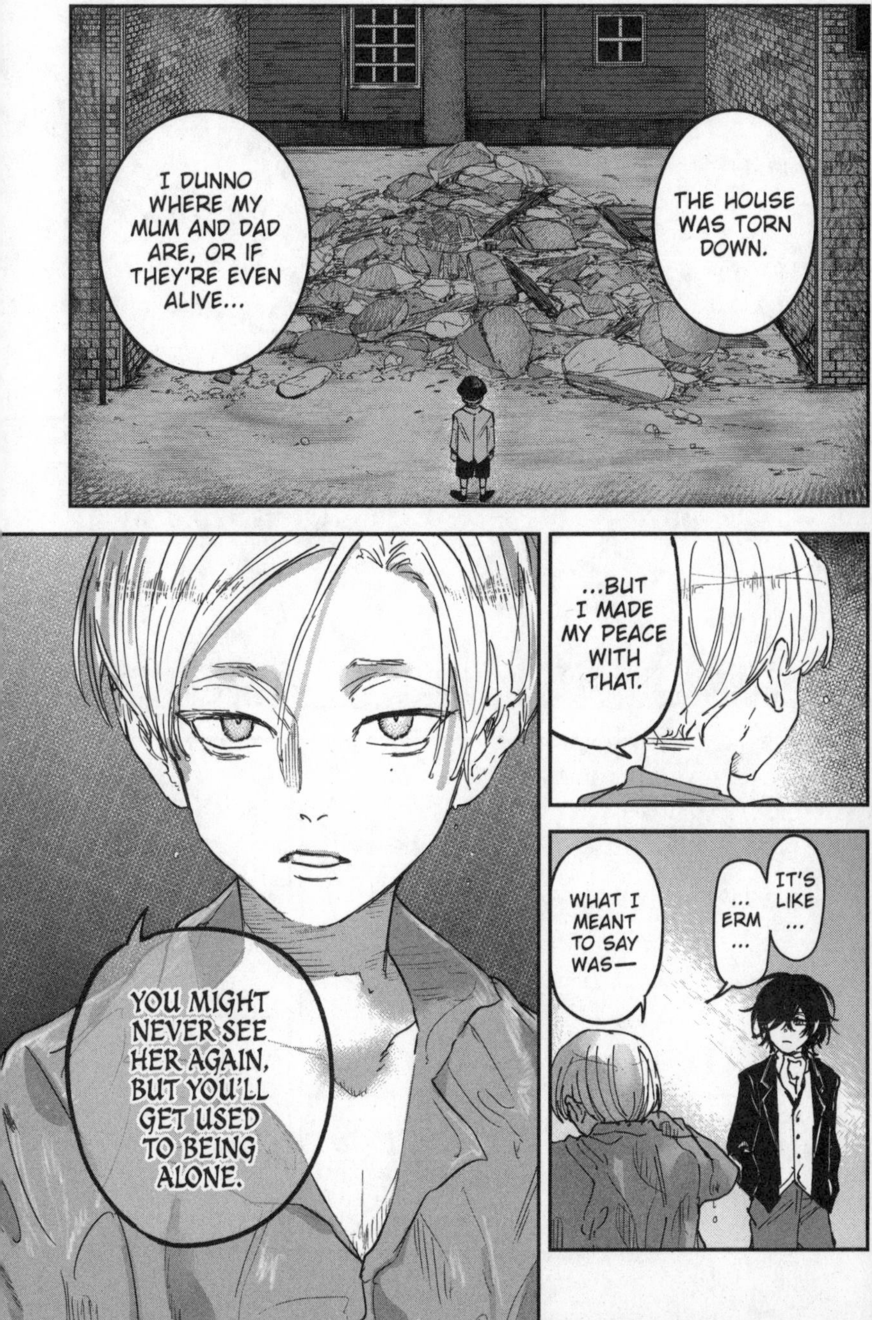
THE HOUSE WAS TORN DOWN.
I DUNNO WHERE MY MUM AND DAD ARE, OR IF THEY'RE EVEN ALIVE...
...BUT I MADE MY PEACE WITH THAT.
IT'S LIKE...
...ERM...
WHAT I MEANT TO SAY WAS—
YOU MIGHT NEVER SEE HER AGAIN, BUT YOU'LL GET USED TO BEING ALONE.

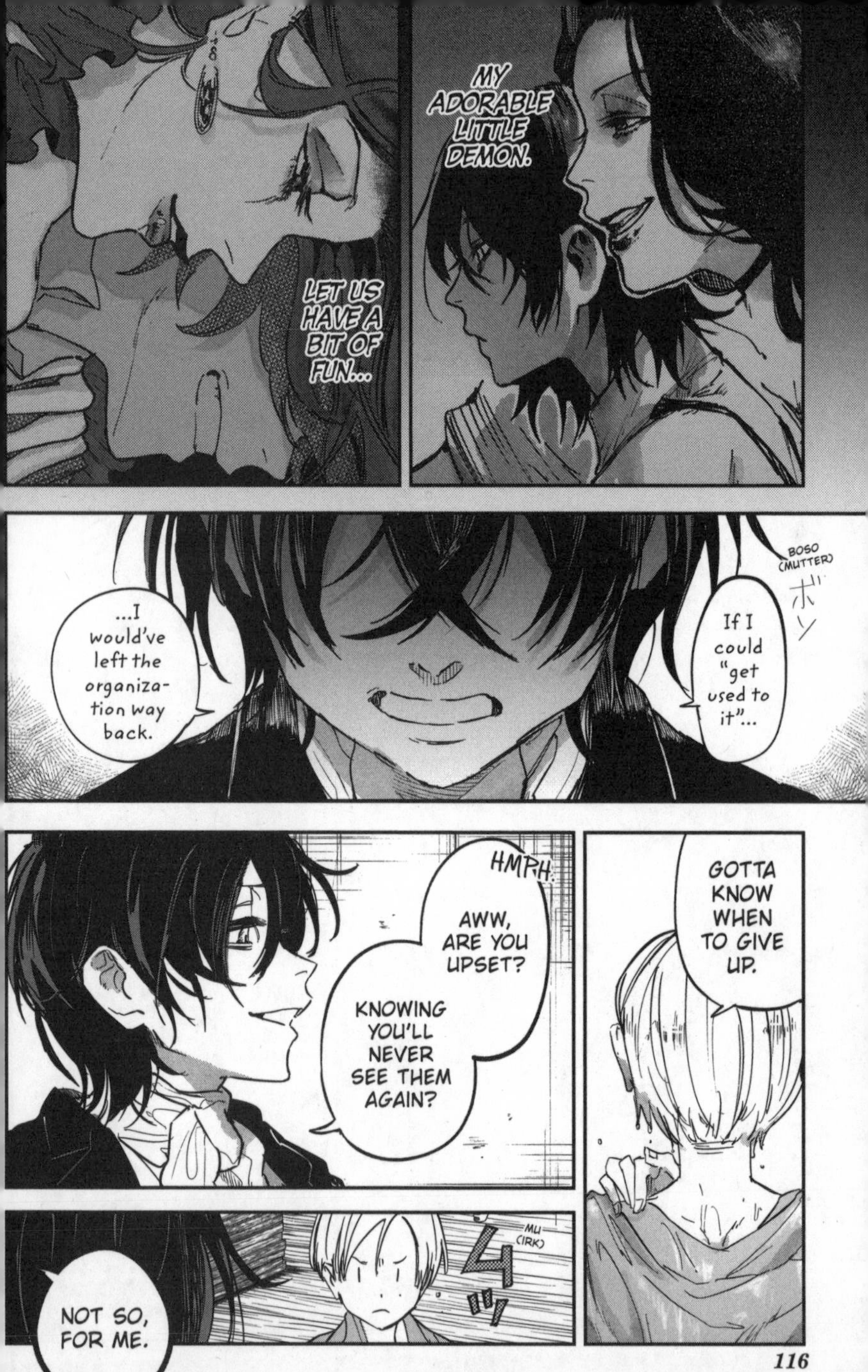
MY ADORABLE LITTLE DEMON.
LET US HAVE A BIT OF FUN...
BOSO (MUTTER)
ボソ
If I could "get used to it"...
...I would've left the organization way back.
GOTTA KNOW WHEN TO GIVE UP.
HMPH.
AWW, ARE YOU UPSET?
KNOWING YOU'LL NEVER SEE THEM AGAIN?
MU (IRK)
NOT SO, FOR ME.

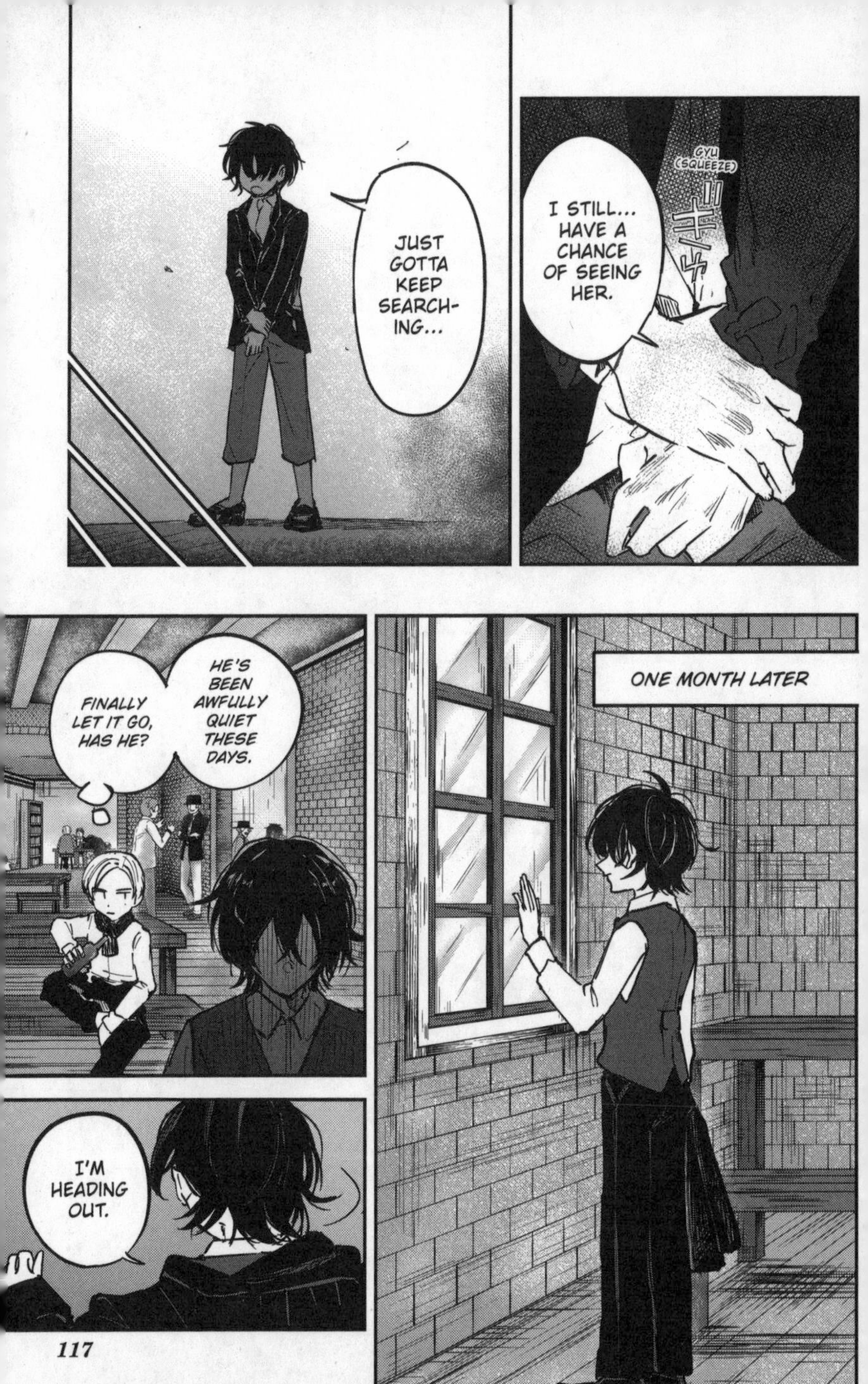
GYU (SQUEEZE)
I STILL... HAVE A CHANCE OF SEEING HER.
JUST GOTTA KEEP SEARCHING...
ONE MONTH LATER
HE'S BEEN AWFULLY QUIET THESE DAYS.
FINALLY LET IT GO, HAS HE?
I'M HEADING OUT.

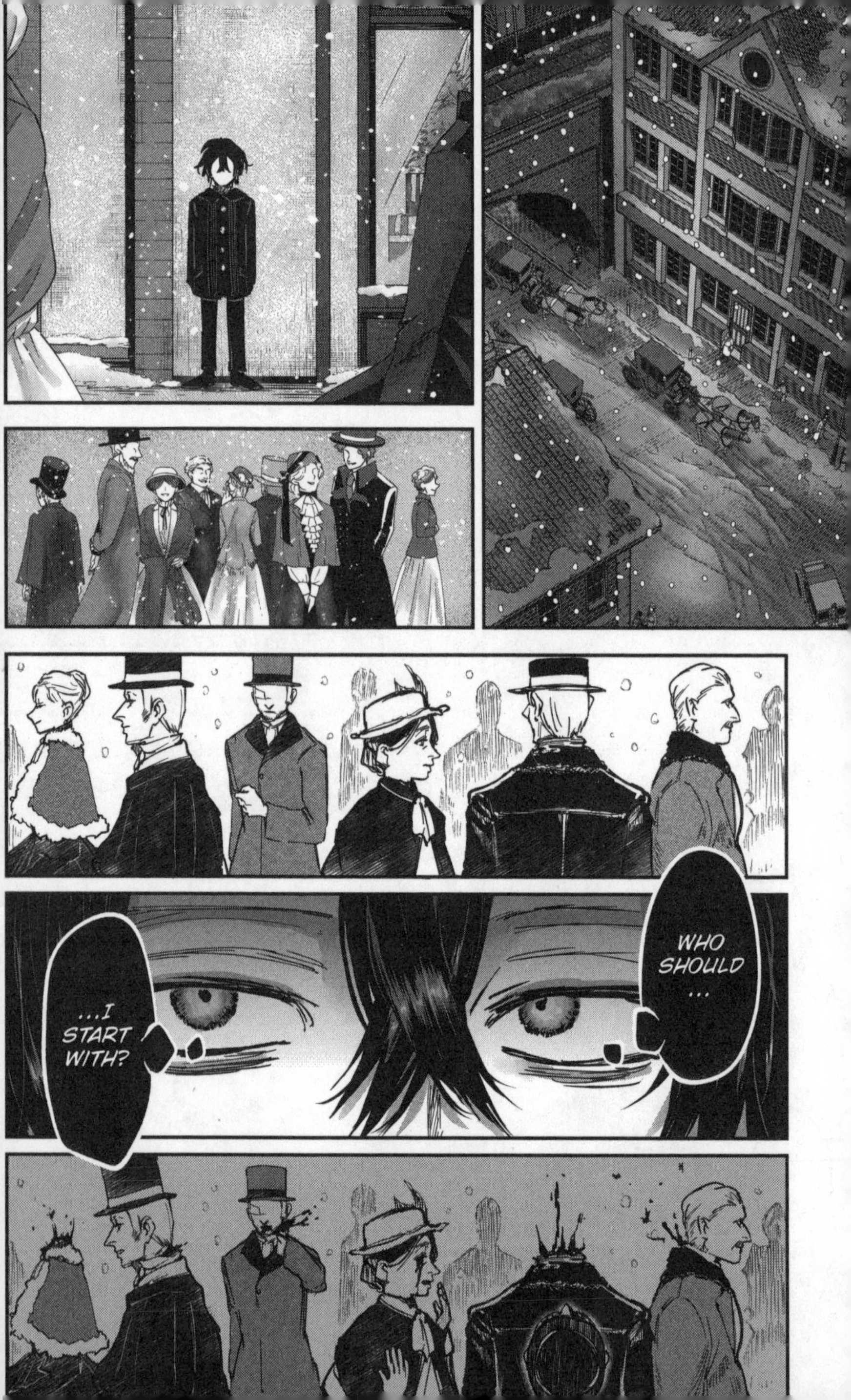
WHO SHOULD...
...I START WITH?

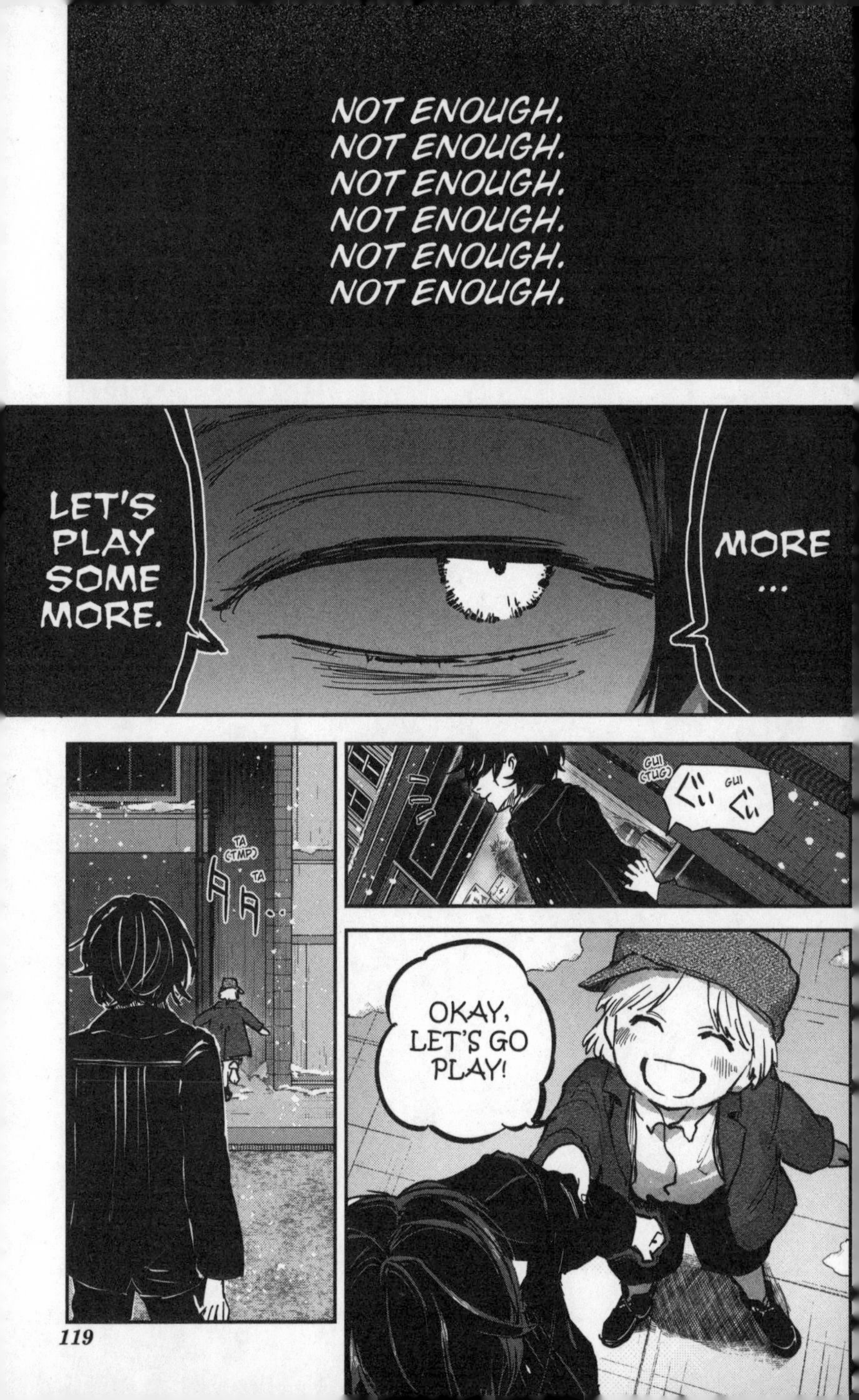
NOT ENOUGH.
NOT ENOUGH.
NOT ENOUGH.
NOT ENOUGH.
NOT ENOUGH.
NOT ENOUGH.
MORE ...
LET'S PLAY SOME MORE.
GUI (TUG)
ぐい
GUI
ぐい
OKAY, LET'S GO PLAY!
TA (TMP)
TA

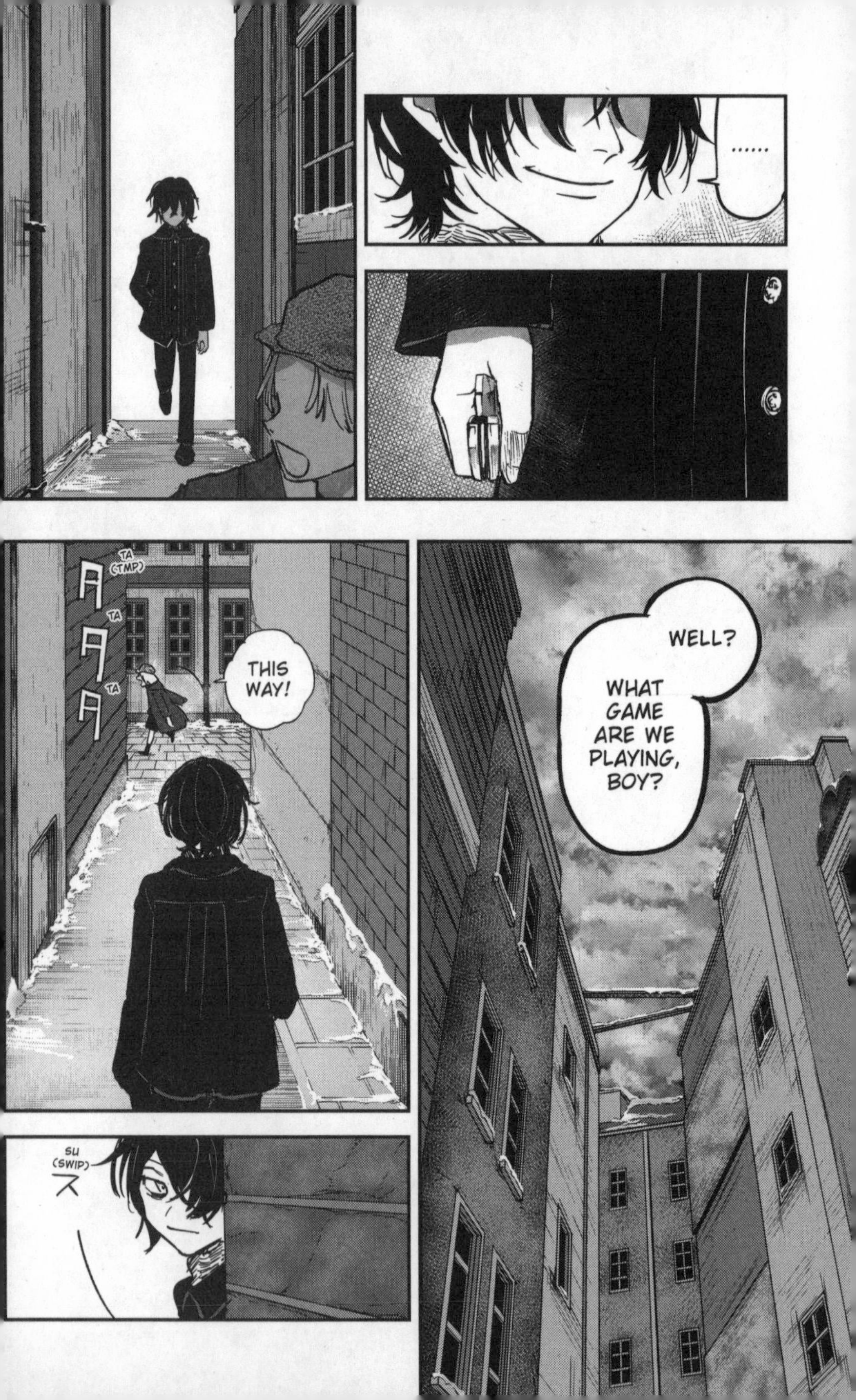
......
WELL?
WHAT GAME ARE WE PLAYING, BOY?
タ TA (TMP)
タ TA
タ TA
THIS WAY!
ス SU (SWIP)

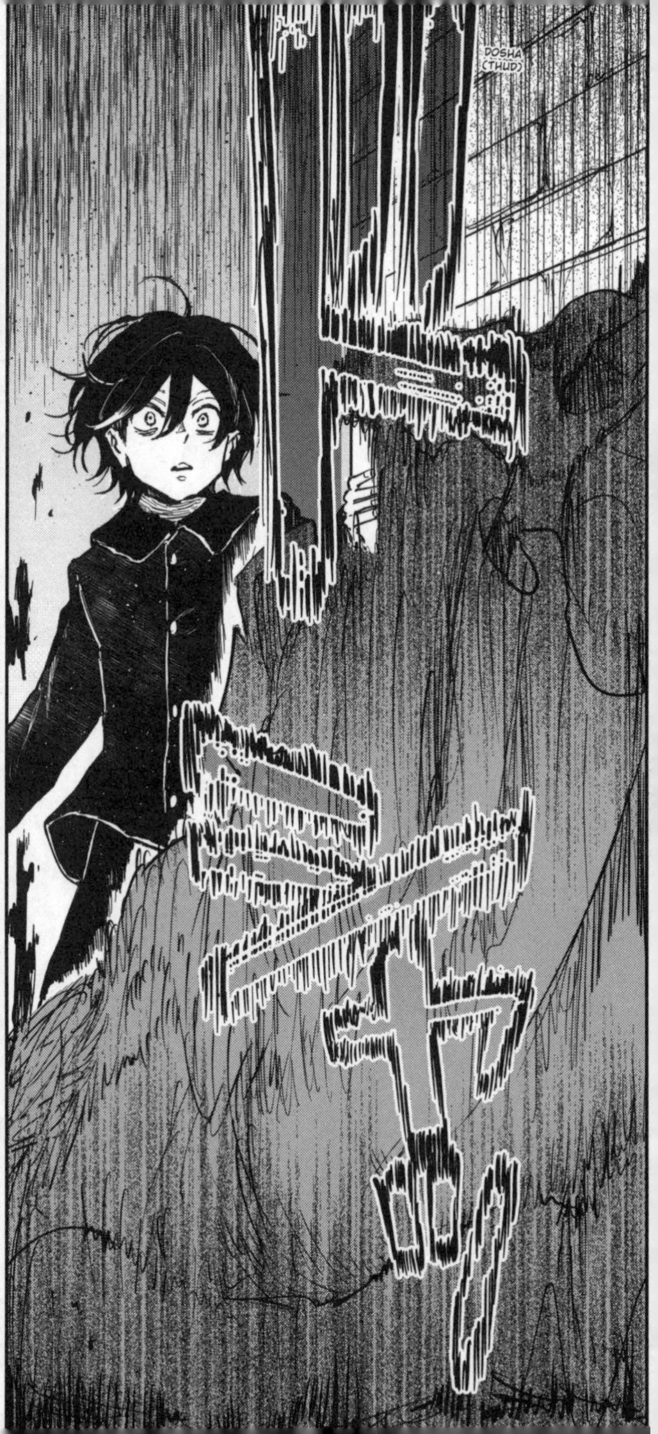
DOSHA (THUD)
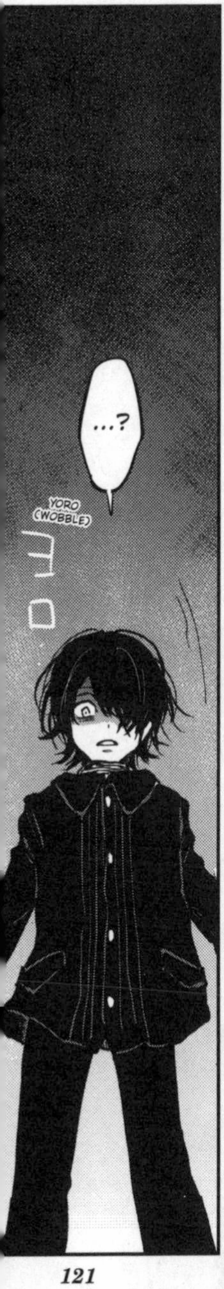
...?
YORO (WOBBLE)

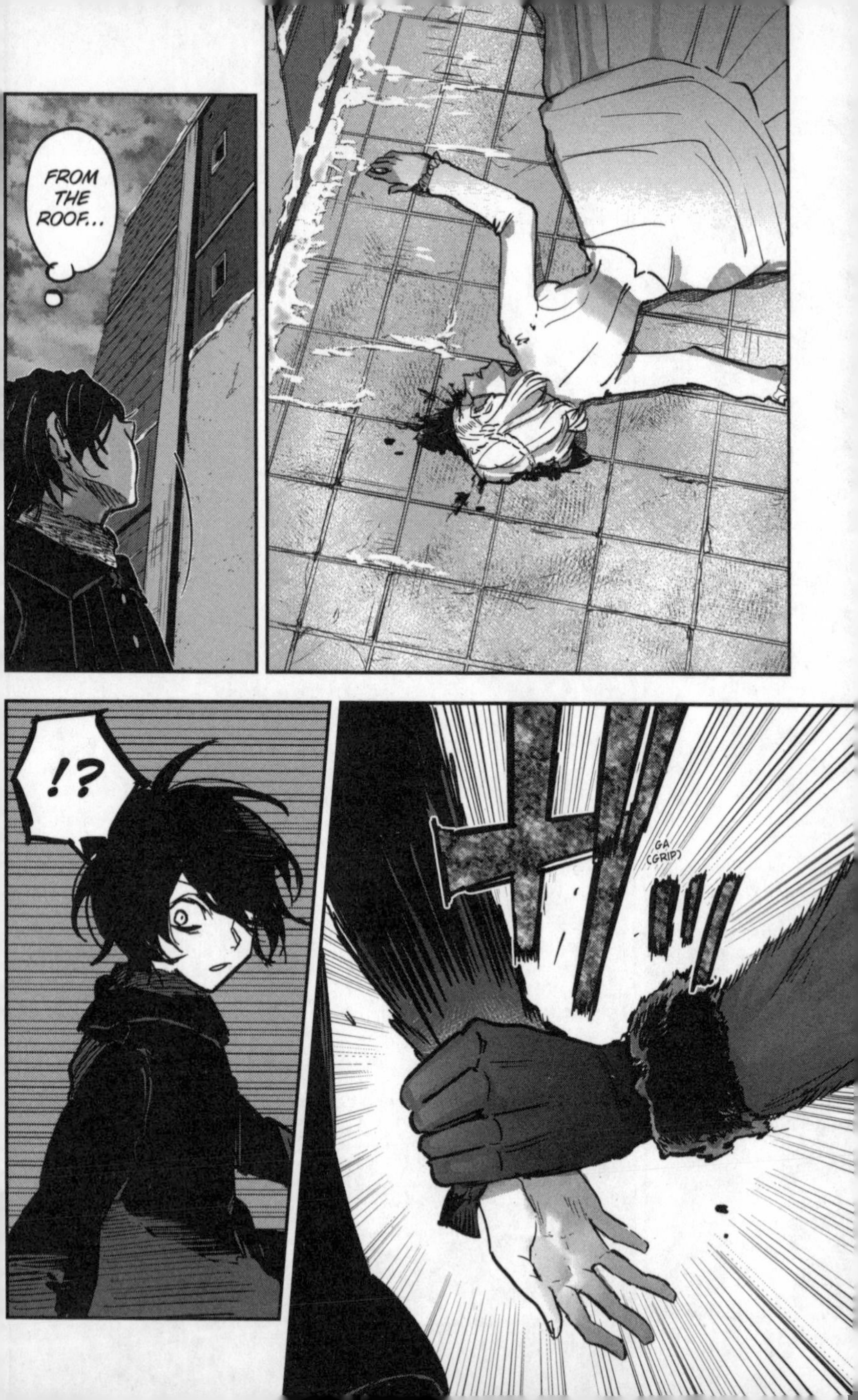
FROM THE ROOF...
GA
(GRIP)
!?

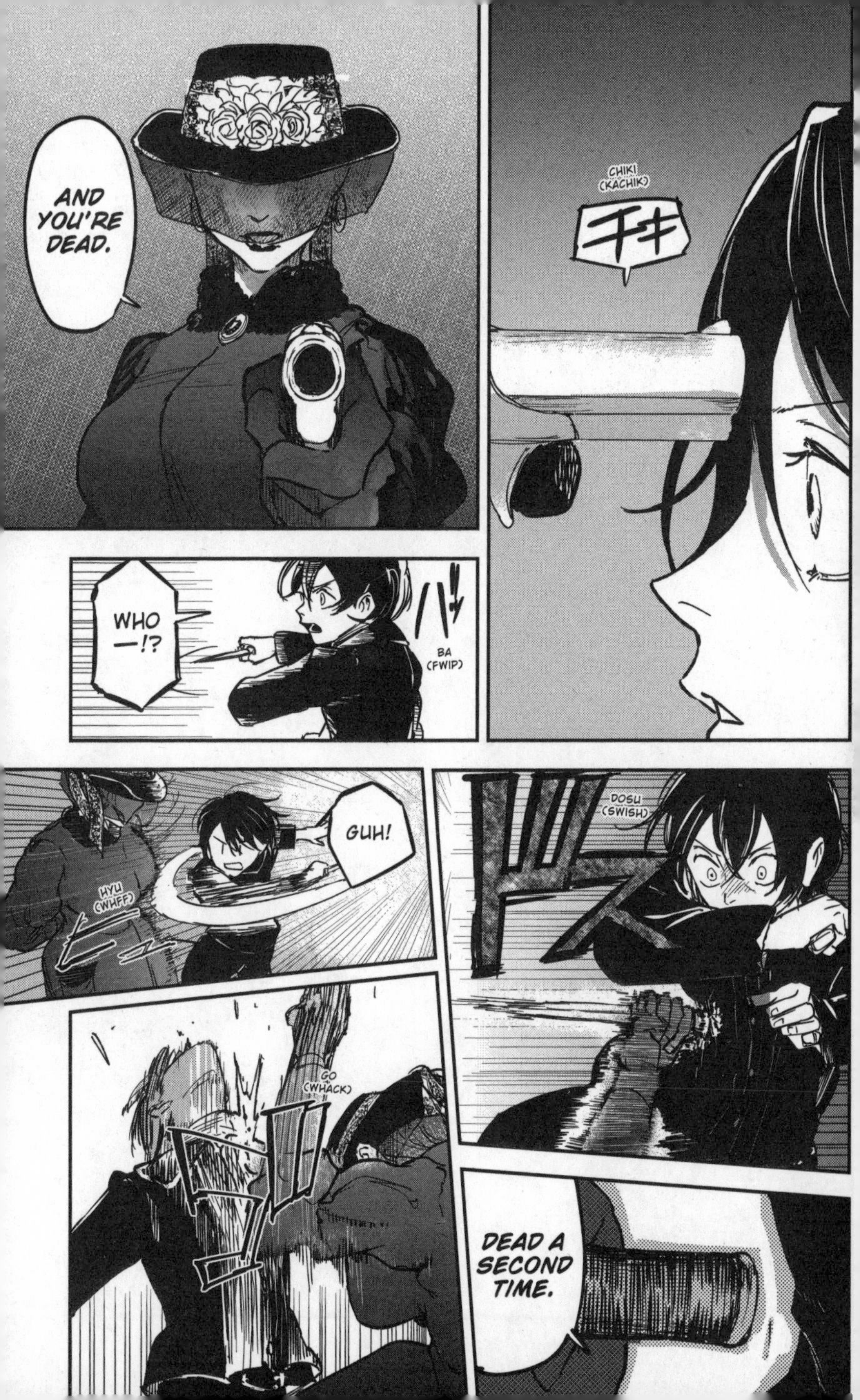

CHIKI (KACHIK)
チキ
AND YOU'RE DEAD.
WHO—!?
BA (FWIP)
DOSU (SWISH)
GUH!
HYU (WHFF)
DEAD A SECOND TIME.
GO (WHACK)

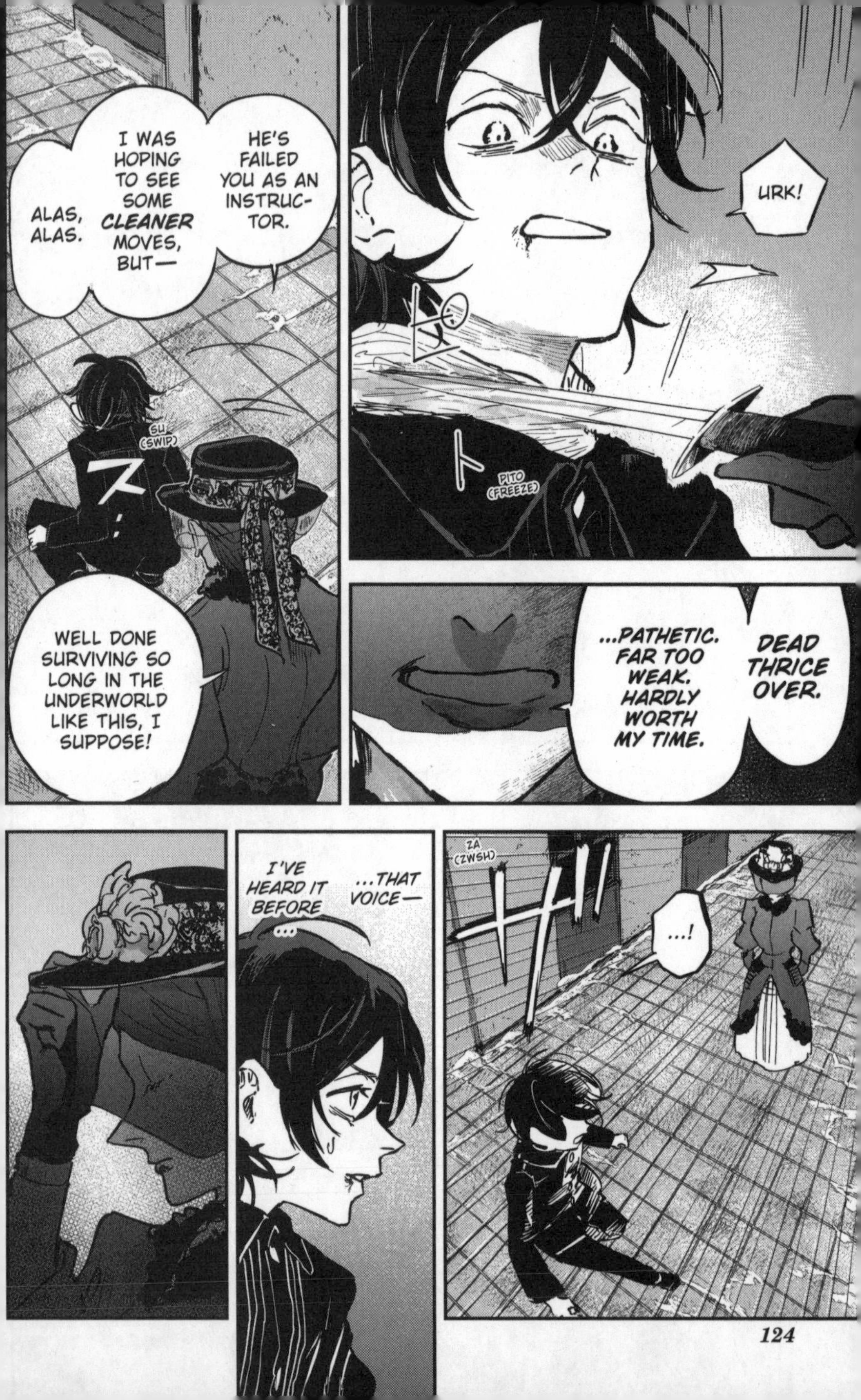
URK!
PITO (FREEZE)
DEAD THRICE OVER.
...PATHETIC. FAR TOO WEAK. HARDLY WORTH MY TIME.
HE'S FAILED YOU AS AN INSTRUCTOR.
I WAS HOPING TO SEE SOME CLEANER MOVES, BUT—
ALAS, ALAS.
SU (SWIP)
WELL DONE SURVIVING SO LONG IN THE UNDERWORLD LIKE THIS, I SUPPOSE!
ZA (ZWSH)
...!
...THAT VOICE—
I'VE HEARD IT BEFORE ...

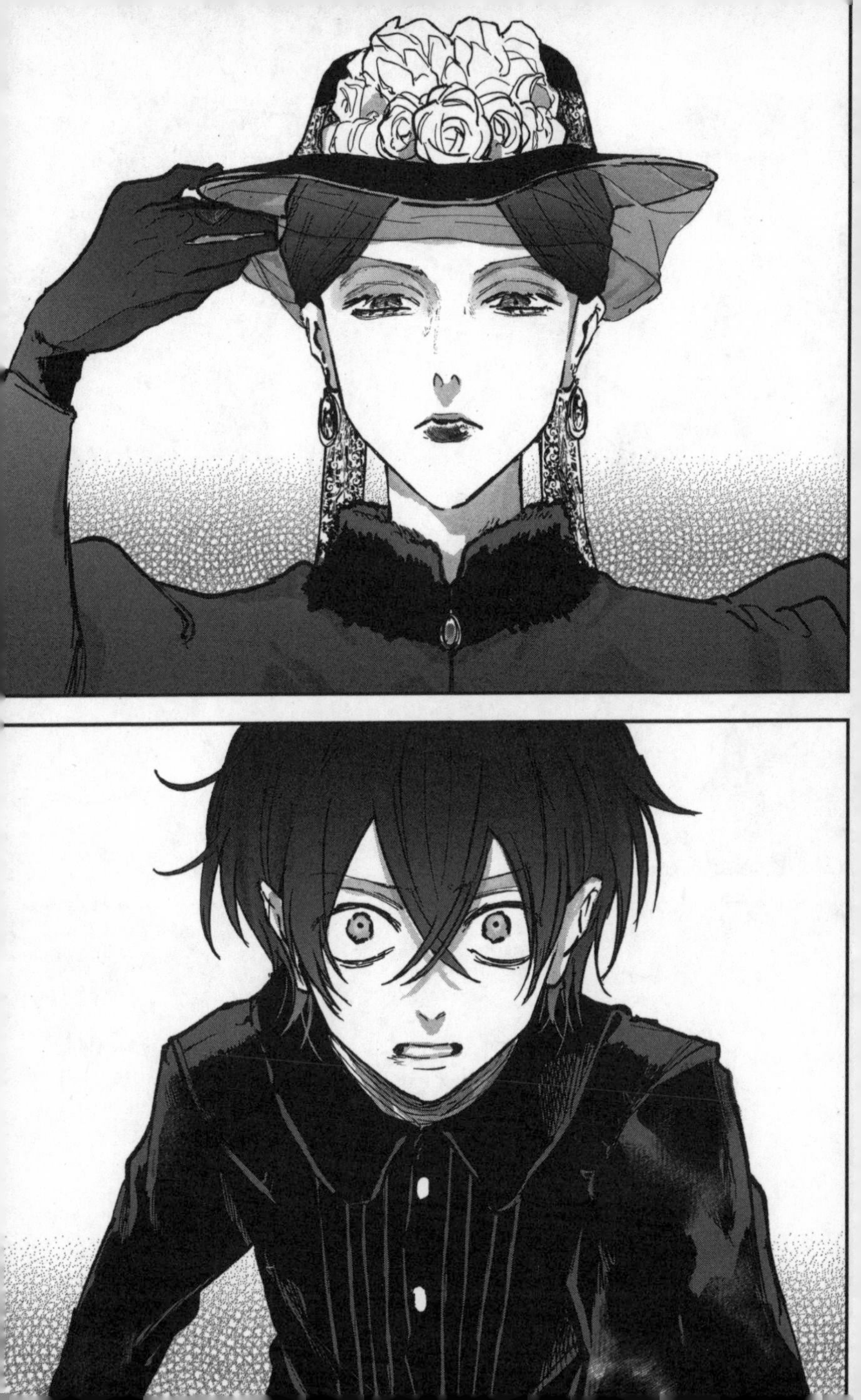

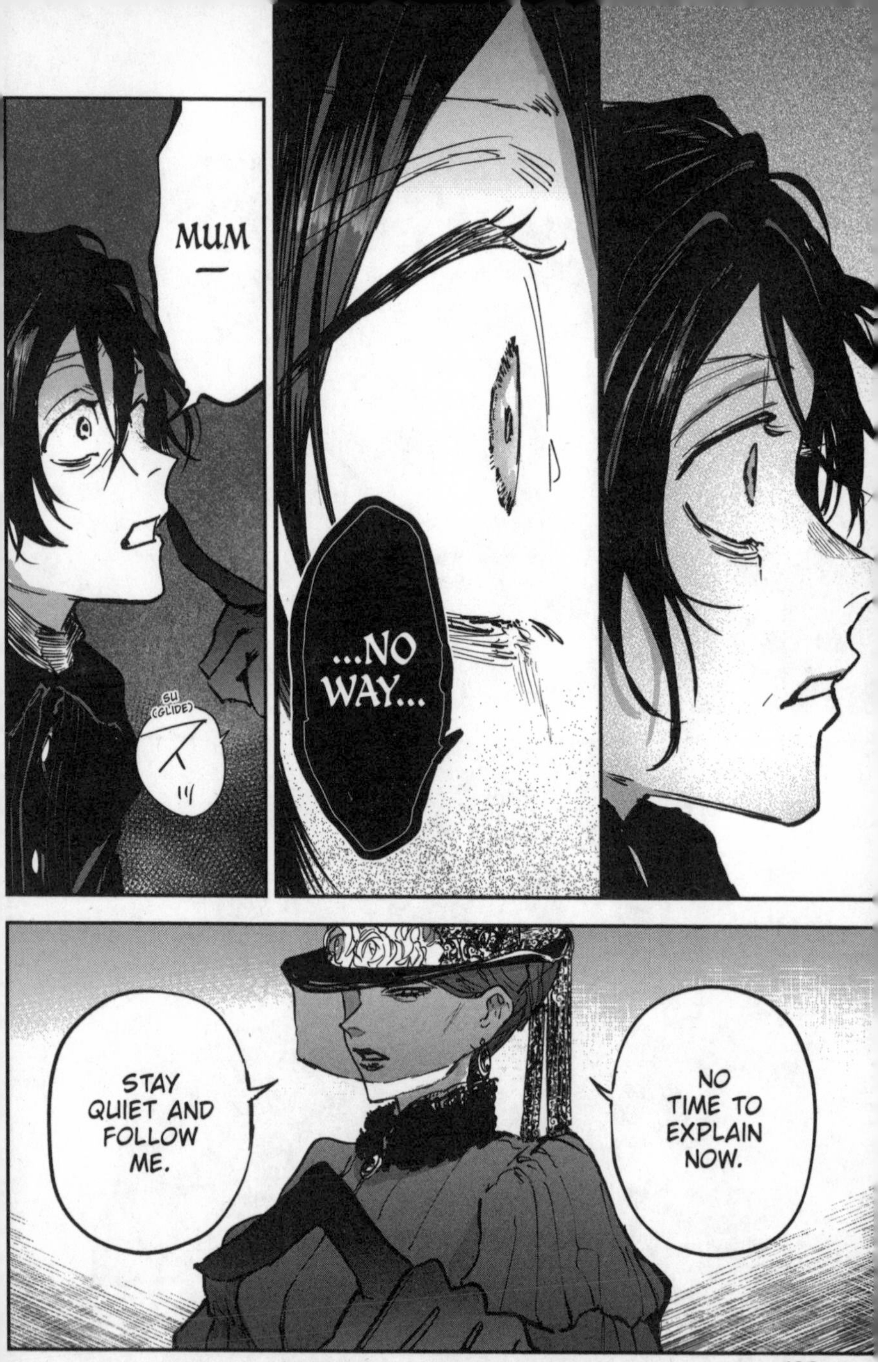
...NO WAY...
MUM—
SU (GLIDE)
NO TIME TO EXPLAIN NOW.
STAY QUIET AND FOLLOW ME.

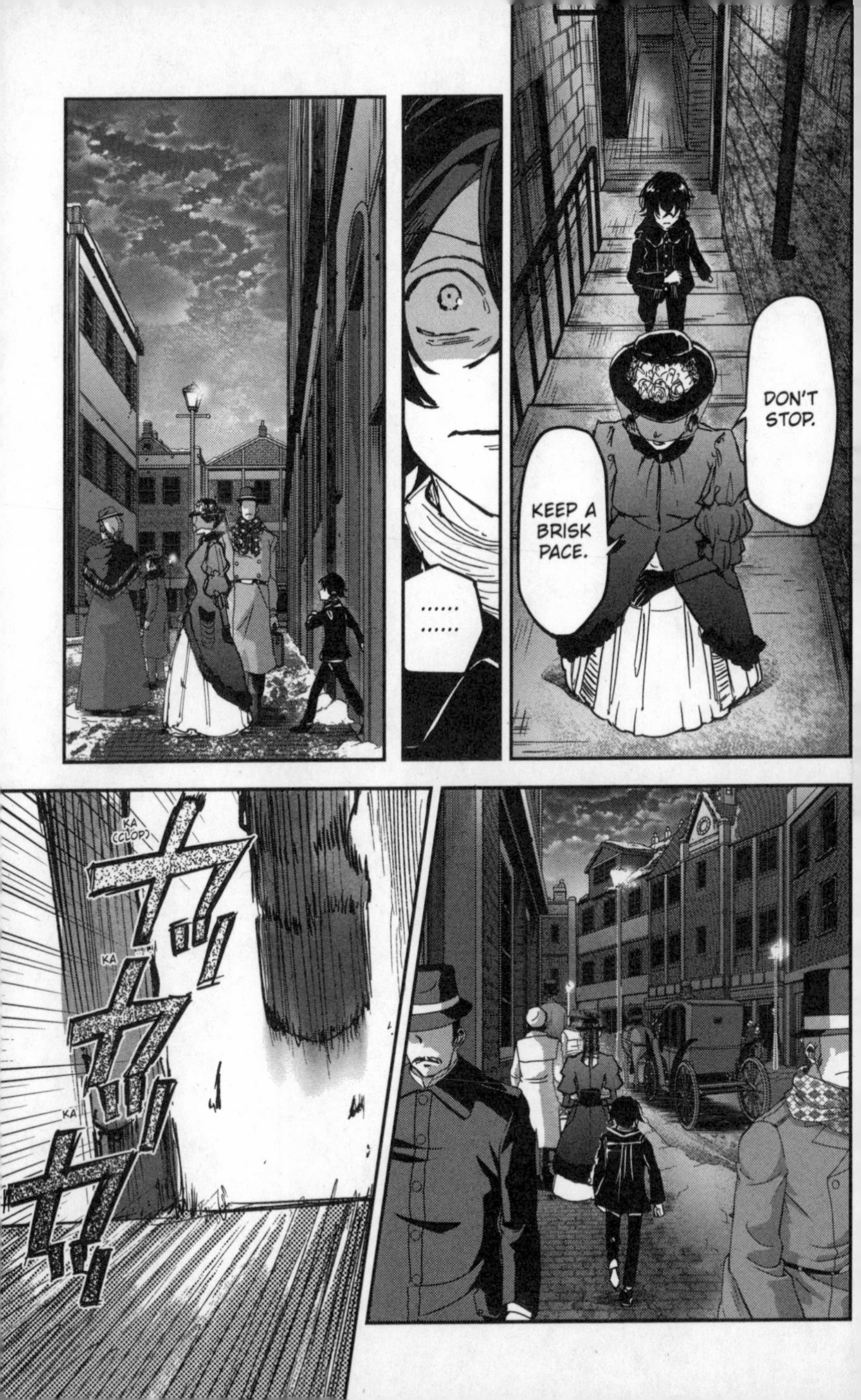
DON'T STOP.
KEEP A BRISK PACE.
......
......
KA (CLOP)
KA
KA

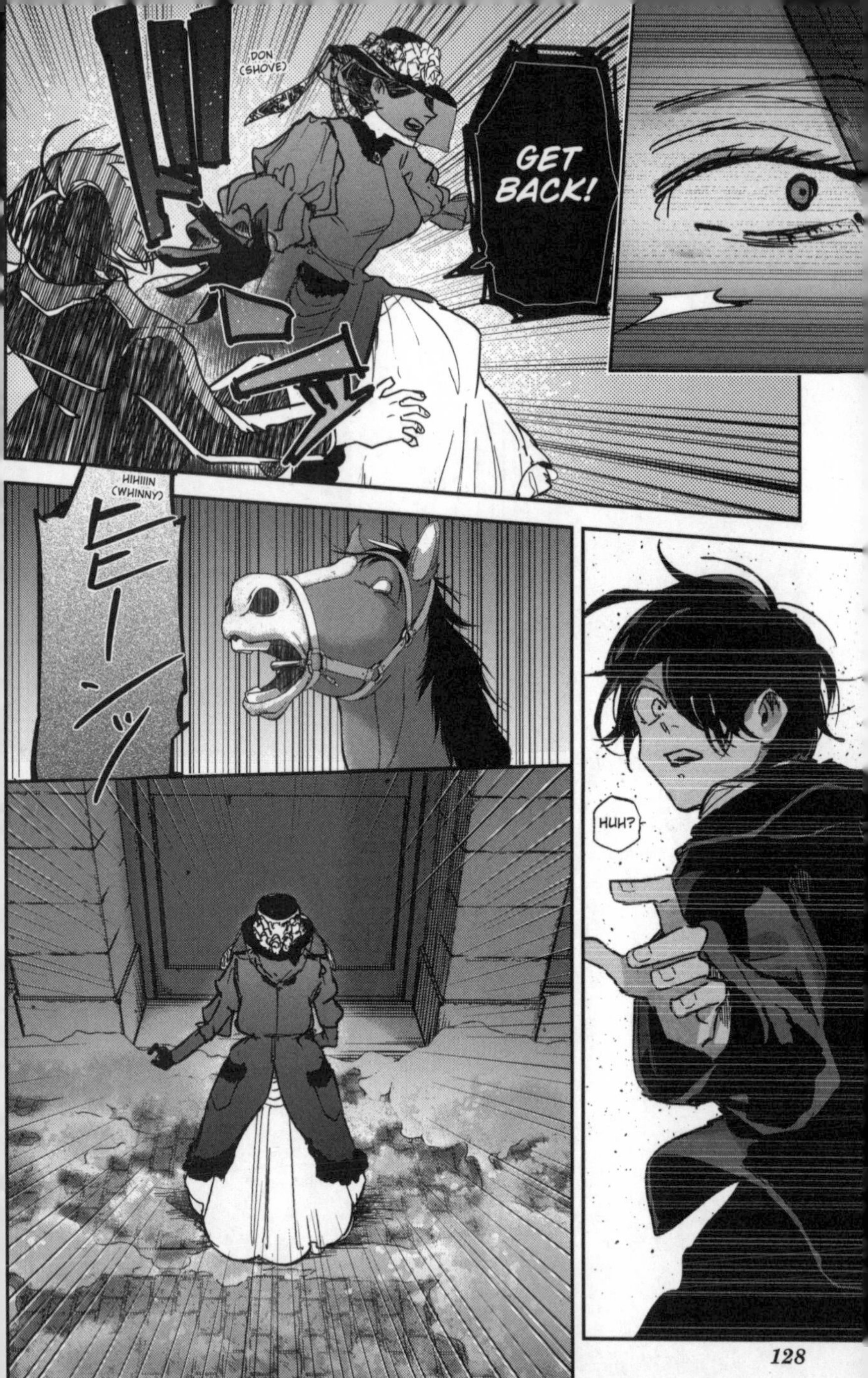
DON
(SHOVE)
GET BACK!
HUH?
HIHIIIN
(WHINNY)
ヒヒーンッ

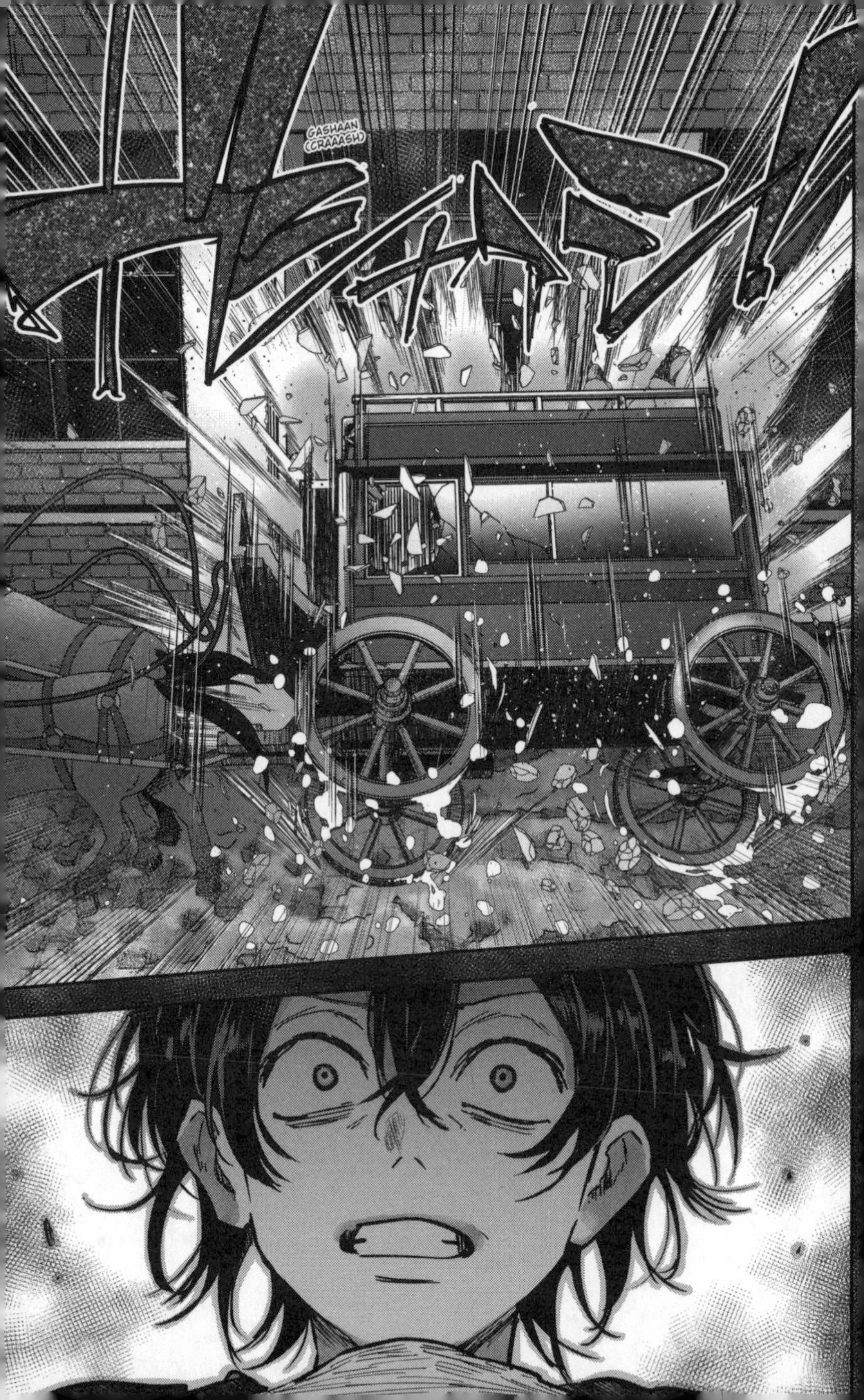
GASHAAN
(CRAAASH)

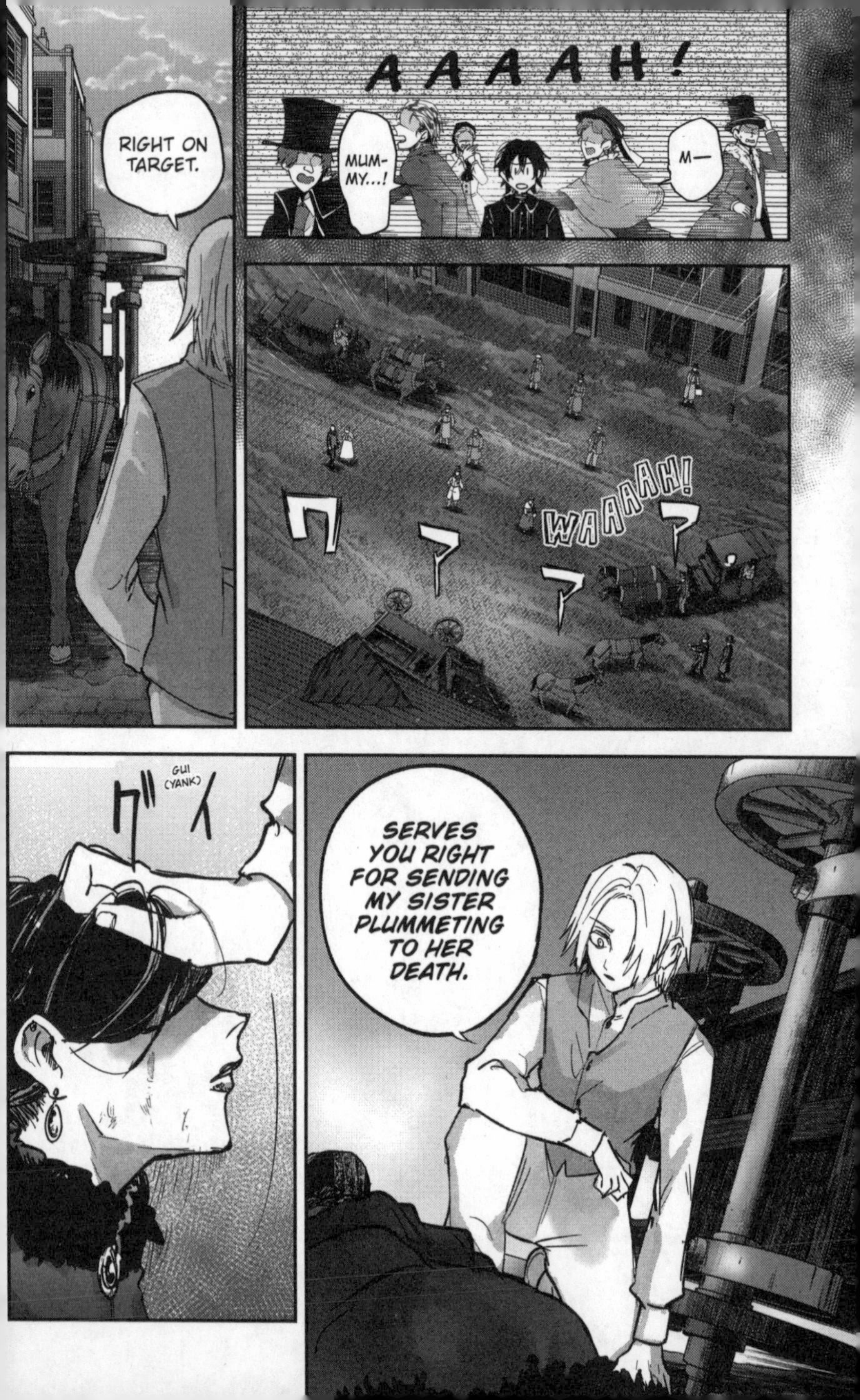
AAAAH!
M—
MUM-MY...!
WAAAAH!
RIGHT ON TARGET.
SERVES YOU RIGHT FOR SENDING MY SISTER PLUMMETING TO HER DEATH.
GUI (YANK)

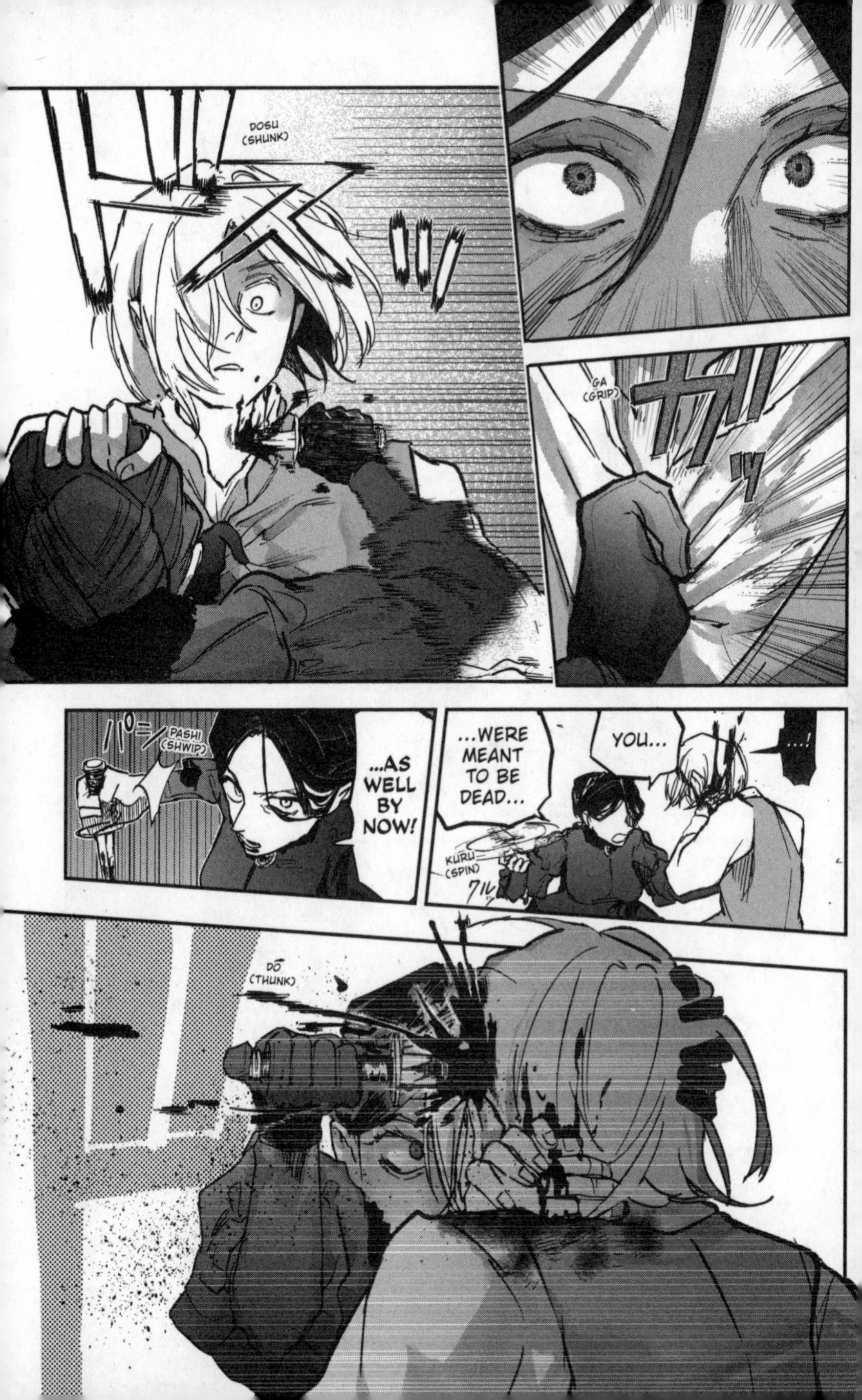
GA (GRIP)
DOSU (SHUNK)
...!
YOU...
...WERE MEANT TO BE DEAD...
KURU (SPIN)
PASHI (SHWIP)
...AS WELL BY NOW!
DO (THUNK)

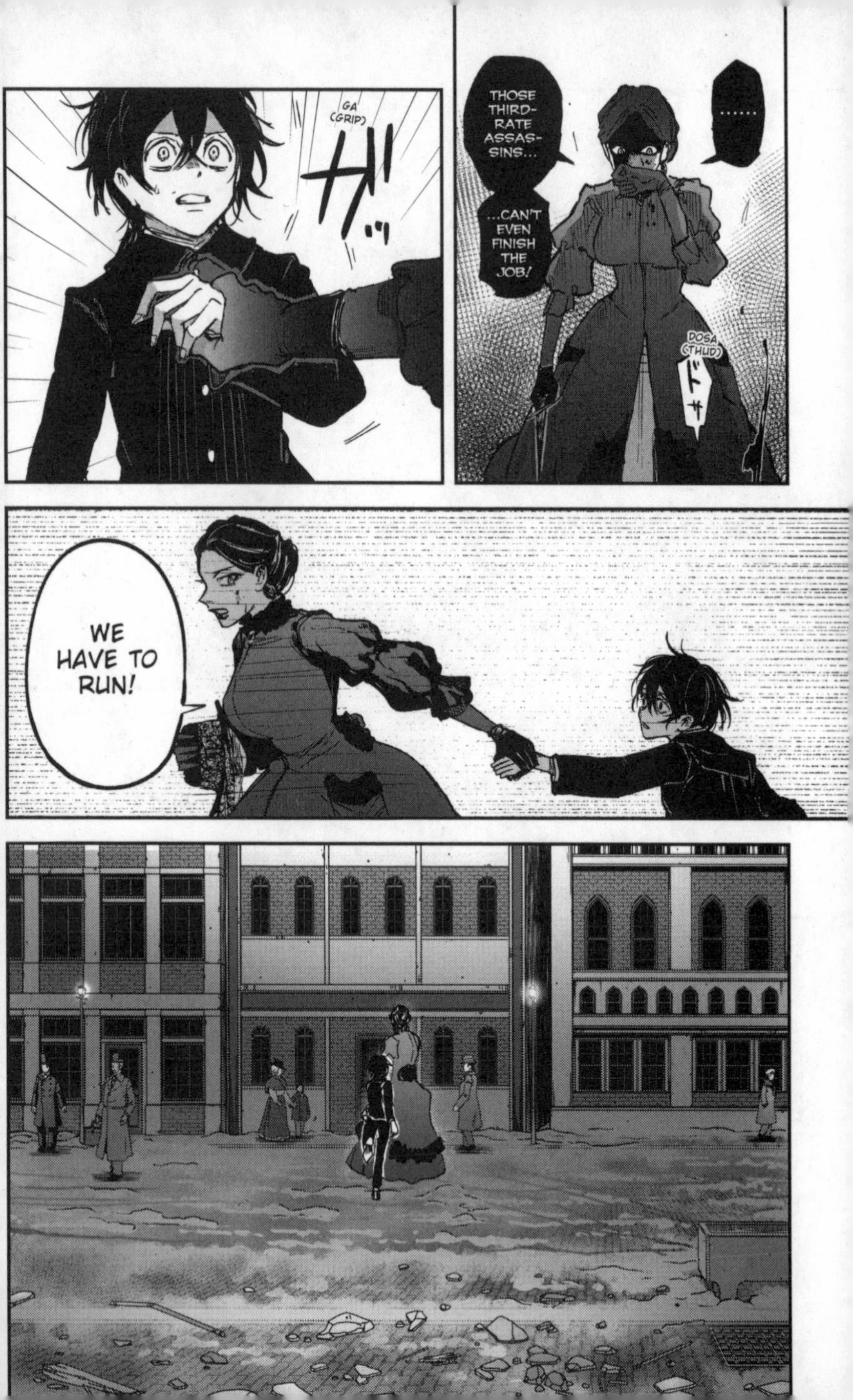

......
THOSE THIRD-RATE ASSASSINS...
...CAN'T EVEN FINISH THE JOB!
DOSA (THUD)
ドサ
GA (GRIP)
ガッ
WE HAVE TO RUN!

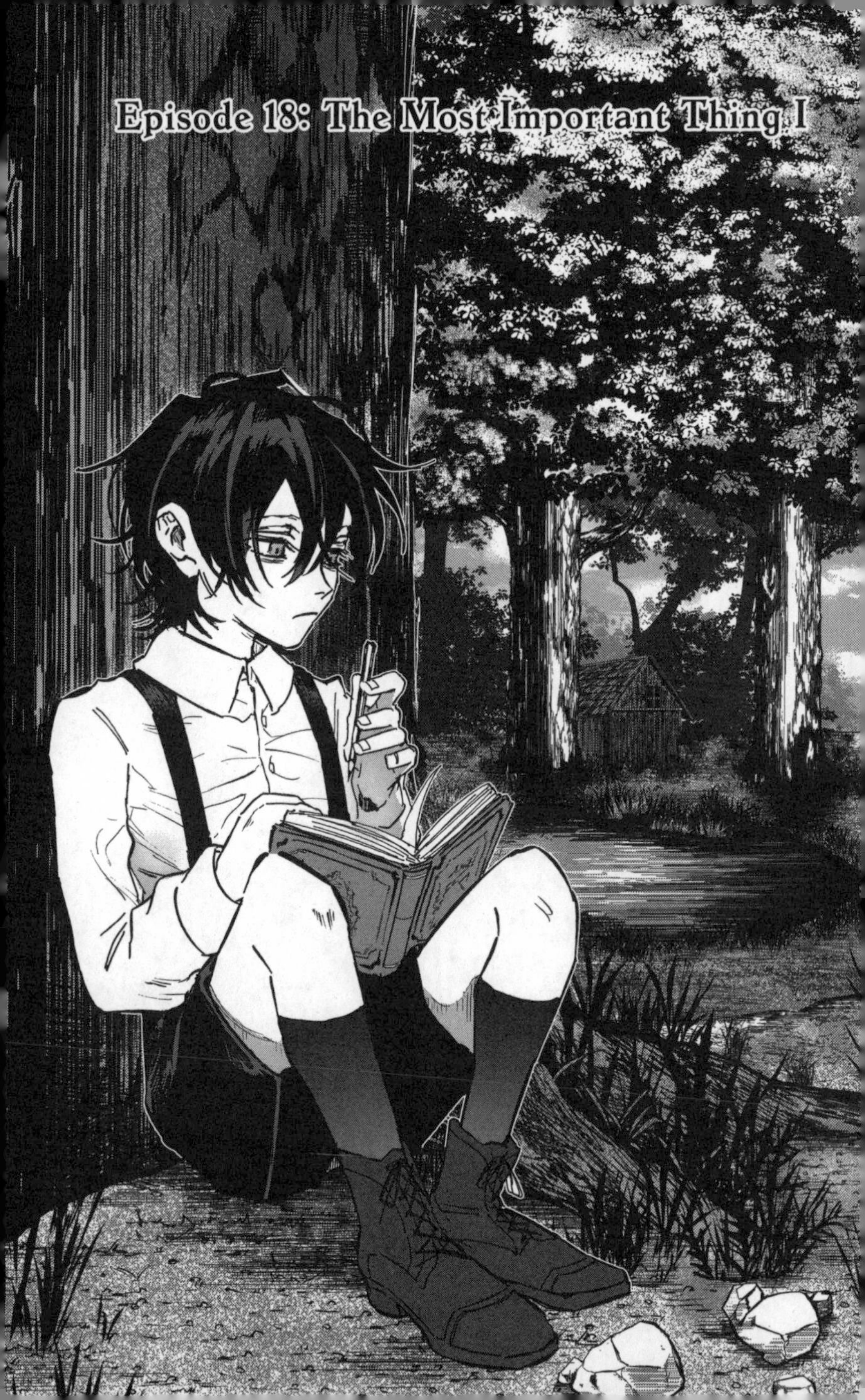
Episode 18: The Most Important Thing I

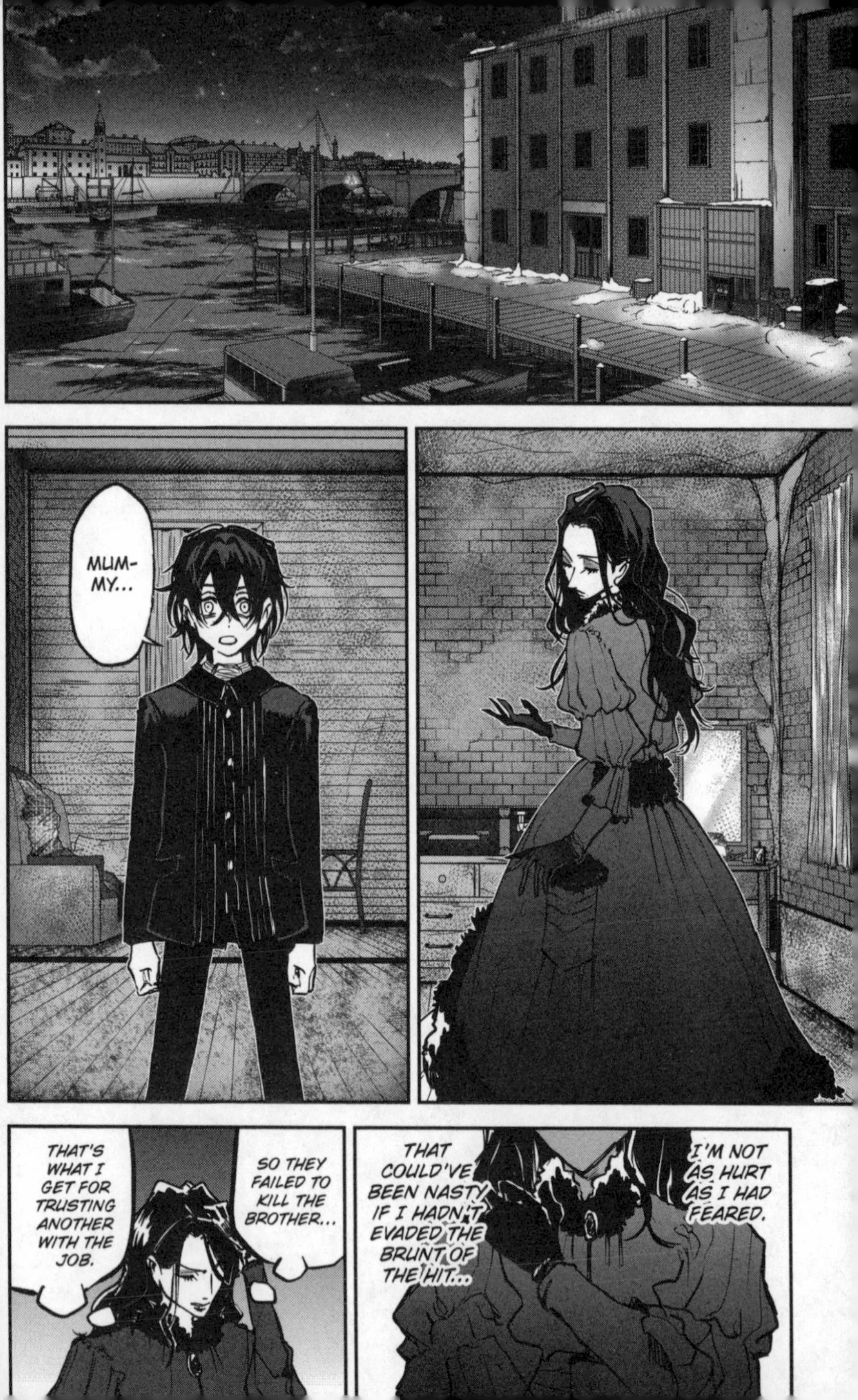
MUM-MY...
I'M NOT AS HURT AS I HAD FEARED.
THAT COULD'VE BEEN NASTY IF I HADN'T EVADED THE BRUNT OF THE HIT...
SO THEY FAILED TO KILL THE BROTHER...
THAT'S WHAT I GET FOR TRUSTING ANOTHER WITH THE JOB.

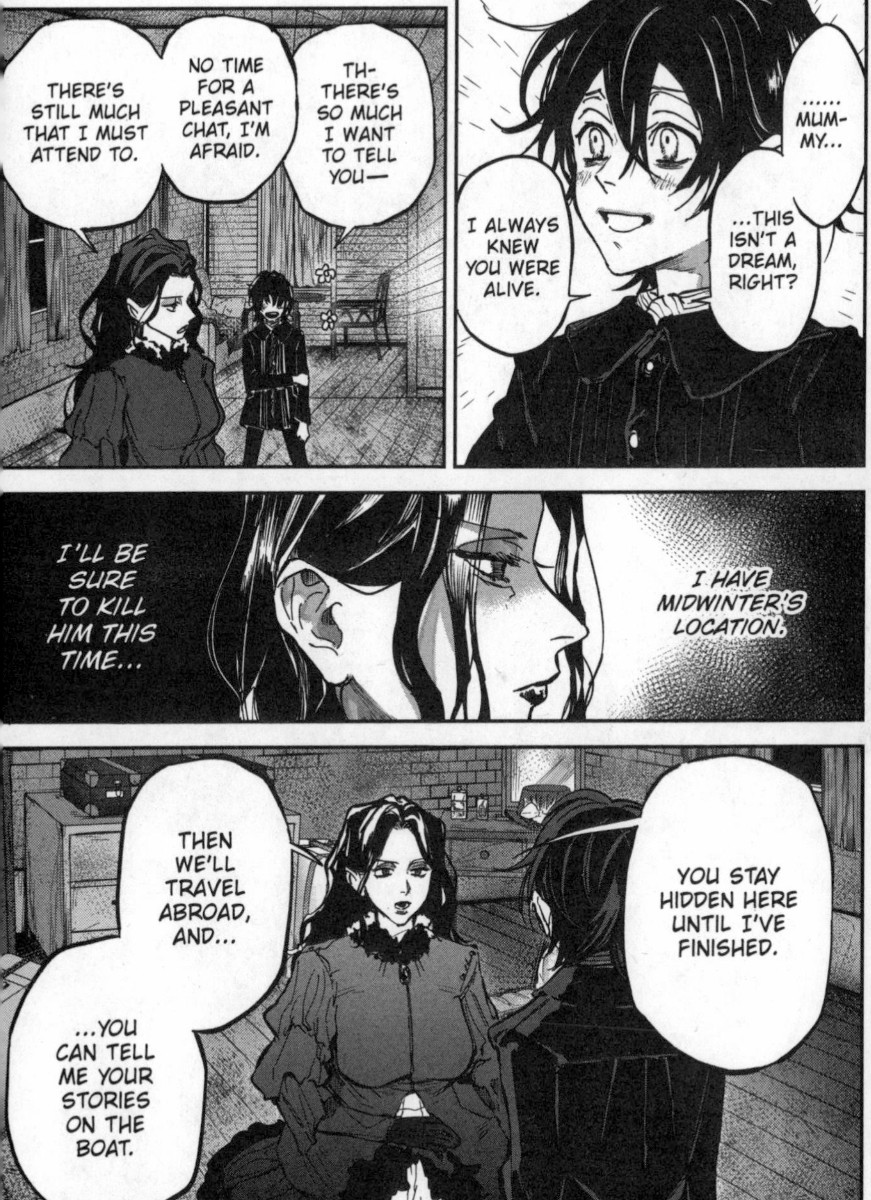
......MUMMY...
...THIS ISN'T A DREAM, RIGHT?
I ALWAYS KNEW YOU WERE ALIVE.
TH-THERE'S SO MUCH I WANT TO TELL YOU—
NO TIME FOR A PLEASANT CHAT, I'M AFRAID.
THERE'S STILL MUCH THAT I MUST ATTEND TO.
I HAVE MIDWINTER'S LOCATION.
I'LL BE SURE TO KILL HIM THIS TIME...
YOU STAY HIDDEN HERE UNTIL I'VE FINISHED.
THEN WE'LL TRAVEL ABROAD, AND...
...YOU CAN TELL ME YOUR STORIES ON THE BOAT.

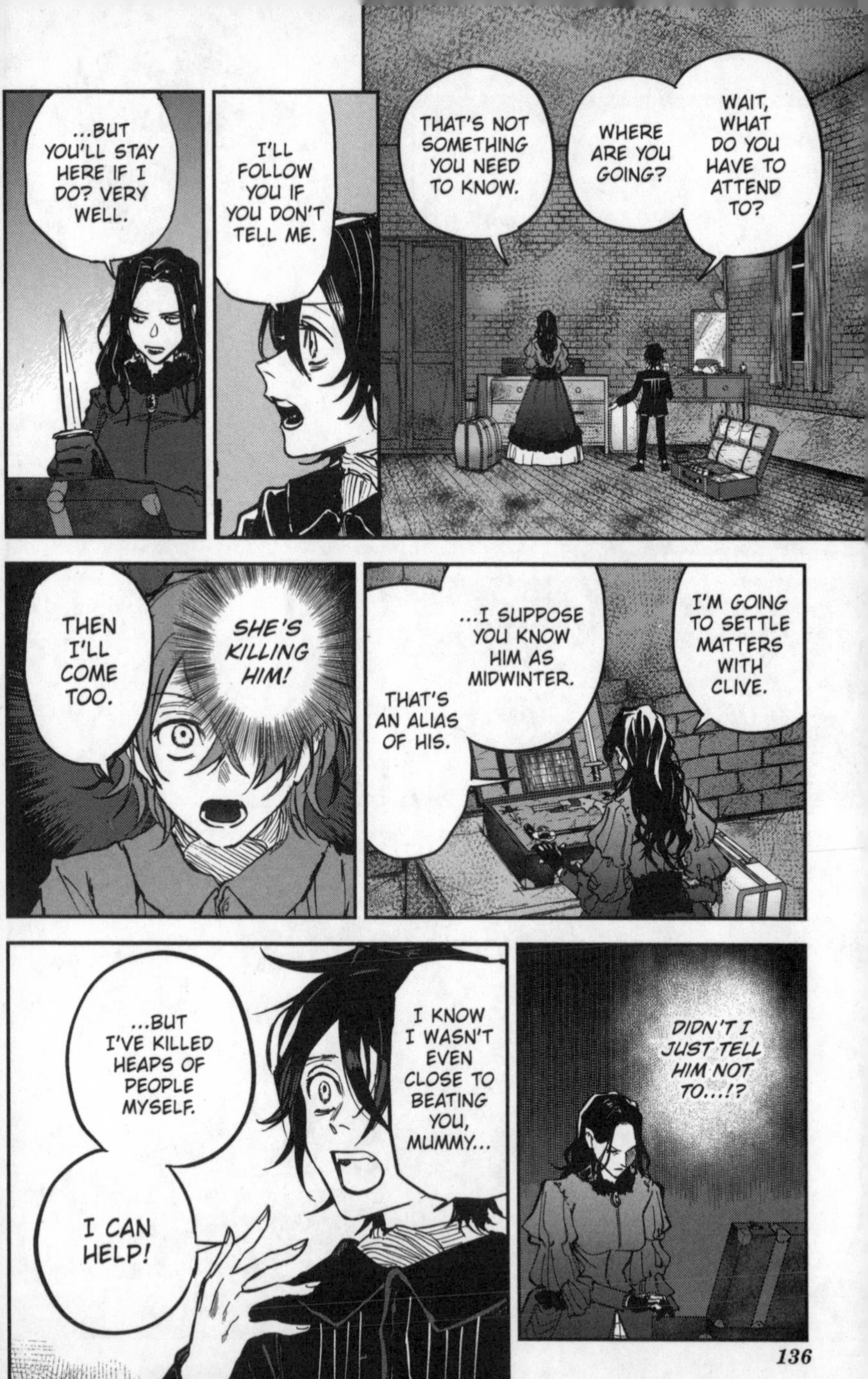
WAIT, WHAT DO YOU HAVE TO ATTEND TO?
WHERE ARE YOU GOING?
THAT'S NOT SOMETHING YOU NEED TO KNOW.
I'LL FOLLOW YOU IF YOU DON'T TELL ME.
...BUT YOU'LL STAY HERE IF I DO? VERY WELL.
I'M GOING TO SETTLE MATTERS WITH CLIVE.
...I SUPPOSE YOU KNOW HIM AS MIDWINTER.
THAT'S AN ALIAS OF HIS.
SHE'S KILLING HIM!
THEN I'LL COME TOO.
DIDN'T I JUST TELL HIM NOT TO...!?
I KNOW I WASN'T EVEN CLOSE TO BEATING YOU, MUMMY...
...BUT I'VE KILLED HEAPS OF PEOPLE MYSELF.
I CAN HELP!

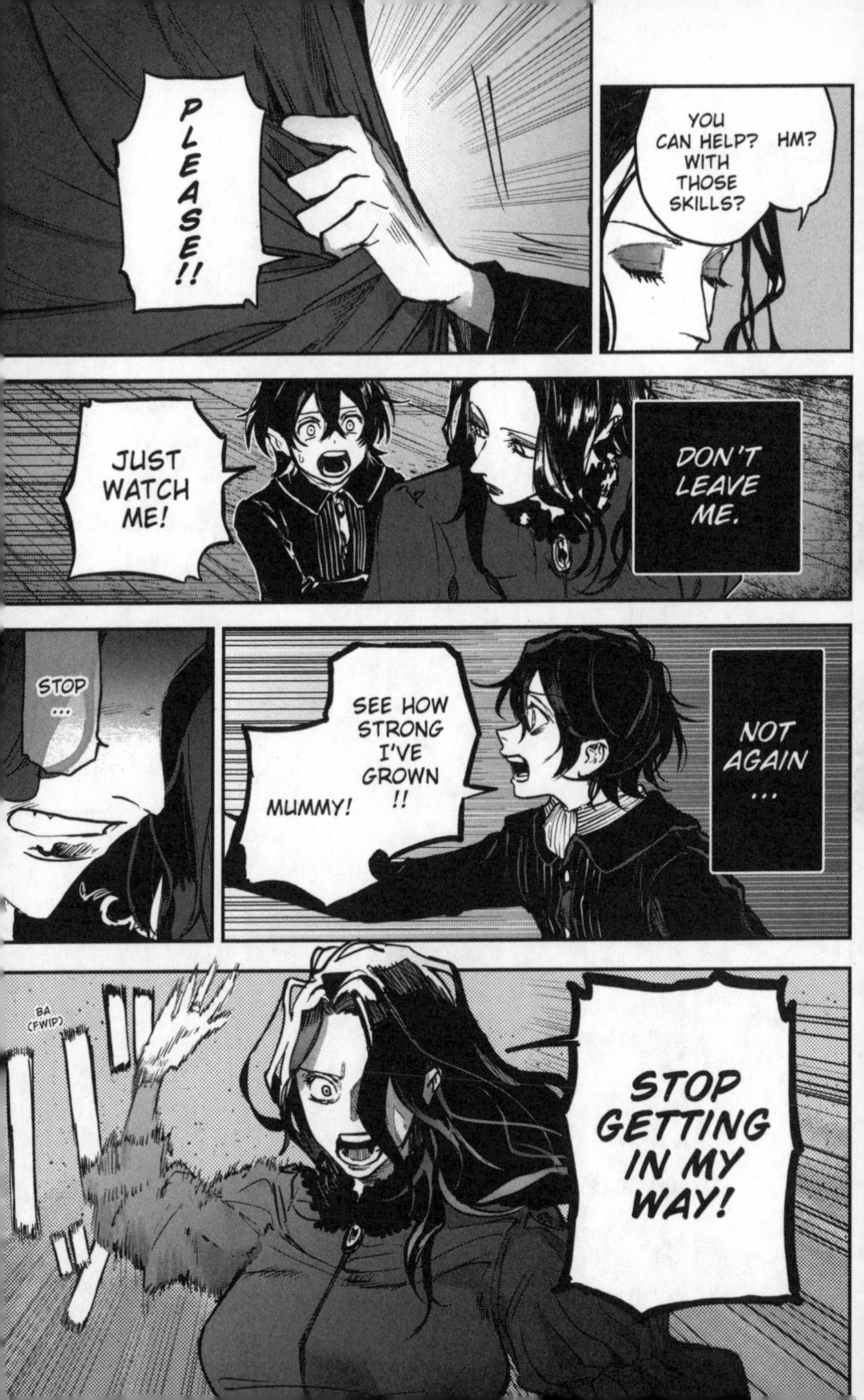
YOU CAN HELP? HM? WITH THOSE SKILLS?
PLEASE!!
DON'T LEAVE ME.
JUST WATCH ME!
NOT AGAIN...
SEE HOW STRONG I'VE GROWN!!
MUMMY!
STOP...
STOP GETTING IN MY WAY!
BA (FWIP)

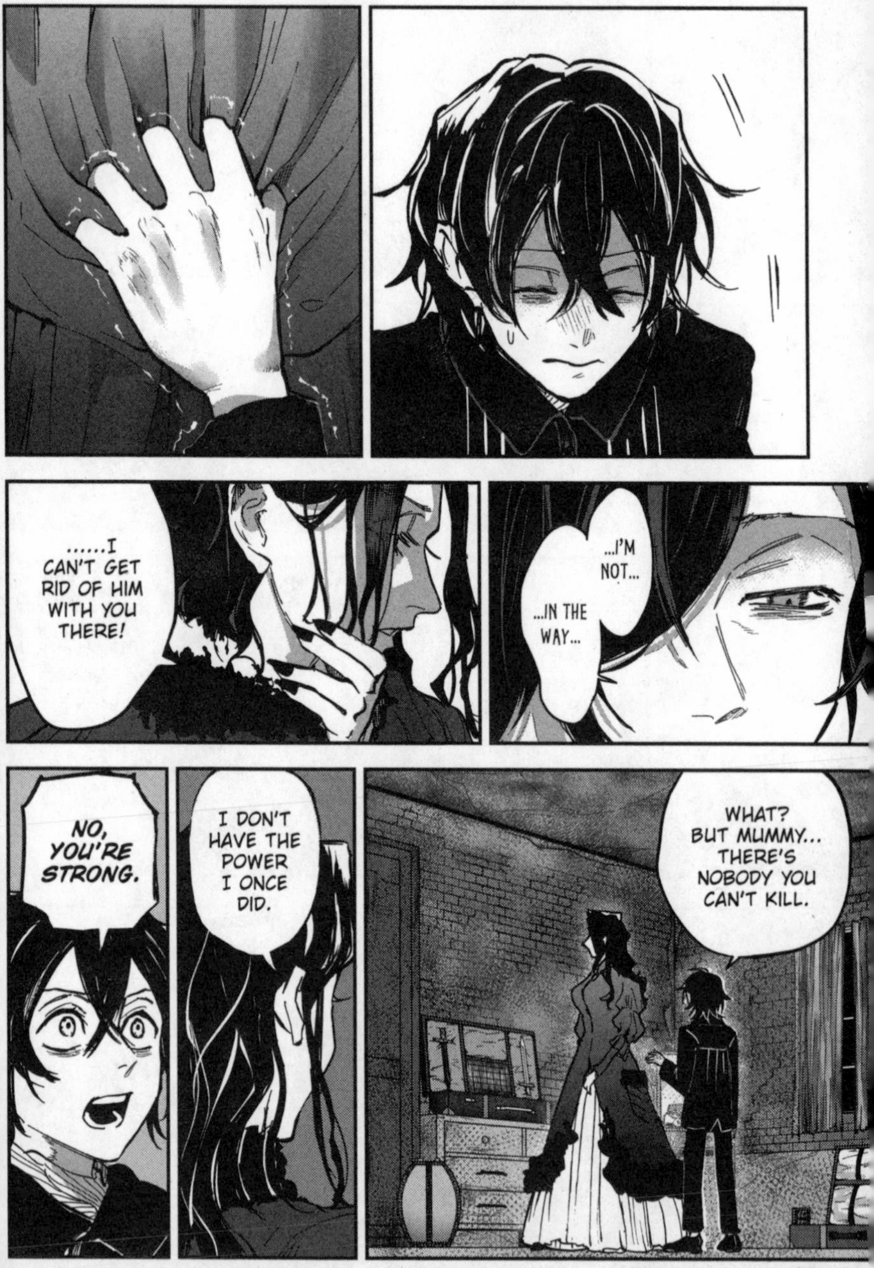
...I'M NOT...
...IN THE WAY...
......I CAN'T GET RID OF HIM WITH YOU THERE!
WHAT? BUT MUMMY... THERE'S NOBODY YOU CAN'T KILL.
I DON'T HAVE THE POWER I ONCE DID.
NO, YOU'RE STRONG.

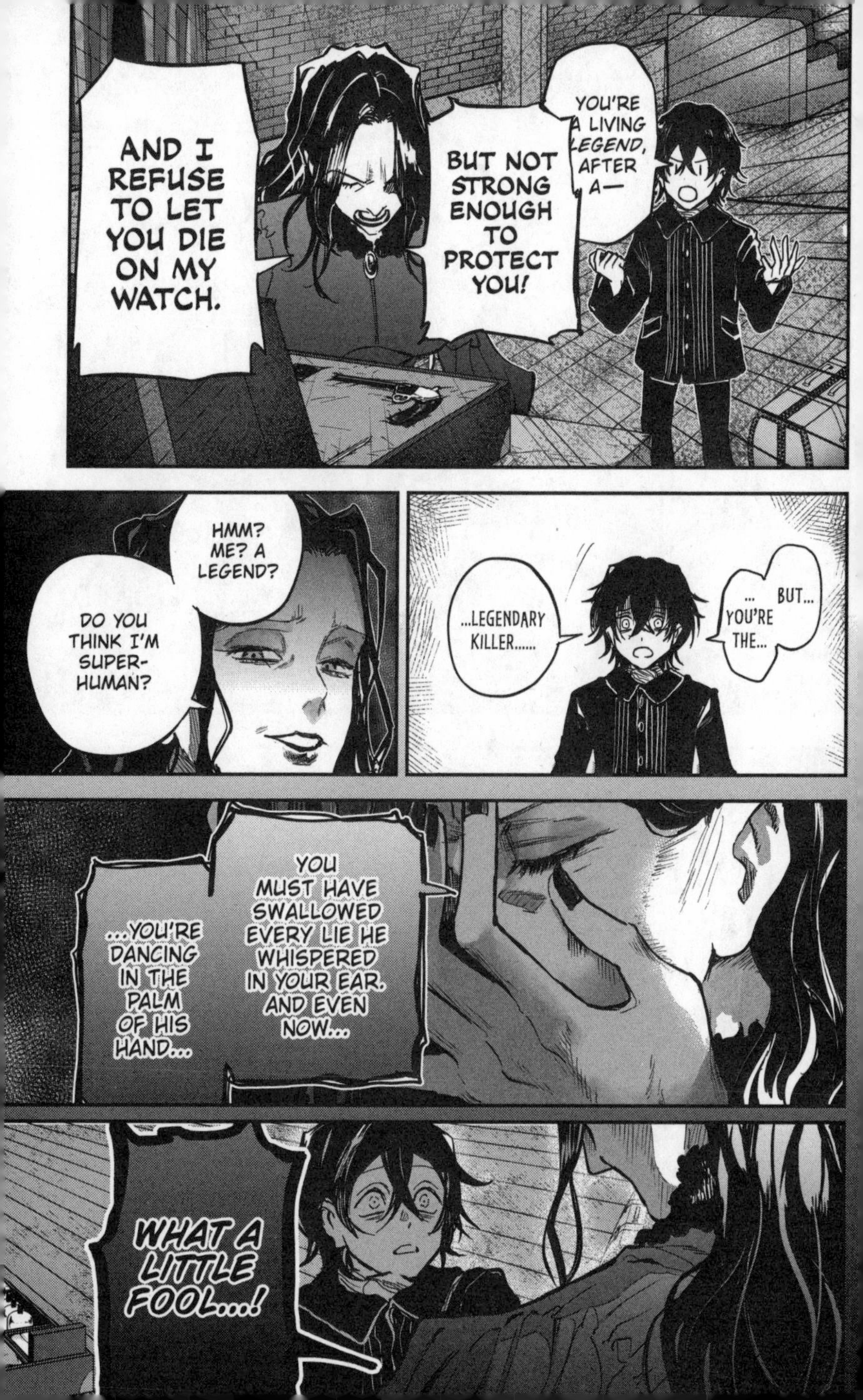
YOU'RE A LIVING LEGEND, AFTER A—
BUT NOT STRONG ENOUGH TO PROTECT YOU!
AND I REFUSE TO LET YOU DIE ON MY WATCH.
... BUT... YOU'RE THE...
...LEGENDARY KILLER......
HMM? ME? A LEGEND?
DO YOU THINK I'M SUPER-HUMAN?
YOU MUST HAVE SWALLOWED EVERY LIE HE WHISPERED IN YOUR EAR. AND EVEN NOW...
...YOU'RE DANCING IN THE PALM OF HIS HAND...
WHAT A LITTLE FOOL...!

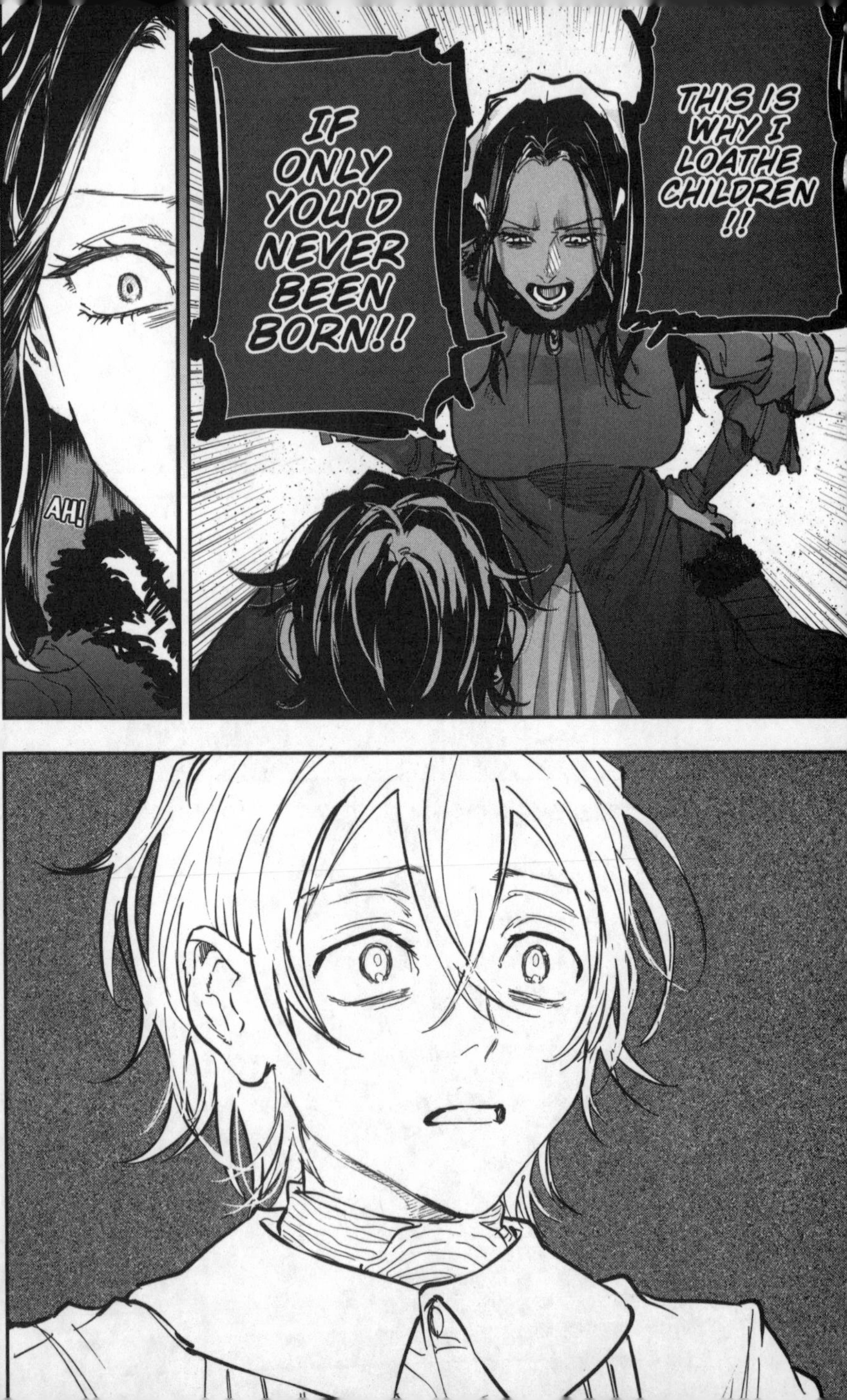
THIS IS WHY I LOATHE CHILDREN!!
IF ONLY YOU'D NEVER BEEN BORN!!
AH!

I...

...I-
I...

... JUST ...

THIS WON'T DO...

ONCE HE'S STANDING RIGHT THERE IN FRONT OF ME, I HAVEN'T THE FAINTEST IDEA HOW TO INTERACT WITH HIM...

... WHAT'S WITH THAT FACE?

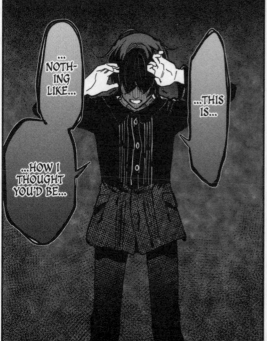

...NOTH-ING LIKE...

...THIS IS...

...HOW I THOUGHT YOU'D BE...

WHAT?

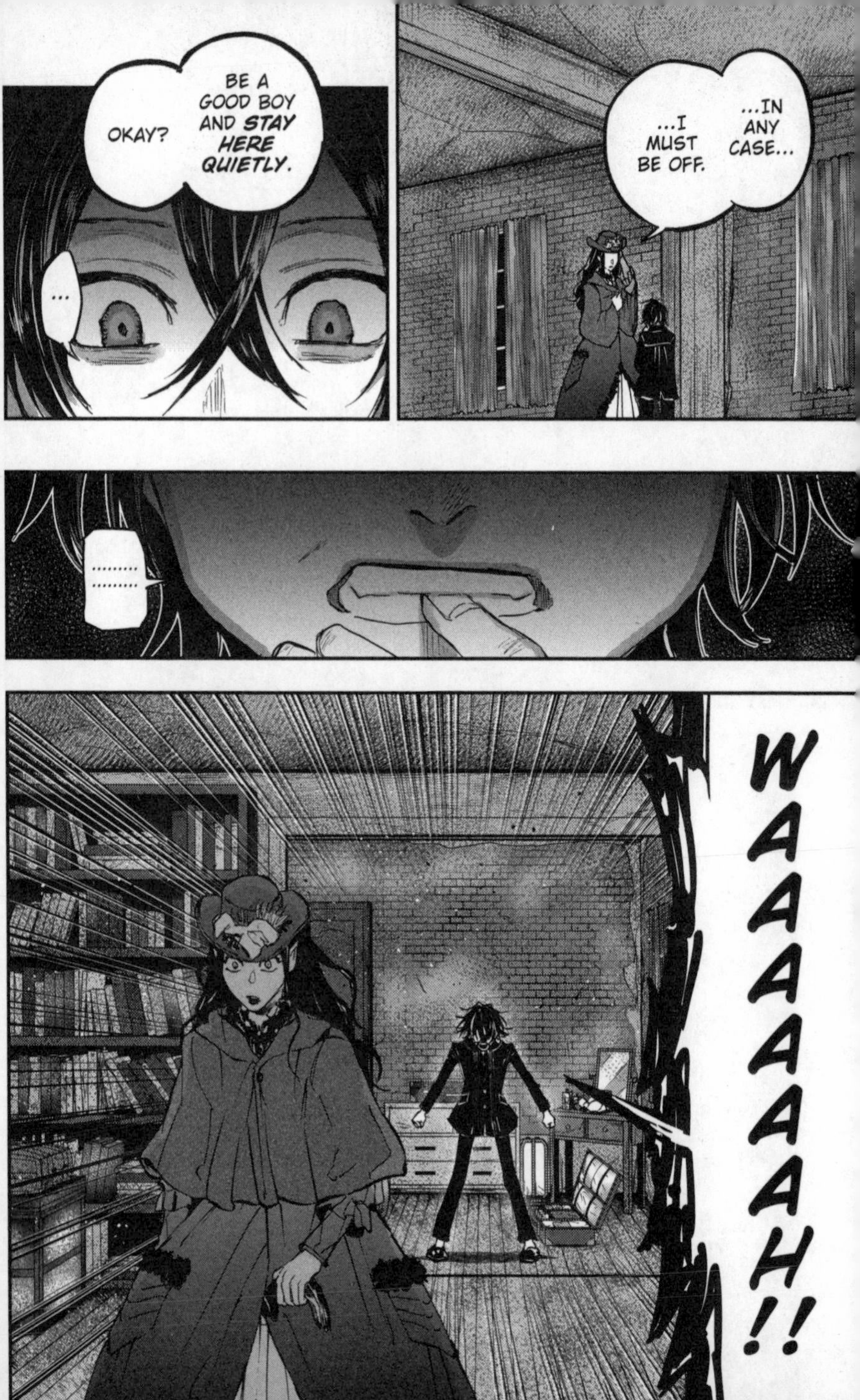
...IN ANY CASE...
...I MUST BE OFF.
BE A GOOD BOY AND STAY HERE QUIETLY.
OKAY?
...
....
....
WAAAAAAH!!

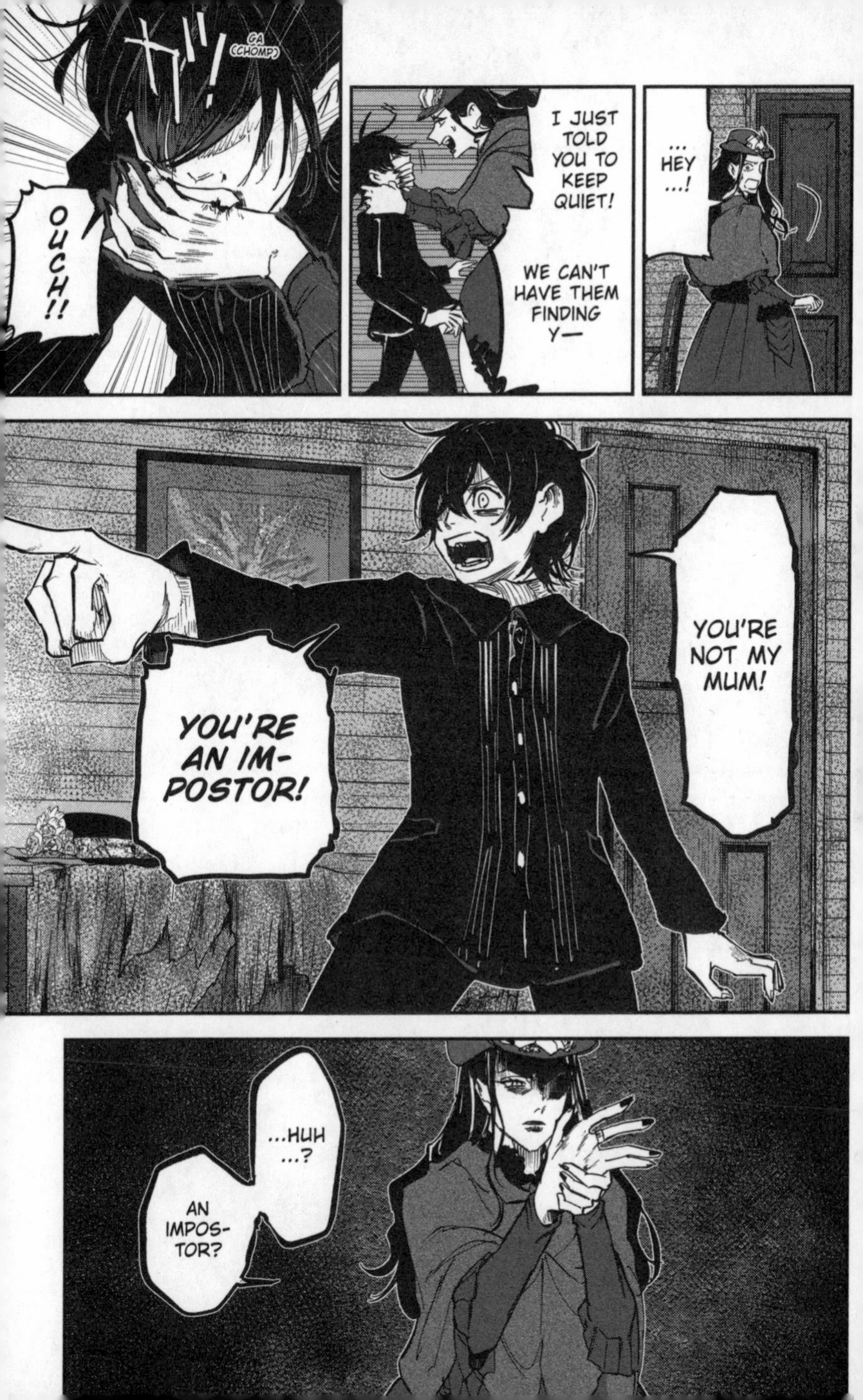
...HEY ...!
I JUST TOLD YOU TO KEEP QUIET!
WE CAN'T HAVE THEM FINDING Y—
GA (CHOMP)
OUCH!!
YOU'RE NOT MY MUM!
YOU'RE AN IM-POSTOR!
...HUH ...?
AN IMPOS-TOR?

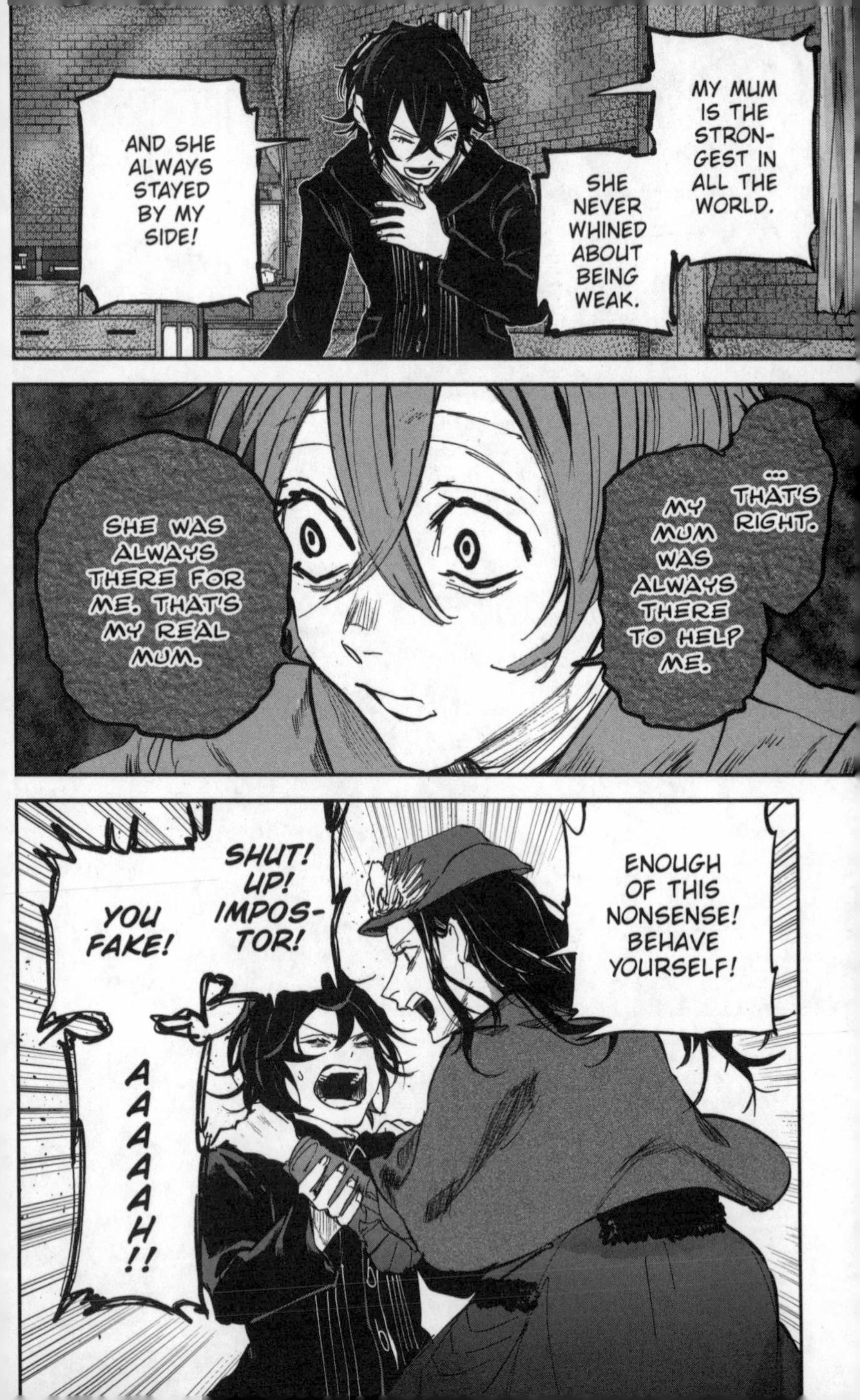
MY MUM IS THE STRON-GEST IN ALL THE WORLD.
SHE NEVER WHINED ABOUT BEING WEAK.
AND SHE ALWAYS STAYED BY MY SIDE!
...THAT'S RIGHT.
MY MUM WAS ALWAYS THERE TO HELP ME.
SHE WAS ALWAYS THERE FOR ME. THAT'S MY REAL MUM.
ENOUGH OF THIS NONSENSE! BEHAVE YOURSELF!
SHUT! UP! IMPOS-TOR!
YOU FAKE!
AAAAAAH!!

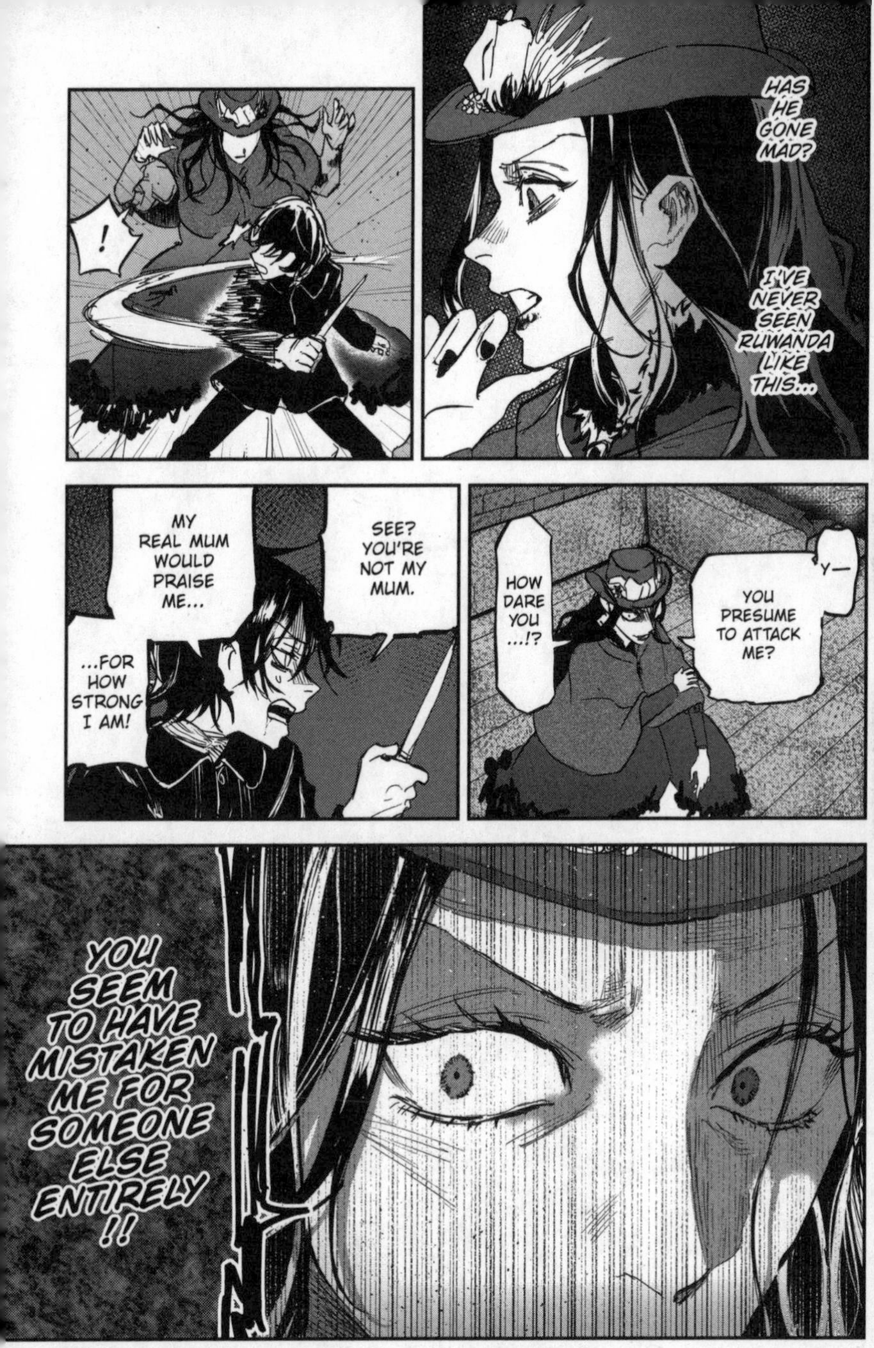
HAS HE GONE MAD?
I'VE NEVER SEEN RUWANDA LIKE THIS...
!
Y—
YOU PRESUME TO ATTACK ME?
HOW DARE YOU ...!?
SEE? YOU'RE NOT MY MUM.
MY REAL MUM WOULD PRAISE ME...
...FOR HOW STRONG I AM!
YOU SEEM TO HAVE MISTAKEN ME FOR SOMEONE ELSE ENTIRELY!!

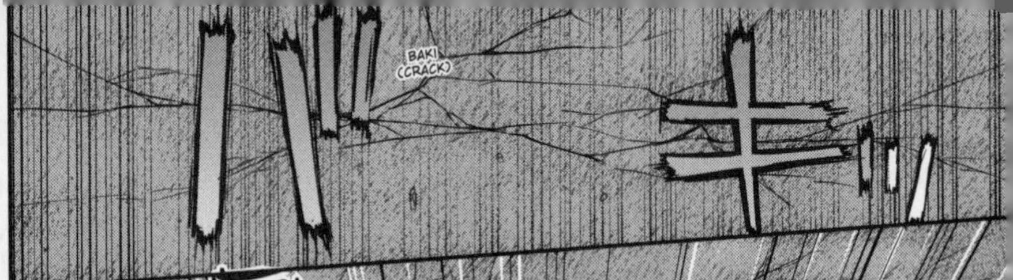
BAKI
(CRACK)
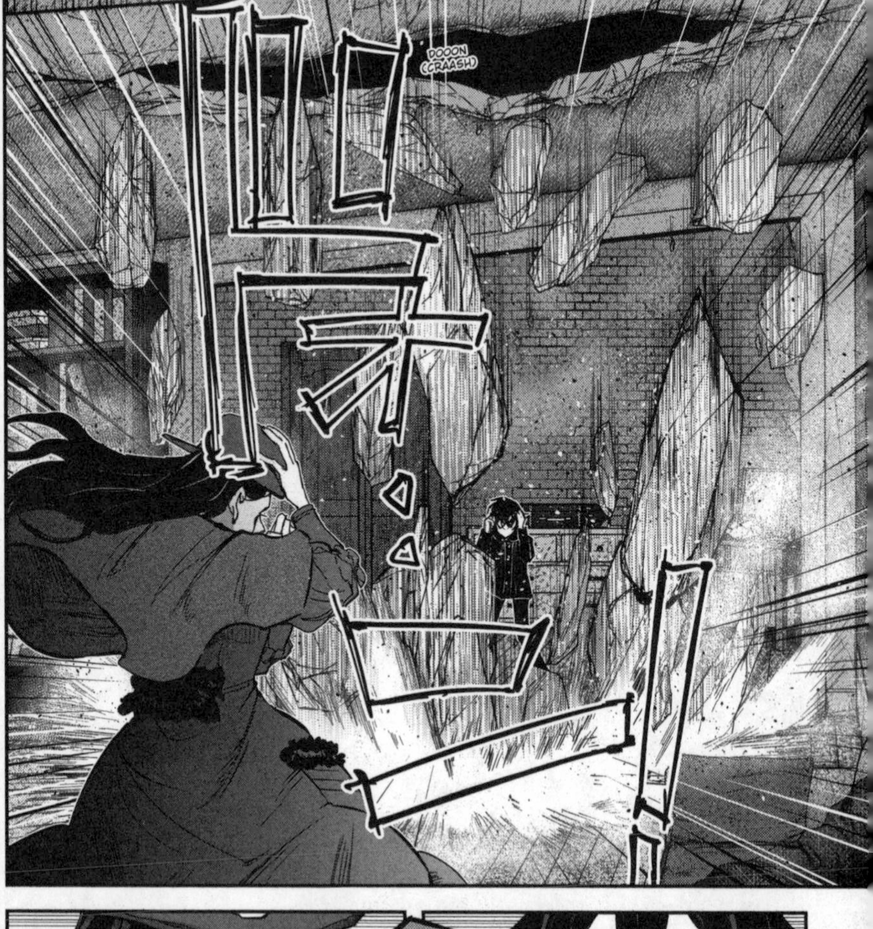
DOOON
(CRAASH)
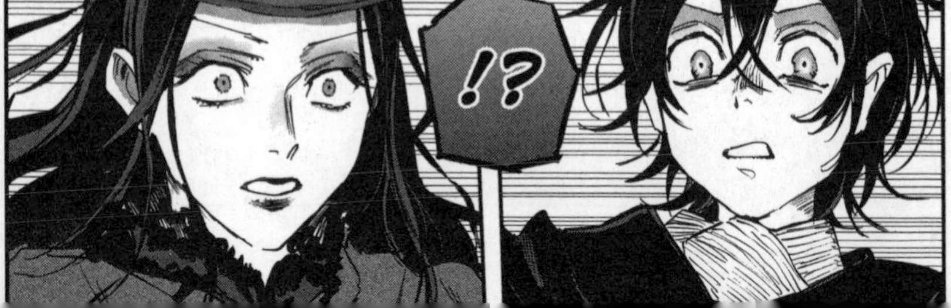
!?

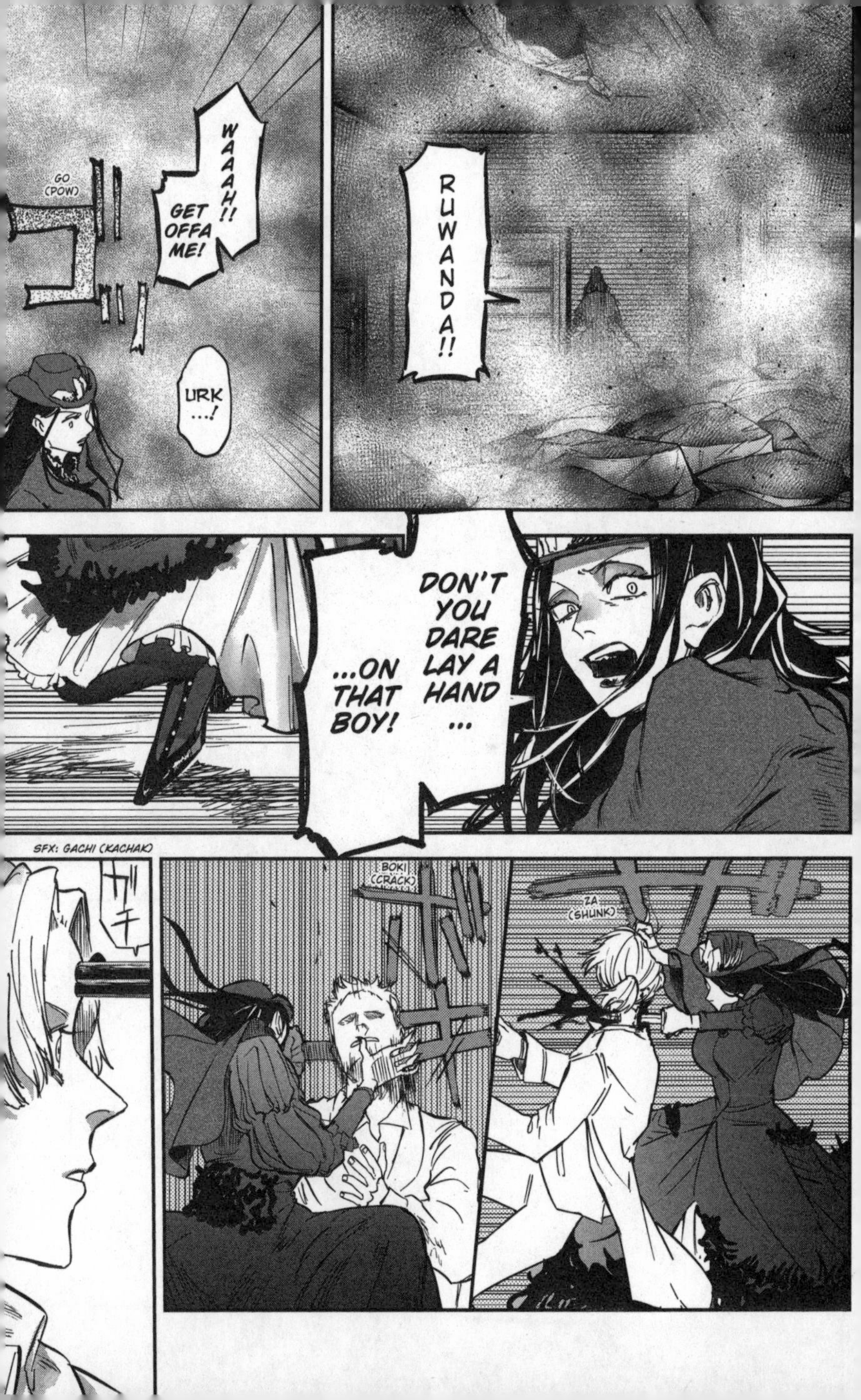
RUWANDA!!
WAAAAH!! GET OFFA ME!
GO (POW)
URK...!
DON'T YOU DARE LAY A HAND...
...ON THAT BOY!
ZA (SHUNK)
BOKI (CRACK)
SFX: GACHI (KACHAK)

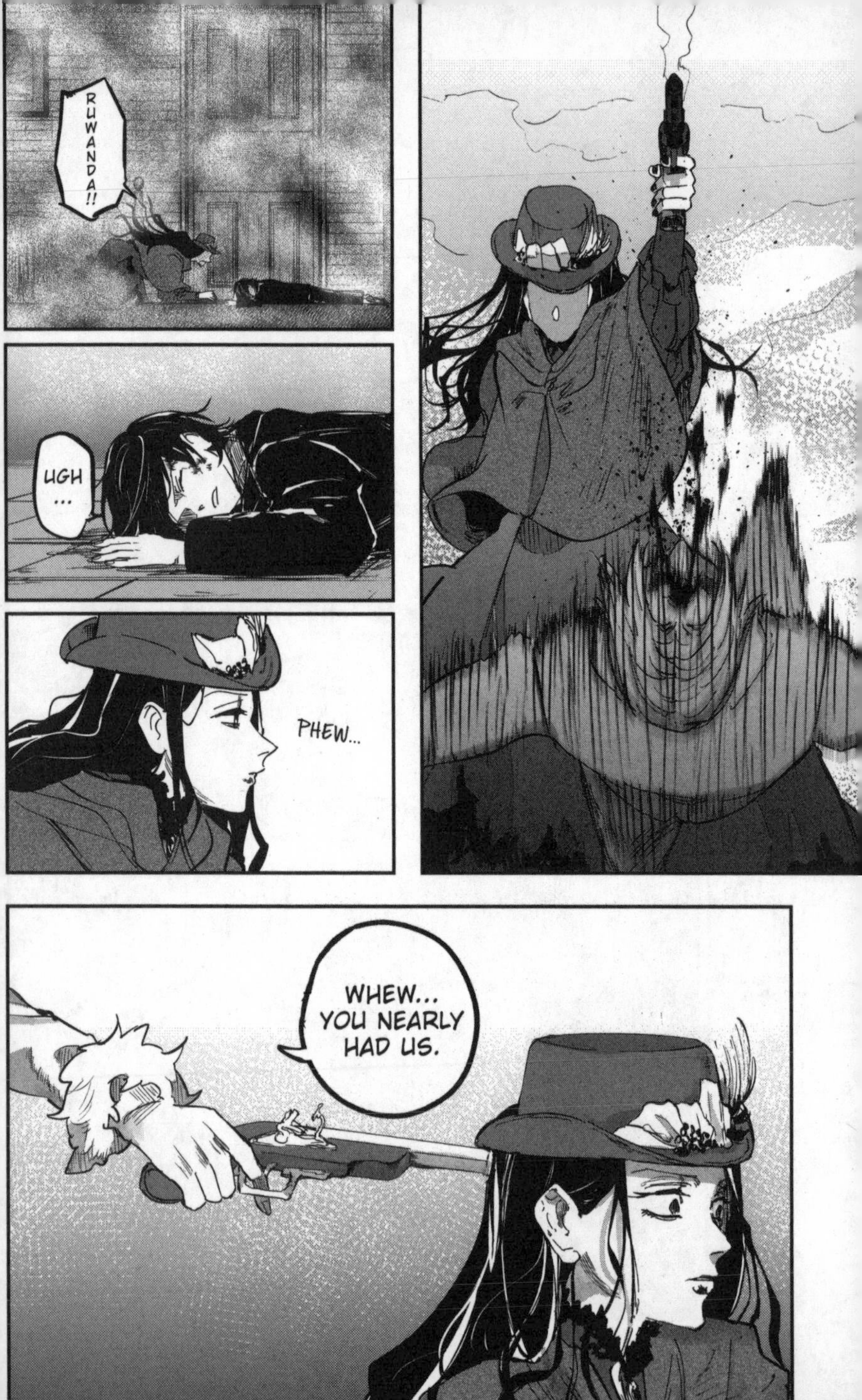
RUWANDA!!
UGH...
PHEW...
WHEW... YOU NEARLY HAD US.

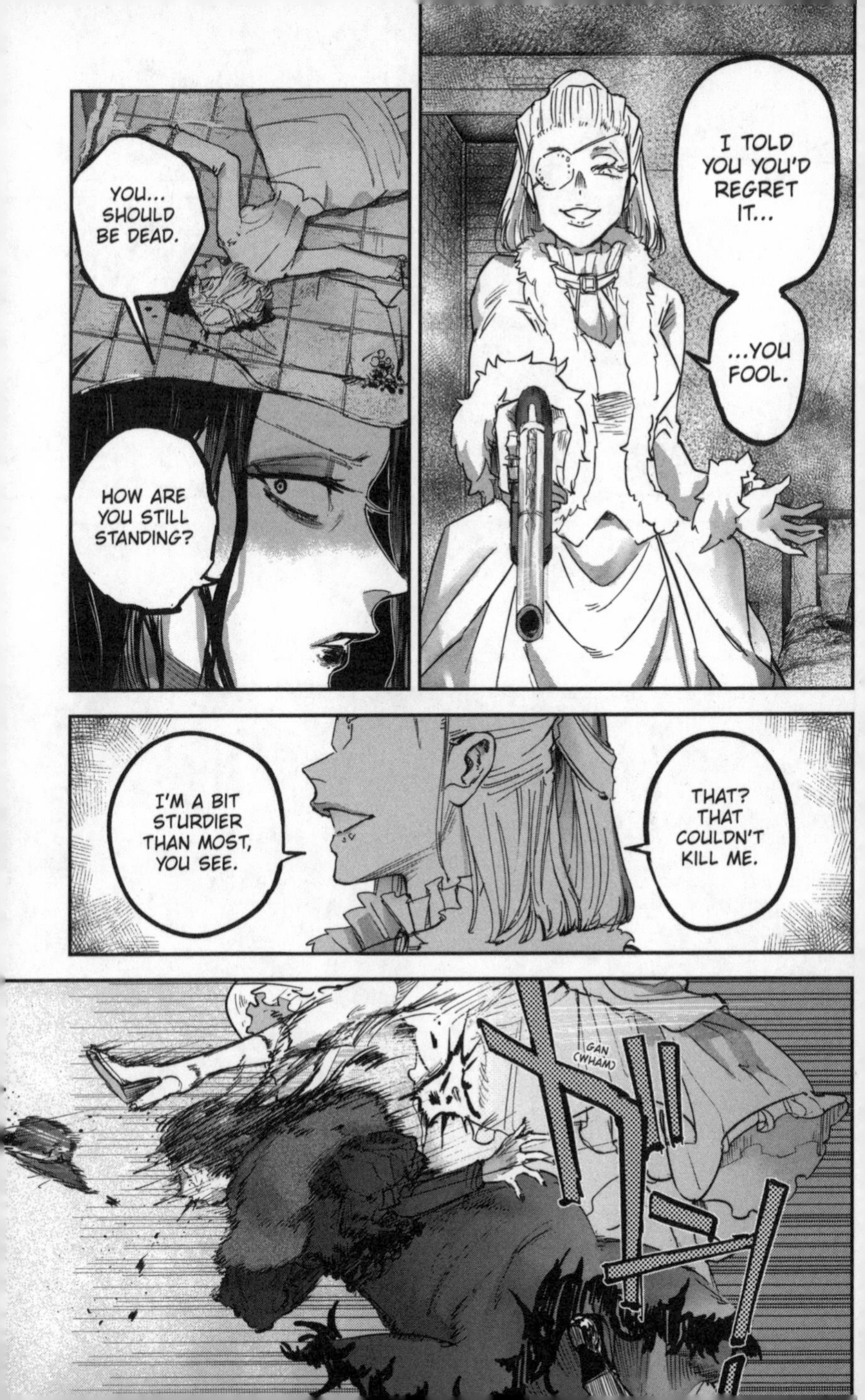
I TOLD YOU YOU'D REGRET IT...
...YOU FOOL.
YOU... SHOULD BE DEAD.
HOW ARE YOU STILL STANDING?
THAT? THAT COULDN'T KILL ME.
I'M A BIT STURDIER THAN MOST, YOU SEE.
GAN (WHAM)

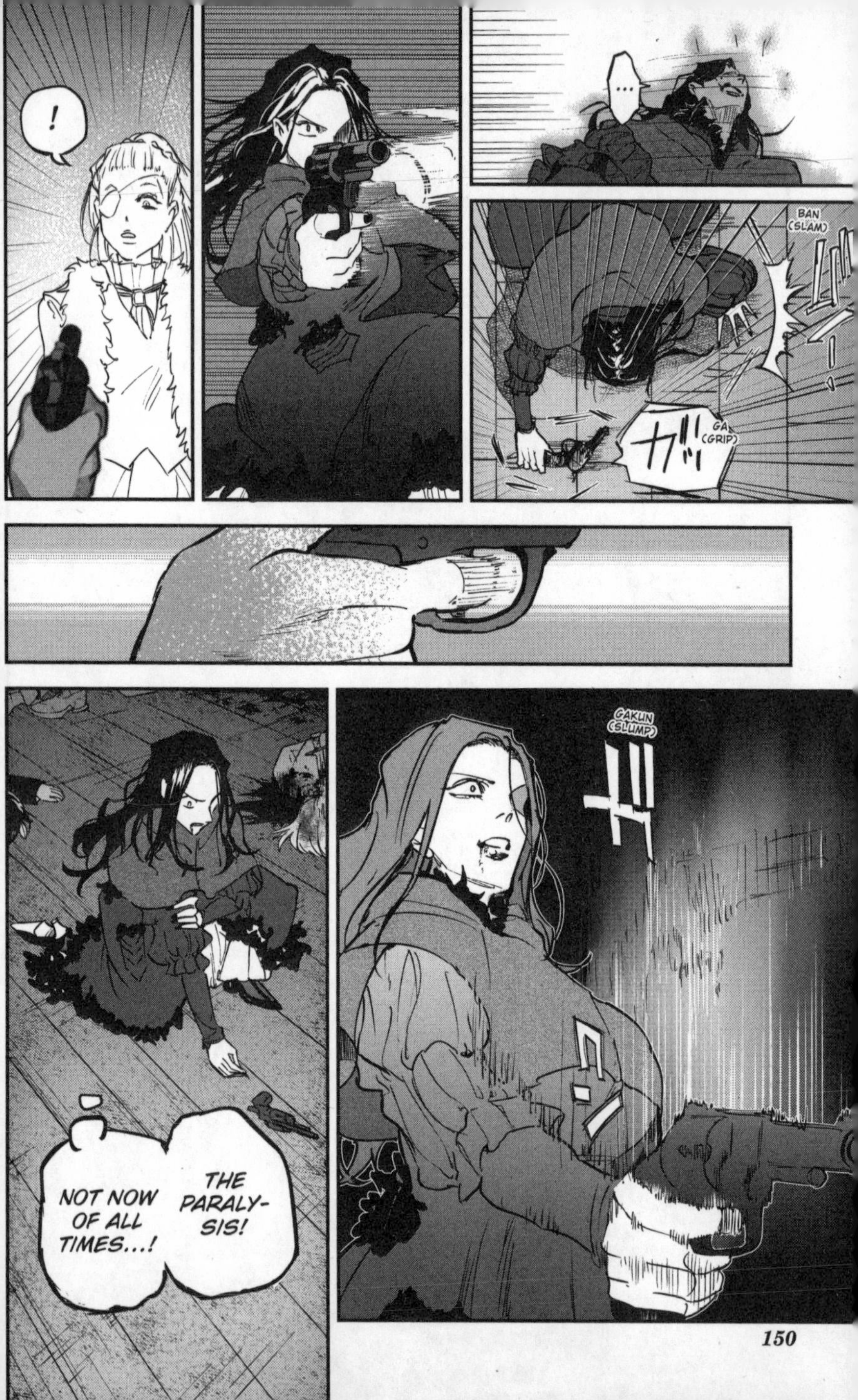
...
BAN (SLAM)
GA (GRIP)
!
GAKUN (SLUMP)
THE PARALY-SIS!
NOT NOW OF ALL TIMES...!

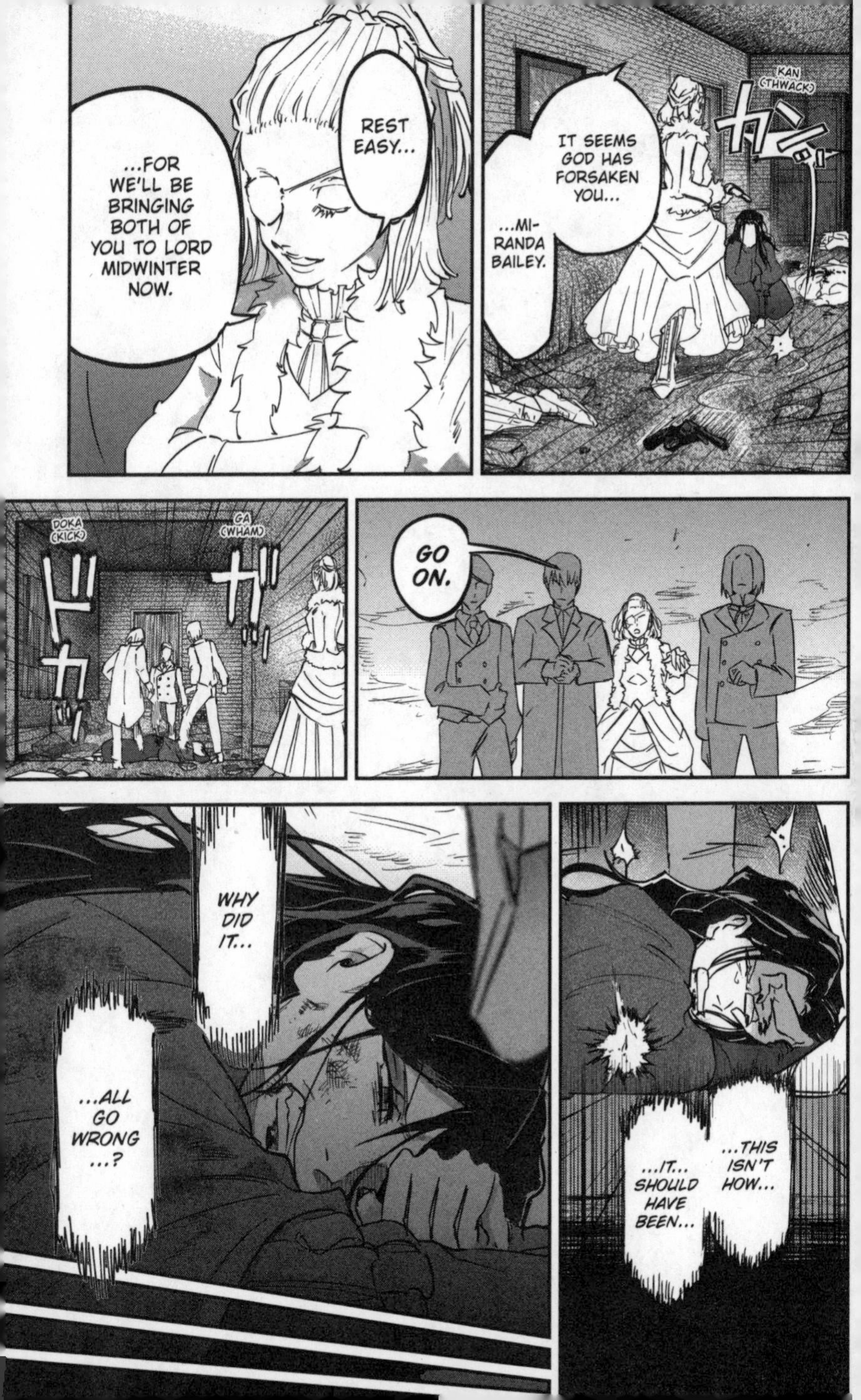
KAN (THWACK)
IT SEEMS GOD HAS FORSAKEN YOU...
...MI-RANDA BAILEY.
REST EASY...
...FOR WE'LL BE BRINGING BOTH OF YOU TO LORD MIDWINTER NOW.
GO ON.
GA (WHAM)
DOKA (KICK)
...THIS ISN'T HOW...
...IT... SHOULD HAVE BEEN...
WHY DID IT...
...ALL GO WRONG ...?

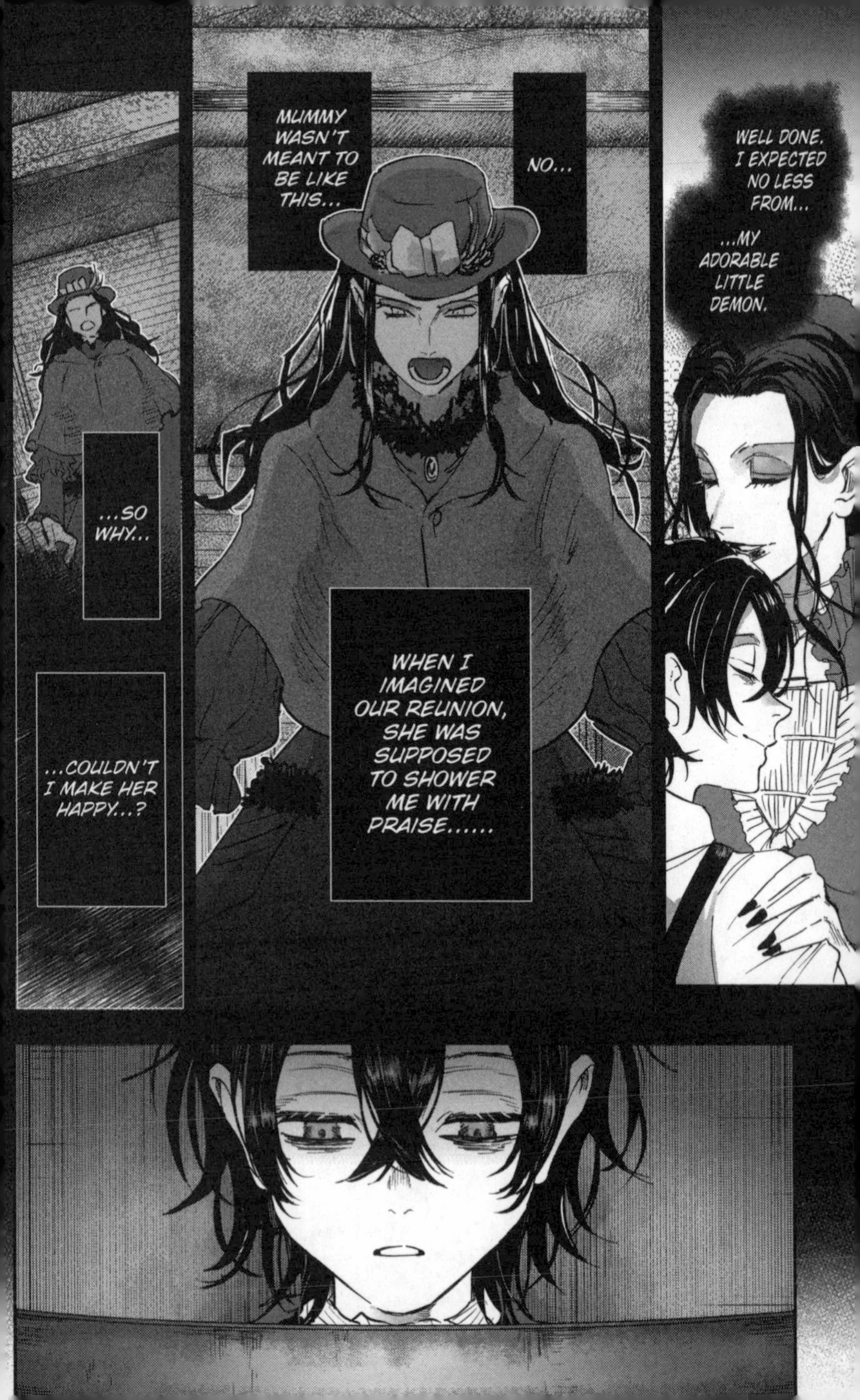
WELL DONE. I EXPECTED NO LESS FROM...
...MY ADORABLE LITTLE DEMON.
NO...
MUMMY WASN'T MEANT TO BE LIKE THIS...
WHEN I IMAGINED OUR REUNION, SHE WAS SUPPOSED TO SHOWER ME WITH PRAISE......
...SO WHY...
...COULDN'T I MAKE HER HAPPY...?

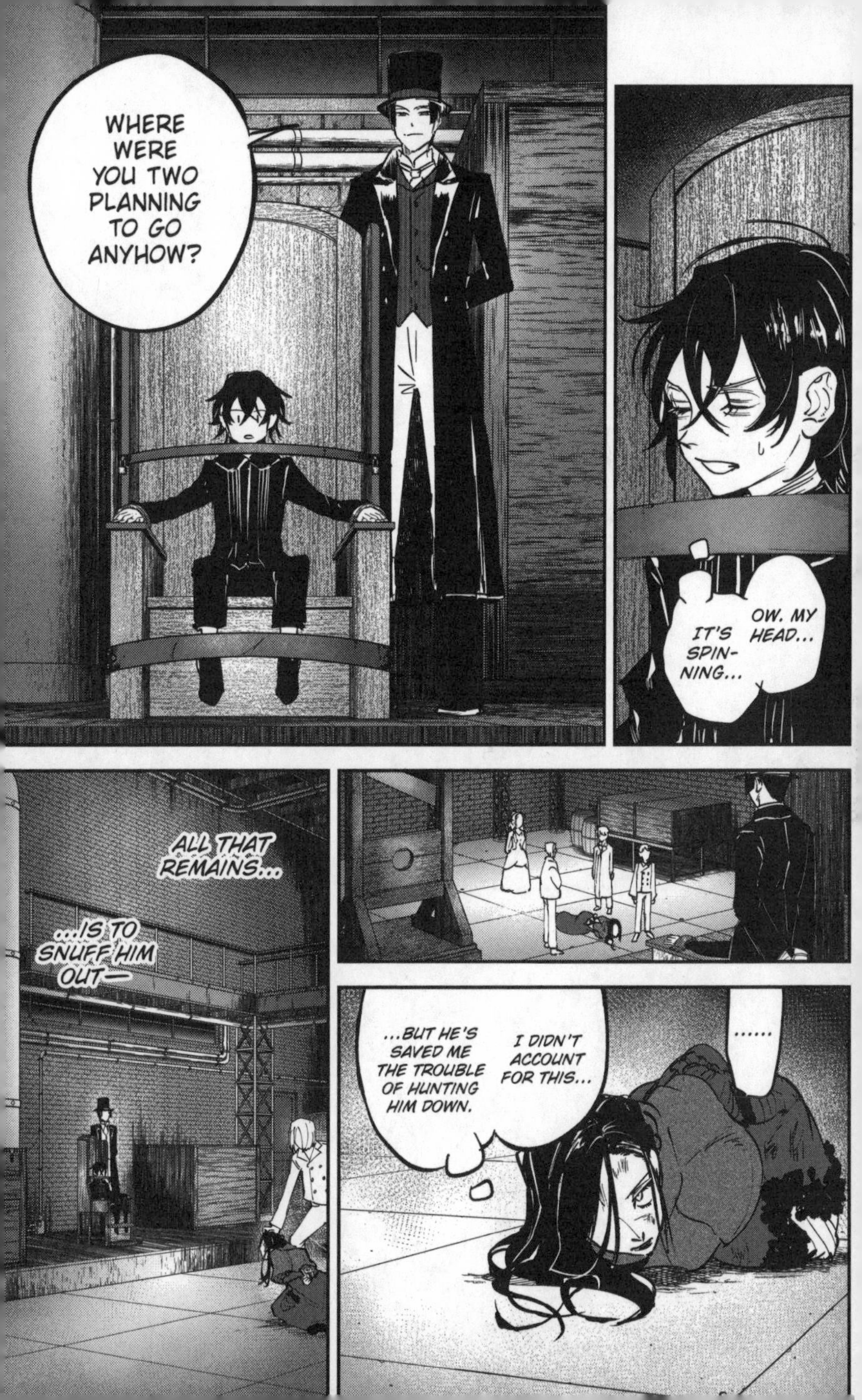
OW. MY HEAD... IT'S SPINNING...
WHERE WERE YOU TWO PLANNING TO GO ANYHOW?
......
I DIDN'T ACCOUNT FOR THIS...
...BUT HE'S SAVED ME THE TROUBLE OF HUNTING HIM DOWN.
ALL THAT REMAINS...
...IS TO SNUFF HIM OUT—

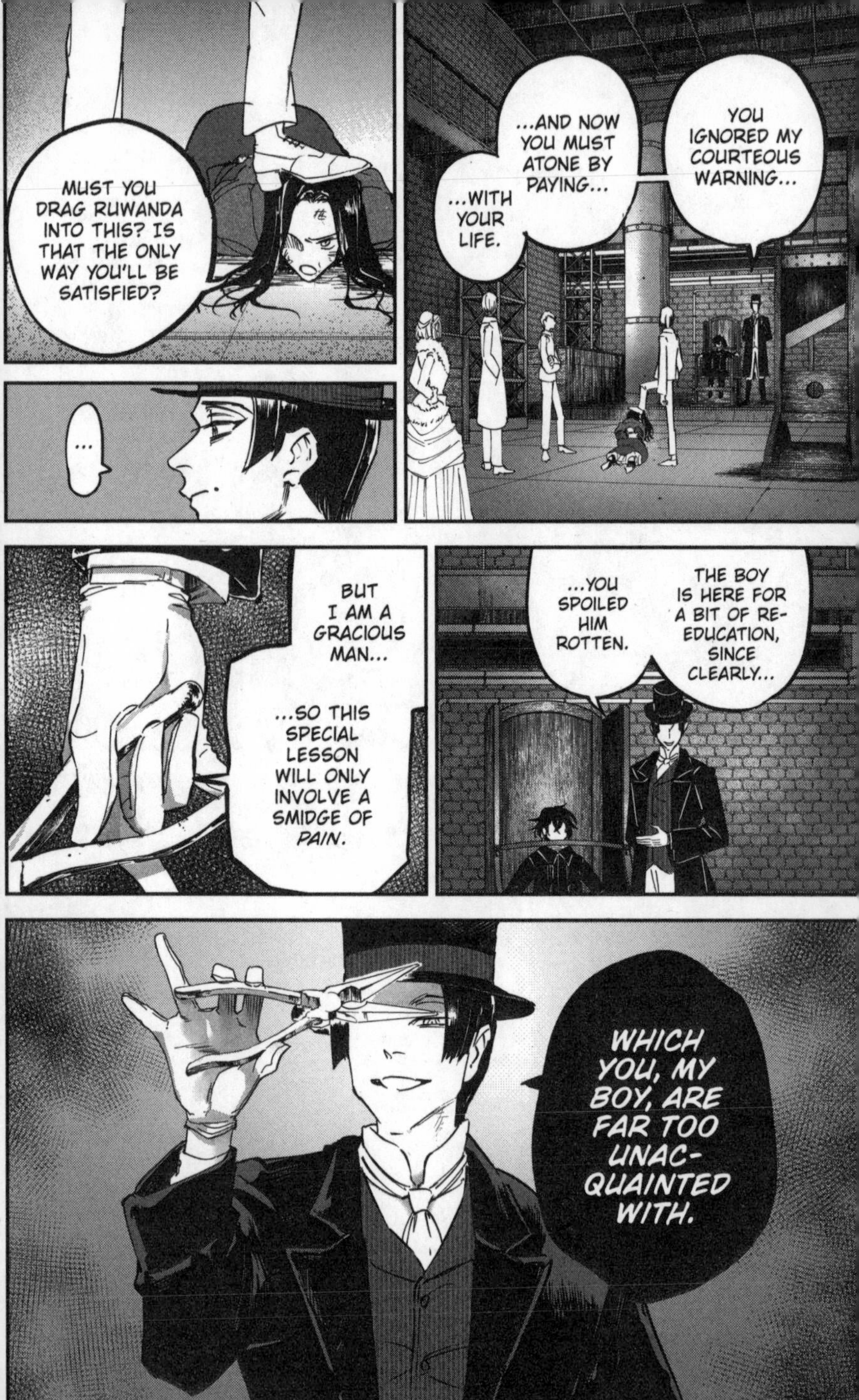
YOU IGNORED MY COURTEOUS WARNING...
...AND NOW YOU MUST ATONE BY PAYING...
...WITH YOUR LIFE.
MUST YOU DRAG RUWANDA INTO THIS? IS THAT THE ONLY WAY YOU'LL BE SATISFIED?
...
THE BOY IS HERE FOR A BIT OF RE-EDUCATION, SINCE CLEARLY...
...YOU SPOILED HIM ROTTEN.
BUT I AM A GRACIOUS MAN...
...SO THIS SPECIAL LESSON WILL ONLY INVOLVE A SMIDGE OF *PAIN*.
WHICH YOU, MY BOY, ARE FAR TOO UNAC-QUAINTED WITH.

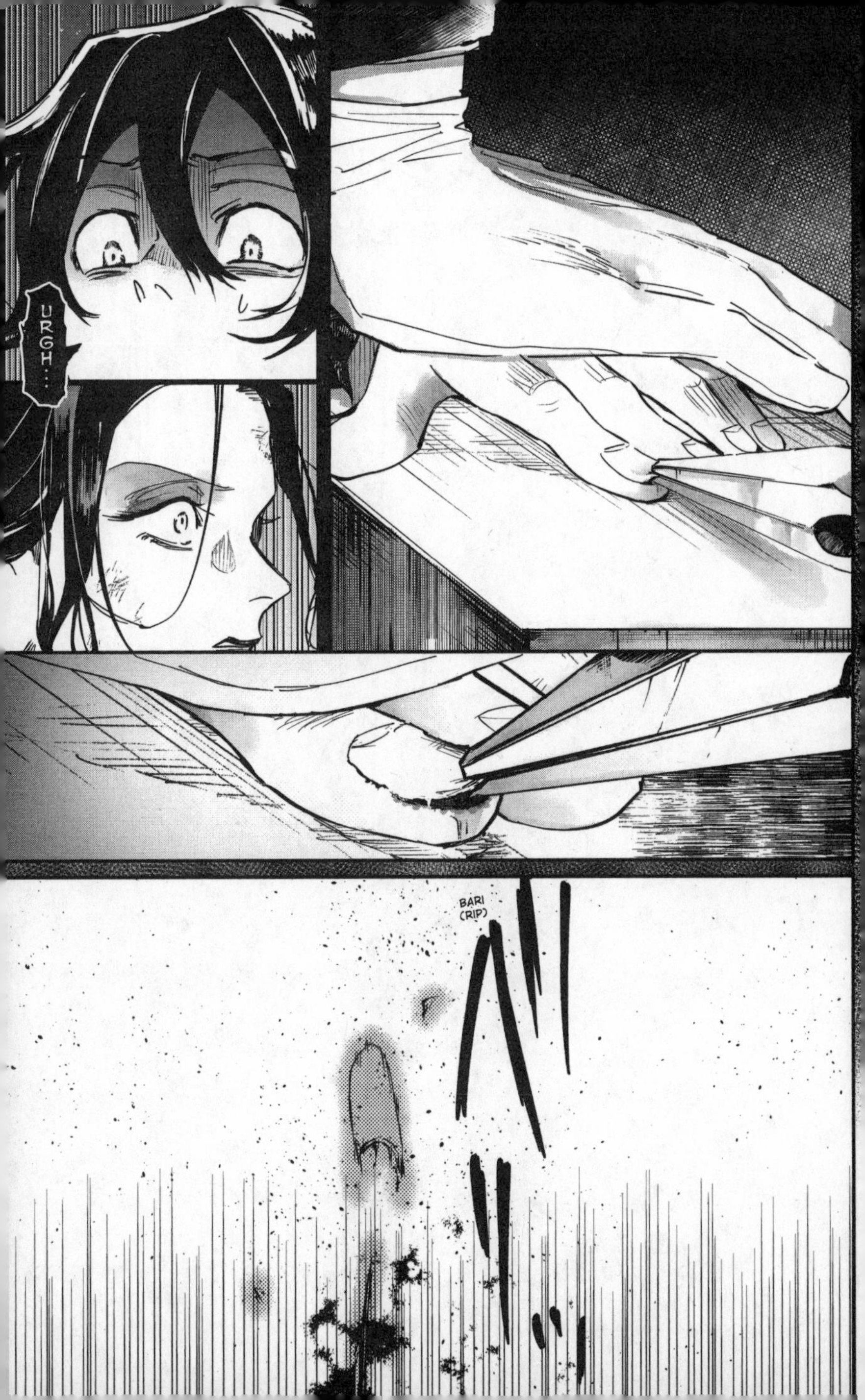
URGH...
BARI (RIP)

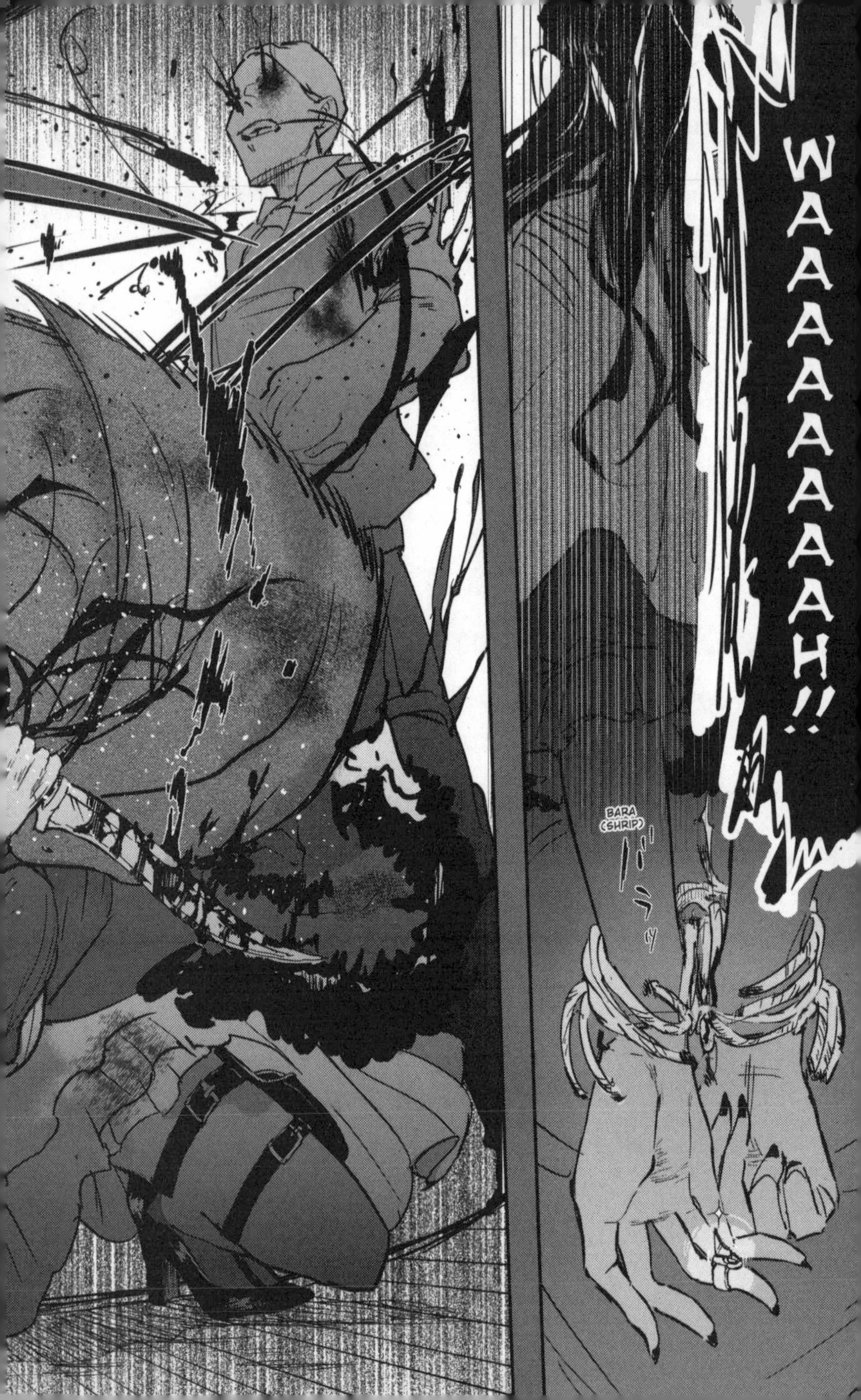
WAAAAAAAAAAAH!!
BARA (SHRIP)

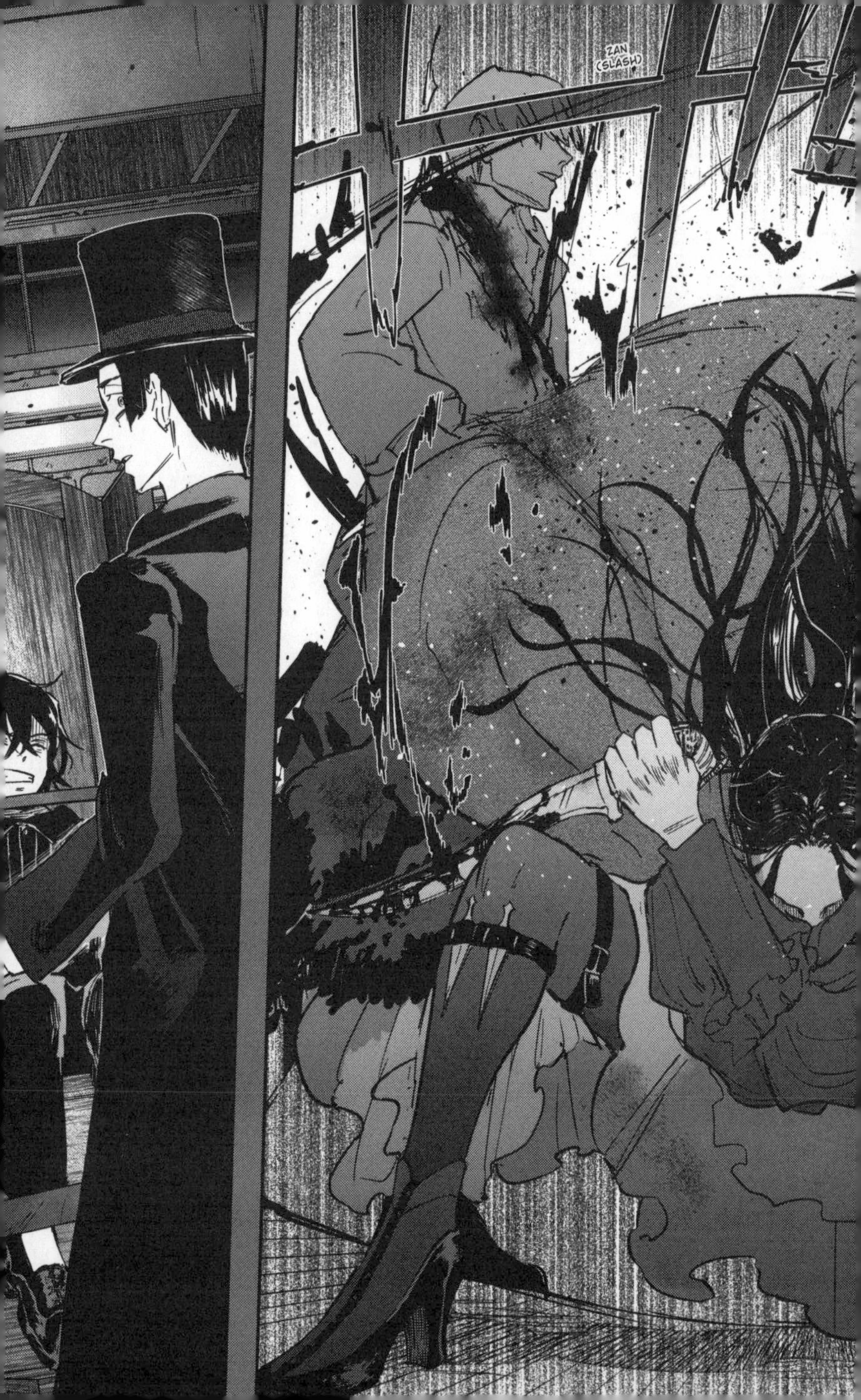
ZAN
(SLASH)

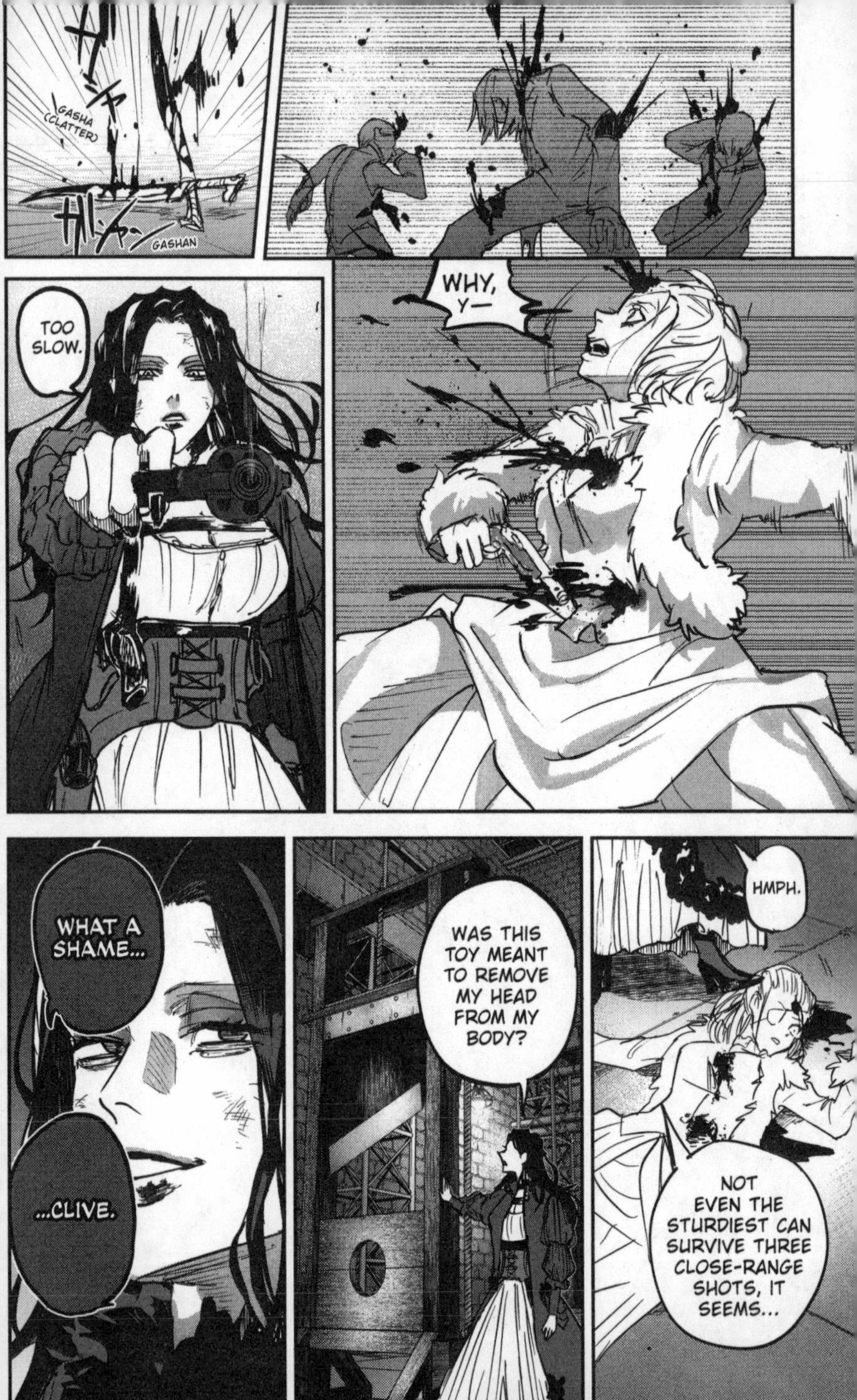
GASHA (CLATTER)
GASHAN
TOO SLOW.
WHY, Y—
HMPH.
NOT EVEN THE STURDIEST CAN SURVIVE THREE CLOSE-RANGE SHOTS, IT SEEMS...
WAS THIS TOY MEANT TO REMOVE MY HEAD FROM MY BODY?
WHAT A SHAME...
...CLIVE.

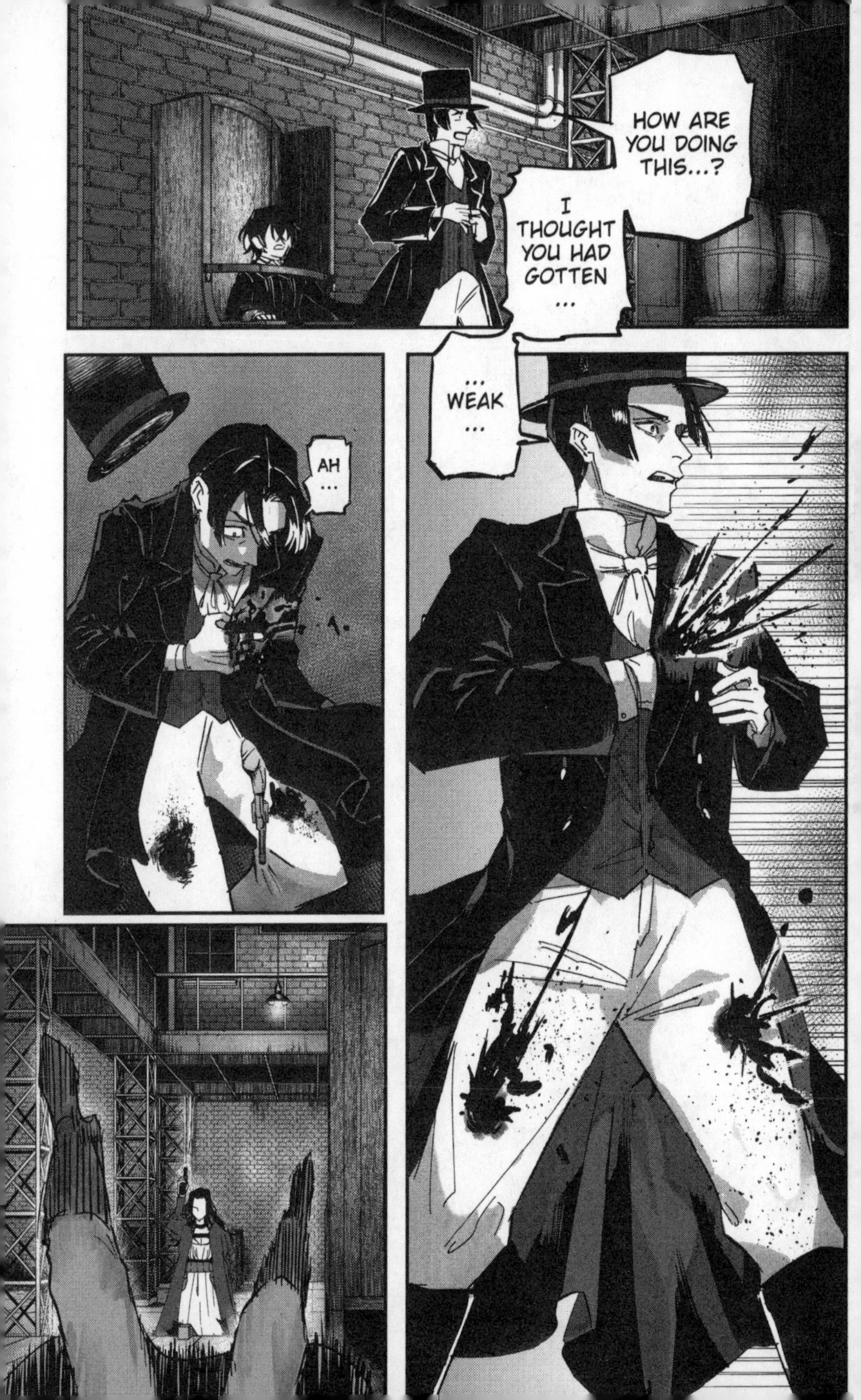
HOW ARE YOU DOING THIS...?
I THOUGHT YOU HAD GOTTEN ...
... WEAK ...
AH ...

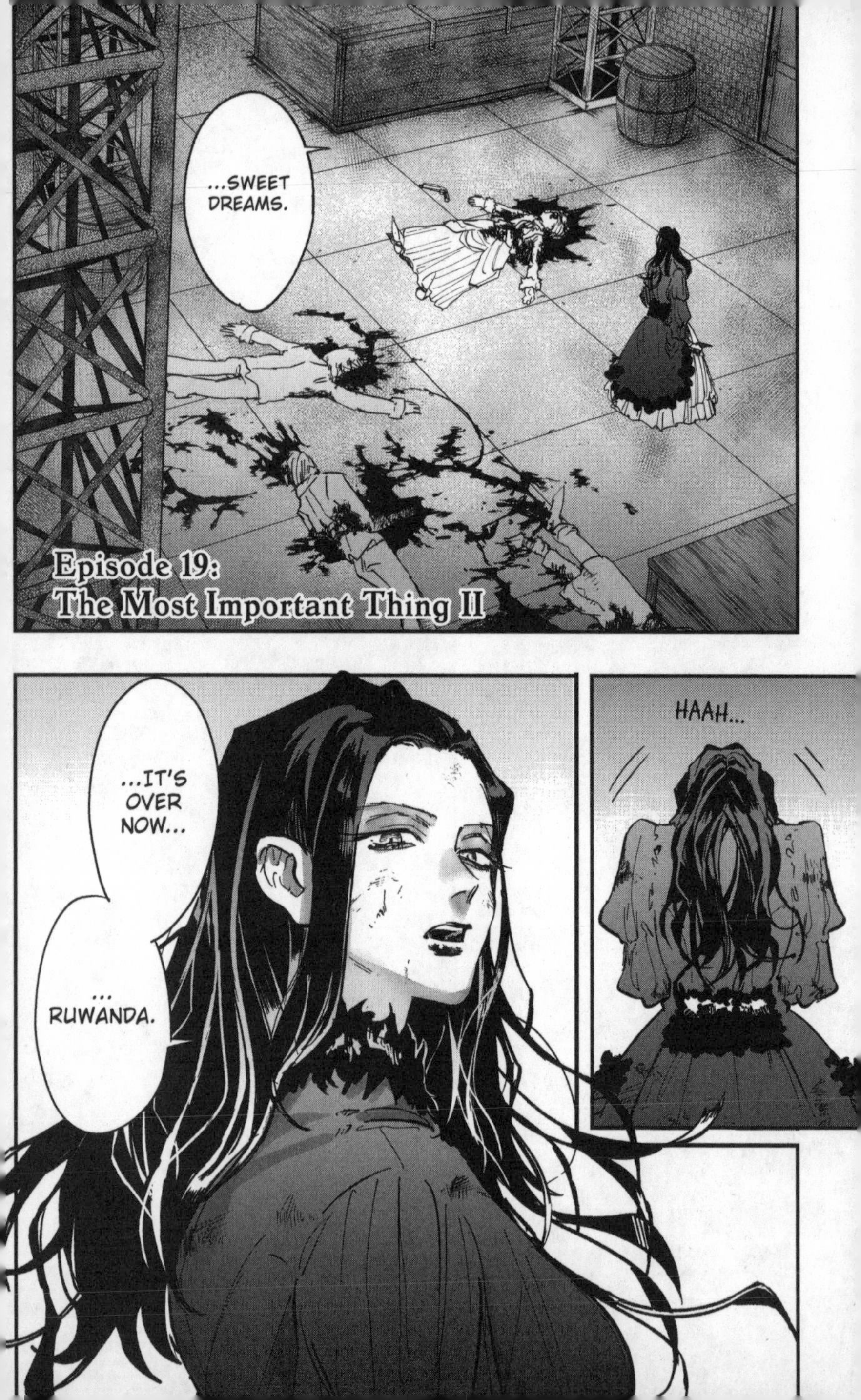
...SWEET DREAMS.
Episode 19: The Most Important Thing II
HAAH...
...IT'S OVER NOW...
... RUWANDA.

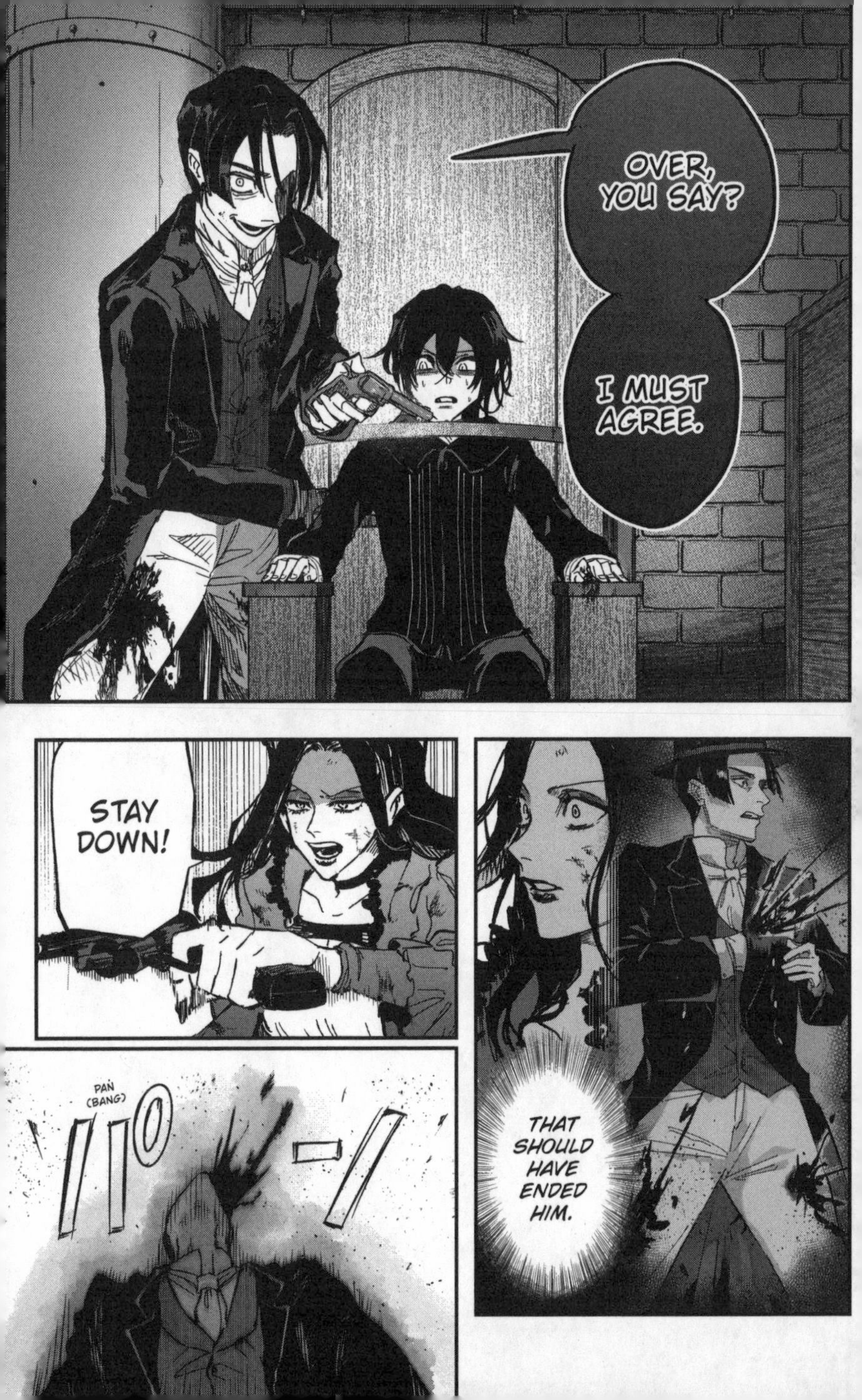
OVER, YOU SAY?
I MUST AGREE.
THAT SHOULD HAVE ENDED HIM.
STAY DOWN!
PAN
(BANG)

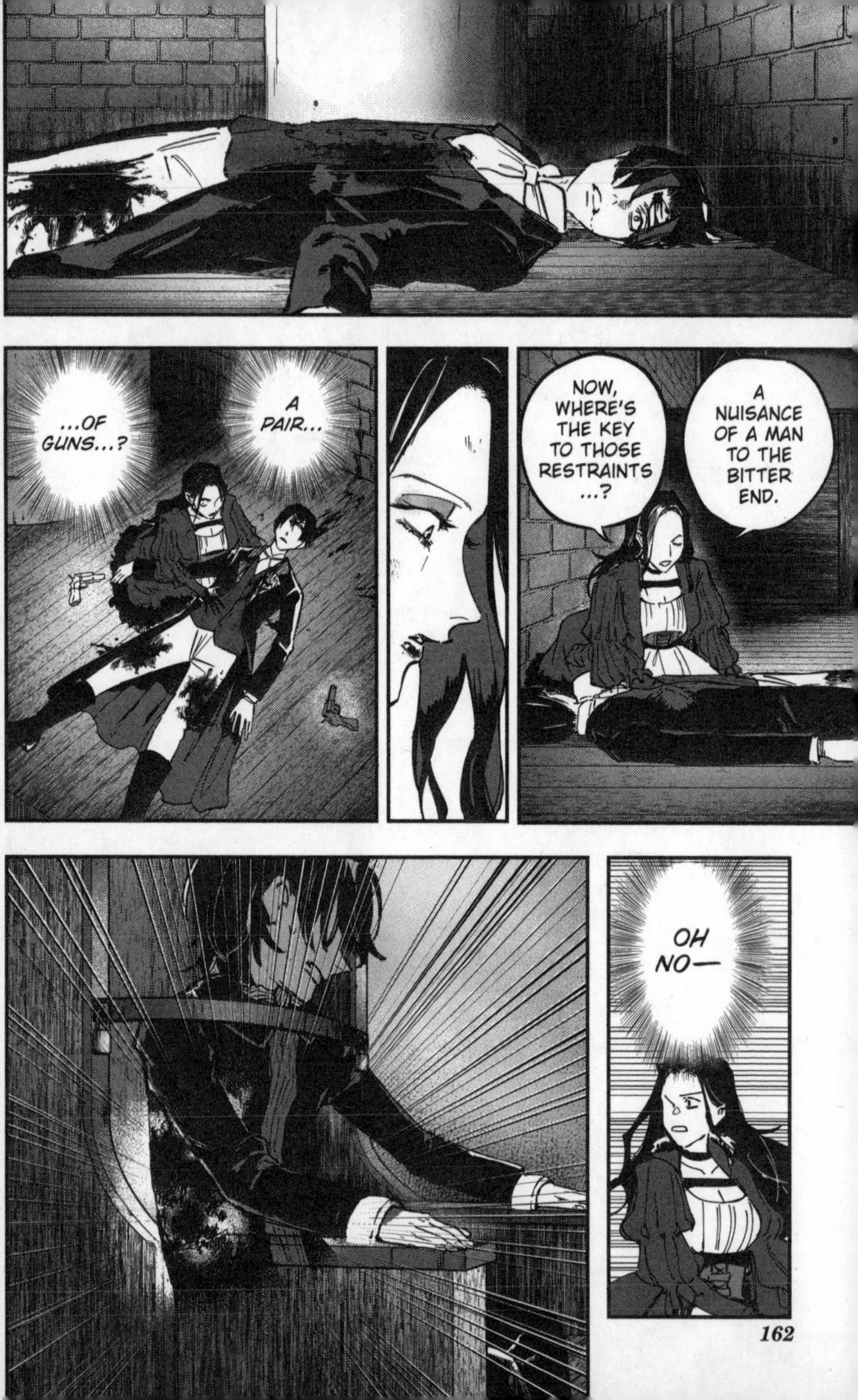
A NUISANCE OF A MAN TO THE BITTER END.
NOW, WHERE'S THE KEY TO THOSE RESTRAINTS ...?
A PAIR...
...OF GUNS...?
OH NO—

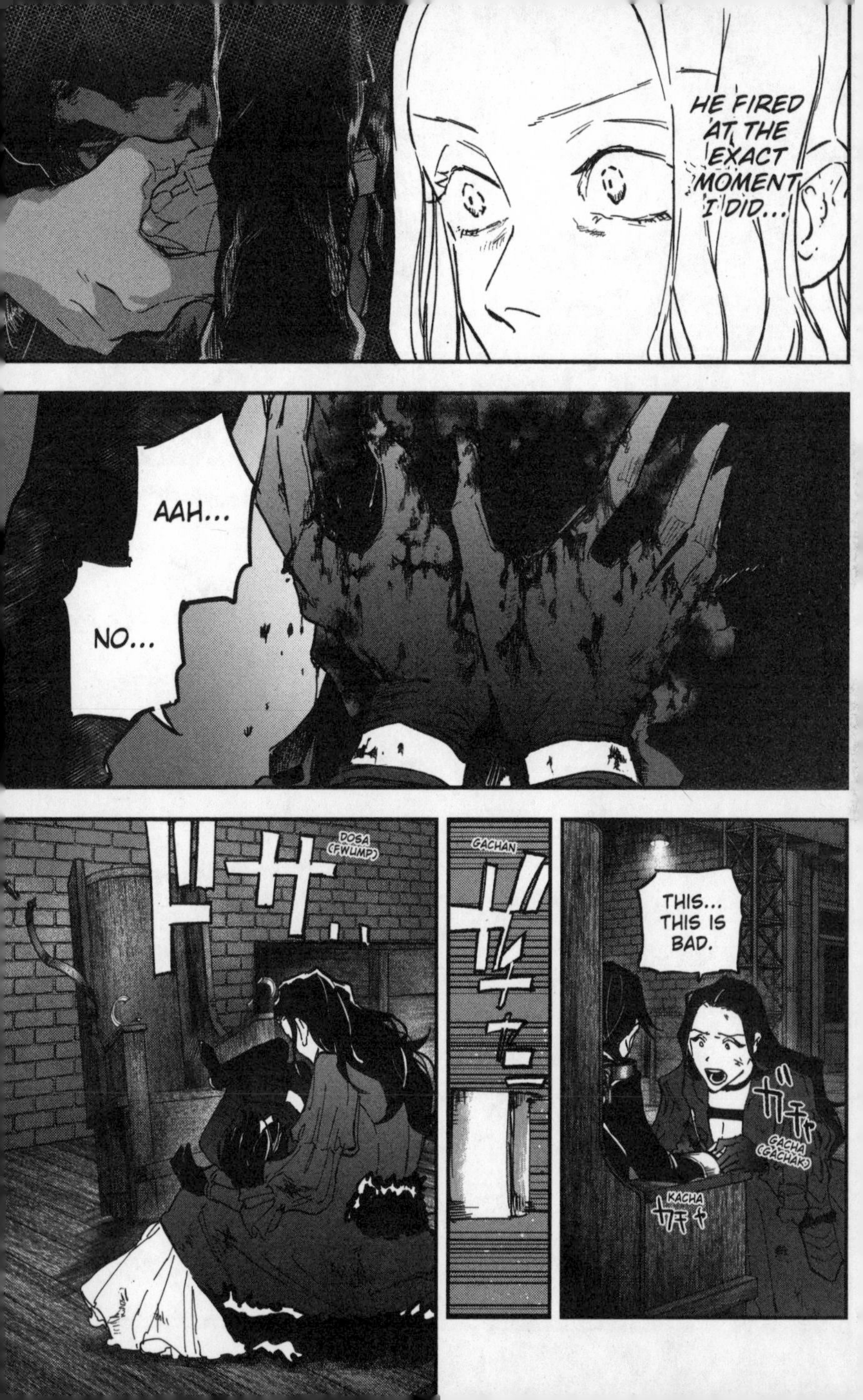
HE FIRED AT THE EXACT MOMENT I DID...
AAH...
NO...
THIS... THIS IS BAD.
ガチャ
GACHA (GACHAK)
KACHA
カチャ
GACHAN
ガチャン
DOSA (FWUMP)
ドサッ..

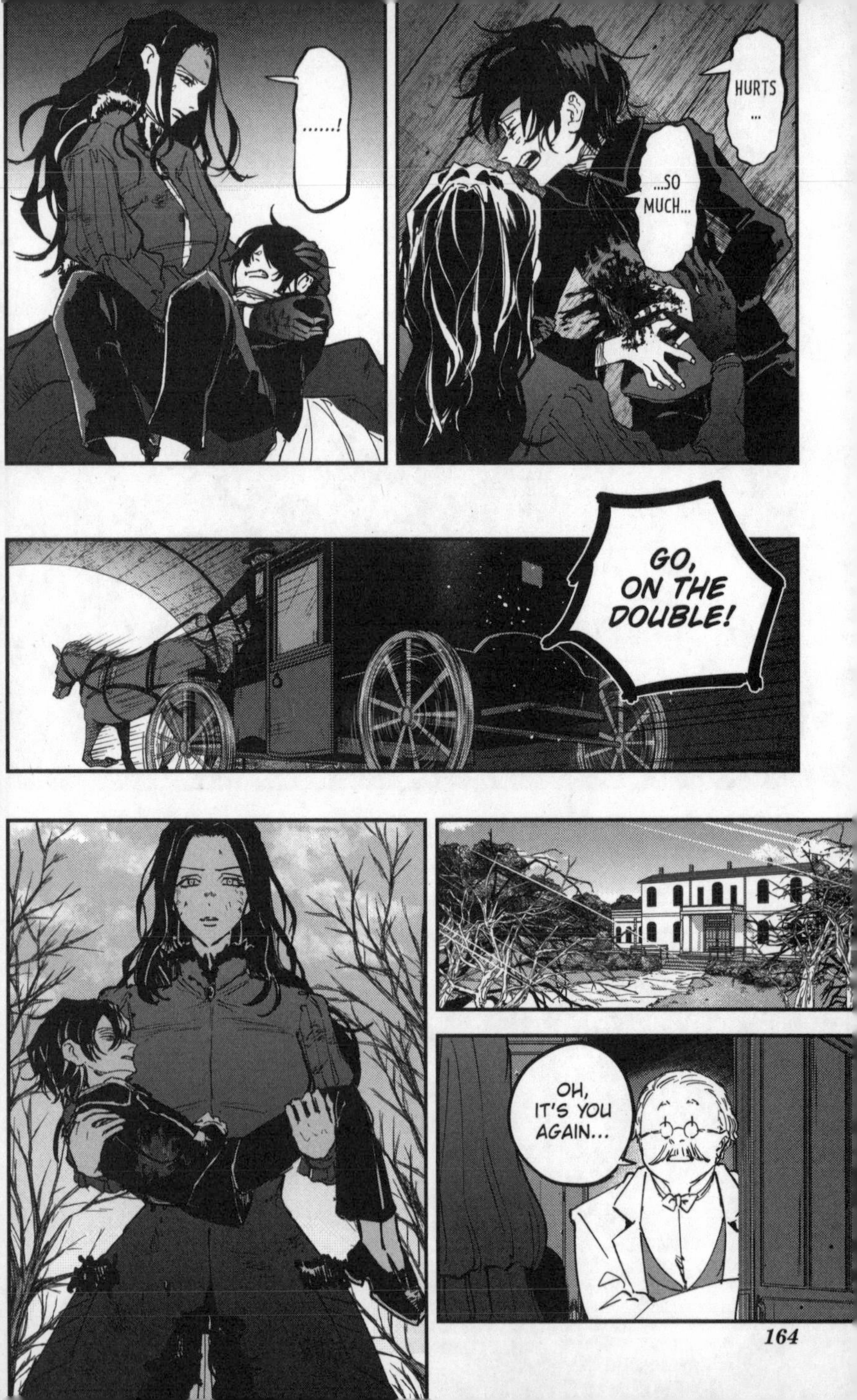
HURTS ...
...SO MUCH...
......!
GO, ON THE DOUBLE!
OH, IT'S YOU AGAIN...

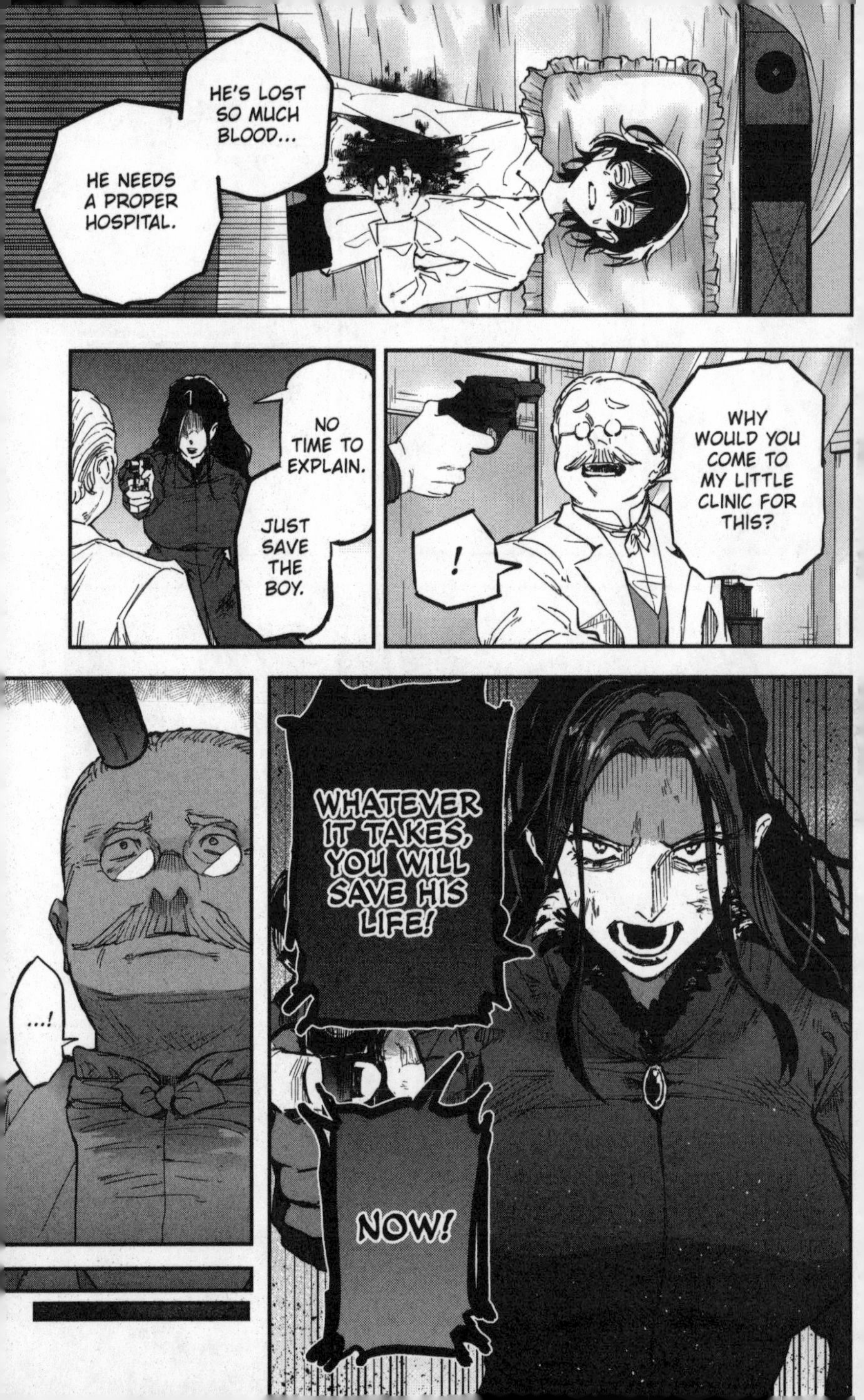
HE'S LOST SO MUCH BLOOD...
HE NEEDS A PROPER HOSPITAL.
WHY WOULD YOU COME TO MY LITTLE CLINIC FOR THIS?
!
NO TIME TO EXPLAIN.
JUST SAVE THE BOY.
WHATEVER IT TAKES, YOU WILL SAVE HIS LIFE!
NOW!
...!

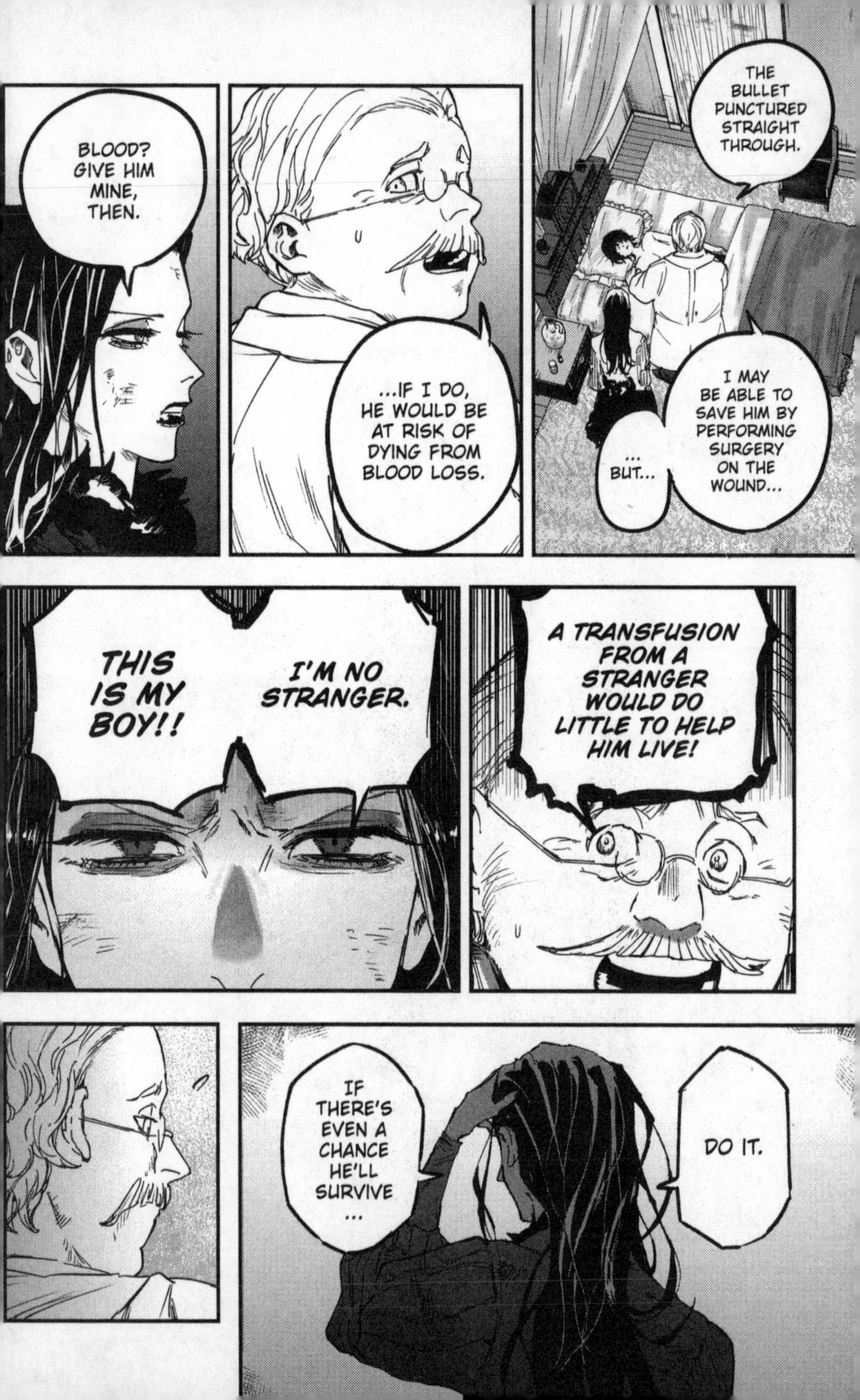
THE BULLET PUNCTURED STRAIGHT THROUGH.
I MAY BE ABLE TO SAVE HIM BY PERFORMING SURGERY ON THE WOUND...
... BUT...
...IF I DO, HE WOULD BE AT RISK OF DYING FROM BLOOD LOSS.
BLOOD? GIVE HIM MINE, THEN.
A TRANSFUSION FROM A STRANGER WOULD DO LITTLE TO HELP HIM LIVE!
I'M NO STRANGER.
THIS IS MY BOY!!
DO IT.
IF THERE'S EVEN A CHANCE HE'LL SURVIVE ...

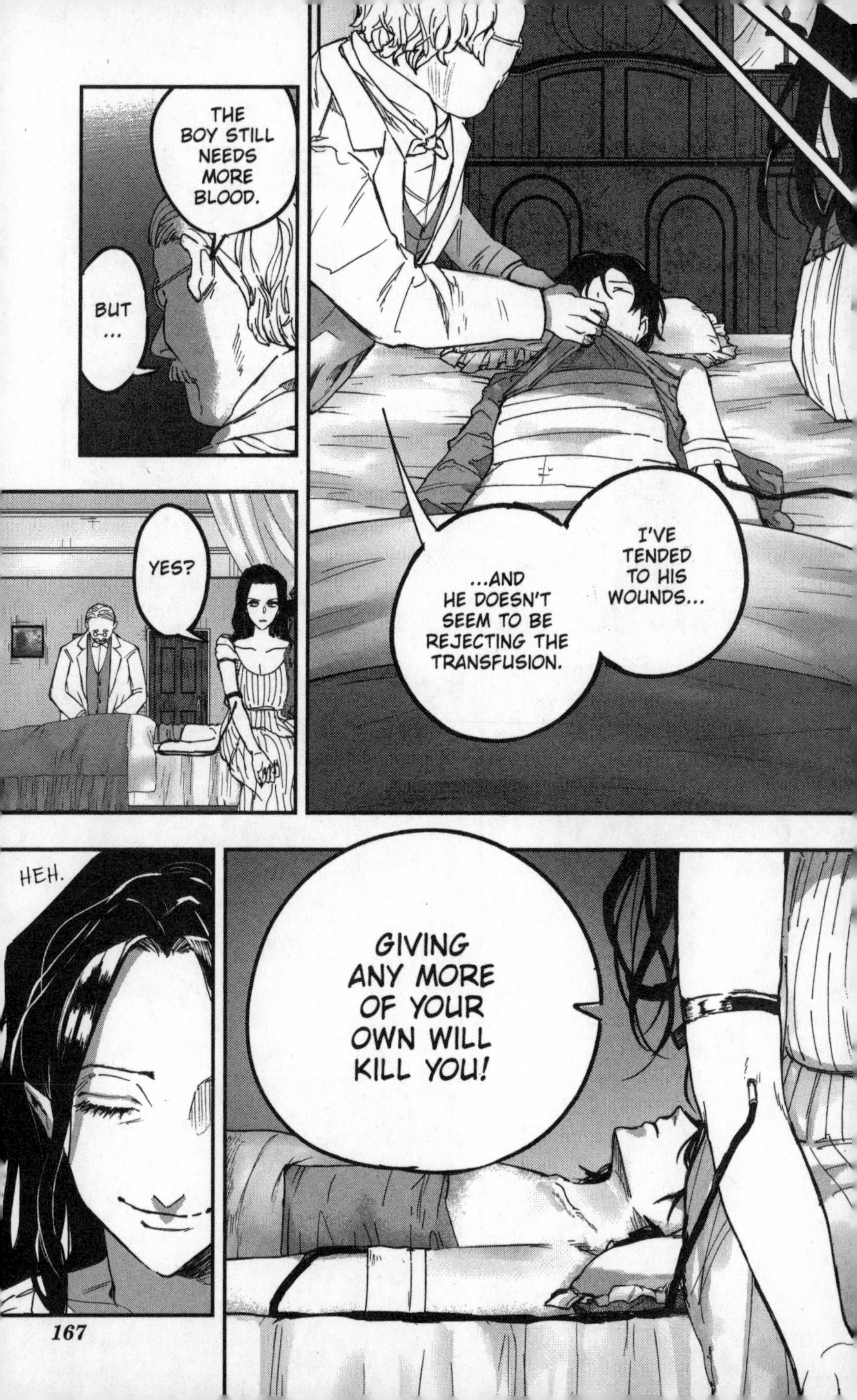
I'VE TENDED TO HIS WOUNDS...
...AND HE DOESN'T SEEM TO BE REJECTING THE TRANSFUSION.
THE BOY STILL NEEDS MORE BLOOD.
BUT ...
YES?
GIVING ANY MORE OF YOUR OWN WILL KILL YOU!
HEH.

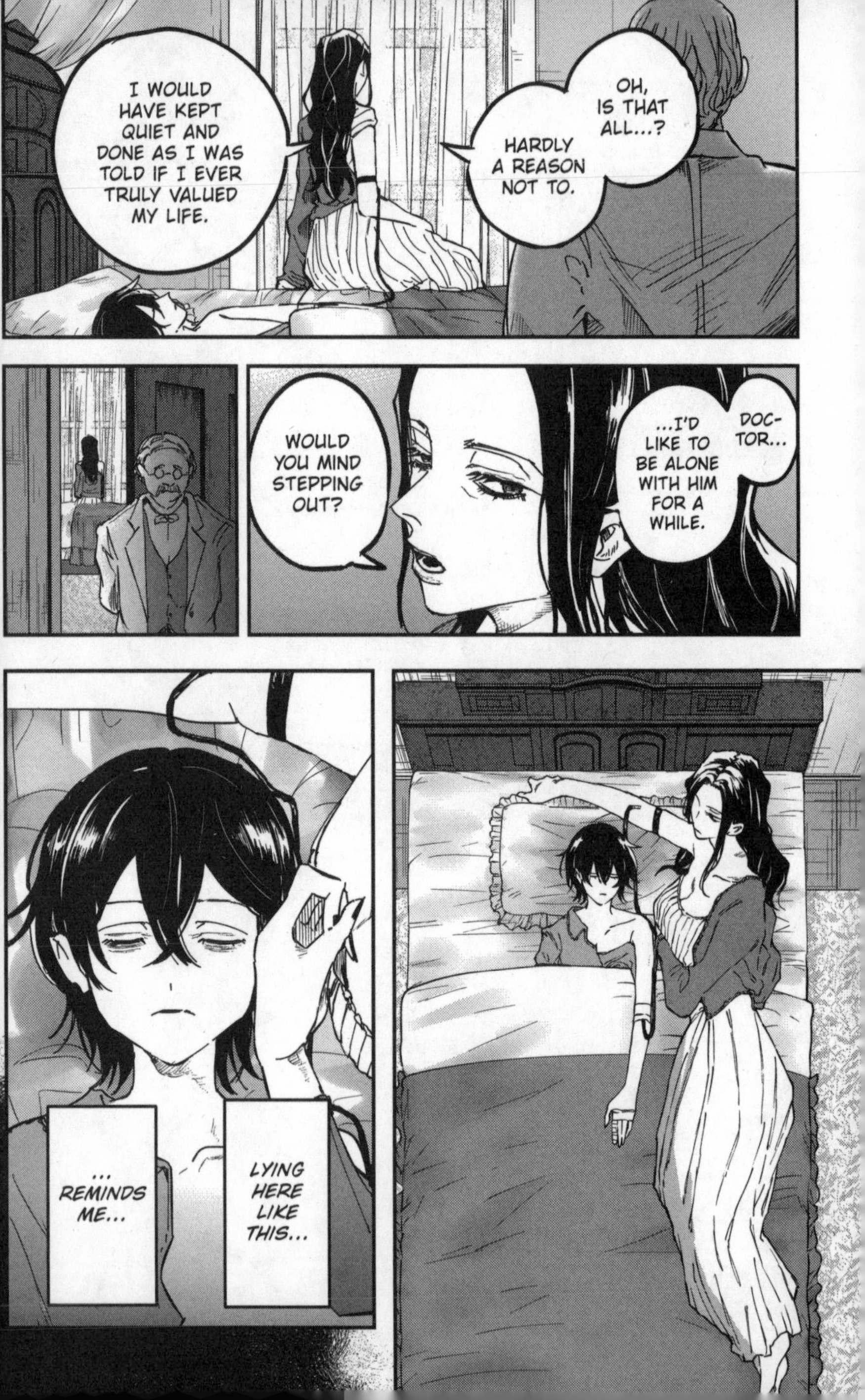
OH, IS THAT ALL...?
HARDLY A REASON NOT TO.
I WOULD HAVE KEPT QUIET AND DONE AS I WAS TOLD IF I EVER TRULY VALUED MY LIFE.
DOC-TOR...
...I'D LIKE TO BE ALONE WITH HIM FOR A WHILE.
WOULD YOU MIND STEPPING OUT?
LYING HERE LIKE THIS...
... REMINDS ME...

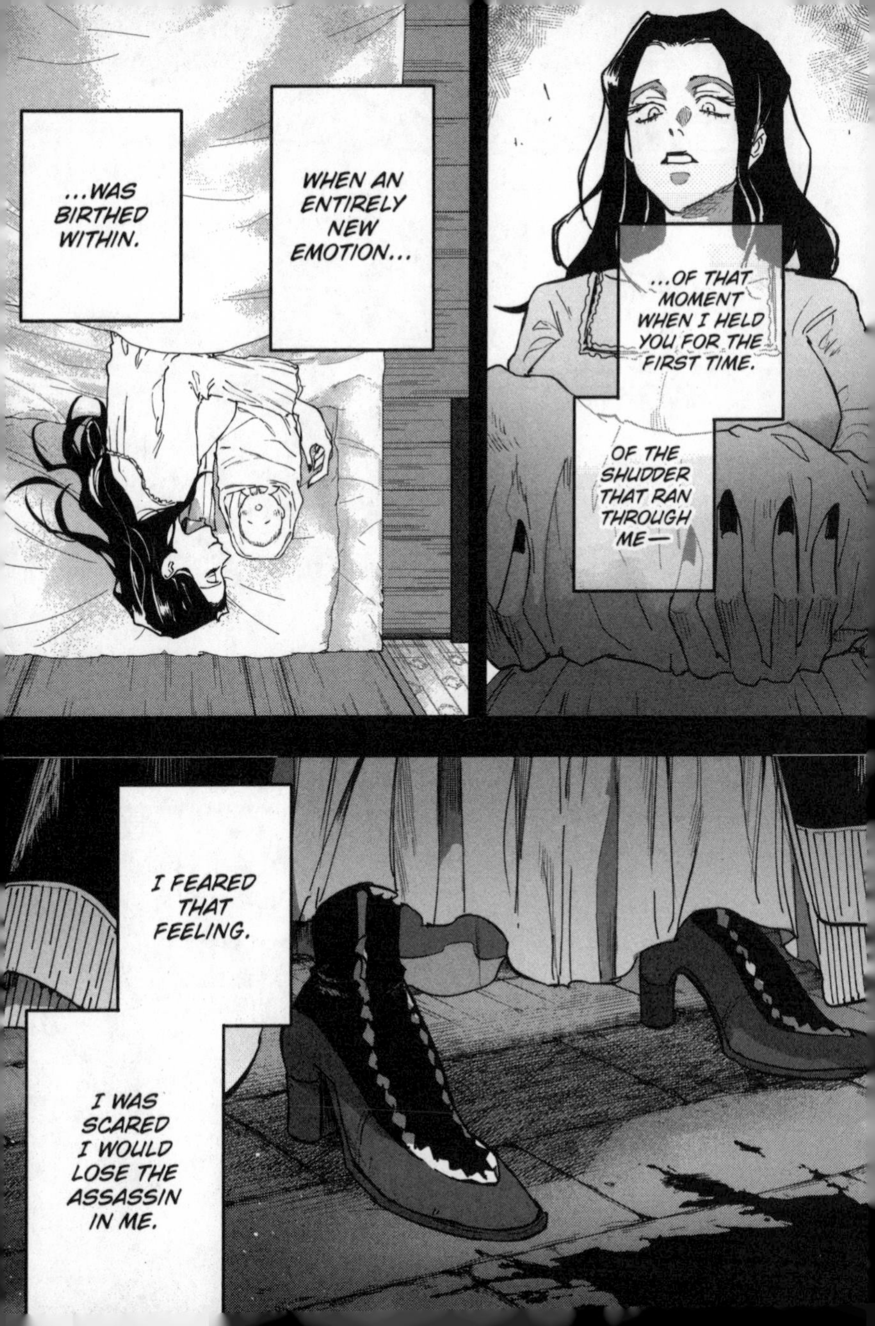
...OF THAT MOMENT WHEN I HELD YOU FOR THE FIRST TIME.
OF THE SHUDDER THAT RAN THROUGH ME—
WHEN AN ENTIRELY NEW EMOTION...
...WAS BIRTHED WITHIN.
I FEARED THAT FEELING.
I WAS SCARED I WOULD LOSE THE ASSASSIN IN ME.

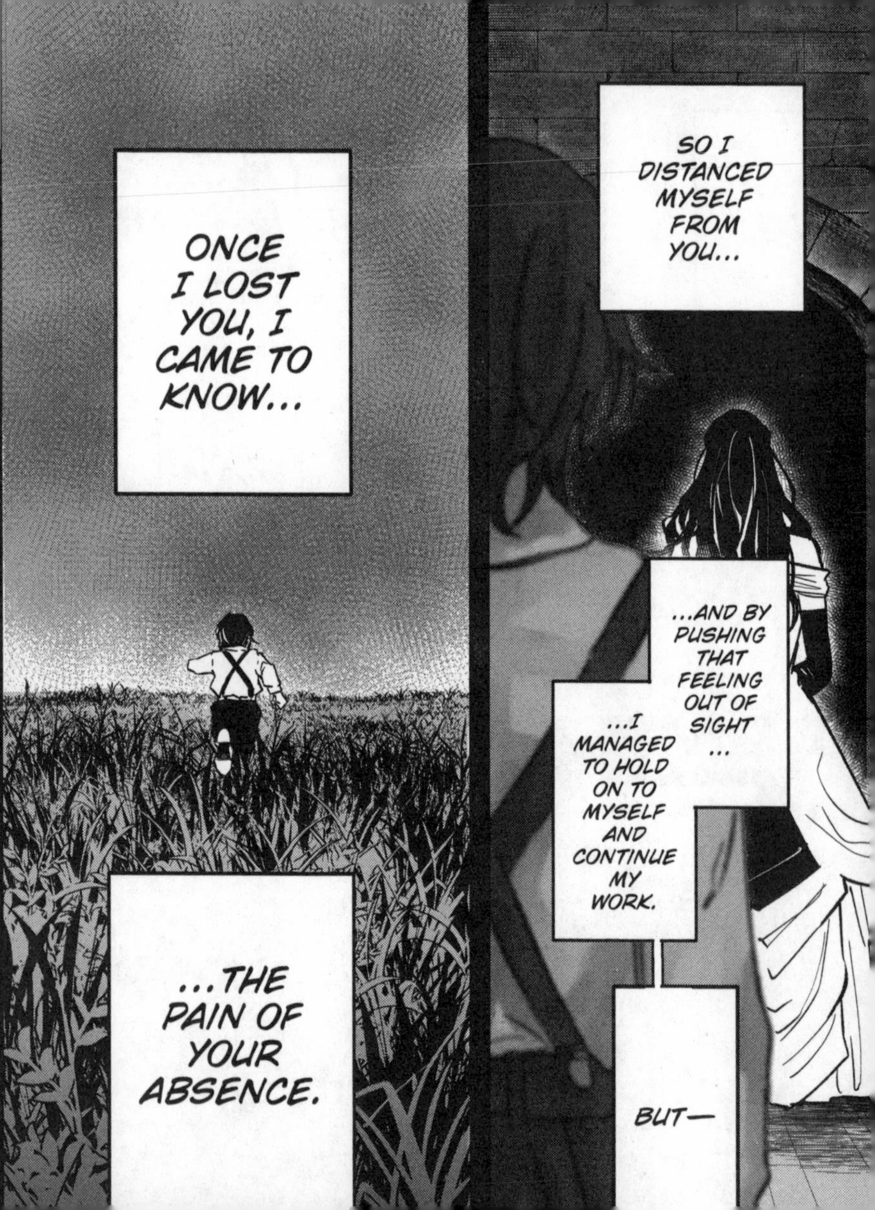
SO I DISTANCED MYSELF FROM YOU...
...AND BY PUSHING THAT FEELING OUT OF SIGHT...
...I MANAGED TO HOLD ON TO MYSELF AND CONTINUE MY WORK.
BUT—
ONCE I LOST YOU, I CAME TO KNOW...
...THE PAIN OF YOUR ABSENCE.

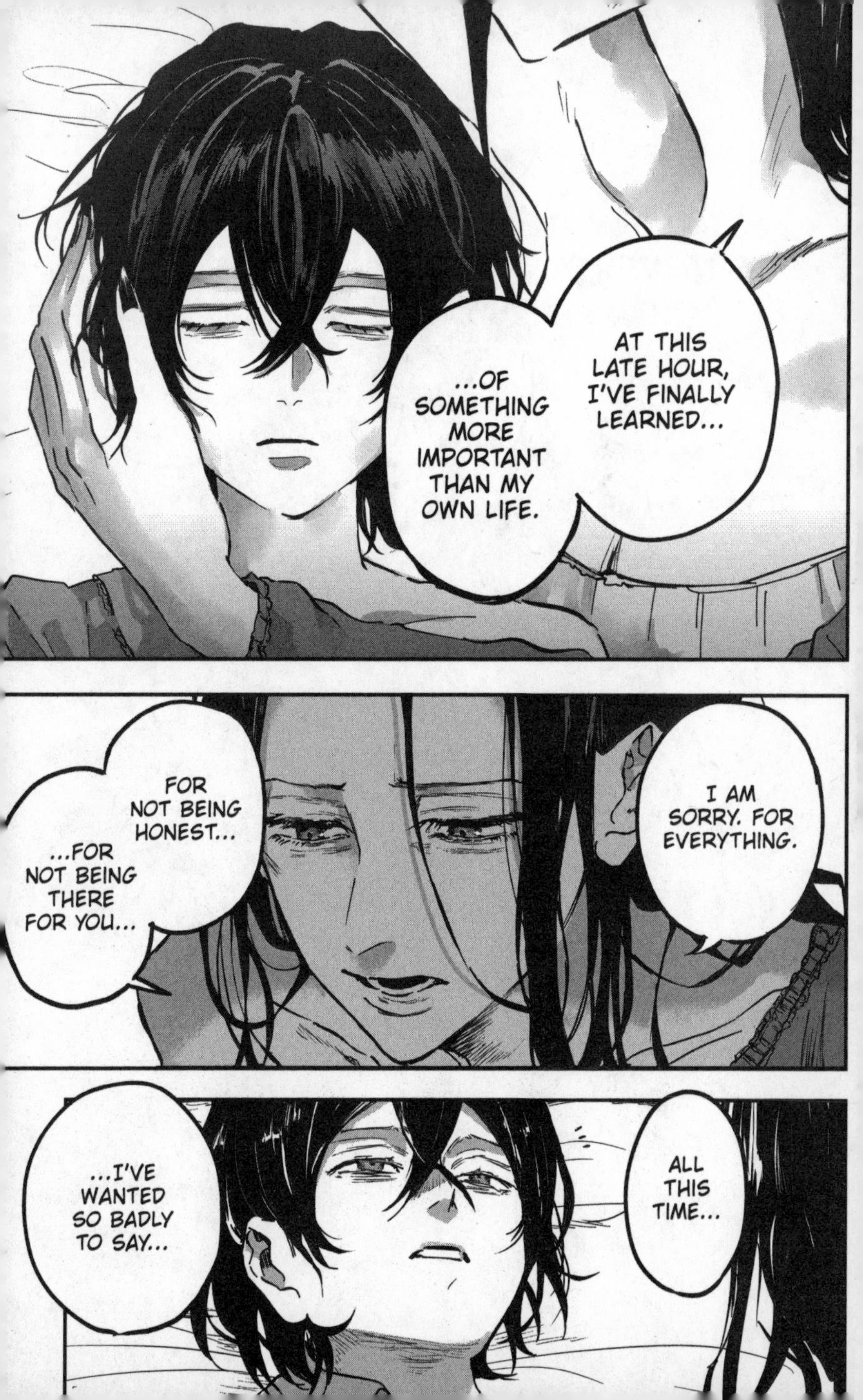
AT THIS LATE HOUR, I'VE FINALLY LEARNED...
...OF SOMETHING MORE IMPORTANT THAN MY OWN LIFE.
I AM SORRY. FOR EVERYTHING.
FOR NOT BEING HONEST...
...FOR NOT BEING THERE FOR YOU...
ALL THIS TIME...
...I'VE WANTED SO BADLY TO SAY...

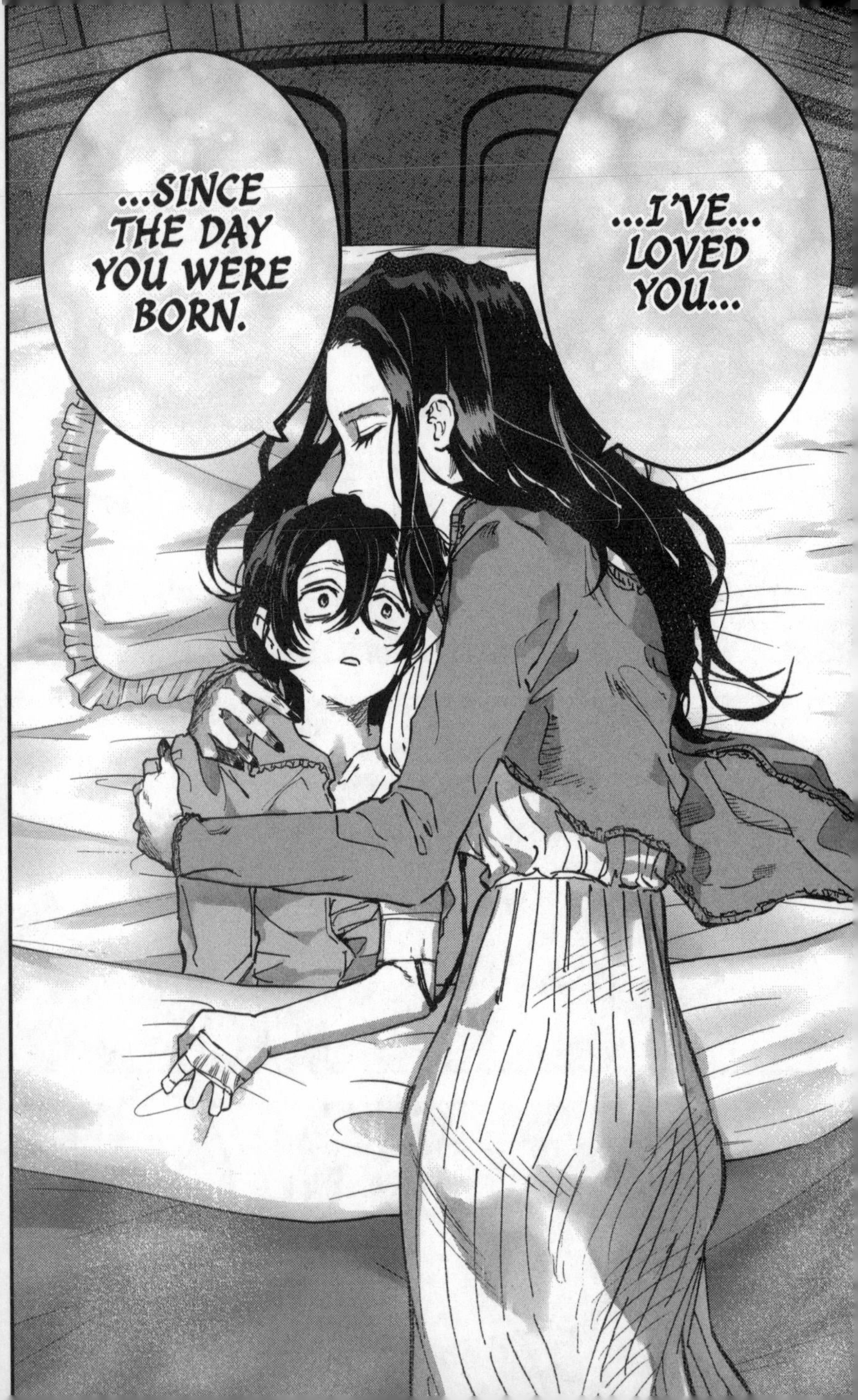
...I'VE... LOVED YOU...
...SINCE THE DAY YOU WERE BORN.

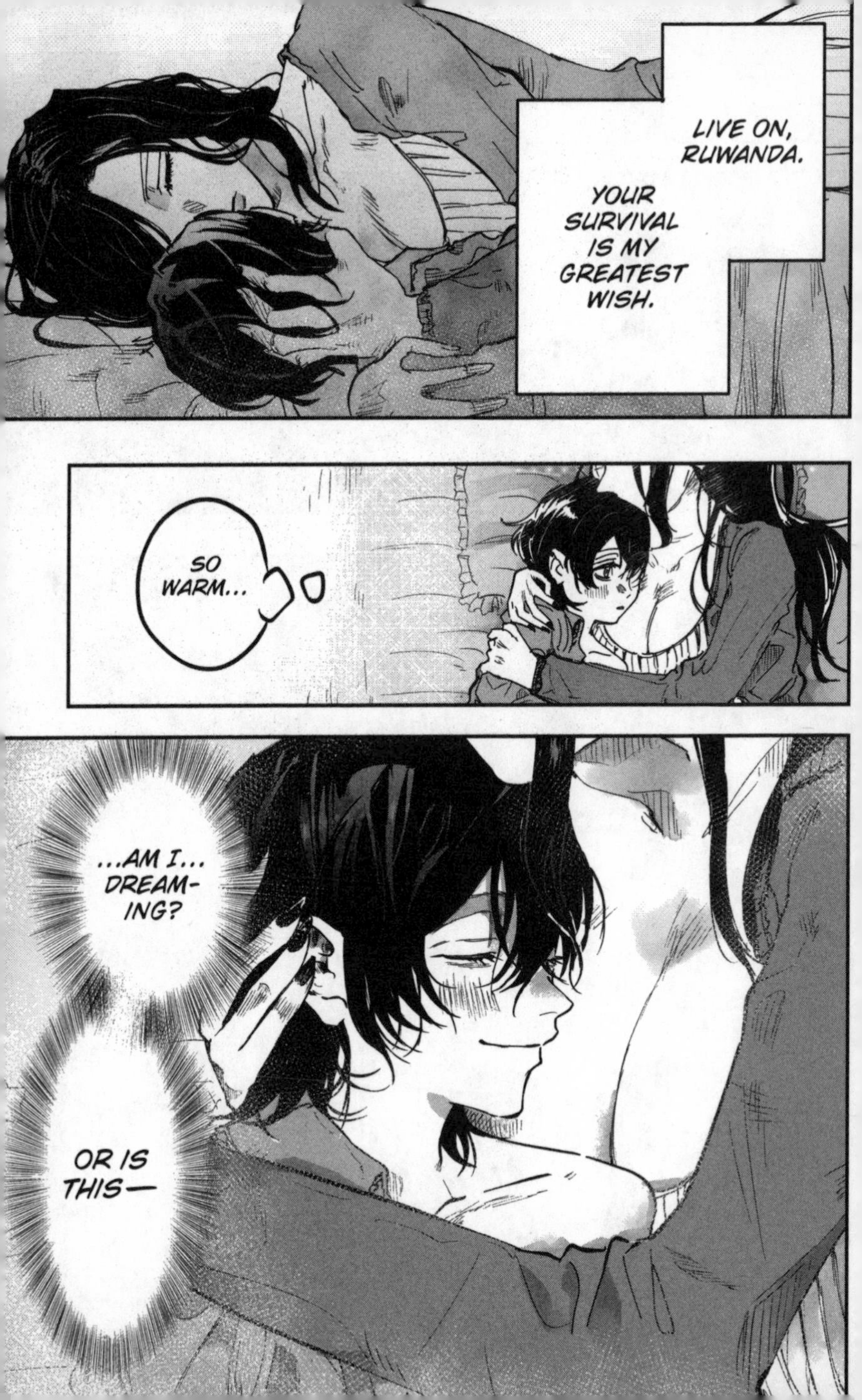
LIVE ON, RUWANDA.
YOUR SURVIVAL IS MY GREATEST WISH.
SO WARM...
...AM I... DREAM-ING?
OR IS THIS—

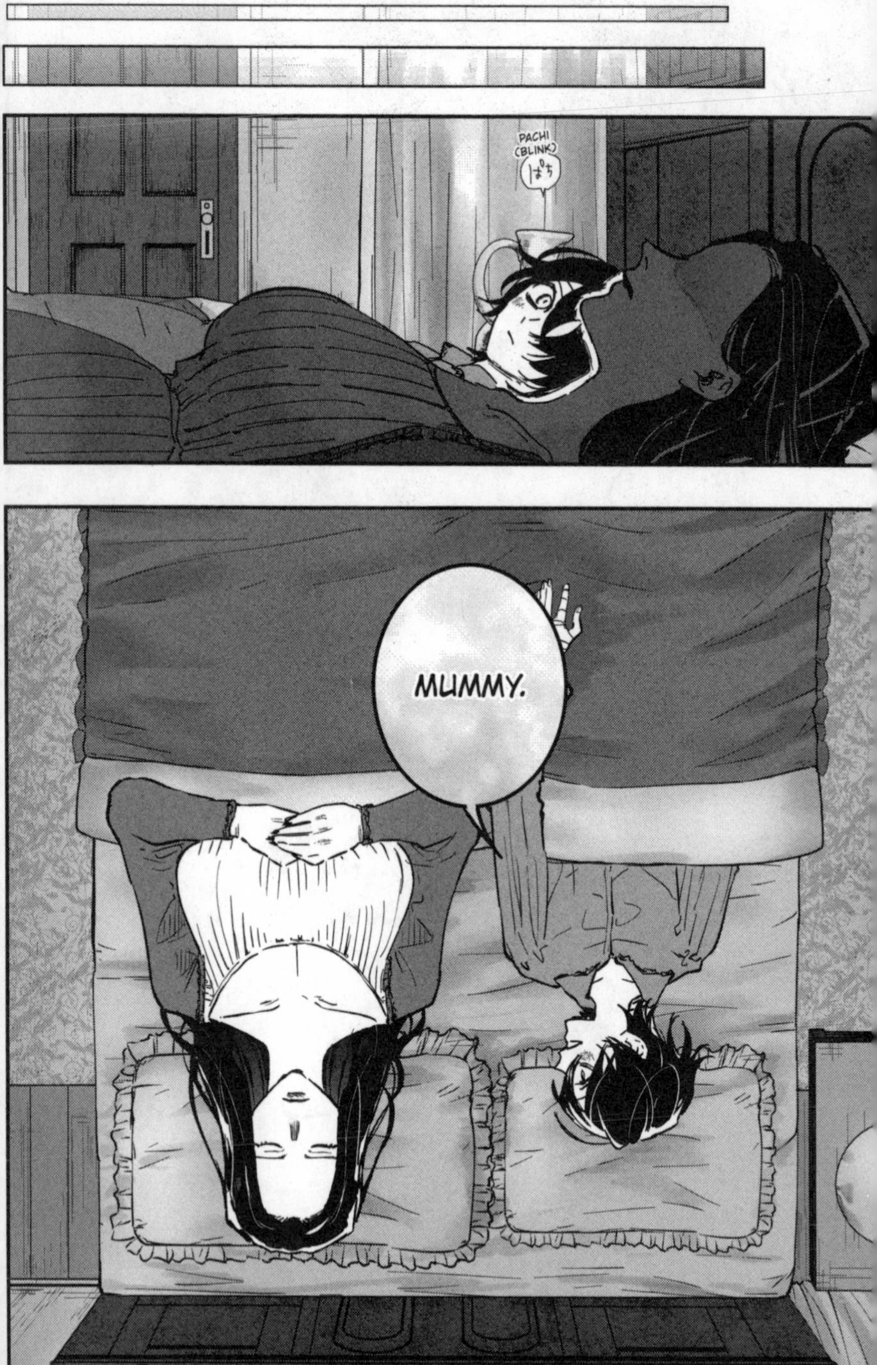
PACHI (BLINK)
ぱち
MUMMY.

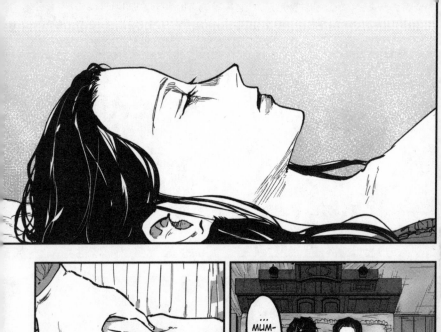

... MUM-MY?

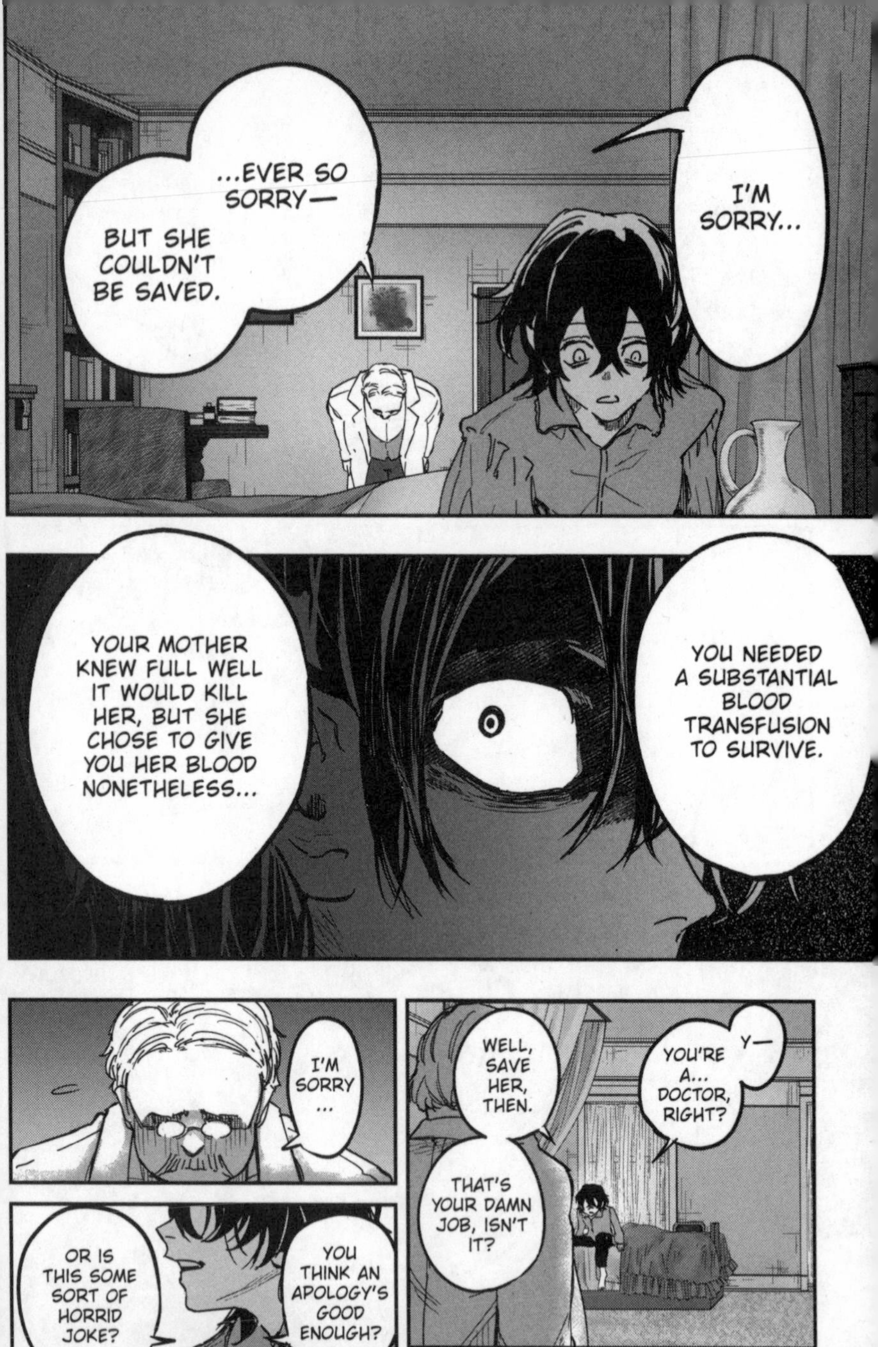
I'M SORRY...
...EVER SO SORRY— BUT SHE COULDN'T BE SAVED.
YOU NEEDED A SUBSTANTIAL BLOOD TRANSFUSION TO SURVIVE.
YOUR MOTHER KNEW FULL WELL IT WOULD KILL HER, BUT SHE CHOSE TO GIVE YOU HER BLOOD NONETHELESS...
Y— YOU'RE A... DOCTOR, RIGHT?
WELL, SAVE HER, THEN.
THAT'S YOUR DAMN JOB, ISN'T IT?
I'M SORRY ...
YOU THINK AN APOLOGY'S GOOD ENOUGH?
OR IS THIS SOME SORT OF HORRID JOKE?

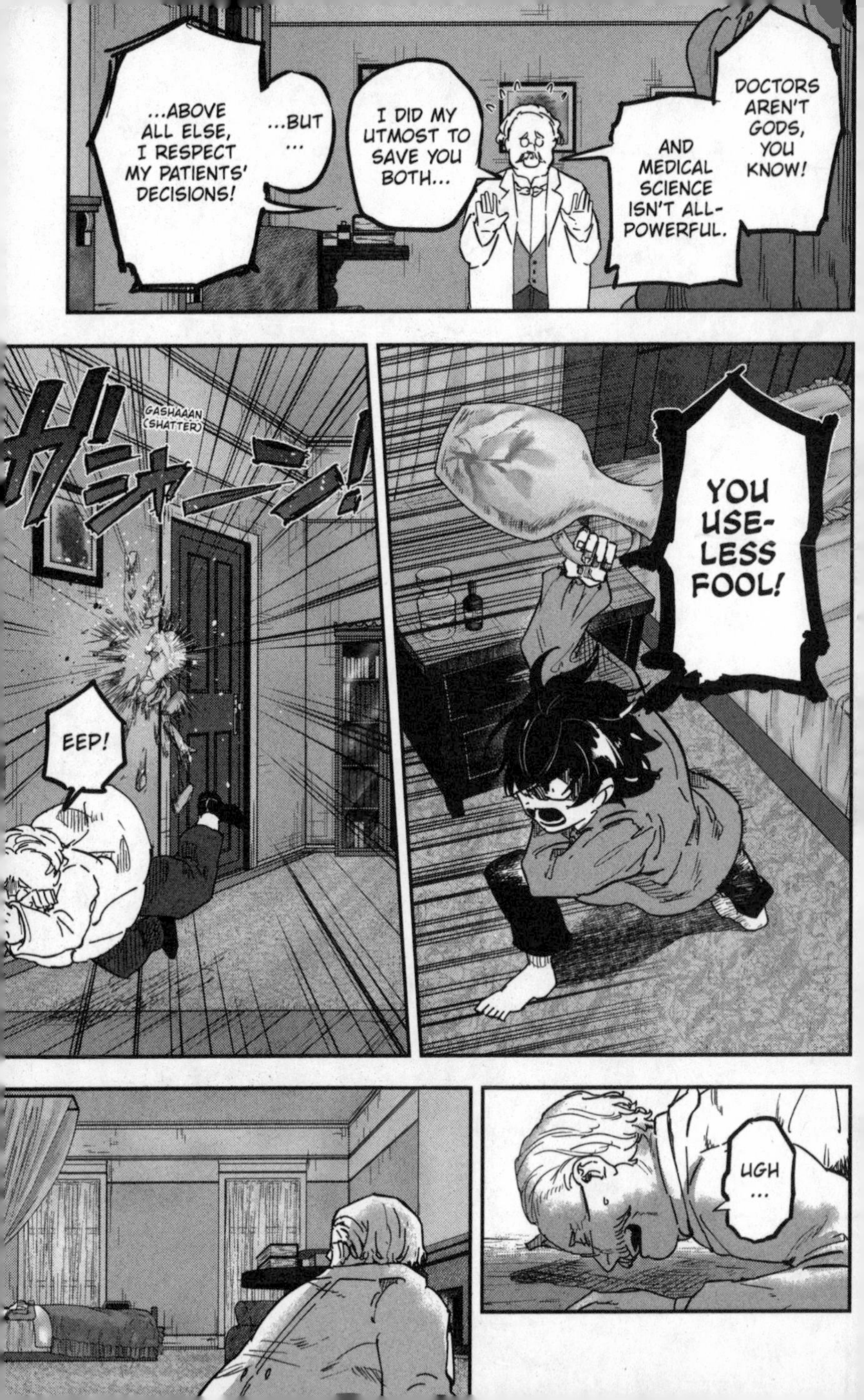
DOCTORS AREN'T GODS, YOU KNOW!
AND MEDICAL SCIENCE ISN'T ALL-POWERFUL.
I DID MY UTMOST TO SAVE YOU BOTH...
...BUT ...
...ABOVE ALL ELSE, I RESPECT MY PATIENTS' DECISIONS!
YOU USE-LESS FOOL!
ガシャーン!
GASHAAAN (SHATTER)
EEP!
UGH ...

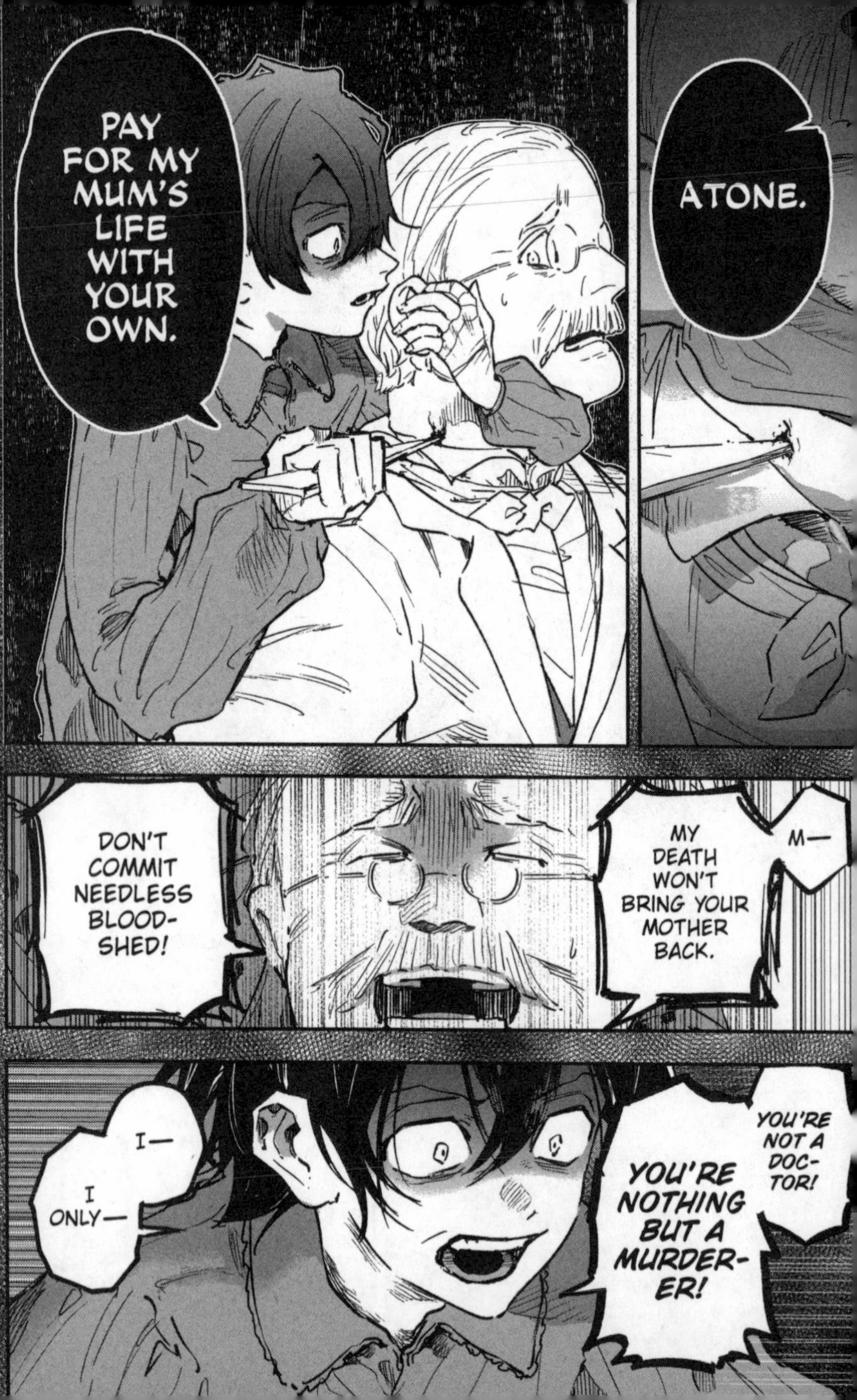
ATONE.
PAY FOR MY MUM'S LIFE WITH YOUR OWN.
M—
MY DEATH WON'T BRING YOUR MOTHER BACK.
DON'T COMMIT NEEDLESS BLOODSHED!
YOU'RE NOT A DOCTOR!
YOU'RE NOTHING BUT A MURDERER!
I—
I ONLY—

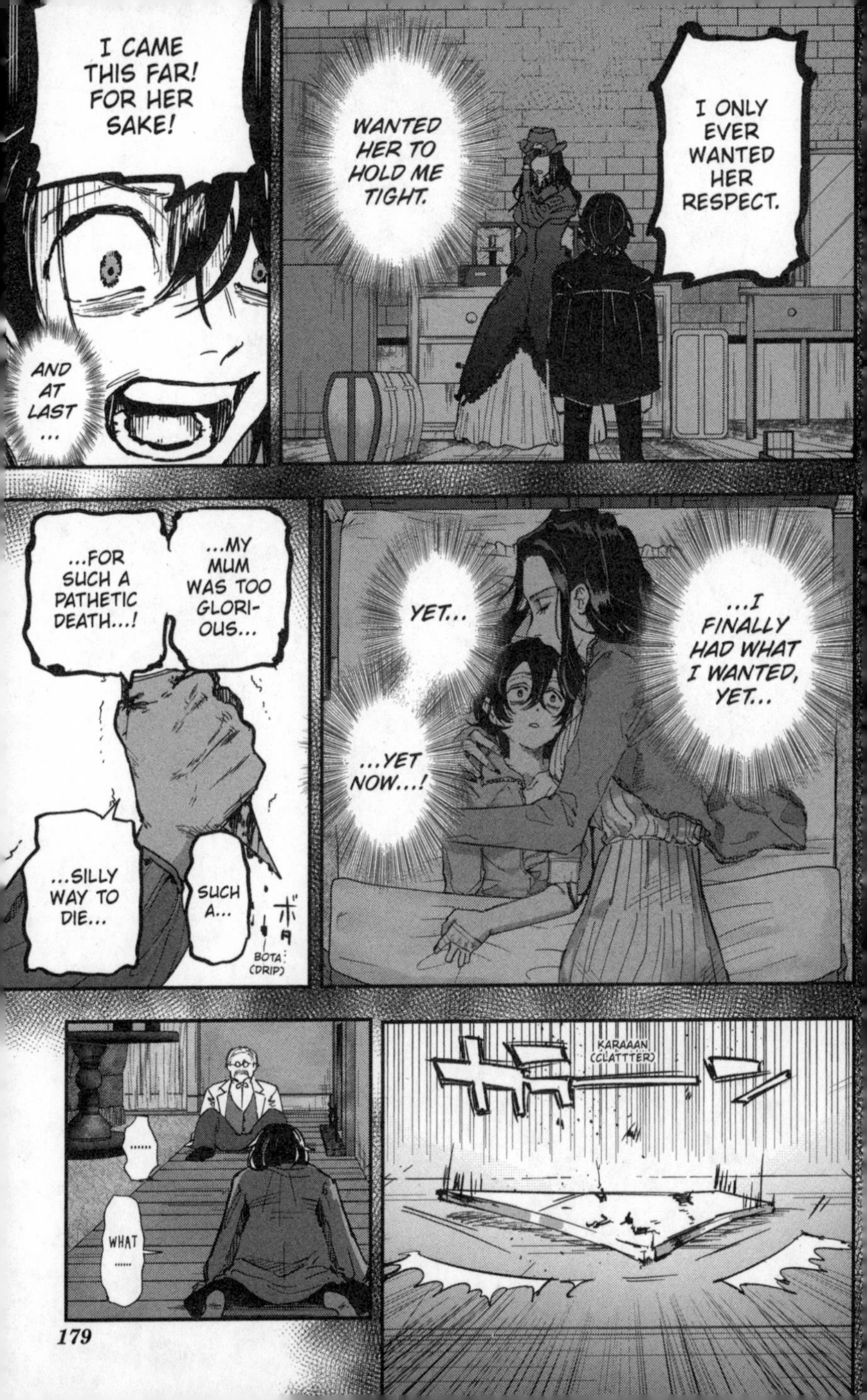
I ONLY EVER WANTED HER RESPECT.
WANTED HER TO HOLD ME TIGHT.
I CAME THIS FAR! FOR HER SAKE!
AND AT LAST ...
...I FINALLY HAD WHAT I WANTED, YET...
YET...
...YET NOW...!
...MY MUM WAS TOO GLORIOUS...
...FOR SUCH A PATHETIC DEATH...!
ボタ
BOTA (DRIP)
SUCH A...
...SILLY WAY TO DIE...
KARAAAN (CLATTER)
......
WHAT ......

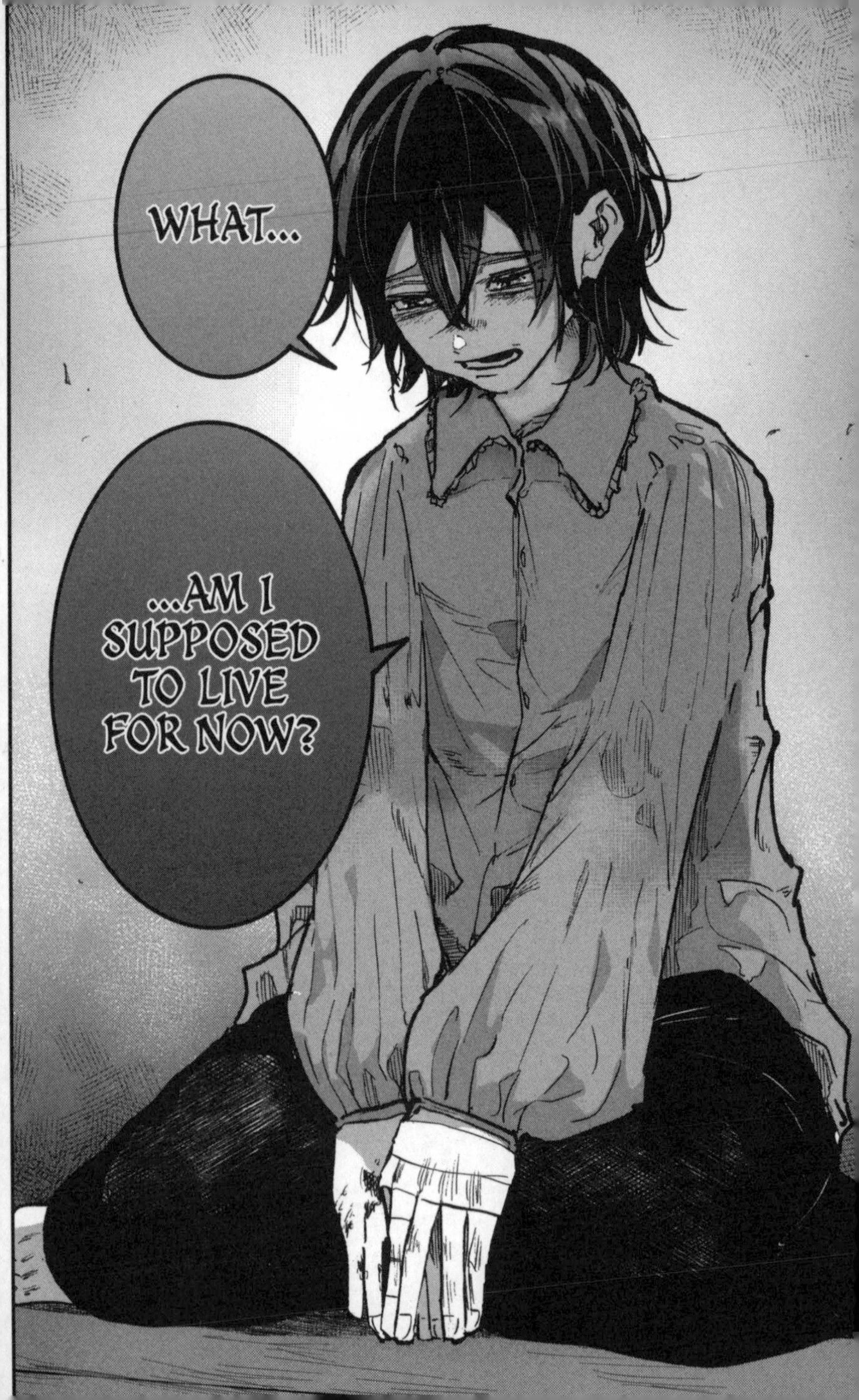
WHAT...
...AM I SUPPOSED TO LIVE FOR NOW?

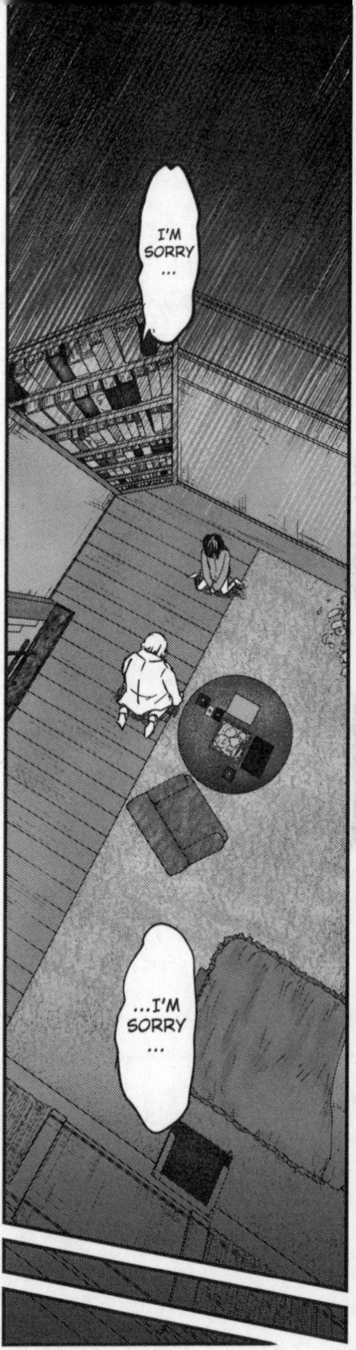
I'M SORRY ...
...I'M SORRY ...
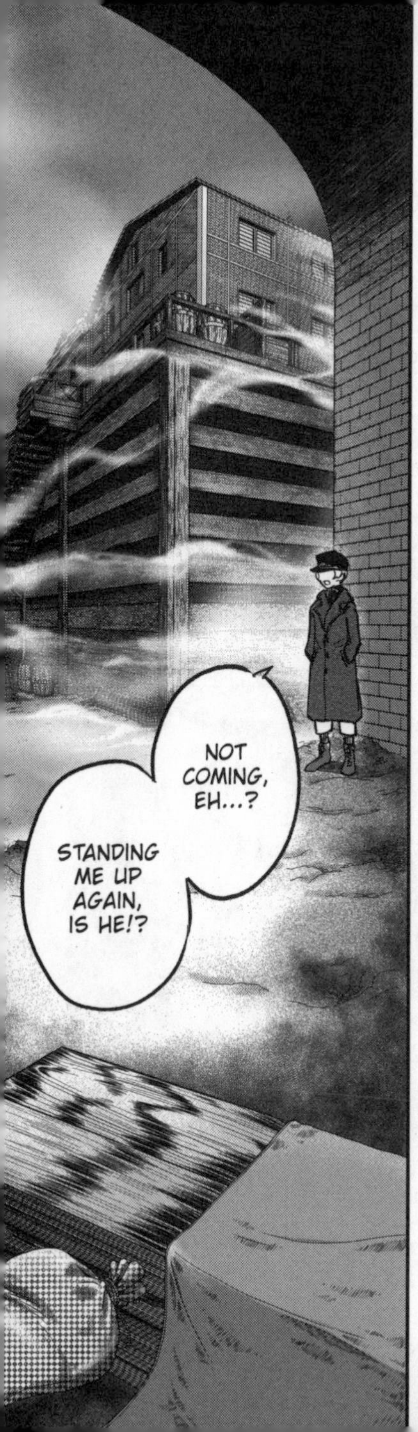
NOT COMING, EH...?
STANDING ME UP AGAIN, IS HE!?

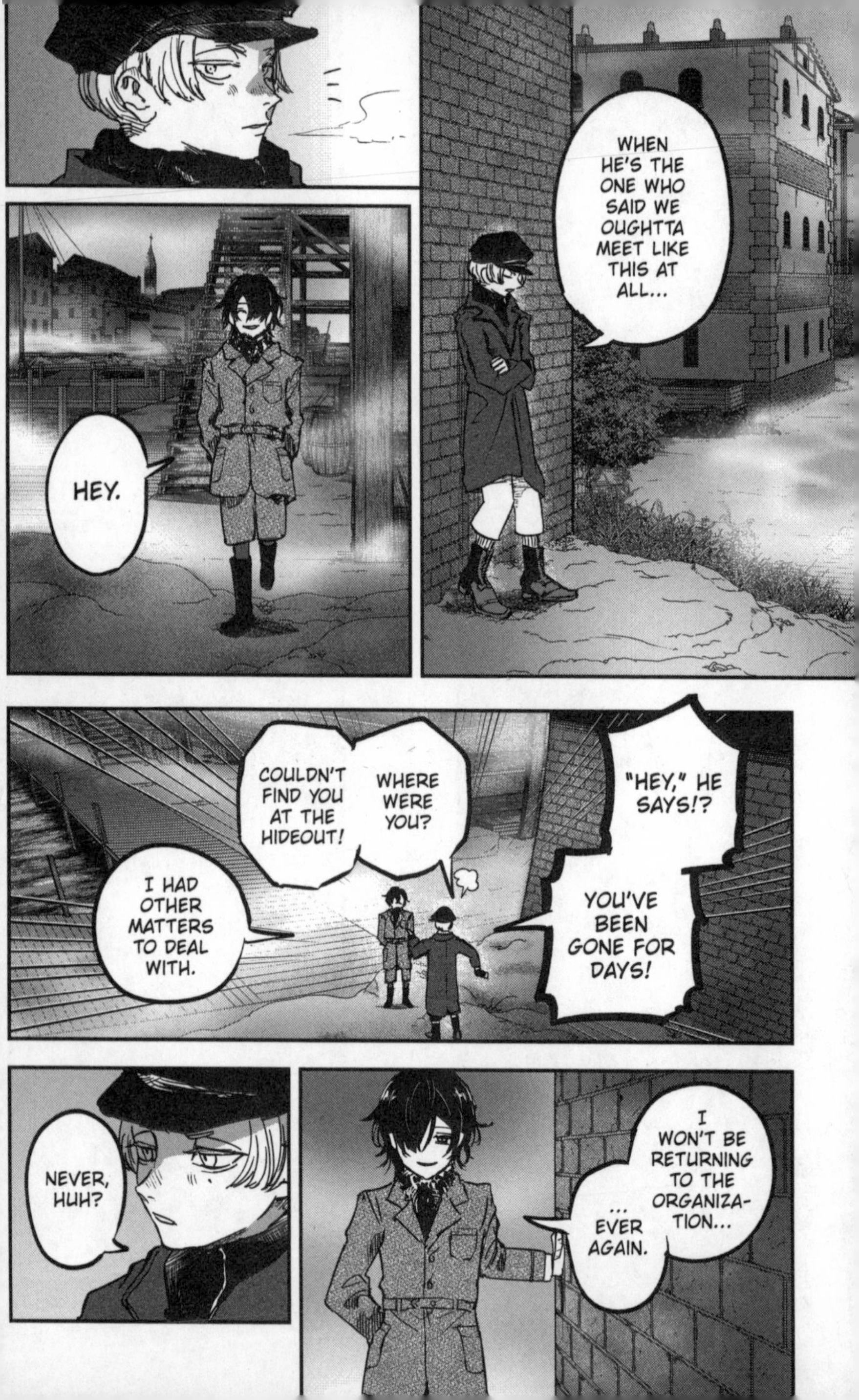
WHEN HE'S THE ONE WHO SAID WE OUGHTTA MEET LIKE THIS AT ALL...
HEY.
"HEY," HE SAYS!?
YOU'VE BEEN GONE FOR DAYS!
WHERE WERE YOU?
COULDN'T FIND YOU AT THE HIDEOUT!
I HAD OTHER MATTERS TO DEAL WITH.
I WON'T BE RETURNING TO THE ORGANIZA-TION...
...EVER AGAIN.
NEVER, HUH?

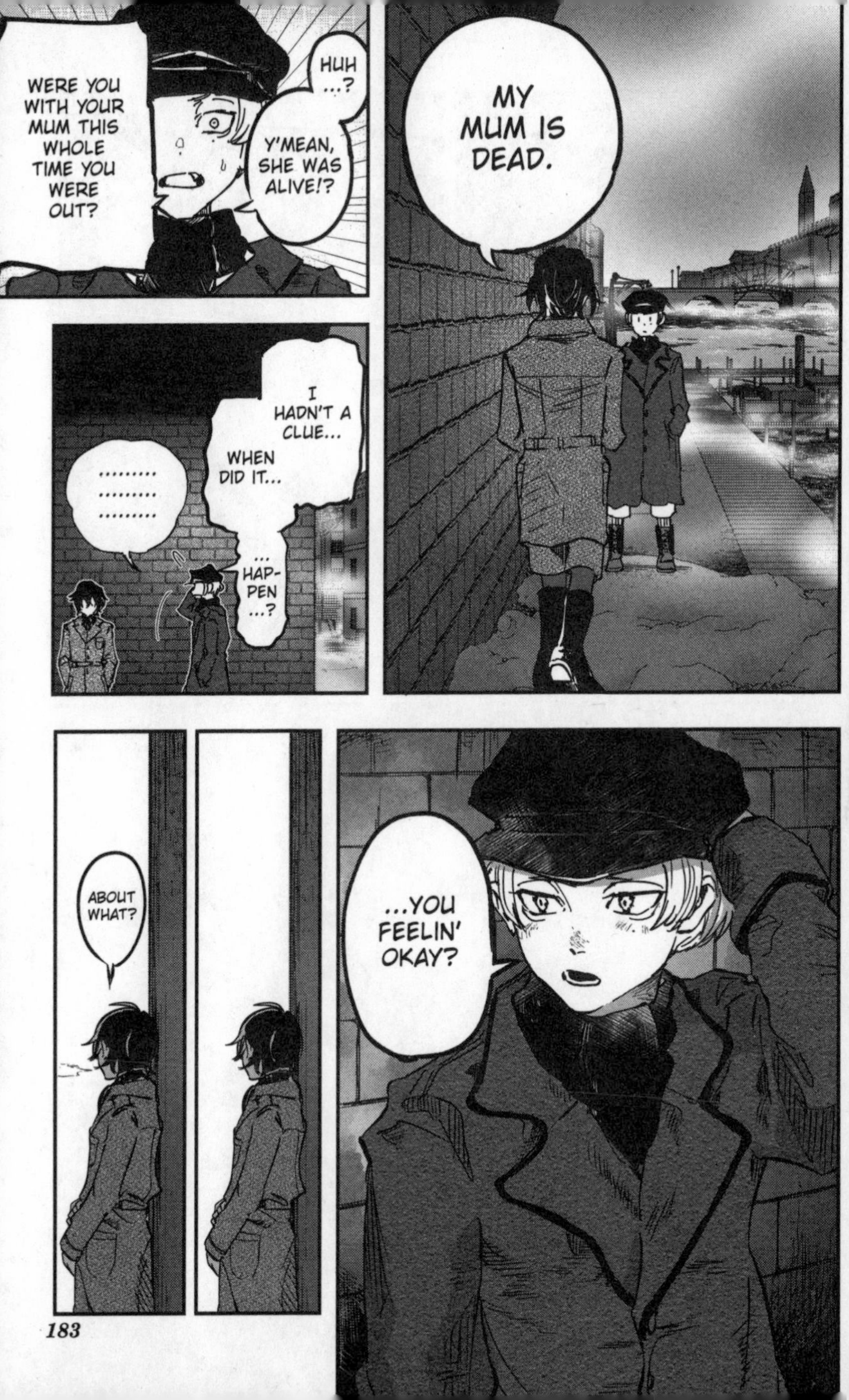
MY MUM IS DEAD.
HUH ...?
Y'MEAN, SHE WAS ALIVE!?
WERE YOU WITH YOUR MUM THIS WHOLE TIME YOU WERE OUT?
I HADN'T A CLUE...
WHEN DID IT...
... HAP-PEN ...?
....
....
....
...YOU FEELIN' OKAY?
ABOUT WHAT?

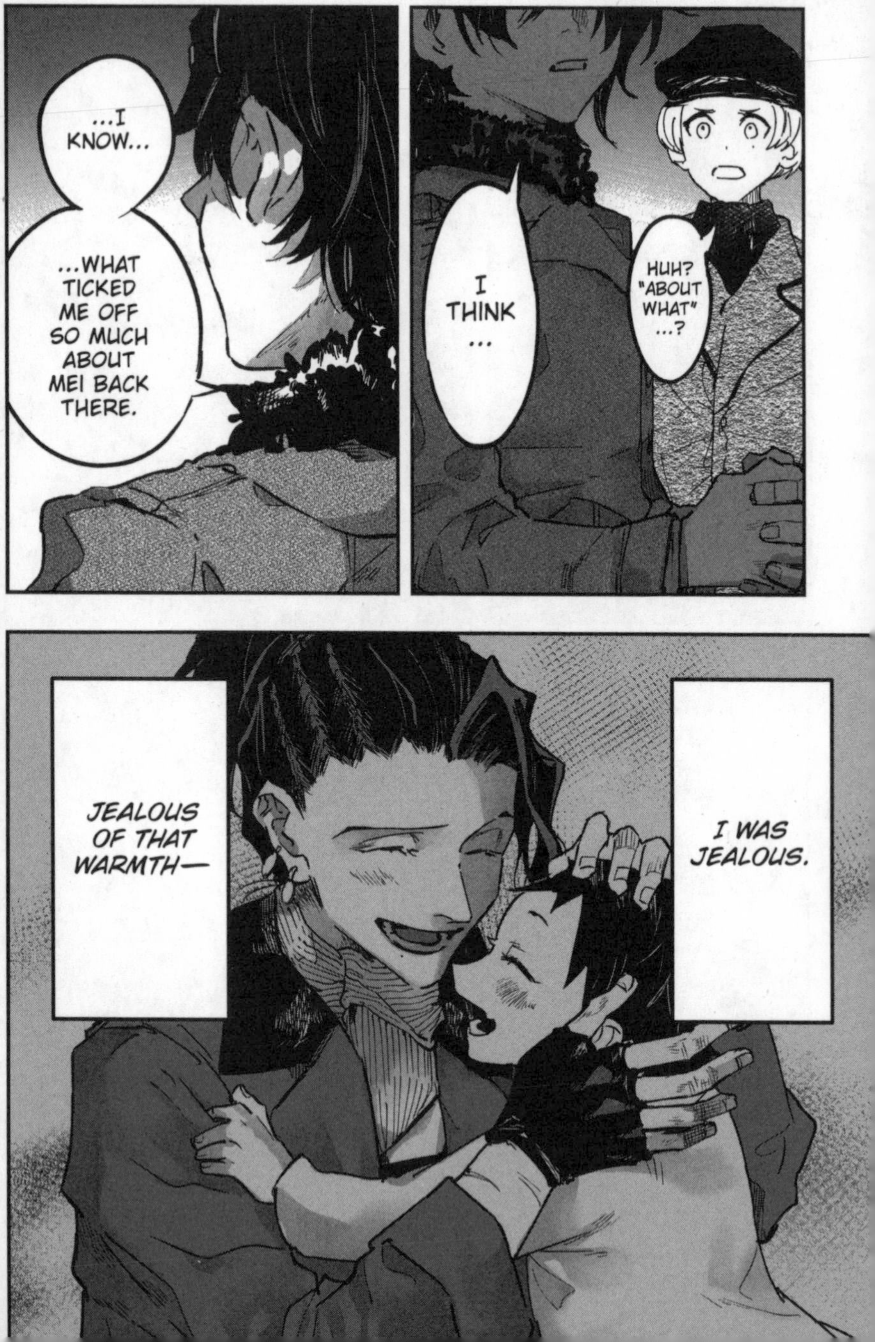
I THINK ...
HUH? "ABOUT WHAT" ...?
...I KNOW...
...WHAT TICKED ME OFF SO MUCH ABOUT MEI BACK THERE.
I WAS JEALOUS.
JEALOUS OF THAT WARMTH—

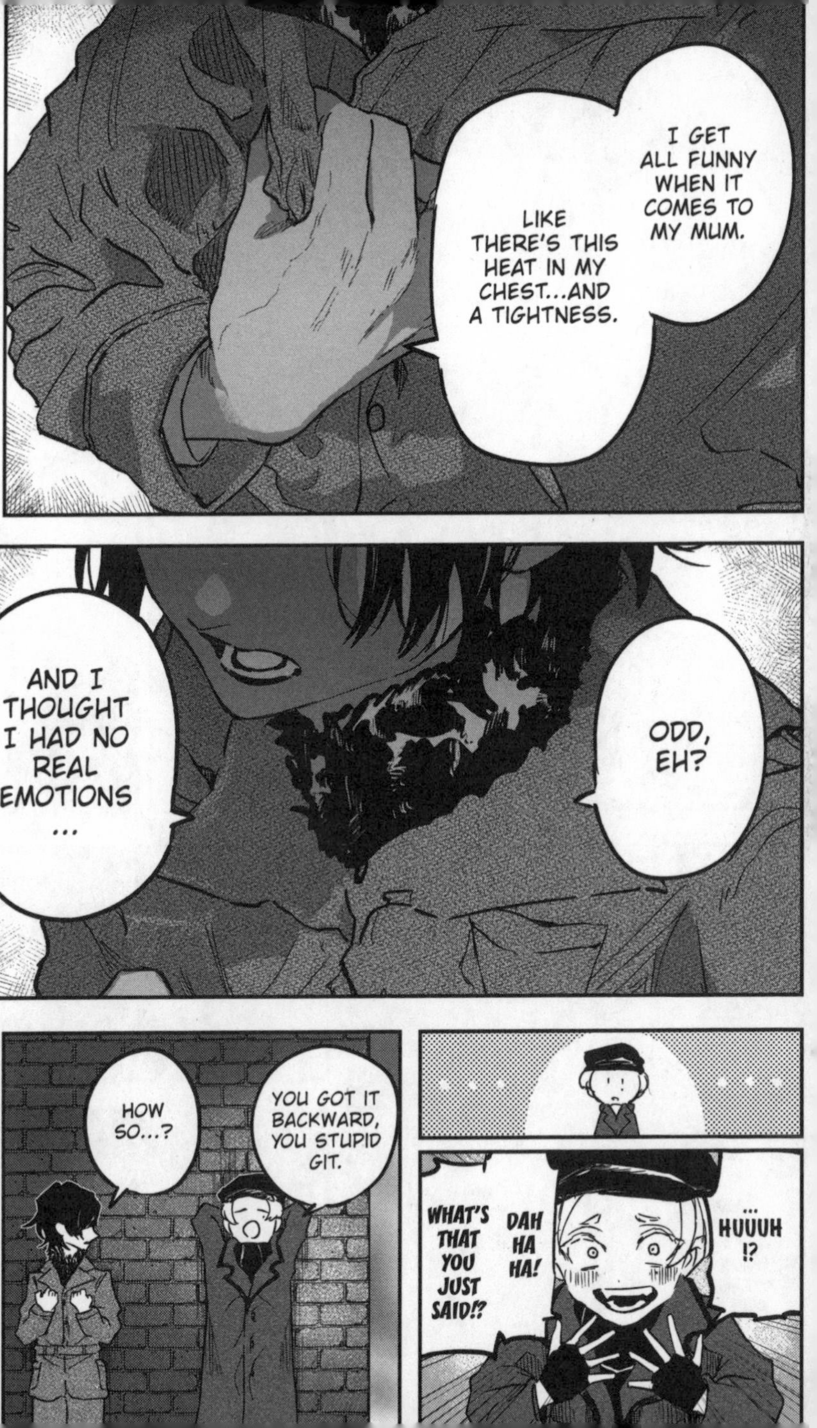
I GET ALL FUNNY WHEN IT COMES TO MY MUM.
LIKE THERE'S THIS HEAT IN MY CHEST...AND A TIGHTNESS.
ODD, EH?
AND I THOUGHT I HAD NO REAL EMOTIONS ...
......
...HUUUH !?
DAH HA HA!
WHAT'S THAT YOU JUST SAID!?
YOU GOT IT BACKWARD, YOU STUPID GIT.
HOW SO...?

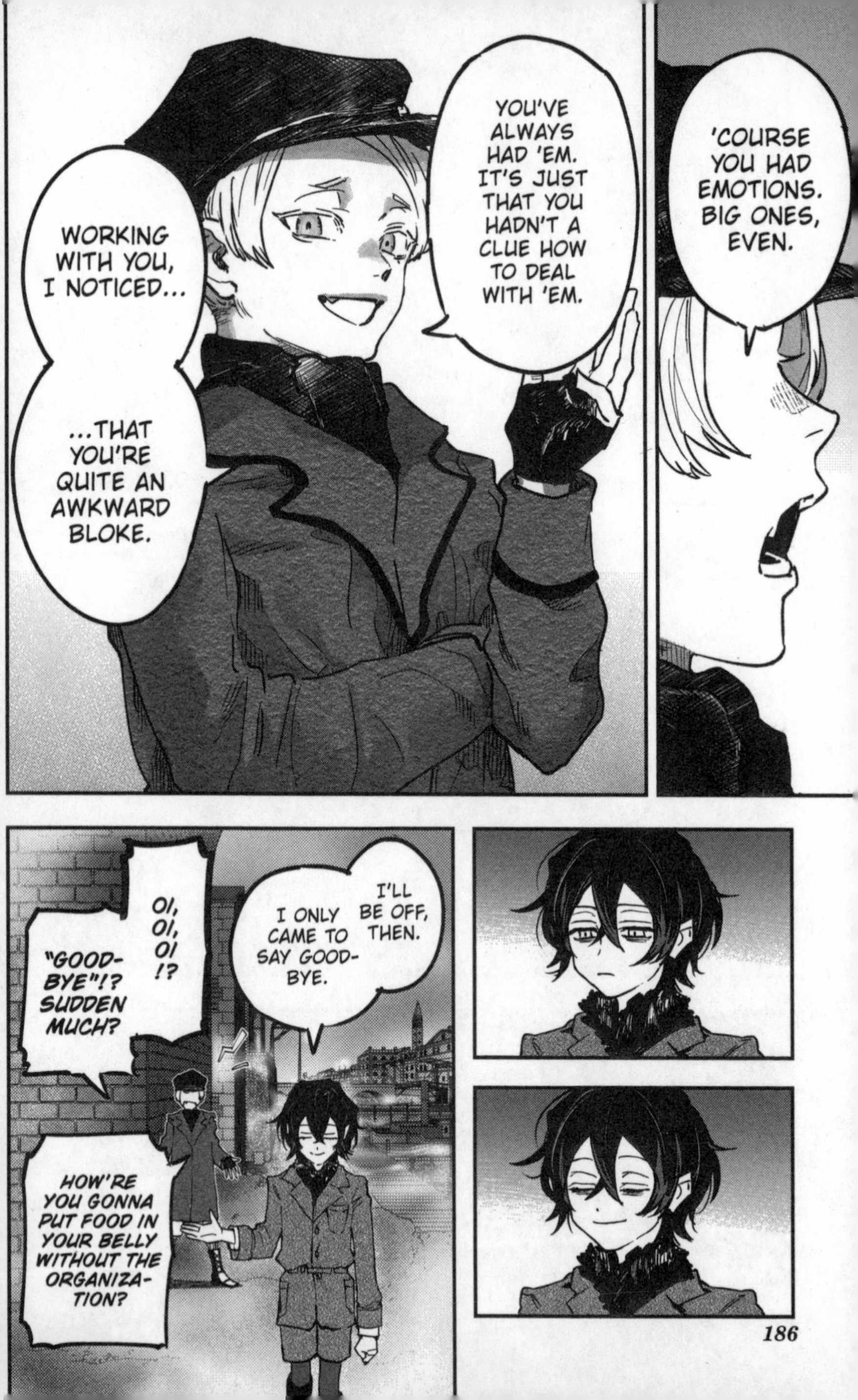
'COURSE YOU HAD EMOTIONS. BIG ONES, EVEN.
YOU'VE ALWAYS HAD 'EM. IT'S JUST THAT YOU HADN'T A CLUE HOW TO DEAL WITH 'EM.
WORKING WITH YOU, I NOTICED...
...THAT YOU'RE QUITE AN AWKWARD BLOKE.
I ONLY CAME TO SAY GOOD-BYE. I'LL BE OFF, THEN.
OI, OI, OI!?
"GOOD-BYE"!? SUDDEN MUCH?
HOW'RE YOU GONNA PUT FOOD IN YOUR BELLY WITHOUT THE ORGANIZA-TION?

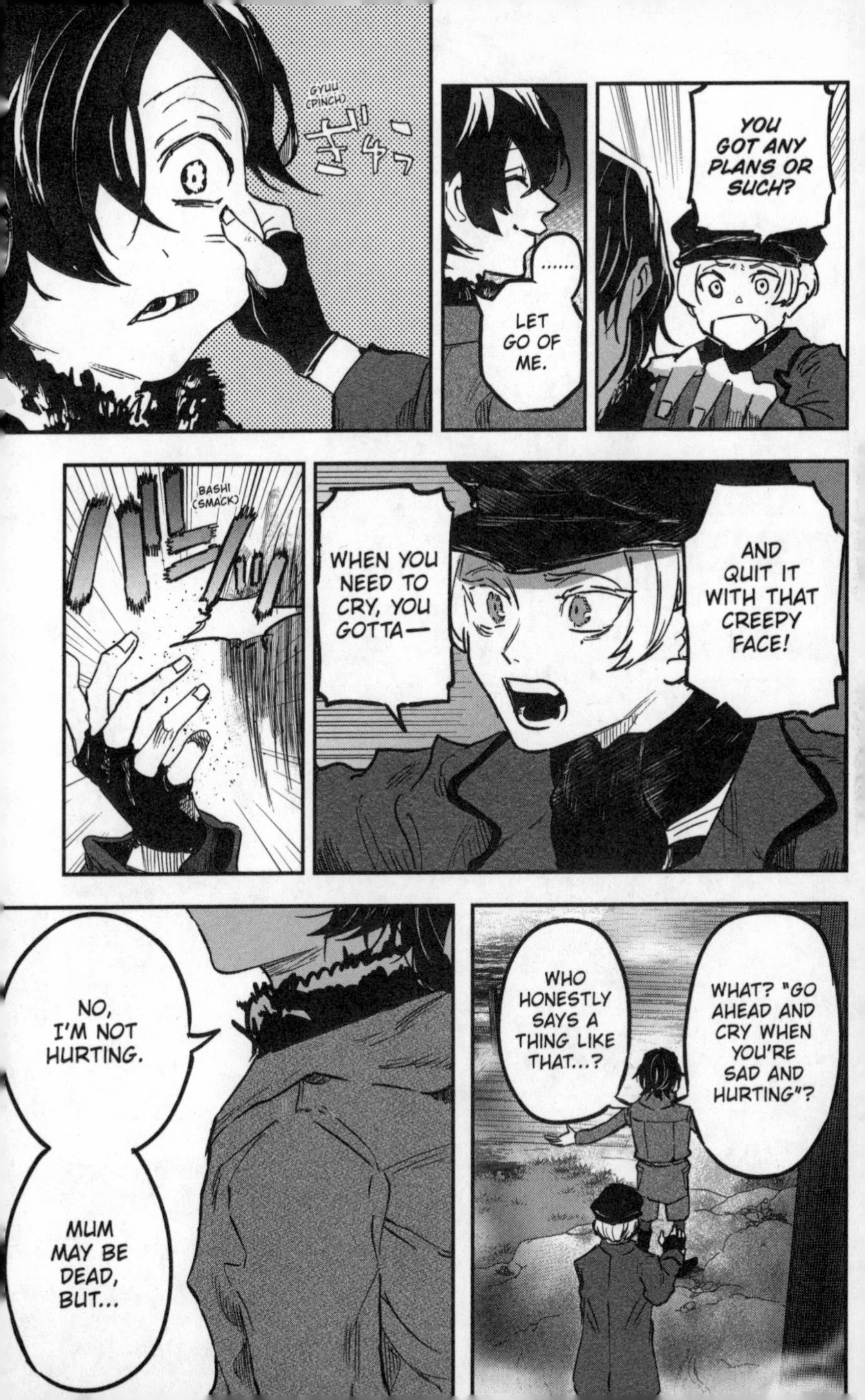
YOU GOT ANY PLANS OR SUCH?
......
LET GO OF ME.
GYUU (PINCH)
AND QUIT IT WITH THAT CREEPY FACE!
WHEN YOU NEED TO CRY, YOU GOTTA—
BASHI (SMACK)
WHAT? "GO AHEAD AND CRY WHEN YOU'RE SAD AND HURTING"?
WHO HONESTLY SAYS A THING LIKE THAT...?
NO, I'M NOT HURTING.
MUM MAY BE DEAD, BUT...

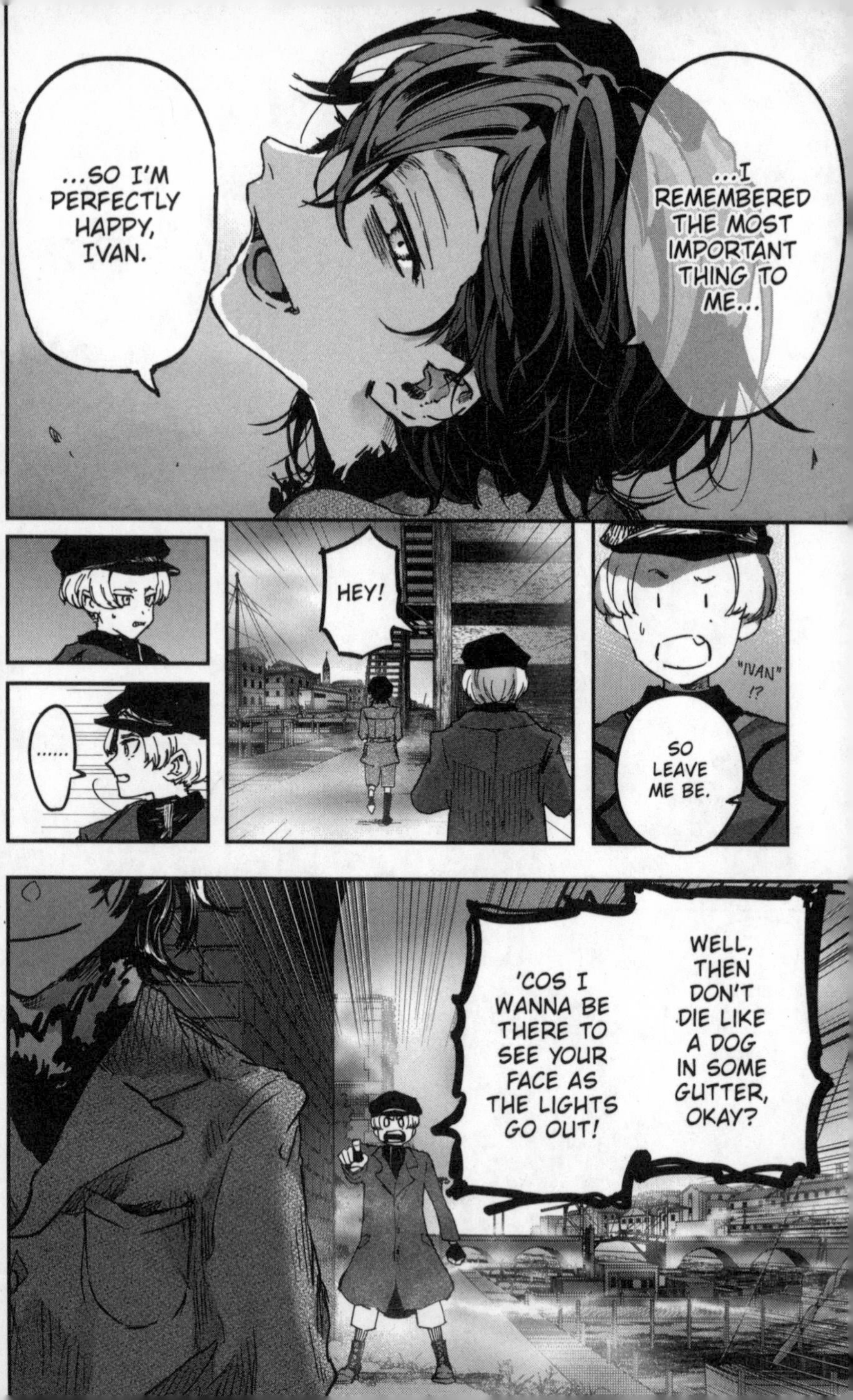
...I REMEMBERED THE MOST IMPORTANT THING TO ME...
...SO I'M PERFECTLY HAPPY, IVAN.
"IVAN" !?
SO LEAVE ME BE.
HEY!
......
WELL, THEN DON'T DIE LIKE A DOG IN SOME GUTTER, OKAY?
'COS I WANNA BE THERE TO SEE YOUR FACE AS THE LIGHTS GO OUT!

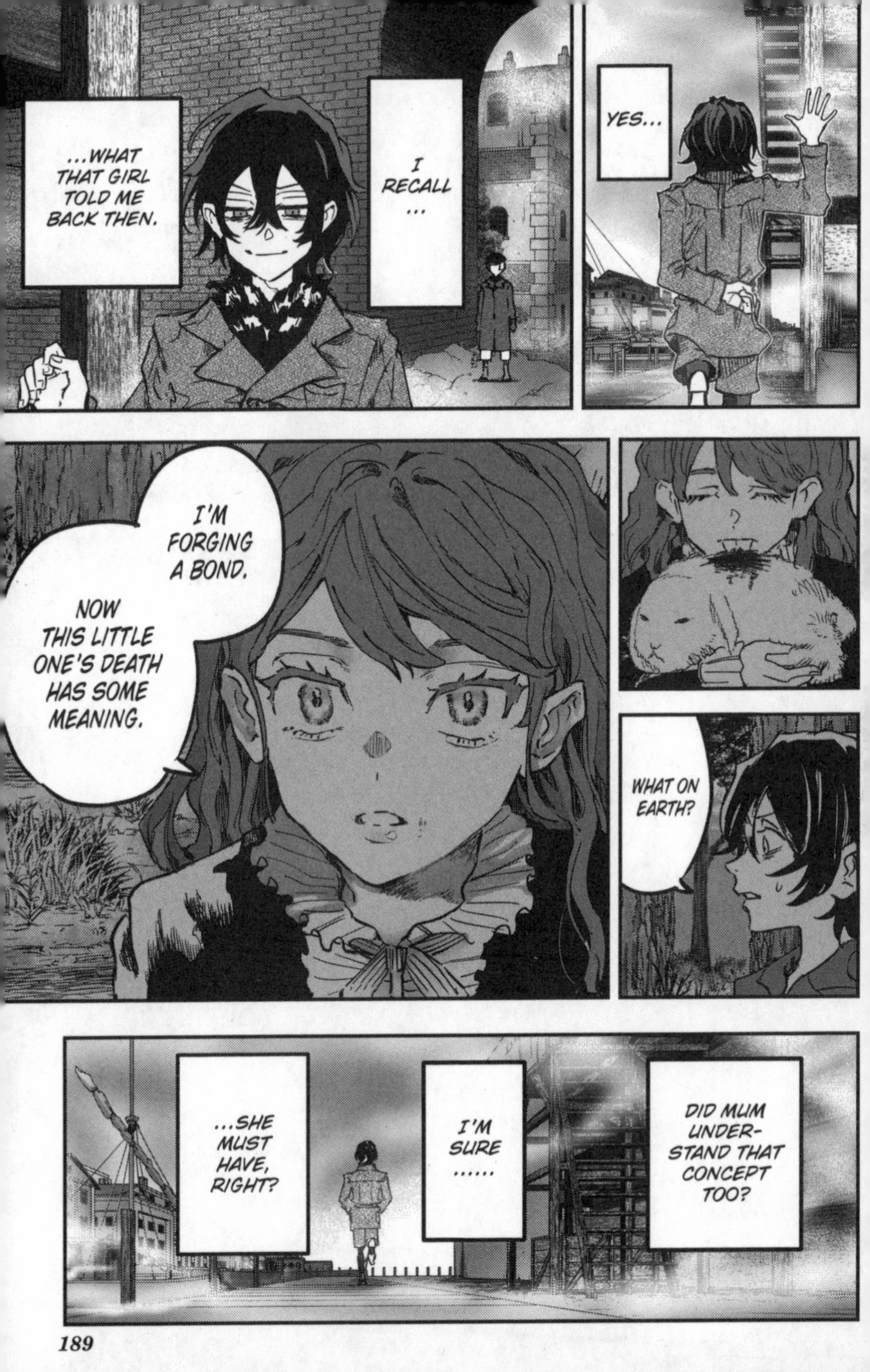
YES...
I RECALL...
...WHAT THAT GIRL TOLD ME BACK THEN.
WHAT ON EARTH?
I'M FORGING A BOND.
NOW THIS LITTLE ONE'S DEATH HAS SOME MEANING.
DID MUM UNDER-STAND THAT CONCEPT TOO?
I'M SURE......
...SHE MUST HAVE, RIGHT?

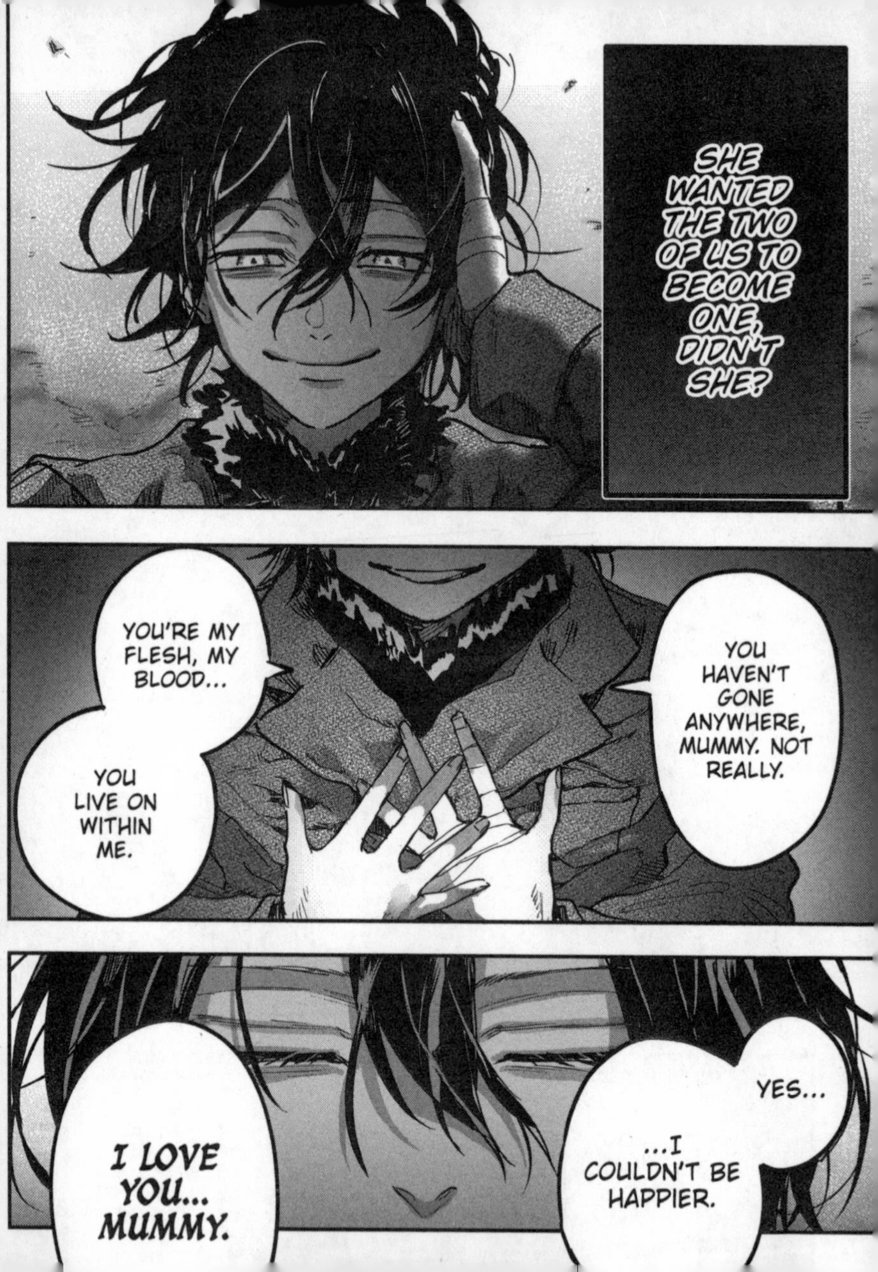
SHE WANTED THE TWO OF US TO BECOME ONE, DIDN'T SHE?
YOU HAVEN'T GONE ANYWHERE, MUMMY. NOT REALLY.
YOU'RE MY FLESH, MY BLOOD...
YOU LIVE ON WITHIN ME.
YES...
...I COULDN'T BE HAPPIER.
I LOVE YOU... MUMMY.

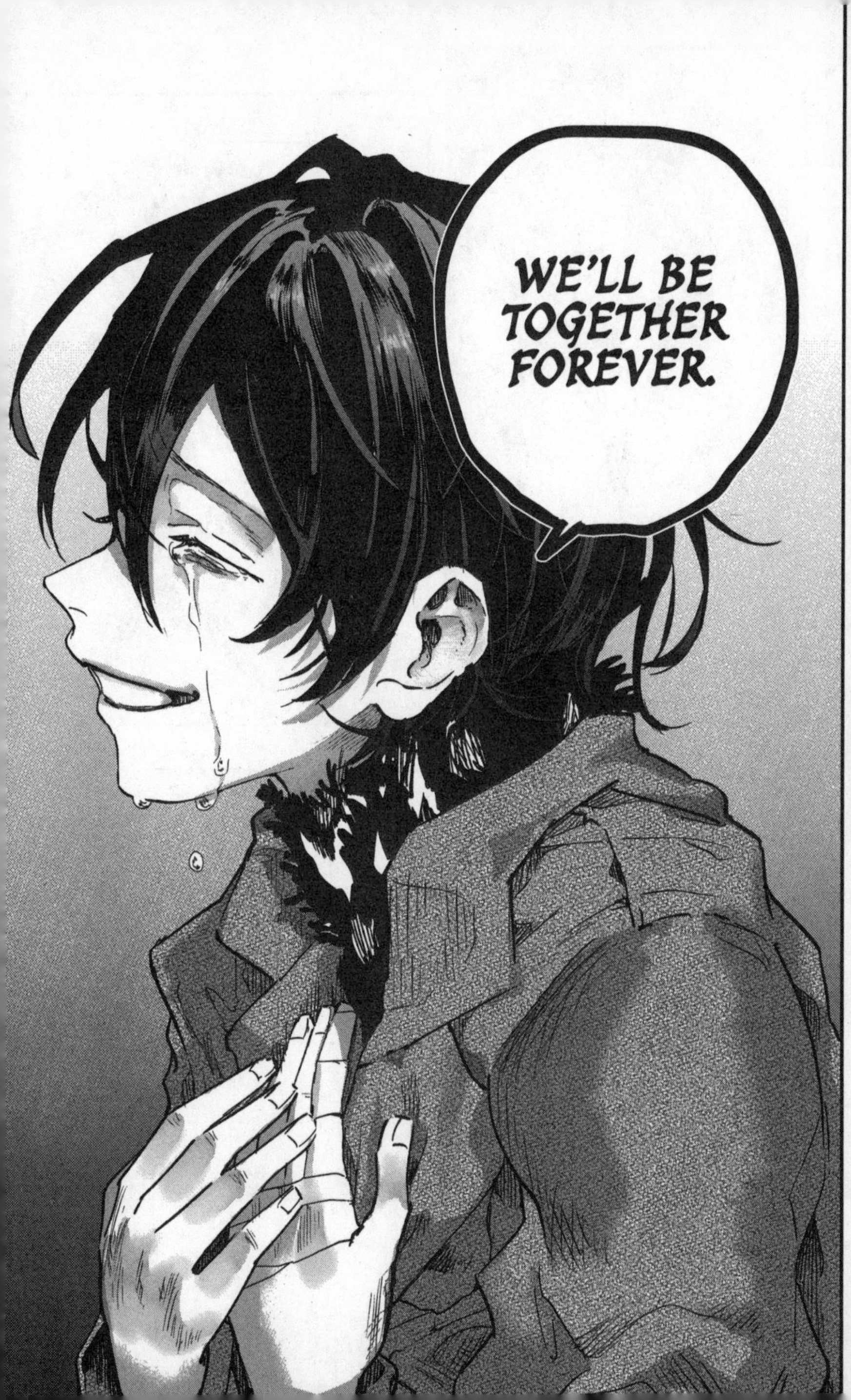
WE'LL BE TOGETHER FOREVER.

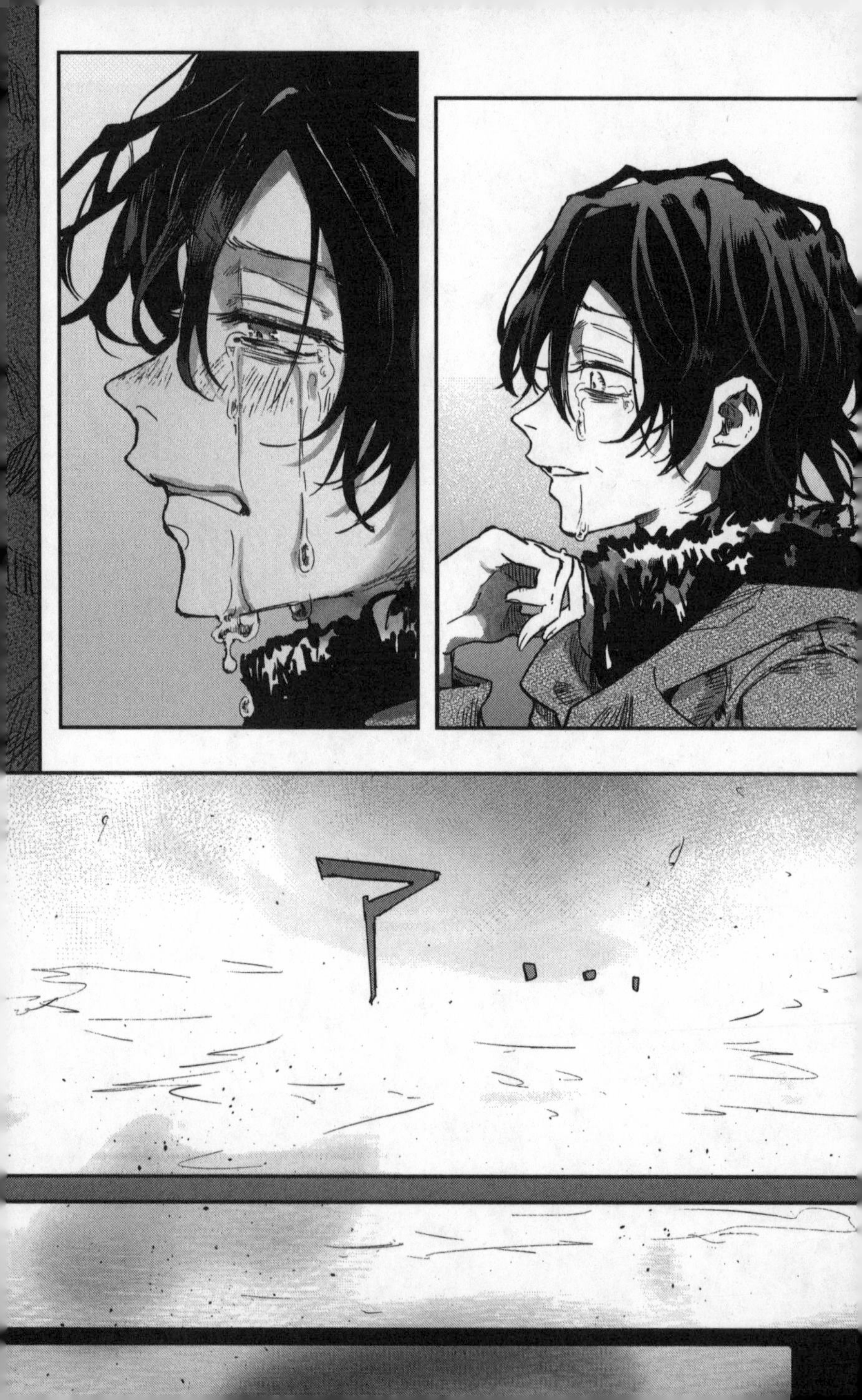
ア…

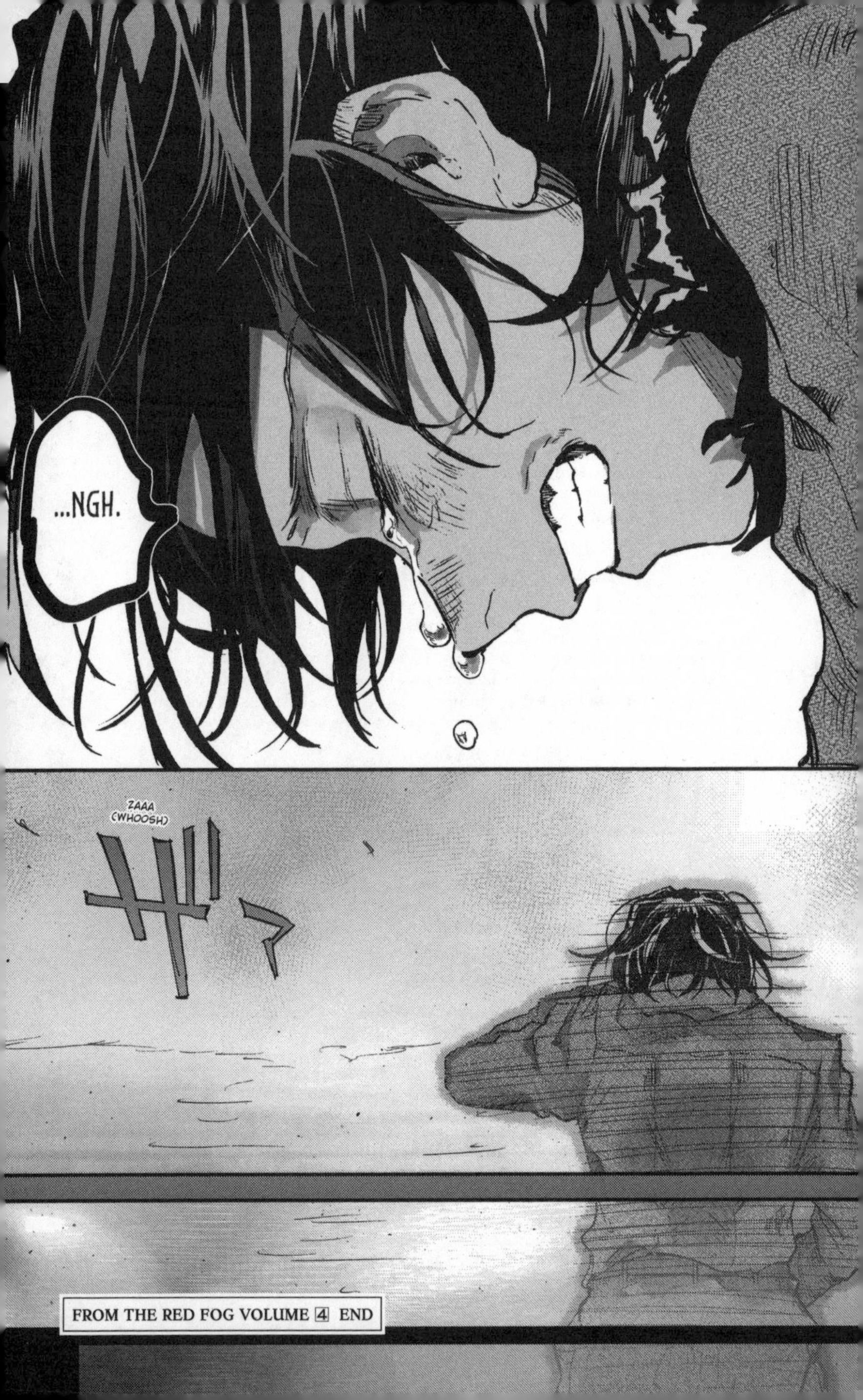
...NGH.
ZAAA (WHOOSH)
FROM THE RED FOG VOLUME 4 END

Mosae Nohara

Translation: Caleb D. Cook

Lettering: Chiho Christie

AKAI KIRI NO NAKA KARA Volume 4
©2022 Mosae Nohara/SQUARE ENIX CO., LTD.
First published in Japan in 2022 by SQUARE ENIX CO., LTD.
English translation rights arranged with SQUARE ENIX CO., LTD.
and Yen Press, LLC through Tuttle-Mori Agency, Inc.

English translation ©2023 by SQUARE ENIX CO., LTD.

Yen Press
150 West 30th Street, 19th Floor
New York, NY 10001

Visit us at yenpress.com · facebook.com/yenpress · twitter.com/yenpress · yenpress.tumblr.com · instagram.com/yenpress

First Yen Press Edition: April 2023
Edited by Yen Press Editorial: Jacquelyn Li, Danielle Niederkorn
Designed by Yen Press Design: Jane Sohn, Andy Swist

Yen Press is an imprint of Yen Press, LLC.
The Yen Press name and logo are trademarks of Yen Press, LLC.

The publisher is not responsible for websites (or their content)
that are not owned by the publisher.

Library of Congress Control Number: 2021949718

ISBNs: 978-1-9753-5117-5 (paperback)
978-1-9753-5118-2 (ebook)

1 3 5 7 9 10 8 6 4 2

WOR

Printed in the United States of America